FIFTY YEARS' MARCH

The Rise of the Labour Party

BY THE SAME AUTHOR

General:

    War by Revolution
    Democracy's Last Battle
    Ten Angels Swearing
    Press, Parliament and People
    The Triple Challenge

Fiction:

    No Man is an Island
    A Provincial Affair

Copyright T.1149.1R.R.

Made and Printed in Great Britain by
Odhams (Watford) Ltd., Watford

KEIR HARDIE
Apostle of British socialism—born 1856, died 1915.

FIFTY YEARS' MARCH

The Rise of the Labour Party

BY

FRANCIS WILLIAMS

FOREWORD BY

THE RT. HON. C. R. ATTLEE
C.H., M.P.

ODHAMS PRESS LIMITED
LONG ACRE, LONDON

FOREWORD

THE Liberal and Conservative Parties in this country have long histories. They have evolved from their predecessors the Whigs and the Tories. Fifty years ago the Labour Party was born. The ideals which inspire it derive from many sources. Socialists can claim fellowship with many fighters for freedom in the past, but as an organized political movement resulting in the establishment of a completely new addition to the major parties in the State the Labour Party is unique in our history.

Previous attempts to send independent representatives to Parliament to express the political aspirations of the workers had failed. In this book Francis Williams tells with a wealth of detail how and why the meeting of Trade Unionists and Socialists at Memorial Hall in February, 1900, succeeded and how it resulted eventually in the great Labour victory of 1945. It is a story well worth the telling. Mr. Williams shows how the different strands in the Labour and Socialist movement were woven together. He indicates the contribution made to that achievement by men and women of different mentalities and of varied social backgrounds and indicates with fairness and lucidity the qualities which they brought to the service of the movement.

It is a story very characteristic of Britain, showing the triumph of reasonableness and practicality over doctrinaire impossibilism. Most of the events which he relates are fresh in the memories of men and women of my generation. Some of the founders are still with us, while many of the foremost figures have only recently passed on.

Mr. Williams has given a well-balanced history and his judgments are notably fair, while throughout he understands and expresses the spirit of the movement.

I hope that the book will be widely read both at home and in other countries. I hope especially that it will be read by the younger generation who will learn from it the difficulties which their elders had to overcome and the faith and vision which inspired them.

C. R. Attlee

10, Downing Street,
  London.

CONTENTS

PART III: CRISIS AND CONFLICT

Part IV: FORWARD TO GOVERNMENT

PART ONE

THE LABOUR PARTY
IS BORN

CHAPTER

THE DECISION IS TAKEN

IT IS only rarely that history fully lives up to its spectacular possibilities. It did not do so on Tuesday, 27 February, 1900, when in the Memorial Hall, Farringdon Street, London, the Labour Party was born.

Here was an occasion which, as it falls into its true place against the moving background of great events, is seen to possess a dramatic significance of the highest quality. The Party born on that grey February day in a drab commercial street off Fleet Street was to contribute decisively in the brief course of less than a quarter of a century to the almost total eclipse of one of the two great traditional parties of the State, one moreover, at the moment, moving to the very summit of its prestige and power. It was to mobilize behind it and become the chief instrument of a political uprising of the working-classes of Britain that was to change the social and economic face of the country out of all recognition. It was to reach parliamentary maturity and political power at a speed unexampled in British political history. Two vast wars, bringing with them the total disruption of great nations and the downfall of famous dynasties, were each to add immensely to its strength and stability. Within half a century it was to reach, entirely by parliamentary and democratic means, the position of the greatest party in the State, and was to carry through Parliament, with the support of a massive majority in which men and women of every class were represented, a programme which would have seemed the wildest and most revolutionary utopianism to those passing along Farringdon Street about their ordinary business on that February day in the first year of the new century. And not only to the passers-by who took little interest in the groups of working-class men, interspersed here and there with a few of a more professional kind, who made their way through the doors of the Memorial Hall, but to most of the delegates within the hall itself.

These delegates, who had come from most parts of Britain, from Stepney and the Mile End Road, from Canning Town, Barking, Battersea, Shepherd's Bush, from Glasgow and Manchester, Liverpool, Birmingham, Sheffield, Bradford, Oldham, Middlesbrough, Huddersfield, Bristol, from almost every industrial area in the country, were the advance guard of a great army. They were part of the wave of the future. But they were also the legatees of the past.

Behind them was a long, proud and often tragic story going back through the centuries, a story of immense effort and stubborn achievement, of victory and disaster, of nobility and betrayal—but always of struggle. A story in which men had fought and laboured and sacrificed themselves and in which some had died for the right to combine together to secure the barest necessities for themselves and their families; in which starvation, imprisonment and transportation had been the weapons used to beat them down; in which again and again there had been defeat, but in which after every defeat the struggle had been resumed and slowly, slowly, inch by painful inch, the advance had gone on.

And now, on that February morning in 1900, the curtain was rising on a new act in this tremendous drama; an act of the most decisive character, yet one which, to the superficial eye, had few of the lineaments of history to mark it out. The newspapers of the day found it unworthy of space. They were busy with matters which seemed to them of more public interest and permanent importance, such as the imperialist excitements of the Boer War, then in its fifth month and beginning at last to go a little better for Britain now that General Roberts, "Lord Bobs," had taken charge. Scarcely a flicker of public inquiry was aroused by the Memorial Hall Conference. Even among the great mass of manual workers throughout the country it aroused little excitement or enthusiasm. As for the delegates themselves, many had, as Ramsay MacDonald said later, come to bury in good-humoured tolerance the attempt to found a Labour Party, and some had come to make sure that burial would be its fate. Fortunately, the majority were of a different mind.

It was a business meeting. Its purpose was to consider certain proposals and discuss various resolutions. By its nature it could not help but seem somewhat humdrum to such few outside observers as concerned themselves with it even in slight degree. It is not easy to give to the formally-worded resolutions of a conference of practically-minded delegates the dramatic value that their true content and actual historic significance may justify.

Even now, with the added knowledge that distance gives and the ability bestowed by the passage of time to place this meeting correctly in relation to both the past and the future, it is not always easy to see, behind the superficially commonplace proceedings of the conference and of the discussions at the Trades Union Conference that led up to it, the raw material of great history. Yet it is there, and because it is there, and because in the light of events it is possible to realize how much hung on the phrasing of a particular resolution, the outcome of a particular controversy long since ended, almost every detail of this conference has its significance. It laid the foundations of the Labour Party and because these foundations were laid in one way rather than another, because this view prevailed rather than that, the history of the Labour Party and indeed the history of Britain has taken the course it has rather than one quite different.

If the circumstances of the conference had little of an obvious dramatic quality nevertheless a singular appropriateness marked its meeting-place. For the Memorial Hall was built as a commemoration to men who suffered imprisonment for conscience' sake and for their right to dissent from what they held to be wrong, and it stands, like a declaration of the victory of man's conscience over man's selfishness and cruelty, upon the site of the old Fleet Prison.

Here then, in this hall built to commemorate the struggle of men to worship God in their own way and think and speak according to the compulsions of their own conscience, on a plot of land that has known as much of misery and degradation, of the consequences of poverty and the fruits of man's inhumanity to man, as any in England, the delegates to the Conference on Labour Representation met: here the Labour Party was born.

There were one hundred and twenty-nine delegates. They came from sixty-five trade unions and three Socialist societies and represented between them 568,000 organized workers and members of Socialist groups—less, that is, than half the total number of the workers in trade unions affiliated to the Trades Union Congress at the time and only a tiny percentage of all the millions of manual workers in the country. They were there to consider the formation of a new political party. But those for whom they could speak— even if they were all of one mind, which was far from being the case—did not number more than a twelfth of the total electorate even on the restricted register of the time. To such of the politicians and industrial leaders of the older political parties as bothered to take even a passing interest in this new stirring of political life among the lower orders it must have seemed an affair of the utmost insignificance.

The great trade unions of today with their mass membership had not then been born. The largest trade union represented was the Amalgamated Society of Engineers with 85,000 members. But of the sixty-five trade unions which sent delegates thirty-seven had a membership of less than 5,000 and eleven of less than 1,000. Only thirteen had more than 10,000 members and only four besides the Engineers' more than 20,000. These four were the Amalgamated Society of Railway Servants with 54,000, the Gas Workers' and General Labourers' with 48,038, the Boot and Shoe Operatives' with 31,000, and the Miners' Federation of Lancashire and Cheshire with 29,000. Among those at the other end of the scale were the Chain Makers' with 985 members, the Electrical Trades Union with 950 (a sharp reminder this of how little the industrial pattern of that time resembled our own and how much of modern industrialism was to come), the Vellum Bookbinders' with 536, the Barge Builders' and the Match Makers' with 400 each, and the Waiters' Union with 200.

The Socialist societies represented were the Independent Labour Party which had 13,000 members, the Social Democratic Federation which had 9,000, and the Fabian Society which had 861—an almost

12

derisory number this, until one remembers the formidable intellectual equipment of the individuals who made it up. The Co-operative movement had been invited to send delegates but had not accepted.

For the most part, the delegates who assembled at the Memorial Hall were solid, sensible, matter-of-fact trade unionists, men with good records within their own societies but little fame outside them. But there were some such as Keir Hardie, John Burns, Ben Tillett, Will Thorne and James Sexton, who already had national and, indeed, international reputations as "political agitators," "strike leaders" and "working-class orators." And there were others such as Ramsay MacDonald, Philip Snowden, F. W. Jowett, J. R. Clynes, whose names, before they were done, were to be known the length and breadth of the country and beyond. There were—it is a commentary on the times—no women delegates.

The conference had been called because of a resolution passed in the previous September at the Trades Union Congress, then in its thirty-first year of life as the great assembly of the organized workers. This resolution had been presented to the Congress by a delegate of the Railway Servants', J. H. Holmes, and seconded by James Sexton of the Liverpool Dockers', but it had in fact been drafted by Keir Hardie and Ramsay MacDonald in the offices of the *Labour Leader*, the official organ of the Independent Labour Party. It represented the culmination of a long campaign fought under the leadership and with the passionate inspiration of Keir Hardie, the Scottish miner who more than any other single man is responsible for the existence of the British Labour Party as we know it. Its purpose was to bring into being an alliance of the trade unions and the new Socialist societies which would be strong enough to fight the political battle of the working-classes in Parliament and at the same time gradually convert the trade unions to the burning Socialist conviction which dominated all Keir Hardie's actions. Only if men were moved, he believed, by the warm-hearted, idealistic gospel of socialism could there be created a new economic and social order in which all men should have a true chance of happiness, and the long-established industrial pattern of exploiters and exploited be ended.

That was the purpose, the dream, behind the resolution. But the pedestrian words of the resolution did not sing of the dream.

Keir Hardie knew that he must not frighten those—and they were many—among the practical leaders of trade unionism at that time who feared any excursion into politics or else were convinced that the political hopes of trade unionism lay in a junior—a very junior—partnership with the Liberal Party, which still carried with it into the new century the tremendous echoes of Mr. Gladstone's moral authority.

Only a few years earlier the Trades Union Congress had shown how influential still was the political word of its older members by passing a resolution excluding all delegates, including Keir Hardie himself, who, whatever their working-class background, were not either actually at work in their trade at the time or engaged as trade-union officials. They had passed it, moreover, with the avowed purpose of freeing the trade unions from "the influence of Socialist adventurers."

The new militant trade unionists—the men who were busy struggling to organize the unskilled and semi-skilled workers, the dockers, the gas stokers, the agricultural labourers, the sweated employees of the tailoring trades; the ninety per cent of workers with whom the old craft unions had not concerned themselves— the men and women who had fought and won the London match girls' strike and the great London dock strike—did not feel this way. They wanted, as Keir Hardie did, a trade-union movement which would organize the workers politically as well as industrially, although not all of them shared his faith in a Socialist movement that should transcend all barriers of class. But it was necessary to move cautiously. The older trade unions must on no account be hurried.

What was important was that they should agree to discuss measures which could, if not immediately, then in due course, pro-duce an alliance which would give socialism those firm roots in the organized Labour movement which it must have if it was to become strong: an alliance capable also of harnessing to the organization of the trade unions the enthusiasm and the idealism of the men and women of all classes whom the conception of democratic socialism had begun to attract. The resolution presented to the Trades Union Congress in the previous September, that historic resolution which was to have such profound consequences to the political, social and

14

economic structure of Britain—had therefore read prosaically enough. This is how it ran:

> "That this Congress, having regard to its decisions in former years, and with a view to securing a better representation of the interests of Labour in the House of Commons, hereby instructs the Parliamentary Committee to invite the co-operation of all the co-operative, socialistic, trade-union, and other working-class organizations to jointly co-operate on lines mutually agreed upon, in convening a special congress of representatives from such of the above-named organizations as may be willing to take part to devise ways and means for securing the return of an increased number of Labour members in the next Parliament."

No trumpet call to social revolution there, it will be seen, no appeal to idealism, no finger pointing prophetically to the future, only a businesslike assertion that it might be useful to consider the advantage of returning specifically Labour members to Parliament. Yet even so innocently-worded a resolution as this met with strong resistance from many of the older trade unionists. They feared the consequence of any move that seemed to be directed to changing their own conception of a trade union as a craft organization primarily concerned with safeguarding the interests of its members by direct negotiation with individual employers and by the provision of Friendly Society benefits.

The views of this group were voiced at the T.U.C. by Thomas Ashton, secretary of the Cotton Spinners'. It was, he declared, a sheer waste of time to bring such a resolution before the Congress. It should not, he said, even be discussed, for not one trade unionist in ten thousand would give such a proposal a moment's consideration even if it were passed. Moreover, if trade unionism were to turn itself into a political party it would inevitably come to grief.

Nevertheless, despite his objections, the resolution was discussed and, having been discussed, was passed after a speech from James Sexton who brought to its support all the fire and cleverness of his Irish eloquence, and a calm, common-sense appeal from Miss Margaret Bondfield, then the assistant secretary of the Shop Assistants' Union, who thirty years later was to be Minister of Labour in a Labour Government and the first woman Cabinet Minister.

15

But it was passed only by a comparatively narrow majority—546,000 votes to 434,000. It was passed, but that might well have been the last heard of it—as it had been of other not vastly dissimilar, if not quite so significant, resolutions on earlier occasions —if its supporters had not been energetic and clever. In the normal way of things, such a resolution after being approved by Congress would have been referred for consideration to what was known as the Parliamentary Committee of the T.U.C. Had that happened on this occasion there would almost certainly have been no conference at the Memorial Hall four months later. And the Labour Party would not have been born so soon as it was.

Most of the members of the Parliamentary Committee disliked the purpose behind the resolution. They were ready, as in duty bound, to consider it. But they had already made up their minds to take no action on it if it came before them. The sponsors of the resolution were aware of the danger. They persuaded Congress, therefore, to refer the resolution not to the Parliamentary Committee as a whole, but, instead, to a special joint committee of four members of the Parliamentary Committee and two members of each of the three powerful Socialist societies: the Independent Labour Party, the Social Democratic Federation, and the Fabian Society.

This having been agreed, the Parliamentary Committee made a further tactical error. It accepted as two of the members of the special committee W. C. Steadman and Will Thorne, both of whom had become convinced of the necessity of parliamentary action and were opposed to the majority of their colleagues on this issue. The Parliamentary Committee's remaining representatives, Sam Woods and R. Bell, were both Liberals. They had little chance against the advocates of a Labour alliance. Not only were they outnumbered, they were heavily out-gunned. For the Socialist societies sent to the Committee the formidable combination of Bernard Shaw and E. R. Pease for the Fabians, Keir Hardie and Ramsay MacDonald for the I.L.P., and Harry Quelch and H. R. Taylor for the S.D.F.

The Socialists knew exactly what they wanted. They knew on what to compromise and on what to stand firm. As a result the special committee was quickly committed to the convening of another conference to consider resolutions recommending that the working-class should be represented in the House of Commons by men sympathetic with the aims and demands of the Labour movement. It agreed also to suggest that a distinct Labour Group should be set up in Parliament having its own whips and its own policy, although as a gesture of conciliation to the Parliamentary Committee of the T.U.C. it was added that it must be willing to co-operate with any group engaged on promoting legislation in the direct interest of Labour or with any party opposing measures which were against the interests of Labour. Furthermore, the special committee recommended that the proposed conference should be asked to set up a permanent committee representing the trade unions, the Co-operative societies, if they would agree to come in as a body, and the Socialist societies.

It was with this very practical agenda before it that the Memorial Hall Conference met. It met, it will be seen, to consider the establishment of something unique and in its way peculiarly British—certainly quite unlike any development of the working-class movement in any other part of the world: an alliance, or federation, of the organizations of industrial labour and of those Socialist societies which recruited their members from all classes. Elsewhere the Socialist and Labour Parties, although they appealed specifically to the organized workers and looked to them for their main membership, recruited and continued to recruit their members individually. The conception of a Labour alliance in which the organized workers would participate not as individuals but *en bloc* through their trade unions was a specifically British conception and one which, as time was to show, was to give the British Socialist movement a strength and, above all, a stability that none of the Continental Socialist movements could achieve.

But for the moment the alliance the conference met to consider was not a specifically Socialist one—it was not indeed to become so for many years. The conference itself, it has to be remembered, was by no means fully representative even of the industrial workers organized in the trade unions affiliated to the T.U.C. Its purpose was not to found a Socialist Party but the more restricted one of returning to Parliament men who would represent the interests not of one particular trade union or group of trade unions, but of the trade-union and Labour movement as a whole. When they were returned they would, it was hoped, co-operate in

17

a common policy. But the scope and content of that policy was not defined.

Nor were the hundred and twenty-nine delegates who assembled in the Memorial Hall by any means united in their view as to what the purpose of such an alliance, if it were to be formed, should be and what policy Labour members, if there were to be Labour members, should follow.

There were among them three sharply defined groups of opinion. The first wanted a federation whose sole purpose should be that of promoting the election of working men and no others to Parliament. The second wanted such a federation to promote the election of all candidates sponsored by one or other of the affiliated organizations and sympathetic to the general aims of the Labour movement irrespective of whether they were working men or not. The third wanted the federation to establish a political party based upon recognition of the class war and to sponsor only candidates specifically pledged to the socialization of the means of production, distribution and exchange.

If either the first or third of these groups had had their way it is doubtful whether the British Labour Party would ever have risen to political power; certainly its history would have been very different from that of the Labour Party as we know it.

The first would have turned it into a purely trade-union pressure-group robbed of the contribution that the crusading fervour, the broader vision and the intellectual energy of the Socialists of all classes could bring. The third would have turned it into a Marxist party on the Continental model, which would, at the very start, have antagonized both a large part of the trade-union support upon which the new movement so depended for its numerical strength and those of all classes who, under the inspiration of the I.L.P., the Fabian Society, the *Clarion* and the Christian Socialists were moving towards an ethical conception of democratic socialism very different from the materialistic conception of the Marxists. Fortunately, the middle view prevailed.

But first the conference, opening with a formality certainly not behind that of more established and more traditional political gatherings, heard an address of welcome to the delegates from J. T. Chandler, chairman of the Parliamentary Committee of the

T.U.C. He, in cautious phrases, expressed the hope that "the outcome of our deliberations will be the evolution of a scheme which will command the support of the trade unionists and of the non-unionists of the country and that, as a result, we will have a much larger number of friends in the House of Commons in the future than we unfortunately have at the present moment."

The conference then unanimously elected as its chairman W. C. Steadman, who had been a member of the preliminary committee and who was a delegate of the small but sturdy Barge Builders' Union with its four hundred members. Steadman, in addition to being a trade unionist, was also a Fabian. He was, however, not by any means a convinced Socialist. On the contrary, he was himself a Lib-Lab M.P., that is, a Labour man who had been returned to Parliament with the support and agreement of the Liberals and who in general worked and voted with the Liberal Party in the House of Commons. He had been returned for Stepney two years previously in a straight fight with a Conservative, receiving (an evidence of the smallness of the electorate at that time) 2,492 votes to his opponent's 2,472. Nevertheless, although he had been elected to Parliament as at least half a Liberal, he had become convinced of the need for specifically Labour M.P.s.

> "I have," he said, "been a member of the House of Commons but a short time, but I have been there sufficiently long to know that every interest is represented and protected in that House, especially when privilege and monopoly are attacked, but the interest of labour. The great industrial army of the country, the men who are endeavouring to raise mankind not by the shedding of human blood but by the peaceful conquest of the ballot box, are the only class who are insufficiently represented in the House of Commons."

He wound up his opening speech amidst the cheers of the delegates with the declaration: "Whether we form a Labour Party or ally ourselves to other political parties in the State, let us be represented by men of character."

So much was common ground: labour, by which was meant in the main the manual workers, needed more representatives in Parliament. After much struggle the Reform Act of 1867 had given the vote to many of the better-paid urban workers—to those who were householders, paid rates and had resided in a constituency for one year, or who lodged in rooms with an annual rental of £10 —and the Act of 1884 had widened the franchise in the rural areas. Now the question to be considered in the light of working-class experience since the Reform Acts was how this right to vote could best be organized and used—how were the voters to be so mobilized that the interests of the manual workers, the largest and most unrepresented class, should be given their due weight.

That the manual workers needed more adequate representation —on that, all in the Memorial Hall were agreed. But were these representatives to be organized in a new party—a Labour Party —or were they to be allied to other political parties? They should be men of character—that, too, was of course accepted by all. But were they to be working men only? They were to advance the interests of labour—yes, but how? By advocating certain restricted measures of industrial reform, by fighting the class war on a wide front or by some middle way?

As soon as the chairman sat down the divisions within the conference on all these issues became apparent. At once the delegate of the Upholsterers' Union, R. W. Jones, moved the uncompromising resolution: "That this Conference is in favour of the working-classes being represented in the House of Commons by members of the working-classes as being most likely to be sympathetic with the aims and demands of the Labour movement." This proposal for an exclusively working-class and trade-union party was seconded by the delegate of the tiny Waiters' Union, Paul Vogel.

It was answered by George N. Barnes, general secretary of the Engineers' Amalgamated Society, the largest of the trade unions represented at the conference. Barnes, who had begun his own working life in a weaving shed at the age of eleven and become apprenticed to an engineer before he was twelve, was one of the pioneer members of the I.L.P. He had no patience with the narrow doctrine preached by Jones and Vogel. He moved as an amendment: "That this Conference is in favour of working-class opinion being represented in the House ot Commons by men sympathetic with the aims and demands of the Labour movements and whose candidatures are promoted by one or other of the organized movements represented at this Conference" (the last three words were later altered to "represented by the constitution which this Conference is about to frame," in order to make room for the Co-operative societies if they would agree to join).

This was seconded by John Burns, Independent Labour M.P. for Battersea. Burns was later to move farther and farther from the Labour movement, and in 1905 to become President of the Local Government Board in Campbell-Bannerman's Liberal administration and thus the first man of working-class origin to reach Cabinet rank. But at this time he was at the height of his national power and prestige as a left-wing organizer, agitator and leader of the unemployed. He had roused the sympathy of the whole nation for the London dockers in their strike for sixpence an hour—"the full round orb of the dockers' tanner," as he called it. He was recognized as one of the supreme mob-orators of his own or indeed any other day—a vital, pugnacious, egotistical, blustering genius of a man who found it always almost as easy to quarrel with his own side as to attack those whom he regarded as his own and the workers' enemies.

Now he scornfully attacked the proposal that Labour representation should be rigidly restricted to members of the working-class. "I am getting tired of working-class boots, working-class brains, working-class houses and working-class margarine," he said, with a gesture of contemptuous dismissal, and he told the delegates that they should no longer be prisoners to class prejudice, but should consider parties and policies apart from all class organizations.

It may well be that Burns's objectives even at this time were not the same as those of the others who shared his dislike of the proposal of a purely working-class party. While they thought in terms of a Socialist party which should embrace men of goodwill of whatever class, he was concerned, no doubt, to avoid barring the door to association with Liberals with whom he found himself increasingly in sympathy. Be that as it may, the resolution proposing working-class members was rejected and George Barnes's amendment was carried by 102 votes to 3. A number of delegates abstained from voting on this basic question, presumably because they felt that they had not received definite instructions from their trade unions.

The conference was over its first hurdle. The door to a classless

Socialist party had been left open. The next hurdle came immediately. James Macdonald of the Social Democratic Federation, who was also secretary of the London Trades Council and a strong Marxist Socialist, proposed that "the representatives of the working-class movement in the House of Commons shall form there a distinct party with a party organization separate from the capitalist parties based upon a recognition of the class war and having for its ultimate object the socialization of the means of production, distribution and exchange."

This resolution struck at the whole conception of what they were about held by most of the trade-union delegates present. It was denounced by James Sexton, representing the Liverpool dockers, as designed to revive a spirit which had been responsible for more recrimination and bad feeling in the Labour movement than anything else. Frederick Rogers, the delegate of the small Vellum Bookbinders' Union, who, like many of his fellows, had come into the Labour movement by way of the Christian faith, saw it as ruinous because it would label across the front of the conference the words "Class War." In an attempt to prevent any such sweeping policy from holding the field, the Shipwrights' delegate, A. Wilkie, then moved an amendment by which the functions of a Labour group in Parliament would have been limited to the support of a specifically trade-union platform of four or five planks to be drawn up by the conference as "embracing questions upon which the vast majority of the workers in the country are in agreement." On all "purely political questions," said this amendment, Labour M.P.s should be left "entirely free."

This proposal, it will be seen, would have had the effect of turning Labour M.P.s into members of a purely pressure-group organized to promote action on a restricted number of issues of trade-union concern and without any other purpose or common political philosophy.

Yet so strong was the feeling among the delegates against anything that might seem to involve the trade unions in specifically Socialist activities, and so deep the suspicion of anything savouring of the Marxian doctrine of the class war, that the amendment was at once carried. But it is clear from the voting—59 to 35 with 35 abstentions—that many delegates were not happy about so restrictive

22

a solution of the problem of what was to be the function of the Labour parliamentary group for which they had voted a few minutes earlier.

Keir Hardie, although he more than any man had been responsible for the movement of opinion which had made possible the calling of this conference, had so far taken little part in its discussions. Now he intervened decisively to rescue the conference from the impasse into which it had got itself and to save from destruction by an ill-considered vote the conception of a true alliance between the trade unions and socialism, to which goal his efforts had long been devoted.

He proposed a further amendment which, instead of committing the Party either to a harshly materialist programme of class war, as the Social Democratic Federation wanted, or turning it into a mere pressure-group concerned only with a few trade-union questions, as the amendment just carried by the conference would have done, had, in his own words, the purpose of forming in the House of Commons a Labour Party. This should have its own political policy and its own whips, it should act in all that concerned the welfare of the workers in a manner free and unhampered by entanglements with other parties, and should be composed of men selected as candidates by one or other of the affiliated organizations without let or hindrance. The one condition should be that every candidate should be required to undertake that, if returned to Parliament, he would join the Labour group and act in harmony with its decisions.

Keir Hardie's amendment has great historic significance. It was so worded as to avoid, on the one hand, antagonizing any of the trade-union groups who were afraid of a purely Socialist policy, while also avoiding, on the other, an inflexibility of aim that would have made future development difficult. Wilkie, although his own proposal had just been carried, at once offered to withdraw it in favour of Hardie's amendment, and this amendment was then carried unanimously by the conference after only a short discussion. Thereafter the principles it embodied determined the composition of the Labour Party for many years and provided the foundation upon which the Party was able to develop and expand at a rate unequalled by any other democratic movement in British history.

23

Yet its wording is without dramatic quality or distinction of style. It was accepted and it made possible a political, social and economic achievement far beyond the hopes or expectations of any at the conference because, like many other decisions of decisive importance in British history, it represented a compromise exactly suited to the conditions and moods of the time. While establishing the essential principle of independence it left the ultimate purpose for which that independence was to be used sufficiently undefined not to invite counter definitions and disputations which would have wrecked the new party at its start. Its terms, which followed closely the recommendations of the original joint committee, were as follows:

"That this Conference is in favour of establishing a distinct Labour Group in Parliament who shall have their own whips and agree upon their policy, which must embrace a readiness to co-operate with any party which, for the time being, may be engaged in promoting legislation in the direct interest of labour, and be equally ready to associate themselves with any party in opposing measures having an opposite tendency; and, further, members of the Labour Group shall not oppose any candidate whose nomination is being promoted in terms of Resolution 1."

With the passing of this resolution and the earlier one referred to in it, by which George Barnes had defeated the attempt to restrict Labour representation to members of the working-classes, the Labour Party was born, although six years were to pass before it was formally given that title.

It was not yet a Socialist party and was not indeed to become specifically so until the passage of eighteen years and the experience of a world war. But it was established as a party independent of all other political parties, although sometimes ready to work with them for particular ends, and one in which trade unionists and Socialists could work together in friendly alliance in pursuit of a distinctly Labour policy and programme.

The content of that policy and the scope of that programme were not defined. These were wisely left at this stage for consideration and agreement by the members of the Parliamentary Party themselves, guided by the decisions of those organizations which had selected them and promoted their parliamentary candidatures.

In this both Keir Hardie and the delegates to the conference showed their practical wisdom and their understanding of the British political character. That character thrives best in a constitutional framework which does not impose upon it the rigidness of a doctrinaire philosophy or even of a narrowly defined practical programme. but leaves, instead, sufficient freedom for the interpretation of events and needs and the common-sense application of fundamental philosophies according to the circumstances of the time.

With this accomplished the conference adjourned until the following day, Wednesday, 28 February.

Having decided that it was desirable to form a distinct Labour group in Parliament, and having agreed on the considerations which should determine the composition and functions of such a group, the conference, when it met the next day, turned at once to the question of forming a permanent political organization to support these policies. On the first day it had been concerned with the formation of what is now the Parliamentary Labour Party. On the second day it set itself to consider the measures which were to bring into being what is now the national Labour Party.

As a beginning the conference agreed that an executive committee should be appointed consisting of seven representatives of the trade unions, two representatives each from the I.L.P. and the Social Democratic Federation and one Fabian. And it was agreed that the members of the committee should be elected not by the conference as a whole but by their representative organizations. This embodied a principle of great importance and one that distinguished this new Labour Party from other political parties.

Thus it was made clear that this new political party was in fact not to be a party in the strict sense at all but a federation—a federation of trade unions and Socialist societies which would retain their individual identities and elect their own executive members. This federal pattern was to become the permanent pattern of the Labour Party, and although, by a resolution passed at the very end of the conference, local trades councils were added to those entitled to federate, the main pattern laid down in 1900 was not otherwise amended in any important particular until 1918. Only then for the first time was the constitution altered and widened to permit of individual as well as organizational membership. And even after this change the federal pattern continued to exist, as it still does, for individual members were required to join local constituency Labour parties, not the national body, and the constituency parties were added to the federation with the right to send delegates to the annual conference and elect their own representatives on the executive.

The members of the first committee were Frederick Rogers, of the Vellum Bookbinders'; Thomas Greenhall, Miners' Federation; R. Bell, Amalgamated Railway Servants'; Pete Curran, Gas Workers'; A. Gee, Textile Workers'; A. Wilkie, Shipwrights'; and J. Hodge, Steel Smelters', representing the trade unions; Keir Hardie and James Parker, representing the I.L.P.; James Macdonald and Harry Quelch, representing the Social Democratic Federation, and Edward R. Pease, representing the Fabian Society. Frederick Rogers was the first chairman.

Rogers represented in his character and personality so much of the ethical and radical tradition that distinguished early Labour and trade-union movements and stamped them with an impress so different from that common to many of the Continental movements, that his election had its own significance.

Rogers was fifty-four when he became the first chairman of the Labour Representation Committee and was to live until close on eighty, a fine-built, vigorous old man, proud of his craft of bookbinding, deeply read in English literature, particularly Shakespeare, Ruskin and Browning, and inspired by a moral faith that coloured all the activities of his life. He had been born in Whitechapel and was apprenticed early to the trade of vellum bookbinding. As a serious young apprentice interested in reading books as well as binding them, he was immensely influenced by the teachings of Frederick Denison Maurice and Charles Kingsley and the Christian Socialists. He was himself indeed a practical Christian of a kind which has fortunately been frequent in the British Labour movement and of which, later, George Lansbury was so typical and so noble an example.

He sought to translate his deep belief in the brotherhood of man into terms of a political philosophy and to live it in his daily life. This made him a radical and a trade unionist. He was interested in everything which would make men happier and had himself

26

an immense enthusiasm for knowledge. He lived frugally and saved hard so that he could travel abroad and see for himself the master-pieces of art and architecture of which he had read in Ruskin's writings. By his own studies he made himself a considerable Elizabethan scholar who was proud of being invited by Sir Henry Irving to advise him on several of his Shakespearean productions. He was one of the pioneers of the University Extension Movement and a most active member of the Browning Settlement in south-east London, and of Toynbee Hall in the days of Canon Barnett.

A fluent, popular and engaging speaker on all kinds of topics, he toured the country as the century opened, working day in and day out and addressing hundreds of meetings in chapels and working-men's institutes, literary societies and ethical clubs to arouse interest in a scheme for old-age pensions. All this activity he combined with an energetic career as a trade-union organizer—and in such spare time as he had left over liked best to entertain himself and his friends by reciting with great verve and not inconsiderable art the more patriotic passages from Shakespeare's historical dramas. He was a lovable and many-sided character, one of those many who by their personality helped to give to the political struggle of the workers in Britain its humanity, its kindliness and its tolerance, and who brought to everything they did a quality of good-humoured tolerance, combined with a habit of blunt plain-speaking when their emotions were aroused, that, one likes to think, has something about it peculiarly English.

There were many at that first conference more intellectually able than Frederick Rogers, many who understood more clearly than he the economic and social forces they must fight, and who could perceive better than he what lay ahead. There were not a few who were to achieve a place in the political and industrial history of the movement and the nation to which he could not aspire. But perhaps no man among them all could better have represented the qualities which have given the British Labour movement its special character, nor more clearly typified the nature of its roots in the British tradition, than this self-taught vellum bookbinder.

Having elected an executive committee, the conference then proceeded to choose a secretary. And here it made a decision which was to prove of the utmost significance and to have for good and

27

ill a profound influence on the history of the Labour Party for more than thirty years. The first name suggested was that of Sam Woods, a member of the Parliamentary Committee of the T.U.C., but it was ruled that as the conference had taken over the functions of the Parliamentary Committee in this matter of Labour representation, and as Mr. Woods was not a delegate, he could not be nominated. A Manchester councillor, F. Brocklehurst, who was an I.L.P. delegate, then suggested that there should be two secretaries, but this met with no favour, and J. Hodge, the Steel Smelters' delegate, who had just been elected as a trade-union representative on the committee and who was also a Manchester man, proposed that Brocklehurst himself should be secretary. This was seconded by another Manchester man, J. B. Williams, of the Amalgamated Musicians'. Brocklehurst, however, declined to stand and instead nominated his fellow-member of the I.L.P., Ramsay MacDonald. This was seconded by A. Wardle, one of the Railway Servants' delegates, and Ramsay MacDonald was unanimously elected.

MacDonald had taken little public part in the conference so far. He had not spoken in any of the debates, but he had been, with Keir Hardie, one of the prime movers in the events which led to it, and during his membership of the preliminary joint committee had been the powerful draughtsman of the conference agenda. He was then thirty-four years of age and was already widely known as one of the most brilliant of Socialist speakers, with a style of oratory which, although in retrospect it seems over-elaborate and shot through with an excessive delight in romantic analogies, fell graciously upon the ears of contemporary audiences. He had a most beautiful speaking voice and a remarkably handsome and romantic presence. Moreover, he was a writer and journalist of considerable distinction who had written much on socialism and had won a discriminating audience.

Although born and brought up in acute poverty in the little Scottish fishing village of Lossiemouth, the natural son of a farm labourer, he had been fortunate in the influence exercised on him by two remarkable women, his mother and his grandmother. Both of them had to a high degree the tenacity and love of learning that characterized so many humble Scottish women of their class and age. And, like many poor Scots boys before him he owed much to the village dominie who rescued him from the plough to which he seemed destined, and trained him as a pupil teacher. By the time the Labour Representation Conference met he had already moved far from his early beginnings, partly by his own exertions and talents and partly by his marriage to Margaret Ethel Gladstone, the daughter of Dr. J. Hall Gladstone, Faraday's successor at the Royal Institution. Mrs. MacDonald was a niece of Lord Kelvin and was herself a woman of remarkable sympathy, character and intelligence. Her early death was a tragedy not only for MacDonald personally but indirectly for the Labour Party, since it removed one whose character complemented his and gave it a stability the lack of which was in the end to bring tragedy.

MacDonald at the time of his election was already a man of wide interests. He had trained himself as a biologist before turning to journalism and politics, had had an excellent education in the technique of politics as secretary to a Liberal M.P., had fought an election as an Independent Labour candidate, had spoken, lectured and written in many parts of the country, and had travelled more extensively than any other among those gathered to form the new party—to Canada, America, South Africa, Australia and India, as well as on the Continent.

By his natural talents, the good fortune of his voice and presence, his gifts of persuasion and his experience, he was marked out for political leadership—and was fully conscious that he was. He had worked indefatigably and skilfully with Keir Hardie to bring this conference into being. More than any man, other than Keir Hardie—but with a different, a more intellectual and, in some ways, if a less visionary yet a more practical understanding than Hardie's —he perceived what needed to be done to create a Labour Party and the vast potentialities that lay ahead if it were to be done right.

To some the post of unpaid secretary to the new committee might have seemed a routine and unimportant one—as no doubt it did to Messrs. Wardle, Hodge and Williams when they made their preliminary proposals. MacDonald knew differently. He knew that with the wrong man as secretary this committee might peter out into well-meaning futility, but that with the right man it could be forged into a genuine Socialist Party, despite the misgivings of some of the trade unionists there. He felt that he was the right man

—as indeed he was at the time. Yet, since he was cast in the mould of parliamentary leadership rather than that of the organizer and administrator, the secretaryship was for him a stepping stone rather than, as it was for his successor nine years later, Arthur Henderson, a post which itself offered an unparalleled opportunity for unselfish devotion in building the most successful party machine in the country.

MacDonald's election to the secretaryship was thus a decisive development, although possibly only a few of those at the conference realized it. The principles upon which alone an independent Labour Party could be founded had been laid down—MacDonald's election ensured that those principles would be given action and practical life.

Three other important decisions remained to be taken before all that was necessary to bring a Labour Party into being should have been accomplished.

The first was to give the new Labour Representation Committee some authority in determining who were and who were not to be regarded as truly representative of the Labour interest at parliamentary elections and endorsed as official Labour candidates. The second was to ensure that the Socialist and trade-union interests represented at the conference should continue to act together. And the third was to provide the new committee with funds.

On the first issue a conflict of views occurred. Ben Tillett proposed that the committee should collect information about candidates who pledged themselves to support the policy of the Labour group and should recommend the "United Labour Party" to support them.

Will Thorne, with a greater realism, moved as an amendment that the committee should prepare a list of candidates promoted in accordance with the first resolution passed by the conference, that is, by one or other of the organizations affiliated to the Labour Representation Committee, and should publish it as the official list of the United Labour Party and recommend the candidates in it for the support of working-class electors.

He was backed in this by Keir Hardie. Hardie attacked Tillett's proposal with great force. "Such a proposal," he said, "would bind us to support any adventurer or scallywag, no matter how unprincipled, who might come before us with a promise to support our programme." Moreover, it would make it easy for the Liberal Party to split the new movement by putting up candidates who promised to support Labour aspirations. Fortunately for the new party, Hardie's view and that of Will Thorne prevailed. The amendment to Ben Tillett's original resolution was carried with only two votes against it.

A resolution that the committee should keep closely in touch with all organizations running Labour candidates, and should convene a Labour Representation Conference each year, was then put and carried unanimously. There was to be no splitting up again into individual political units without contact with each other after this conference. The decision was taken which was to establish the long series of annual conferences that were to formulate Labour policy over the years and give the Parliamentary Party roots in a great national movement that could act as a constant guide and director of policy.

When the question of finance arose it at once became clear, however, that those present, although they had laid the foundations for a great political party, were still far from being ready to accept all that it implied. A proposal made by the delegate of the Printers' Warehousemen, a small union with only 573 members, that all the affiliated organizations should pay an annual contribution to a central political fund of one penny per member, was negatived practically unanimously with hardly any discussion. Yet within four years the absolute necessity of contributions on at least this scale was to become recognized and a levy per member of exactly that amount made compulsory.

At this first conference, however, the most that the delegates would agree to was an annual contribution from each organization of ten shillings for every thousand workers—a rate which brought in an income of £210 10s. in the first year of the Labour Representation Committee's existence. Today the Labour Party's income from this source alone is only just short of £100,000 a year and the annual affiliation fee is 6d. per member.

But in 1900 even a contribution of ten shillings per thousand members seemed a considerable sum to many of the delegates, and it was only after a debate in which Will Thorne, while strongly

31

supporting the proposal, warned the conference that many trade unions would have difficulty in getting the money, that it was agreed.

Thus with an unpaid secretary and financial resources of the scantiest, but with agreement on principles and on organization the practicability and the durability of which were to be demonstrated over and over again as the years passed, a Labour Representation Committee, which was in effect a Labour Party and was formally to take that name within six years, was launched.

The hundred and twenty-nine delegates had met for two days. To the observer lacking the vision that the perspective of history gives, their proceedings must have seemed of a humdrum character. They had discussed quietly, and with a formality and good sense characteristic of the trade-union movement from which so many of them came, a number of not very excitingly worded resolutions. They represented organizations embracing not many more than half a million of the many millions of workers in the country. And even of the 545,000 trade unionists represented at this first conference, more than a third, including the Miners, the Engineers and three of the other largest unions, were, when its recommendations went back to them, to reject, for the time being, the proposal that they should affiliate to the new body. As a result the total trade-union membership that could be reported, when the first annual report was made, was only some 350,000.

Yet those who had met at the Memorial Hall had, as time was soon to show, participated in a significant moment in history. They had turned over a page and begun a new era in the political life of the British people. What they had done was to have results more far-reaching than most of them could have dreamed. Yet what had been begun in that hall had only been possible because the movement these men spoke for was rooted in the past. They had laid the foundations for a unique synthesis of Socialist and trade-union thought, a unique alliance of men and women of many classes and diverse backgrounds, a coming together of movements of opinion that flowed from many sources and had their beginnings in many different circumstances, economic, industrial, social, ethical and intellectual.

It was because this conference, so undramatic in its external appearance, came at a moment of intense dramatic value in the

JOHN BURNS

His oratory roused the nation's sympathy for the London dockers in their strike for sixpence an hour. He was the first working-class M.P. to reach Cabinet rank.

R. B. CUNNINGHAME GRAHAM

The aristocratic hero of the clashes in Trafalgar Square and president of the first Scottish Labour Party, 1888.

H M. HYNDMAN

An early Marxist and founder of the Social Democratic Federation.

history of working-class and Socialist thought in Britain that it achieved what it did. Its unique significance cannot be comprehended, nor the developments that flowed from it properly understood, unless one looks to the circumstances, of which it was the natural culmination. It must be set against the background of the men and events that made it possible if one is to understand its true meaning.

CHAPTER II

THE BACKGROUND TO THE DECISION: THE FIRST PHASE

FOUR movements converged to make the modern Labour Party. All of them, inevitably, were affected during their development by world forces and by the impact of Socialist and revolutionary thought in other countries. But each of them transmuted the international influences to which it was subjected into a peculiarly British form—although one of them did so to a less degree than the others—with the result that the Socialist movement they created developed its own specifically British political method, its own unique organizational pattern and in large part its own philosophy. All of them were much less influenced by theory in their development than by the economic, political and social pattern of British society at the time and the one most influenced by theory made the least impact on British Socialist history. All were coloured in their philosophy and practice by the British tradition and were fed by many tributaries having their sources in the moral and intellectual history of the British people.

The first of these four movements which between them had so decisive an influence on the pattern of the Labour movement in Britain, and thus on the future course of British political history, was the new trade unionism. This came into existence in the closing years of the nineteenth century in response to the desperate need of the unskilled and semi-skilled workers in whom the established craft unions had little or no interest.

The second was the Social Democratic Federation—the only one among the immediate forebears of the British Labour Party to be specifically Marxist in inspiration. It became, for a short period, the political spearhead of working-class revolt against intolerable conditions, only to wane in influence as the brief insurrectionist phase of the Labour attack on the established economic and social order came to an end, and to dwindle into insignificance by reason of its adherence to a conception of the class war to which the great majority of the British working-classes were wholly unsympathetic.

The third was the Independent Labour Party, which, drawing upon moral and idealistic resources to which the Social Democratic Federation had little access, mobilized the awakened social conscience of men and women of all classes and brought into political life a crusading and evangelical spirit that had long been absent from it.

The fourth was the Fabian Society, which gave to British socialism much of its intellectual content. Although itself a profoundly unrevolutionary body, it contributed to the Labour movement a philosophy as truly revolutionary, in the sense of causing a fundamental change in men's outlooks, as any contribution made to economic and political thought by Marxism, and one much more rooted in the realities of the British situation and the natural attitude of mind of the British people.

Other movements had their part in the creation of the Labour Party: the Co-operative movement, which, although it refused to ally itself directly to the new party, had a profound influence on shaping the political attitude of many workers and in giving them self-confidence; Henry George and the single-taxers who were inspired by his book *Progress and Poverty* and by his lecture tour throughout Britain; Blatchford and the *Clarion* group who brought to the Socialist movement a gaiety, a sense of fellowship and a directness of appeal that was of incalculable value; and beyond and wider than these the ethical societies, the Christian Socialist movement and the great tradition of nonconformity which gave so many working men and women moral beliefs to which all the conditions imposed upon them by industrial capitalism were alien.

Like all organizations which possess the quality of permanence, the Labour Party had indeed not one source from which it drew its strength but many. It was a true product of the national life in that it derived from that life at many points. Nor was the personal factor missing. Its history was shaped not simply by the vast anonymous development of events, but by many great and diverse personalities—individual genius both of character and of mind had a great part in its growth.

Nevertheless, these four movements, the new trade unionism, the S.D.F., the I.L.P., and the Fabian Society, the social forces they represented and mobilized and the men and women most intimately associated with them, had the major role.

The most decisive of them all, because it was by reason of its development that the alliance between the organized industrial workers and the Socialists became possible, was the new trade unionism. The new trade unionism could not of itself have brought into being the Labour Party which began in February, 1900. For that the Socialist societies, and particularly the Independent Labour Party, were needed also. But without it the Socialist societies which consciously worked for that creation would have lacked the means to make their dream a reality.

Yet this new trade unionism was not, in its beginnings, political. It was, as was natural, concerned first and foremost with industrial action. It arose and grew in strength in response to industrial needs, and in its industrial responses it was an inevitable product of the growth of nineteenth-century capitalism. It represented the instinctive challenge of the disinherited to conditions which, at the height of Britain's material wealth and international prestige, condemned them to poverty and degradation.

How deep was that poverty, how bitter and hopeless that degradation, was made plain for all time in a fully documented investigation into the social conditions of the people of London financed by a great social reformer and wealthy Liverpool shipowner, Charles Booth, in the closing years of Victoria's reign.

There is something peculiarly appropriate to the British tradition in that this survey which had an effect on public opinion of the most far-reaching character, and which confirmed, and much more than confirmed, the accusations previously made by those who were dismissed as "Socialist agitators," should have been initiated by a man of wealth who was also a man of great public spirit.

In the annals of the Labour Party the name of Charles Booth, rich merchant and shipowner, deserves a place of honour. Not because he was himself a Socialist, for he was not, but because he

held fast to the fine liberal tradition that the truth should be un-
covered and told, however uncomfortable it might be and whatever its implications for the society which had made him wealthy.
He was not a creator of the new trade unionism, that was created
by the conditions which the survey he financed brought into the
public light of day. But he was, however undeliberately, its greatest
single ally. The facts he published created a public opinion and
a public sympathy which enabled the new trade unions of the
unskilled workers to achieve victories that would otherwise have
been infinitely more difficult for them and perhaps impossible. He
was concerned only to serve the truth. By serving it he served also
the cause of all who were trodden down in the ruthless pursuit
of wealth.

The first fruits of the survey he initiated appeared between the
years 1889 and 1891—some ten years before the Labour Representation Conference at the Memorial Hall. It was published under the
title *Labour and Life of the People*. It provided irrefutable evidence,
based on the most elaborate inquiry statistically verified, that over
a million and a quarter people in the capital city of the wealthiest
empire known to the world were at that very moment dragging
out an existence far below a poverty line which itself had been set
at a level making no allowance for anything but the very barest
necessities of life. As the evidence he collected was examined it
showed that 32 per cent of the entire population of London was
living in the most acute and degrading poverty and that in the
East End of London the proportion was 60 per cent. Later investigations, based on Booth's methods and carried out in provincial towns
and in the rural areas, showed that what was true of London was
true of the rest of Britain.

Triumphant Victorian capitalism was seen to be founded on a
system of economic oppression and moral and material degradation
that was an affront to the Christianity it flaunted. The efficiency it
boasted was in large part an efficiency made possible only by the
inhuman exploitation of many millions of workers throughout the
country.

Yet if the disclosures made by Booth and others stirred the
social consciousness of many of the middle-classes and thus gave
the Labour movement important allies for the future, they did little

to persuade industrialists to alter the conditions that were so profitable to them. Only trade-union organization, supported by political action, could do that.

Even fifteen years after the publication of the first volumes of Booth's *Labour and Life of the People*, 25 per cent of the adult workers of the United Kingdom were still earning less than 25s. a week. In the cotton trade the proportion was 40 per cent. In the jute industry nearly 50 per cent of the workers were paid less than £1 a week. The average wage of agricultural workers throughout the country was 18s. 6d. a week. In Dorset it was only 12s. 6d. a week.

Half of all the women in industry, according to figures compiled by the Board of Trade, were paid less than 10s. a week. Yet it was estimated that, with the cost of living at its then level, 15s. a week was the lowest amount on which any woman living by herself could exist.

In the tailoring trade 13s. a week was a high wage for a 58-hour week. Home workers were paid rates that forced them to a level of economic desperation that beggars description. The wage for completely making a man's coat was 4d. to 9d., that for making a pair of trousers 4d. to 8½d. Shirts were paid for at the rate of 8½d. a dozen. A hook and eye carder in Birmingham earned 4s. a week working ten hours a day. The average weekly earnings of matchbox makers working a 12-hour day were 5s.

These last were the sweated industries. These were the industries in which the workers were not organized—the industries in which Victorian capitalism was free to do what it pleased without let or hindrance. Yes, but in the 'eighties when the new unionism began to stir, 90 per cent of the workers in British industry were unorganized—and 90 per cent of the industries of Britain were sweated industries.

It was possible for the Parliamentary Committee of the Trades Union Congress to state in its annual report of 1884 that it saw little advantage in an international conference of trade unions because "the position we assume is that we are so well organized, so far ahead of foreign workmen that little can be done until these are more on a level with the skilled workers of Britain." But it was possible only because the Parliamentary Committee was thinking exclusively in terms of the 10 per cent or so of skilled workers organized in the trade unions then represented in the Trades Union Congress, and not at all of the 90 per cent of skilled and semi-skilled workers outside.

The existing trade unions were primarily—although not entirely, for the miners' organizations were an exception—craft unions concerned only to organize workers highly skilled in a particular craft. They were not concerned with workers in industries which depended mainly on unskilled labour or even with the less skilled workers in the industries in which their craftsmen members were employed.

Moreover, the trade-union scene was dominated by a group of "amalgamated societies" of which the Engineers' Amalgamated Society was the greatest example. Having brought into one group the local unions into which members of their craft had organized themselves in the past they had developed into rich composite societies no longer concerned solely with the organization of their members for industrial purposes, but equally with the provision of sick benefits, provident benefits and superannuation. They were Friendly Societies as much as, or even more than, trade unions.

It is true that they still organized to secure advantages through collective bargaining. They still included among their purposes the employment of the strike weapon if need be and the payment of strike pay during a dispute. But they were preoccupied with safe-guarding the funds they administered for Friendly Society and similar purposes. The need to safeguard these funds acted as a constant brake on their militancy. They avoided, if they could, any action that might lead to their having to use funds to finance a strike.

Moreover, the very fact of the large non-industrial benefits they offered to their members put their subscription rates at a level far beyond the reach of any but the better-paid workers. They were not for the unskilled and the ill-paid.

Their leaders had in the past done great and lasting service to the cause of the working-class. They had for the first time established organizations sufficiently strong financially to stand up against the economic depressions that had previously always wrecked workers' organizations. They had demonstrated the existence in the trade-union movement of men with the integrity and ability to manage large organizations and administer great funds. But they had fallen victims to their own success. They were so concerned to hold on to what they had that they had no interest in doing the job of organization that was crying out to be done.

Not only were they uninterested in the unskilled workers, but, so long as they dominated trade-union thought, organization for political purposes in the interests of labour as a whole was ruled out. They believed that their members could do better by direct negotiation with employers than by legislative action.

Thus year after year at the Trades Union Congress they fought the proposal that the trade unions should combine politically to obtain a legally enforced eight-hour day for all workers. Hours and conditions of labour must, they declared, be left exclusively to negotiations between trade unions and employers. It would be an intolerable interference with industrial liberty if the State were allowed to determine the hours of work of adult workers. They were satisfied with a position in which the only restriction on hours was that secured by one of the first working-class members of Parliament, Alexander Macdonald, restricting the hours of juvenile workers to ten a day. Beyond that they were for a very long time not prepared to go.

Between them and the underpaid workers of the new unskilled industries there was, as the Webbs said later, no more affinity than between those same unskilled workers and the House of Lords.

But the movement of events could not be stayed by those who, although with the most honest intentions, thought merely in terms of maintaining for a relative few what had been won by past struggle and organization. Depression and mass unemployment, intolerable conditions and starvation wages brought their own ferment. The new trade unionism—the trade unionism of the hitherto unorganized—arose because it was the only, the inevitable answer to the conditions of the time. Inevitable, but confronted with immense difficulties. For how could the unorganized workers of the depressed industries, living constantly under the threat of dismissal with little chance of finding a new job if they fell foul of their employers, be taught to organize? How could they, with their scanty wages, hope to accumulate the resources which alone would enable them to fight with some chance of success against their wealthy employers?

The first effort to do so, made by Ben Tillett in 1886, when he tried to organize the London dockers, failed. The dockers at Tilbury struck and were heavily defeated. The membership of Tillett's union, the Tea Operatives and General Labourers', fell to only three hundred. The prospect of successful organization seemed remote.

And then almost out of the blue and from a most unexpected quarter the answer came. In 1888, without organization and without money, the London match girls struck against the conditions in the East End match factories of Bryant and May's and won their fight. By so doing they set aflame a movement which was to prove a great turning point in British working-class history.

Like many decisive events, the match girls' strike came without premeditation, in response to a sudden passionate anger against a wanton act of oppression and injustice. It succeeded because it mobilized behind it forces greater than any the match girls themselves could command. Most important of these forces was a public opinion deeply stirred by the disclosures of Booth's survey of London. This was to provide the ally that the new unionism needed for its success.

In a small journal, named *The Link*, there had been appearing a series of articles exposing the appalling conditions under which the girls in the match factories had to work.

The editor of this paper and the author of these articles was Mrs. Annie Besant, one of the most remarkable women of her own or indeed any other day. She was a person of immense vitality, courage and charm and one of the greatest women orators there have ever been. Her personal magnetism on a platform was amazing: she could carry great crowds with her to the highest emotional peaks. Her pen was not so unrivalled a weapon as her voice, but she wielded it with great gusto and a complete disregard for any consideration other than the cause she had at heart. She was a friend of Charles Bradlaugh and a fellow member with him of the Secular Society. Because of her religious principles she had been deprived of her children and even refused permission to enter the Royal Botanic Gardens lest the curator's children who used it should be contaminated by her presence. But no sacrifice, no insult could deter her from what she believed to be right.

She had fought for freedom of principle since she was a girl. As the new movement of socialism came to birth she was naturally, inevitably, drawn into its struggle to improve the conditions of the poor and exploited, just as earlier she had been drawn into the struggle for freedom of conscience. She was one of the earliest members of the Fabian Society and one of the first of the Fabian Essayists: even among that brilliant company her personality shone undimmed. Later she was to turn to mysticism, transfer her passionate allegiance to Theosophy, become the prophet of a new religion and seek in the East a new saint to lead the world to the good life. But in all the tumultuous journeys of her life she was to retain, even into her old age, a passion of oratory and a magnetism of personality capable of moving the greatest crowds. She was an indomitable founder of small propagandist journals—she published, and actually paid for, some of Bernard Shaw's early novels in one of them, a magazine with the oddly unpropagandist title of *Our Corner*. She had started *The Link* as a radical Socialist journal that should be a potent weapon in rousing men and women to an understanding of the social conditions which existed all around them.

She wrote her articles on the conditions of the match girls with all the humane indignation that her nature commanded, combined with that careful documentation of facts that the Fabian method had taught her.

Her principal informant was a girl herself employed in the Bryant and May factory. This fact was discovered by the management of the firm and the girl was summarily dismissed. At once her fellow workers, stirred already to the beginnings of revolt by Mrs. Besant's advocacy of their cause, rallied to her support. They struck and appealed to Annie Besant to aid them.

The appeal was answered at once. All Annie Besant's passionate hatred of injustice and all her human sympathy for the oppressed responded. With the aid of Herbert Burrows, a member of the Social Democratic Federation, to whom she turned for practical advice and aid, she made the match girls' fight for better conditions into a crusade that stirred public opinion as it had never before been stirred on such a matter. She appealed for funds so that the girls should not be defeated by that most powerful of all the weapons that the employers had at their command—starvation. Within a few days £400 was subscribed by men and women of all classes. Within a fortnight public opinion was so roused and public sympathy for the girls was so great that the firm was forced to bow to it. It agreed to the improvement in conditions demanded and reinstated the strikers.

The match girls had won. They had won not because they had behind them, as the skilled workers of the older trades had, a strong organization, but because Annie Besant had known how to turn their very weakness into their most potent weapon. She had used that weakness to appeal over the heads of their employers to the awakened social conscience of ordinary men and women. With the aid of all the instruments of publicity she could mobilize, she had created a public opinion so strong that no employer dared withstand it. She had pointed the way. She had discovered almost by accident the road by which the new trade unionism could travel to success—not as a result of careful planning or prolonged theoretical analysis, but by her instinctive emotional reaction to injustice and her passionate conviction that others would feel as she did if only they knew the conditions under which men and women were being forced to work.

The lesson was quickly learned. The victory of the match girls was an inspiration that brought new hope to workers everywhere.

Its moral was at once seen and understood by a group of working-class leaders who were determined to turn trade unionism into a militant force that should fight the battle of all workers, unskilled as well as skilled. Chief among this group were John Burns and Tom Mann, both of them members of the Engineers' Amalgamated Society who had long been opposed to the exclusive and non-militant policy of the leaders of that union; Ben Tillett, a docker who had fought unsuccessfully to organize his fellow dockers two years before, and Will Thorne, a gas worker.

These four devoted themselves first to organizing the London gas strikers. They were so successful that they forced the three London gas companies to agree to an increase in wages and a reduction in working hours from twelve to eight.

This accomplished, Ben Tillett turned once more to organizing the London dockers. Under the stimulus of his efforts a group of dockers handling a difficult cargo at the South-west London Dock put forward on 12 August, 1889, a demand for a bonus above the 5d. an hour they were being paid, and a rate of 8d. an hour for overtime. Their claim was rejected and they struck. At once John Burns and Tom Mann, who had come to Ben Tillett's assistance, called upon all dock labourers to come out in sympathy. The demand of the South-west London Dock labourers for a bonus was transferred into a flat demand for 6d. an hour for all dockers. Within three days ten thousand men were out; within a week the Port of London was at a standstill.

In the historic struggle that followed, John Burns, then at the height of his power as an organizer and open-air speaker, took the lead with Tom Mann and Ben Tillett as his principal lieutenants. It was his talent for mass organization and his genius as an open-air orator that kept the men together even when, as was several times the case in the first few days, the strike was on the verge of collapse. And it was his gift for dramatic leadership and for publicity on a grand scale that in the end brought them victory.

The methods that had served the match girls so well were used and magnified. Each day a great procession of the strikers and their supporters was organized. With bands and banners they marched through the streets of London to Tower Hill, where Burns and Ben Tillett put forward the case for the docker's tanner with a simplicity that no one could misunderstand. Both Burns and Tillett were magnificent mob-orators. Burns had a voice of immense range. In his early days as a street-corner orator he had been wont to attract a crowd by standing up, opening wide his mouth and letting out a huge roar which went on for as long as two minutes without perceptible pause. He was a big man, black bearded, strong, egotistical and assertive and he had a magnificent command of pungent, homely and racy language that drove home every point. That the crowd should know him better he wore a striking white straw hat.

Ben Tillett was a puny little waif of a man, three years younger than Burns. Born in Bristol twenty-eight years earlier, he had never had more than a few days' schooling in his life. At seven he was put out to work in a brick-making yard and at eight was sent underground as a pit-boy. When he was ten he escaped from the mines and travelled the country as a circus hand and after two years of that became a ship's boy on a fishing smack. He joined the Navy as soon as he was old enough, was invalided out and went as a sailor in the Mercantile Marine at a time when the lot of the sea-going man was hard to the point of desperation. He had been tramp, labourer, docker, agitator. He was small in size and he seemed insignificant until he got up to speak. Then he seemed to grow in stature and he had a voice of silver. He could stir the emotions of a crowd with an almost incomparable virtuosity. He could make it laugh with him and weep with him. He could set it on fire with passionate indignation.

To hear these two on Tower Hill the dockers came in their thousands, and with them came the newspaper-men, hot after a story.

Burns cultivated the reporters. He fed them with news and by so doing got sympathetic statements of the dockers' case in all the important papers. He made the struggle of the dockers into a dramatic battle that caught the imagination of the nation and stirred the social consciences of men and women everywhere.

The dockers had no money. That was remedied by opening a fighting fund to which contributions came from all over the world.

Far away in Australia, workers, made aware by the newspaper dispatches of their common cause with the men who were fighting the battle of the working-classes in the London docks, met and voted large sums to help the dockers to fight on. On one day alone the organized trade unionists of Melbourne cabled £4,000, those of Sydney and Adelaide £1,200 each, those of Brisbane £1,000, and the miners of Broken Hill £500. It was a demonstration of inter-national working-class solidarity such as had seldom been known before, and one to stir men's imagination and steel them to fresh efforts. Altogether £48,736 was raised by public subscription—a phenomenal figure for those days. Of this £30,483 came from overseas—the bulk of it from the Australian Labour movement. £13,730 was subscribed in sums of various sizes by men and women of all classes throughout the length and breadth of Britain; £4,473 was given by the established British trade unions—a sum whose smallness when compared with the magnificent gifts of the Australian workers showed the dislike of the older trade-union leaders for the militant tactics of Burns and his lieutenants.

With this money the three strike leaders were able to organize an extensive system of strike pay. They distributed hundreds of thousands of relief tickets throughout the dock area. They had the means to ensure that this strike should not, as others had so often done before, founder on the hunger of women and children. As the strike continued, public sympathy mounted. Under its pressure the Lord Mayor was persuaded to set up a Mansion House Conciliation Committee, and Cardinal Manning undertook to act as mediator between the strikers and the port employers. Four weeks after the strike had begun the employers capitulated, accepted the men's demands and undertook that there should be no victimization.

The mobilization of public opinion as an ally in the struggle of the workers had once again, as in the match girls' strike, but on an infinitely greater scale, proved of decisive consequence. Three years earlier Tillett's union could muster only three hundred members. Now under its new name of the Dock, Wharf and Riverside Labourers' Union it had more than thirty thousand. Moreover, the success of the dockers' strike had an immediate effect on other industries. Within a year, getting on for a quarter of a million fresh members were recruited by trade unions both old and new, and by 1890 the number of trade unionists in organizations affiliated to the Trades Union Congress was three-quarters of a million higher than it had been four years before.

Not only in the great cities and packed industrial areas, but in the rural areas also men began to organize and fight. The movement spread from the manual workers, the dockers, the gas workers, the seamen, the agricultural workers and the general labourers to the black-coated workers, the teachers, the clerks, the shop assistants. And almost everywhere they organized themselves not on the model of the old craft unions, but on the model of the new. They did not form and did not wish to form associations with Friendly Society benefits, but fighting organizations open to all the workers in their industry and pledged to devote themselves primarily to militant action to raise wages and improve conditions, "unencumbered," in the words of a resolution of the General Railway Workers' Union in 1890, "by any sick or accident fund."

The leaders who helped to organize these unions and the new leaders they threw up were, moreover, for the most part men and women who saw beyond the need for trade-union action within particular trades to the need for political action to raise the standards of the working-classes as a whole. They were not—or most of them were not—Marxists who thought in terms of an inevitable and continuous class struggle. But bitter personal experience had made them only too well aware of the existence of the class struggle at that moment. Everywhere they saw the effort of the working-classes to achieve decent standards resisted. They were prepared to ally themselves with all who would work for greater social justice of whatever class they might be. But they saw clearly that so long as the interests of Labour, alone among the major interests within the nation, remained unrepresented in Parliament, so long would they be denied the consideration to which they had a right.

The new trade unionism—the trade unionism that was to form the pattern for the great industrial developments of the future and lay the foundations for the vast and powerful general unions of today—had come into being. It had won its first victories. It had yet ahead of it many bitter campaigns. In the depression that came in the early 'nineties many of the unions both old and new were to suffer reverses. Strikes by the Lancashire cotton spinners, the Hull dockers, the Tyneside engineers, the Dundee jute workers, the Welsh, Scottish and Durham miners were to be heavily defeated. The new unions everywhere were to be hit hard by unemployment. They were to be hit, but they were not to crumble.

They stood, they survived and in the end they went on to new strength. They had established a new and permanent pattern of working-class organization. With its establishment, with the new voices that it brought to the counsels of the Trades Union Congress and the new spirit that it engendered among all industrial workers, the day of the Labour Party was brought steadily nearer.

Without the new trade unionism the Labour Party would never have been born. But the new trade unionism, great though its influence was, could not of itself have established such a party. For the Labour Party was never a purely trade-union party. Although its practical achievements have only been possible because of the mass membership and support that trade unionism has given it, it represented from the first, and has always represented, much more than a trade-union point of view. It grew out of the seething ferment of social reform which characterized the closing years of the nineteenth century and which was complementary to, and the result of, reaction against the excesses and social cruelties of the triumphant Victorian capitalism of the day.

This ferment, of which the new trade unionism was the most important industrial product and the Labour Party in due course the political result, took many shapes and brought together at one time and another in the cause of socialism as diverse and brilliant a group of people as have ever been associated in any enterprise.

Well before the new trade unionism won its first successes it had made its impact upon the Church of England, where a young London curate, Stewart Headlam—who later provided Shaw, at any rate in part, with a model for the Reverend James Morell in *Candida*—went into the slums to attack atheism and remained to preach that only by accepting and working for socialism could the Church justify its appeal to the hungry and dispossessed that they should have faith in God.

Headlam owed, as all who wished to bring the Church closer to the needs of the times did, a great debt to Frederick Maurice and Charles Kingsley. They, a quarter of a century or more earlier, had preached that socialism was the truest form of Christianity at a time when to most respectable people it was synonymous with atheism and immorality. Now, under the inspiration of their teaching and the impact of the new forces that were stirring in the world, Headlam went down into the slums of London to find that the Christian teachings of the Church were but a bitter mockery to men and women huddled together in squalor and starvation, sweated and exploited, treated as though they were scarcely human, to be worked like slaves when their work was needed and thrown aside when it was not.

What he found horrified Headlam. He gathered around him a body of clergymen and laymen who faced the bitter opposition and hatred of their ecclesiastical superiors to fight for social justice. They founded schools and missions. They published an exposure of the social evils of the time, *The Bitter Cry of Outcast London*, that shocked the conscience of all those capable of being shocked. They formed the Guild of St. Matthew, set themselves to justify God to the people and proclaimed themselves Socialists in every sense of that word, economic as well as ethical. Their influence in the development of British socialism, which owes very much to Christian ethics, was considerable.

The ferment caught the working men's Radical clubs and the Nonconformist chapels which then provided one of the strongest bulwarks of Gladstonian Liberalism. Nine years before the great dock strike it led to the foundation of what was probably the first specifically working-class Socialist society, the Labour Emancipation League, which came into being as a result of a series of meetings held on Mile End Waste in 1881 by the Stratford Working Men's Radical Club.

And about the same time it caught also—one of the oddest of its captures and one who, although he never understood the trade unions, was indirectly to have no small part in creating the mood that made the new unionism possible—a rich young man, an Old Etonian with a highly aristocratic and autocratic turn of character, an extensive interest in international affairs developed by much foreign travel, a magnificent flaming beard and a habit of never appearing in public except in a frock coat and a top hat, even when, as later, he paraded the Strand selling a Socialist journal. This young man the ferment turned into a fiery revolutionary and the chief British exponent of Marxist socialism.

This was Henry Mayers Hyndman. In 1880, after reading the French edition of *Das Kapital*—no English edition had then been published—which had been recommended to him as worthy of a critical perusal by a Conservative M.P., Hyndman was immediately converted to socialism and hurried off to make Karl Marx's personal acquaintance. His interview with Marx completed his conversion— if completed it needed to be. The powerful intellect and immense erudition of the German philosopher filled him with a profound and permanent admiration. This admiration was not returned. It seldom was in Marx's case. The founder of modern communism met few people in his life whom he could bring himself to like and fewer still whom he could persuade himself to admire. He regarded Hyndman as a news-hunting busybody, a frivolous amateur.

When in June, 1881, Hyndman published a book for English readers entitled *England for All*, in which the Marxian thesis was expounded but without mentioning Marx, the breach between the two became too wide to bridge. Hyndman, although he paid tribute in his preface to the work of "a great thinker and original writer," from whom his ideas had been derived, made in it no direct reference to Marx because he believed that thus he would make the book more acceptable to the English public—which is notoriously distrustful of foreigners. He assumed that what mattered to Marx was that his ideas should be made known and the revolution brought nearer.

In this he was mistaken. He underestimated the vanity of a great man. Although he tried to make amends two years later when he published a second book, *The Historical Basis of Socialism*, in which he quoted Marx liberally, it was no good. Marx throughout his life quarrelled more easily than he forgave. Thenceforward Hyndman had to be a Marxist without Marx: and the first British Marxist party had to get on as best it could without the guidance of the master.

Hyndman was not deterred. He was completely convinced of the validity of the Marxist thesis. He was entirely certain that revolution would come to Britain—perhaps by 1889—and that it would be followed by revolutions all over Europe. To work actively to that end he founded in 1881 the Democratic Federation. This he conceived of from the start as a revolutionary force, although its actual published programme was at first more Radical than Socialist. Four years later it came out into the open, adopted a specifically Marxian Socialist programme, absorbed the Labour Emancipation League and changed its name to the Social Democratic Federation.

For the next twenty years it was at one and the same time the chief propagandist in Britain of the Marxian doctrine of the class war and one of the most potent forces in the organization of working-class discontents. It had an immense influence both in helping to create a new spirit of working-class militancy and thus paving the way for the new trade unionism, some of whose best leaders received their first training in its ranks, and in arousing the social conscience of many of the middle-classes.

It would have had even more influence if it had not been perpetually rent by schisms arising partly from quarrels in policy, partly from revolts against Hyndman's dictatorial methods of leadership, and if it had not made a number of serious tactical errors in its political campaigns.

Nevertheless, it provided a rallying point to which there gathered a group of men and women of amazing energy—some of them recruited in the most unexpected quarters.

Among the glittering if ill-assorted group who were its early leaders were Ernest Belfort Bax, a writer, philosopher and historian of distinction; Eleanor Marx-Aveling—Marx's daughter—a dark, heavily built woman of keen intellect who had read enormously among the Socialist literature of all countries; her husband, Dr. Edward Aveling, who managed to combine a good brain, a magnificent speaking voice and much general capacity with a wildly unstable character; John Burns; J. L. Joynes, a former Eton master and revolutionary poet who had been forced to resign from Eton after touring Ireland with Henry George preaching land reform; Harry Quelch, a dour and bitter working-class fighter, whose soul had been seared by the poverty in which he had been born and who became the editor of the S.D.F. paper *Justice*; Henry H. Champion, an ex-artillery officer who had resigned a commission in the Army to fight for socialism, and who has the double distinction of being Bernard Shaw's first publisher—he brought out a shilling edition of *Cashel Byron's Profession* because the pugilism appealed to him—and of contributing very materially to the success of the dock strike of 1889 by taking command of the pickets and so deploying them according to professional military tactics as to defeat all attempts to break the strike by introducing blacklegs; Walter Crane, an artist of many parts; James Macdonald, a working tailor who became secretary of the London Trades Council; and William Morris.

Morris, world-famous already as a designer and poet, became a Socialist because he hated ugliness and he saw capitalism breeding ugliness everywhere around him. Having become one he insisted on serving in the ranks. He went out in the streets to sell copies of *Justice*, he spoke at street corners, and he took on all the tasks of the propagandist up and down the country; a gusty, angry, bluntly honest, not very successful speaker who could flare up into great rages at one minute and forget he had ever lost his temper the next. He took his socialism with passionate seriousness. He believed a revolution must come, and under Hyndman's tuition, read Marx's *Das Kapital*. But he found it dull reading and remarked very sensibly that he did not need a Labour Theory of Value to tell him that the rich robbed the poor, for he could see it very well with his own eyes.

This brilliant, diverse, passionately sincere and, as it was to turn out, very quarrelsome group under the flamboyant leadership of Hyndman—who was so certain that revolution would come in Britain at any moment that he carried a list of the Revolutionary Cabinet, with himself at the head of it, around in his pocket so as not to be caught unprepared—lacked the cohesion to become an effective Socialist force. But, by its propaganda, it did much to stir men's imaginations and feed the new working-class movement that events were bringing into being. Through the columns of its journal, *Justice*, which was started with a contribution of £300 from Edward Carpenter, the author of *Towards Democracy* and *England Arise*, it spread the gospel of socialism with great vigour and much literary art.

But it was an assembly of individuals, not a coherent organization. At the end of 1884, only six months after it had taken its new name, it split in two. Morris, Bax, Crane, Eleanor Marx-Aveling and her husband left it and went off to form a new body, the Socialist League. Hyndman, Champion, Joynes, Burns and Quelch remained to forge the S.D.F. briefly into an effective spearhead of working-class militant action until it quarrelled first with the trade unions and then with the new Labour Representation Committee it had helped to found, disintegrated internally and became an altogether ineffective little body that lingered on long after its day was done.

As for the Socialist League, it proved one of the outstanding examples of a group possessed of great self-sacrifice, much talent and, in the case of Morris himself, great genius, which, for lack of any organizing ability or sense of the practical, dissipated its energies and disintegrated. Six years after its formation, all those who had founded it had left and it had become a tiny anarchist group of no importance.

Nevertheless, through its paper *The Commonweal*, and particularly through Morris's writings for that paper, it left behind it a legacy greater than itself. To *The Commonweal* Morris gave poems of great beauty which echoed in the minds and hearts of men and women who knew nothing of the Socialist League and its disputations. For it he wrote the *Dream of John Ball* and *News from Nowhere*, imperishable contributions to the literature and the Socialist thought of Britain. He and some of those, such as Belfort Bax, who went with him, gave to British socialism gifts of mind and heart of a kind peculiarly their own. Because of them the Socialist League, despite its inglorious career as an organized body, has a place in Socialist history.

Morris himself, through his writings and his passionate advocacy of a social system in which beauty and social justice should be able to live, awakened in the minds of thousands a dream that inspired them, and through them the Socialist movement, long after his own days as an active Socialist propagandist were ended. Although he became an active Socialist first as a partner, if never in any true sense a comrade, of Hyndman, the dialectical materialist, his own contribution to socialism was to lift men's eyes to the skies, to set their imaginations afire with visions they had not known before, to teach them to dream and to work that the dream should come true. And by his songs he gave them comradeship.

In little dingy halls in the ugly industrial towns he hated, at street-corner meetings held against the dreadful background of the slums that rent his heart with pity and anger, in scattered villages all over England, the England that he wanted to make lovely and gracious to the spirit, they sang:

" *On we march, we the workers, and the rumour that ye hear*
Is the blended sound of battle and deliverance drawing near;
For the hope of every creature is the banner that we bear
And the world is marching on."

And as they sang they knew themselves to be members of a great companionship.

He was never a practical politician. He knew little of economics —why should he? He was wrong in his assessment of the course of events and mistaken in his judgment of the way in which socialism would come in the British context. He got little out of his Socialist activities but disappointment and disillusion. Those he worked with most closely wasted his money and his genius and quarrelled with him. The irreconcilable revolutionary heroes of the platform

in whom he put his trust—and the crowds who cheered them—
for the most part proved very poor revolutionary metal when any
test came. But he gave to socialism without stint his faith, his
genius, his passionate and generous conviction that all men could
live beautifully, and in so doing he wove into the pattern of its
thought strands of an imperishable glory.

The Social Democratic Federation, itself depleted in numbers
by the defection of those who had joined the Socialist League, but
with the advantage of a greater coherence of view than it had
previously held, flung itself into the parliamentary battle which
opened with the General Election of 1885 following the dissolution
of the Liberal Government—and nearly wrecked itself at the start
by a series of ill-considered manoeuvres such as possibly only
Hyndman could have conceived and which for a time threatened to
sink it beneath the contempt and anger of all who should have been
its allies.

Hyndman was at once fantastically optimistic in his judgment
of the strength of the forces he led and quite irresponsibly opportunist in the methods he was prepared to adopt. He managed to
combine a sincere and passionate belief in the rightness and inevitability of a working-class revolution with an arrogant contempt for
the intelligence of the working-classes themselves. He decided that
the S.D.F. must fight, and would undeniably win, a number of
parliamentary seats. The S.D F., however, had no funds. Champion,
therefore, went to call upon his friend Hudson, the rich soap manufacturer, and persuaded him to put up the money to enable John
Burns to fight at Nottingham.

But one contest was far below Hyndman's ambitions. He,
therefore, entered into secret negotiations with the Conservative
Party, worked on their fears of a Liberal victory and persuaded
them to invest in splitting the Liberal vote by putting up the money
for two other S.D.F. candidates, John E. Williams at Hampstead
and John Fielding at Kennington. Both these were, on any sane
assessment of political chances, quite hopeless seats for a Socialist
to fight.

In the election when it came, Burns, although he came at the
bottom of the poll, did not do too badly; he got 598 votes. But the
other two candidates made a lamentable showing. Williams in

Hampstead got 27 votes, Fielding in Kennington got 32. This was bad enough, for it seemed to make completely ridiculous Hyndman's boast, which many people had begun to believe, that the S.D.F. had the support of thousands of London workers.

But the story of how these two contests had been financed, when it came out, was even more disastrous. It destroyed for a time all confidence in Hyndman and ended any hopes he might ever have had of bringing the Radical Working Men's Clubs into the orbit of the S.D.F. To these radical working-men, to accept Tory money was the basest of all treacheries. It was no use Hyndman explaining that Tory money was the same as any other money and that the S.D.F. had given no commitments in exchange for it. Radicals, trade unionists, Socialists, all felt that this was a piece of political dishonesty that nothing could forgive.

It seemed as if the S.D.F. was finished. Yet because Hyndman and Champion, even if they were capable of misjudgments of this kind, were right in their instinctive belief that the time had come for the working-classes to fight back, and because in John Burns they had a working-class leader of genius—although one who very soon sloughed off the Marxism Hyndman had taught him and in the end his socialism also—within two years the S.D.F. recovered from this collapse and reached its highest point as a fighting force.

Its leaders were fools if not worse in their purely political tactics. But they grasped more quickly than anyone else the Socialist implications of the economic depression which was at that time at its lowest depths. They set to work to organize the unemployed. They marshalled them into processions and staged demonstrations and finally they precipitated—not altogether deliberately—a series of events which were to arouse the whole country to excitement and do more than anything else until the dock strike to stir the working-classes to militancy.

The first of these was the Dod Street Affair. Dod Street was a narrow street in Limehouse running between tall warehouses. On Sundays, when the work of the port was at a standstill, it was practically deserted and here the S.D.F. took up their pitch and began to hold public meetings, calling on the people of Limehouse to turn to socialism and to combine.

After one or two meetings the police arrived and ordered them to move on—they refused, standing firm on the principle of the Englishman's right of free speech. There were tussles with the police, and Jack Williams, one of the working-class leaders of the S.D.F., and its candidate in the unfortunate Hampstead election, was arrested and fined 40s. He refused to pay and was sent to prison for a month.

At once all the Radical Working Men's Clubs in the East End and all the other Socialist groups rallied to the side of the S.D.F. They announced that the great fight for free speech was on. The following Sunday they all marched to Dod Street and held a mass meeting of protest at which William Morris among others spoke. The police charged the crowd with batons and arrested Morris. He was brought before the magistrates. When asked who he was he replied with a certain justified arrogance: "I am an artist and a literary man pretty well known, I think, throughout Europe." The magistrates may have been shaken by this reply. At any rate, they discharged him.

The next Sunday a great procession of Social Democrats, Christian Socialists, Socialists, trade unionists and unemployed with banners waving and bands playing marched through the London streets to Dod Street. Hyndman, John Burns, Bernard Shaw, Champion, Stewart Headlam and James Macdonald were at their head. All were determined to make speeches, police or no police, and all had pledged themselves if arrested, to refuse to pay a fine and go to prison.

Before this show of determination, and with their failure to get a conviction against William Morris well in mind, the police at the last minute capitulated and let the meeting go on. This was unfortunate, for history was thus denied the pleasure of recording the spectacle of Bernard Shaw, John Burns, Stewart Headlam and Henry Mayers Hyndman all expressing their Socialist ideas and their opinions of the police from the same dock—an opportunity for immortality not often offered to a Thames-side magistrate's court. The first battle had been won.

But it was only a preliminary engagement. As the economic depression deepened and unemployment rose—unemployment without any payment of benefit or organized relief, unemployment that meant actual starvation for hundreds of thousands—the

S.D.F. organized more and more demonstrations and protest meetings.

They were not alone in the field. A Tariff Reform movement, under the title of "The Fair Traders," had arisen and had enlisted in its service a small group of trade unionists who were in conflict with the mass of the Labour movement and particularly with the S.D.F. Early in 1886, the year after the Dod Street affair, the Fair Traders announced that on Monday, 8 February—Black Monday as it was later to be called in the annals of Labour—they would hold a mass demonstration in Trafalgar Square.

At once the S.D.F. set about organizing a rival demonstration. When the day arrived a mass procession of unemployed, accompanied by not a few rowdies and hooligans who saw the chance of fun and possibly of some profit to themselves from such an affair, arrived, headed by Hyndman, Burns, Champion and Williams, and took possession of the north side of the square.

When the Fair Traders arrived trouble started. The platforms of the Fair Traders were torn down and the police, who were too few in numbers to handle the situation, appealed to Burns, who towered above the crowd by the railings opposite the National Gallery carrying a red flag, to restore order. Burns and Hyndman thereupon agreed to lead their followers in procession to Hyde Park. Headed by Burns with his red flag, the crowd moved off in the direction of Pall Mall.

So far they had been perfectly orderly. But as they came abreast of the Carlton Club, clubmen looking out from their windows at the motley ill-kempt and shabby crowd with the man with a red flag at their head, and confident no doubt that the police were in the offing to see that they were kept in their proper place, began to shout and jeer.

The unemployed had stood much. They were not ready to stand the taunts and laughter of the rich and well fed who, they felt, were responsible for their own poverty. Road repairs were going on in Pall Mall. They picked up paving stones and began to hurl them through the windows of the clubs where those who mocked them were standing. In the confusion some turned down St. James's Street, while others surged into Piccadilly. Terrified shopkeepers, convinced the revolution had started, hurriedly put up their shutters. A number of shop windows were broken by the crowd and some of the rowdies who had attached themselves to the procession took advantage of the disturbance to loot a few shops.

The majority of the crowd reached Hyde Park and there, after being addressed by Burns and Hyndman, quietly dispersed. As Bernard Shaw put it: "The rich men crowded to the windows to see the poor men pass along; and Dives, not noticing the absence of the police, mocked Lazarus. Lazarus, thereupon, broke Dives's windows, and even looted a shop or two, besides harmlessly stoning the carriage of a tactless lady at the Achilles statue."

The affray sent a wave of terror through all the rich streets of Mayfair—to such an extent indeed that Dives, dipping deep into his pocket in a desperate attempt to buy off the revolution he felt was coming, sent a Mansion House Fund that had been opened for the relief of distress without much success, soaring within a few days from £3,000 to over £70,000.

Next day Hyndman, Burns, Champion and Williams were arrested for seditious conspiracy. They were released on bail after a preliminary hearing, William Morris standing bail for them, and immediately proceeded with their campaign. In Hyde Park Burns declared that, if advocating a social revolution was an incitement to sedition, sedition would have to be the charge against him until the grave claimed him.

In April they came up for trial. They were not legally represented and Hyndman acted as the chief counsel for the defence. From the dock Burns delivered a great revolutionary speech which, as soon as the trial was over, the S.D.F. reprinted as a pamphlet under the title *The Man With the Red Flag*. It sold in thousands. Hyndman, Champion and Williams followed with less eloquent but hardly less uncompromising declarations of their revolutionary faith. Much to everyone's amazement, theirs included, the jury acquitted them, although, in so doing, it added a rider that the speeches of Burns and Champion at the Trafalgar Square demonstration had been highly inflammatory and greatly to be condemned.

Well-off London was now thoroughly aroused and alarmed, while the poor and unemployed were conscious of their strength as never before. The wealthy, fearing riots, but quite unready to alter the economic conditions which might understandably create them, called for strong police action to safeguard them against the barbarians of the slums. A new Chief Commissioner of Police, Sir Charles Warren, was appointed to carry out a "strong policy" by the Conservative Cabinet that had come into power at the 1885 election. The police were instructed to wage unceasing war against the Socialists of London.

Undeterred by external authority, although considerably shaken from time to time by its own internal quarrels, the S.D.F., in combination with anyone who would join it, went on with its agitation on behalf of the unemployed.

Champion, who was a tower of strength until, as most men did, he quarrelled with Hyndman and left the S.D.F., combined a professional competence in handling large numbers on the march with a great fertility of ideas and propaganda devices. As the day of the Lord Mayor's procession came round he conceived the idea of organizing a procession of unemployed to follow the pageant through the streets. Sir Charles Warren at once prohibited it. Champion and the other S.D.F. leaders, deciding not to risk a head-on clash with the police, switched their plans and called instead a rally in Trafalgar Square after the Lord Mayor's procession was over. Warren at once prohibited that also. The S.D.F. thereupon decided to fight.

Under Champion's direction, S.D.F. speakers, one of them being Tom Mann, were posted, with supporting groups to defend them from surprise attack, at strategic points in the Square. As soon as the procession had passed they began to address the assembled crowds from vantage points to which their supporters hoisted them. The police charged, but were hampered by the presence of the great crowds who had come to see the Lord Mayor's Show. Including as they did many highly respectable ratepayers, these could not, as Sir Charles Warren knew only too well, be treated with the same scant regard as an unemployed procession. The affair, in which the Socialists clearly came off best, created a great stir and produced an immense deal of useful publicity in the newspapers.

Following this up with their usual high-spirited vigour, Hyndman and Champion made plans for another Trafalgar Square demonstration. Sir Charles Warren, who, under a constant stream of instructions from the Government and adjurations from the

Press to be firm with these agitators, was beginning, perhaps, to lose his sense of proportion. He drew up elaborate plans to stop the meeting taking place—including the placing of artillery in the square. Hyndman and Champion heard of these plans with delight. They at once dispatched a letter to Sir Charles—making sure at the same time that the newspapers knew of it—offering to relieve him of the heavy strain on his forces such a campaign must involve by themselves providing a force of Special Constables to keep the peace.

Champion, as an ex-artillery officer, gave Sir Charles his personal word that these Special Constables should include a sufficient number of competent artillerymen under his own direct command to ensure that the artillery was properly used. The Chief Commissioner was ready to fight all tangible attacks upon the dignity of Government, but his training had not taught him how to deal with ridicule. In face of it he lost confidence, cancelled his plans, and allowed the demonstration to proceed.

Having, even although only very temporarily, defeated the police, the S.D.F. next devoted its attention to the churches. With Burns in the forefront, processions of the unemployed marched to Sunday services at the principal London churches. There they demanded from the clergy sermons suitable for a congregation of men and women hungry and desperate through no fault of their own, but because they were the victims of a system in whose operations they had no voice, and who wished to know if the Christian religion approved of their condition. These Sunday gatherings culminated in a huge procession of six marching columns to St. Paul's Cathedral carrying banners with the message, among others, "My house is a house of prayer but ye have made it a den of thieves." At the conclusion of the service, which was much interrupted when the preacher declared that there must always be rich and poor, John Burns sang a hymn based on "Dare to be a Daniel" and called "Dare to be a Freeman."

By such methods the S.D.F. kept both the plight of the unemployed and the case for socialism well to the forefront of public interest. They allowed no one to forget either. Meanwhile the battles with the police over the right to speak in Trafalgar Square began on a new and even more bitter scale. At one Trafalgar Square meeting

60

twenty of the S.D.F. were arrested. Clashes with the police and broken heads were frequent.

On Sunday, 13 November, 1887—Bloody Sunday as it came to be called—these clashes reached a remarkable climax. A demonstration arranged for that day, not by the S.D.F. or any other Socialist group, but by the Metropolitan Radical Federation, to protest against the imprisonment of the Irish Nationalist, William O'Brien, was banned by Government order. The S.D.F., the Socialist League and many other Radical groups combined with the Metropolitan Radical Federation to defy the ban. Marching columns were mobilized to converge upon Trafalgar Square from every side of London. The Government replied by calling in the military to aid the police in repulsing them. All the Thames bridges were garrisoned in order to beat back the great contingents marching from South London. Trafalgar Square itself was cordoned off and the Life Guards posted ready to go into action. The picture was one almost of preparations for civil war—an indication of the extent to which the S.D.F. and its allies had aroused and frightened the country.

Most of the marchers were driven back before they could reach the Square and many were wounded. But one contingent from North London managed to reach the Square. It was headed by John Burns and R. B. Cunninghame Graham—a Scottish laird and Radical M.P., a wild, quixotic and fantastically distinguished figure who marched forward with aristocratic disdain looking like a Highland chieftain, or still more, perhaps, like a Spanish grandee of immensely ancient lineage. There they were mercilessly attacked by the police. Cunninghame Graham was beaten to the ground, bleeding profusely, and John Burns was also wounded badly.

When the crowd had been driven back by the batons of the police these two were at once arrested and, after their wounds had been attended to, charged. They were released on bail, Stewart Headlam standing bail for Burns and R. B. Haldane—later Lord Haldane—for Cunninghame Graham. Two months later, when they were tried, both were found innocent of riot but guilty of "unlawful assault" and sent to prison for six weeks.

A month after their conviction the struggle for freedom of speech in Trafalgar Square mounted to a new and tragic climax. During a further demonstration the crowd were batoned by the police and a workman named Alfred Linnell clubbed so severely that he died.

At his funeral a vast procession of workers, Socialists, Radicals and unemployed followed his coffin through the streets to the cemetery. There Stewart Headlam took the solemn service and William Morris preached a funeral address.

"Our friend who lies here," he said, with a characteristic directness and simplicity, "has had a hard life and met with a hard death; and if society had been differently constituted his life might have been a delightful, a beautiful and a happy one. It is our business to begin to organize for the purpose of seeing that such things shall not happen; to try to make this earth a beautiful and happy place."

Then the Death Chant that Morris had written was sung, while the great crowd of working men and women whose lives were no less hard than the dead man's had been and who could look forward only to deaths as hard as his if different, stood bareheaded in the open air:

> *They will not learn; they have no ears to hearken,*
> *They turn their faces from the eye of fate,*
> *Their gay-lit halls shut out the skies that darken,*
> *But lo! this dead man knocking at the gate."*

The long struggle of the working-classes for freedom had added another martyr to the already crowded roll.

But the day of riots and demonstrations, of unemployed marches that set the country seething with rumours and alarms but left behind them no permanent improvement in the condition of the people, was passing. In the early 'nineties trade began to improve and, as it improved and unemployment fell, men's minds turned to more permanent ways of bettering their condition than demonstrations and riots in Trafalgar Square, however justified they had been. And, with the new mood, the influence of the S.D.F. waned and its methods lost their appeal. "Insurrectionism," Bernard Shaw wrote in 1892, "after a two years' innings, has vanished from the field and has not since been heard of."

Now a new phase was opening, a phase which called for different men and methods from those of the S.D.F., the phase of the constructive democracy of the I.L.P. and the Fabian Society.

The day of Hyndman and his companions was passing. It had been a short day, but it had made much noise while it lasted and it had helped to create a new and militant mood among the working-classes, a mood that was to have its first big success in the dockers' strike later that year and that was to help to make the new trade unionism a reality.

Hyndman and the others of the S.D.F. had themselves mistaken the tumults of Trafalgar Square for the first rumour of the approaching revolution. They were wrong. They failed to understand how contrary revolution was to the real mood of the British Labour movement, even although men made desperate by unemployment might sometimes seem disposed to desperate courses. For all their dialectical knowledge they failed to see the real nature of the new forces that were on the move in Britain. In the development of these forces, in their consolidation and in their ultimate advance, they had little part to play: that task and that achievement lay with men very differently constituted and possessed of a vision more practical and more constructive.

Nevertheless, in the history of the events that brought the Labour Party into being they have their place, and it is not a little or a mean one. They realized more quickly than most the ferment that lay underneath the unemployment and poverty of the times. They helped to give it a voice. They helped to make men understand the strength that lay in the unorganized and disinherited if only they would act together. They fought bravely for the rights of free speech without which Socialist propaganda would have been crippled. They helped to forge the spirit that made possible the new unionism and they gave the new unionism some of the most effective of its early leaders. The future was not theirs, but they had their part in shaping the past out of which the future could come to birth.

CHAPTER III

THE BACKGROUND TO THE DECISION
THE SECOND PHASE

TEN years before the social conscience of the middle-classes
had begun to be awakened by Booth's *Labour and Life of the
People*, to the horrors upon which their prosperity rested,
and the London match girls and the London dockers, by claiming
that conscience as their ally had shown the way to the victories of
the new trade unionism, two young men, an impecunious young
Irishman of twenty-three, who was trying to write novels, and a
twenty-year-old tax surveyor, met for the first time at an obscure
Hampstead debating club, the Zetetical Society.

In that same year of 1879—two years before Hyndman, hot
from his meeting with Karl Marx, wrote *England for All* and embarked upon that career of social insurrectionism which for a few
years was to seem spasmodically to portend the coming of the
British revolution—another young man, a twenty-two-year-old
miner in Lanarkshire, was dismissed from his job because he had
taken the chair at a meeting of miners and gone on a deputation
to the management. From then on, he was told, he would be boycotted in every pit in Lanark.

And about the same time a somewhat older young man, a
sergeant in the 103rd Regiment, the Royal Dublin Fusiliers, the
son of an unsuccessful strolling player and a small-part actress,
who was himself a great teller of tales and could, to boot, shoot like
an angel, received his discharge from the Army with a certificate
of education which informed all who read it that he possessed the
capacity to read and write and the requisite proficiency in numera-
tion but no more. Having secured this rather unenthusiastic recommendation, he obtained by its means a job as a time-keeper at 30s.

RAMSAY MACDONALD
The first secretary of the Party and the first Labour Prime Minister.

BERNARD SHAW
A brilliant member of the Fabian Society's executive from 1885 to 1911.

a week with the Weaver Navigation Company of Northwich in Cheshire, asked his girl Sarah, whom he had left behind him in Halifax when he'd joined the Army, to marry him and set about writing short stories in the hope of raising his income to a level more appropriate to the status of a married man.

The first two young men were George Bernard Shaw and Sidney Webb. The third was Keir Hardie. The fourth was Robert Blatchford.

It would be untrue to say that the Labour Party owes its present form and philosophy exclusively to any group of individuals. It has been shaped in its ideals and in its organization by many men and women and has drawn abundantly from the rich resources of the British tradition and from the developing social and economic history of its time. But, more than any others, these four shaped modern British socialism in its first days. It was their efforts above all others that made possible the formation of the Labour Party. And it was they who mapped out for it the route that, forty-five years after it was founded, was to bring it to power.

All four were to exercise their greatest influence on the Socialist movement and upon the thinking of the middle- and working-classes when the era of the Trafalgar Square demonstrations and the unemployed marches came to an end, although Shaw took part in many of these demonstrations and, throughout the ten years which culminated in the dock strike, Keir Hardie worked with passion and self-sacrifice for the unorganized and the victimized and during them became the chief trade-union spokesman for independent political action.

But it was in the second phase of the twenty-year period of ferment and struggle and debate that preceded the birth of the Labour Party to 1900 that their influence became most decisive.

The instrument whereby Shaw and Webb took hold of the idealism and the discontents which had brought modern British socialism into being and turned them into a concrete and practical political programme was the Fabian Society. That through which Keir Hardie gave to the Labour movement a moral and political significance it would not otherwise have possessed was the Independent Labour Party. The medium which Blatchford used and every page of which was stamped with his rich and flamboyant character was the *Clarion*.

In point of time and in its intellectual impact upon the course of British socialism the Fabian Society takes precedence. In the number of those whose fervour it roused, and whose lives because of it were dedicated to the Socialist cause, the Independent Labour Party has pride of place. Without Shaw and Webb—and Webb especially—British socialism would have lacked the coherent political philosophy which from the start gave it strength and a practical insight whose validity has been demonstrated ever more remarkably as time has passed. Without Keir Hardie that alliance between trade unionists and Socialists, which from the first gave the British Labour movement its peculiar national character and brought it a durability and stability which has withstood all tests, might never have come into existence.

Not only did most of the ideas and policies of the Socialist movement come from one or other of the organizations with which these three were so intimately concerned, but it was in the service of the Fabian Society and the Independent Labour Party that most of the leaders of the Labour Party received their political training. The debt of the Labour movement to them is not easily to be computed.

If the influence of the *Clarion* was not quite so permanent, nevertheless it brought to British socialism a verve and gaiety all its own. And it probably converted more people to socialism in the early days of the movement than any other single agency.

When that meeting which one way and another was to have such remarkable consequences upon the course of British political history took place at the Zetetical Society in Hampstead, Shaw was an impecunious employee in the way-leave department of the Edison Telephone Company. He was soon to abandon the short-lived and highly uncongenial task of earning his living by honest toil as someone else's employee and was to throw himself on his mother's resources for six years until he managed to earn enough (£112 in twelve months) to keep himself by his pen. He had arrived from Dublin three years before, had written—at the steady pace of five quarto pages an evening—a novel, *Immaturity*, that no publisher would accept, and knew practically no one of his own age in London. He went to the Zetetical Society to learn and practise the art of public speaking—an art in which he was helped by a delightful Irish brogue, a sparkling wit, a great deal of gaiety and a striking presence, and in which he very soon excelled.

Sidney Webb was a surveyor of taxes, a post he had just gained in open competition after a year as a lower division clerk at the War Office. Before that he had spent three years as a clerk in a Colonial broker's office in the City. He was a small, stocky youth, with bulging eyes, glasses, a little beard cut to a point, a weak voice, a fine forehead and small, pretty hands and feet. He rose with complete and absolute self-confidence to take his part in the debate.

"He knew," wrote Bernard Shaw, describing the occasion, "all about the subject of the debate; knew more than the lecturer; knew more than anybody present; had read everything that had ever been written on the subject; and remembered all the facts that bore on it. He used notes, read them, ticked them off one by one, threw them away, and finished with a coolness and clearness that, to me in my then trembling state, seemed miraculous. This young man was the ablest man in England—Sidney Webb."

No doubt only Shaw would have been ready at that time to describe Webb in such terms, but his phenomenal capacity for the rapid digestion of the most complicated subjects, his mastery of facts and his power of logical exposition, cultivated by work as an Honorary Lecturer in Economics at the Working Men's College, already excited the slightly stunned admiration of everyone who met him. He did not then, or later, approach the wit and audacity of the young Irishman who also dazzled the Zetetical Society on that never-to-be-forgotten evening. But an opponent of their views required to make a choice as to which of the two he should engage in action might well have wondered whether it was worse to be made to look a fool by the one or an utter ignoramus by the other.

Neither of them was at that time a member of the Fabian Society, for that remarkable example of the power of a tiny, clear-headed and able group to change the course of much social and political history had not yet come into existence.

It did not do so until five years later, in 1884, when it began its career rather inauspiciously as a by-product of a little ethical-anarchist-communist group founded two years earlier by an eccentric scholar, Thomas Davidson, a Scotsman, who had emigrated to America but who made periodic visits to Britain, where he wandered from town to town lecturing on philosophy and ethics. The somewhat self-conscious name of this group was The Fellowship of the New Life, its purpose "the attainment of a perfect character by all and each," its membership small but distinguished; it included Edward Carpenter, Havelock Ellis and, later, Ramsay MacDonald.

Two of the original group, E. R. Pease and Frank Podmore, finding the attainment of a perfect character somewhat beyond their immediate powers, split off and, both being interested at the time in the teachings of Henry George, decided to form a group to discuss social and economic improvement—the mundane soil in which it seemed to them the new life and the perfect character might alone have a chance to develop. A few others joined in and it was decided that they should form a society whose first purpose should be to clear the minds of its members as a preliminary to any action. They decided to call it the Fabian Society, after Fabius Cunctator the Roman general. Frank Podmore invented an historical quotation to sustain the choice: "For the right moment you must wait as Fabius did most patiently, when warring against Hannibal, though many censured his delays; but when the time comes you must strike hard, as Fabius did, or your waiting will be vain and fruitless." With this motto, a foundation membership of nine, and an initial capital of 13s. 7d. the Fabian Society was started.

The first members of the Society were intelligent, sensible and good-intentioned. By patient reading and discussion they taught themselves much about the social and economic conditions of the day. Among them were several men of talent, like Podmore and Pease, but none with all the qualities needed to make any great impact upon their times. They would probably have progressed calmly but ineffectively from drawing-room meeting to drawing-room meeting, trying to make up their minds whether communism or anarchism would be best for the world, and returning thereafter, soothed by thought, to their nice professional occupations if suddenly they had not fallen within the orbit of the formidable couple who had made each other's acquaintance and recognized each other's qualities at the Hampstead Zetetical Society on that evening in 1879.

The first to arrive at the Fabian Society was Shaw, still in search of audiences upon whom to try out his now considerably more practised talents as a speaker and his skill as a writer. He turned up first as a visitor on 16 May, 1884. He came once or twice after that, and on 5 September was elected a member of the Society. Within a fortnight, with characteristic speed and elan, he had produced a manifesto setting out the aims of the Society of which he was the most recent member. This contained among many other typically Shavian utterances the statement: "The established Government has no more right to call itself the State than the smoke of London has to call itself the weather."

The members of the Society recognized a good thing when they saw it. They decided to issue the statement of their aims as seen by Shaw as a pamphlet. They had already issued one pamphlet, drafted by the only working man ever to belong to that early select little group, a house-painter named W. L. Phillips, with the title *Why Are the Many Poor?*, and called it Fabian Tract No. 1. Shaw's pamphlet was, therefore, published as Fabian Tract No. 2.

If the Fabians recognized Shaw's merits, he recognized theirs also, or rather perceived that this was the sort of group that could very well be used for the Socialist purposes he now had in mind. He persuaded Webb, with whom he had become close friends while striding across Britain, and sometimes France, walking and talking with inordinate energy, to come along to speak to them. Webb addressed the Society on "The Way Out." Two months later Webb became a member. He had by this time promoted himself to the Colonial Office, passing high into the First Division in the Civil Service open examination, and had also been called to the Bar, for which he read in the spare time left over from working at the Colonial Office, lecturing at the Working Men's College, frequenting debating clubs and reading copiously in economics. He at once set to work with Shaw to reorganize society through the agency of this small, intelligent but practically unknown group of middle-class intellectuals.

As a preliminary to doing so he set himself to convince the Fabians themselves that theories were useless without facts. As Webb was the most tireless accumulator and co-ordinator of facts in England, and Shaw was their most brilliant expositor, the two

69

of them were ideally suited for this task. Gradually there gathered around them one of the most brilliant groups of people any society, Socialist or otherwise, has ever possessed, chief among them Sidney Olivier, a colleague of Webb's at the Colonial Office, later Governor of Jamaica and Secretary of State for India, tall, grave and handsome and wearing his velvet jacket with a difference; Graham Wallas, distinguished scholar, writer and educationist; Hubert Bland, a journalist with an immense following in the north of England; Annie Besant and Stewart Headlam. In 1887 Webb produced his first Fabian Tract, *Facts for Socialists*, which had a large and continuing sale, and in 1889, on the eve of the dock strike, the first collection of *Fabian Essays* was published.

This collection of Fabian Essays presented the case for socialism in plain language varnished with wit and gaiety and based most firmly on facts. It could be read and enjoyed by any intelligent person, even if he had never, as the essayists very obviously had, read Marx and Ricardo, Jevons, Bentham and John Stuart Mill. It set out, with that self-confident gay arrogance which was Shaw's special contribution to Fabian method, just as an immense matter-of-fact erudition was Webb's, to prove that although the existing capitalist system might be theoretically the most perfect economic system ever dreamed of by man, it suffered from the grave practical defect that it simply did not work. It must, therefore, be regarded by any sane and sensible man who looked at the facts as an absurd anachronism which should be swept away as rapidly as possible and replaced by socialism, which the essayists were perfectly ready to prove was the natural, logical and inevitable next stage in society. Although the only one of the authors with any public reputation or notoriety at the time was Annie Besant, the Essays were an immediate success. The first edition sold out in a month and altogether sixty thousand were distributed in various editions.

The Fabian Society had arrived. Shaw and Webb had made it into the sort of instrument they wanted and had found the kind of colleagues they needed. That same year an upper-middle-class young woman of twenty-eight wrote to Sidney Webb to say that she was busy on a piece of research into the Co-operative movement and other working-class organizations in the eighteenth century, and a friend had suggested that he, who was said to know everything, might be willing to help her with a list of useful reference material. Her name was Beatrice Potter and she was the eighth of nine daughters of Richard Potter, President of the Grand Trunk Railway of Canada and former Chairman of the Great Western Railway.

Herbert Spencer, Huxley, George Eliot had all been family friends of hers. She was thus well used to mixing on easy terms with people of formidable intellectual equipment and was herself a young lady not only of much charm and social poise but of very great ability in investigating and collecting social data. Spencer, who was one of her very closest friends and her intellectual guide, had encouraged her to take up social investigation as a profession. She had worked with Canon Barnett at the East End settlement, Toynbee Hall, which was one of the most immediately successful products of the Christian Socialist movement, and also on the great survey into the conditions of life and work in London, organized by Charles Booth, who was a relation of hers by marriage.

Sidney Webb at once replied to her letter. They met. He gave her, there and then, a complete list of all the references she could possibly use, including manuscripts in the British Museum, records of State trials, and dates of relevant copies of old Chartist periodicals —and fell in love with her. As an early step in his courtship, he introduced her to the Fabian Society, which she joined in 1900, and then asked her to marry him. She took eighteen months longer than he to make up her mind. When she did so, she did so utterly. In June, 1892, by which time Sidney had resigned from the Civil Service and was keeping himself by writing, they were married and went off for a honeymoon to Dublin and Glasgow to look up old trade-union records.

The great Fabian combination was now complete. It was a remarkable combination of which the complete identification between Sidney and Beatrice Webb, which was so absolute that they seemed to be not two personalities but one, was the most remarkable part. Of that partnership of mind, Beatrice Webb, writing in her diary a year before her marriage, but when she had at last decided that she truly loved Sidney, spoke with a typical clarity of judgment and a much greater restraint than that shown by Shaw on the occasion of the Zetetical Society meeting.

71

"We are both of us," she wrote, "second-rate minds; but we are curiously combined. I am the investigator and he the executant. Between us we have a wide and varied experience of men and affairs. We have also an unearned salary [hers not his]. These are unique circumstances. A considerable work should be the result if we use our combined talents with a deliberate and persistent purpose." A considerable work did indeed result, for if they were, as she said, separately both second-rate minds (and they were only so if second-rate is used in its strictly accurate sense in relation to the great creative thinkers), their minds when working in combination formed a perfect instrument for the purpose to which they devoted themselves.

That purpose was the Fabian purpose of social investigation as a prelude to social action and the permeation of all parties and classes—but particularly what were then the ruling classes—with the Socialist idea as an essential technique of social efficiency and social justice.

As one looks back across the sixty or so years since the Fabian campaign was first started, its success appears phenomenal. Fabianism has not only played a large and in some ways a decisive part in shaping the Labour Party, but it has permeated the most active and constructive minds in every party. Even Winston Churchill, the most eighteenth-century of modern statesmen, has been under its influence from the day in 1908 when, without his being fully aware of what was happening, the then youthful William Beveridge was skilfully planted on him by the Webbs and the first Labour Exchanges were the result. There is no single aspect of twentieth-century social policy which has not been subject to the Fabian influence.

On the Labour Party the influence of Fabianism has been two-fold. In the first place, it provided Labour with a practical philosophy exactly suited to the conditions in which it came to birth and, in the second, it taught it how to become a ruling class.

It is true that in its early days the Fabian Society showed little comprehension of the place and importance of trade unionism. It is also true that for some time its members conceived of socialism as a simple evolutionary process which would be brought into being by the intellectual permeation of the traditional parties rather than by the formation of a specifically Socialist party—a concept which reveals at once the weakness and the strength of the early Fabians.

Being themselves intelligent and socially enlightened people, they tended too much to assume that others were likewise, that the case for social reform had only to be correctly stated to be accepted and that the conflict of self-interest between the classes would dissolve of itself if a memorandum were prepared to show that it was wasteful and unnecessary. They disliked the class-war because it was foolish and untidy as well as immoral. When they destroyed it on paper they sometimes assumed that it had thereupon ceased to exist. In this assumption they were sometimes right when immediate practical issues of social reform were in question, but wrong when it led them, as it sometimes did, to the belief that the possessing classes could simply be argued into giving up their possessions and their privilege.

The early Fabian disregard of the importance of the trade unions in the social and political struggle was manifested to a remarkable degree in the Fabian Essays. The reader of that statement of belief was given no hint whatever of the forces which were already creating the new trade unionism—even although one of the essayists, Annie Besant, had herself been the chief protagonist in the Match Girls' Strike which showed the new trade unionism the way, and the London Dock Strike, which was entirely to transform the trade-union picture, was only just round the corner. In so far as trade unionism was considered it was looked at only to be condemned as an anti-social movement by workers to secure monopolistic advantages for themselves to the detriment of the general mass of people.

The credit for changing the Fabian view on this, and bringing the Fabians to a more realistic understanding of the political and social forces of which trade unionism was the symbol and the instrument, belongs to Beatrice Potter. During the researches into working-class co-operation which had led to her writing to Sidney Webb, she had come to the conclusion that the place of the trade unions had been very much underestimated, and this view she very soon impressed upon Sidney Webb and through him upon the Fabian Society. The immediate result was the Webbs' *History of Trade Unionism*, which appeared in 1894, and has remained the classic work on the subject ever since, and *Industrial Democracy*, three years later.

By setting trade unionism in its true historical perspective, these two books did a great deal both to persuade intelligent Socialists of the need for co-operation with the unions and to provide intelligent trade unionists with an understanding of their own movement and of its historical role in the political and industrial struggle of the workers.

Even before this change in their attitude to trade unionism, the Fabians had begun to realize that their policy of permeation must not stand in the way of efforts to establish a specifically Labour Party. In 1892, on the eve of the General Election which brought Gladstone's fourth administration to power, a Fabian Election Manifesto, written by Bernard Shaw, was issued, in which the working-classes were told that they ought at once to set about forming a party of their own and would do so if they cared as much for politics as they did for horse-racing. A year later, when the Liberal Government had lamentably failed to carry out Campbell-Bannerman's election promise to make the Government the best employer of labour in the country, Shaw and Webb jointly wrote an article for the *Fortnightly Review* entitled, "To Your Tents, O Israel," in which the workers were advised to abandon all allegiance to Liberalism, form a Trade-Union Party of their own and get ready to run at least fifty candidates at the next election. This article was later considerably amplified and the steps necessary to establish a distinct and independent Labour Party set out in some detail. It was then published as Fabian Tract No. 49, *A Plan of Campaign for Labour*. It had a large sale and much influence in developing the Socialist and trade-union attitudes which seven years later made possible the formation of the Labour Representative Committee at the Memorial Hall.

But if the Fabian Society's direct influence on the course of the events which led to the formation of the Labour Party was not small, its indirect influence on those events, and even more on the development of Labour thereafter, was even larger.

It gave British socialism a coherent and practical approach to politics which was neither Marxist nor Liberal and which provided a practical method of advance towards democratic socialism; one, moreover, which took into account the political, economic and social attitudes of the British middle- and working-classes.

In that work Shaw's contribution, and one that only he could give, was to destroy with enormous verve one after another of the Victorian myths which held command over the minds of the middle-classes and through them over a large part of the working-classes also. In the course of his witty and iconoclastic progress he thus cleared the way for new ideas and new attitudes. He broke down the prison walls of Victorian social morality and let in the fresh air. He took the social conceptions that Victorian capitalism had established in its defence, stood them on their heads and pelted them with fireworks—after which they lost their formidable appearance of being laws of nature and the young could take courage to throw them out of the window if need be.

The contribution of the Webbs, and to only a less extent that of Graham Wallas, Olivier and others among the leading Fabians was to offer to British Labour the same sort of theoretical and philosophic support that Jeremy Bentham and James Mill had given to nineteenth-century liberalism and that Marx and Engels gave to revolutionary socialism.

Their revolutionary achievement was to show that revolutionary socialism was, in Britain, out of date. In so doing they provided the Labour Party with the theoretical basis which every political party, and particularly every new political party, must have to give it full self-confidence and coherence—even although the discovery made intellectually by the Fabians had already been felt emotionally by the ordinary workers in their trade unions, their radical clubs and their new Labour groups.

Marx's theory of social revolution had been evolved at a time when the whole force of the State was mobilized on the side of wealth and privilege. It had been born during a period of enormous wealth accumulation by the new middle-classes of the industrial revolution, and when, since the State was undemocratic, there existed no parliamentary means by which the working-classes could hope to improve their position and achieve their rightful influence on the course of affairs. In such circumstances not only was the class-war a positive and powerful fact, but the only hope of the workers' success in a war which their exploiters had forced upon them was to organize themselves for revolutionary purposes. Industrial capitalism presented a solid face which, it appeared, could only be broken by a frontal attack.

This was no longer the case by the end of the nineteenth century. Trade unions had been legalized and the workers had won the political franchise. They possessed constitutional and non-insurrectionist weapons which could give them victory if they could be taught how to use them. Moreover, the implacable face of industrial capitalism had begun to crumble from within. A ferment was at work for which Marx had made no allowance—the ferment of social conscience. The class-war still existed, but it was possible now for the workers to fight on new ground and in so doing to transform the class-war into something greater. They now had the possibility of attracting to themselves allies from the other side and turning what had originally been a war of the classes, a war of the helots of industrial capitalism against their oppressors, into a battle in which the most intelligent and the most humane of the middle-classes themselves would rally to their side—a battle for social reform and for the saner, more efficient and more moral organization of the productive system.

Britain had become a political democracy. The old liberalism, which had grown out of the upsurge of the new middle-class of the industrial revolution, and which had for the time commanded the support also of most of the politically conscious working-class, was disintegrating. Practice had failed to conform to the theoretical assumption on which the Liberal philosophy had been based that individual interest was the best guide to the general good. The recognition was spreading that social reform was essential and that the chief instruments of social reform must be central and local government. The first self-confidence of the middle-classes was passing and with it the ruthlessness which self-confidence had brought in its train.

The Fabians recognized, as the Social Democratic Federation failed to do, that a Socialist theory based on political and social conditions that had passed was simply an encumbrance about the feet of the Labour movement. Champion, the most practically minded of the S.D.F. leaders, had begun to recognize by 1886 that the day of successful revolution by means of workers' riots and street fighting had passed and said so in *Justice*. There was not going to be another French Revolution. But being a soldier rather than a social philosopher, he transferred his affection to dynamite —to dynamite in the hands of a few resourceful, determined and secret groups.

The Fabians had no time for conspiratorial nonsense of this kind in what had become, without the Marxists recognizing the fact, a political democracy and could, therefore, if the workers could be educated to use their political power and the middle-classes be persuaded to help them, be turned by political means into an economic and social democracy also. They recognized that there was a much more potent dynamite to hand than any Champion was thinking of—the dynamite of a public opinion that could be awakened to the need for economic and social change. Their great contribution to socialism was their intellectual appreciation of the fact that the time had come when socialism had to be adapted to democracy and democracy could be adapted to socialism. They did not contribute any new economic theory to the Socialist doctrine. They were not creative political philosophers or creative economic thinkers. They were social scientists. They took over more or less complete the political philosophy of Bentham and John Stuart Mill and the economics of Jevons and Ricardo. But they set themselves to show how these could best be practically applied in the conditions of the day and that such an application led logically, and indeed inevitably, to socialism.

Being social scientists, rather than political philosophers and economic thinkers, they perfected a social science technique to further their political aims, having complete confidence—as Sidney Webb showed later when he used one half of a legacy of £10,000, left to the Fabian Society for purposes of Socialist education, to found the London School of Economics without any political bias —that the more economic facts there were available, and the more widely understood those facts were, the more clear would the case for socialism be. Their technique was based on careful investigation of conditions, followed by the preparation of fully documented demands for social reform. It would not be entirely true to say that they let the facts speak for themselves, but having discovered the facts they used them as the main part of their ammunition in any

77

campaign and they never started a campaign until they had discovered all the facts.

Yet, although a large part of the Fabian effort was devoted to social reform, they were not simply social reformers but Socialists. They aimed, in the words of their declaration of principles, "at the reorganization of society by the emancipation of land and industrial capital from individual and class ownership and the vesting of them in the community for the general benefit." Accordingly they worked "for the extinction of private property in land and of the consequent individual appropriation in the form of rent of the price paid for permission to use the earth, as well as for the advantages of superior soils and sites," and for "the transfer to the community of the administration of such industrial capital as can conveniently be managed socially, for, owing to the monopoly of the means of production in the past, industrial inventions and the transformation of surplus income into capital have mainly enriched the proprietary class, the workers being now dependent on that class for leave to earn a living."

The economic basis of Fabian socialism derived from the theory of rent enumerated by David Ricardo, the great English economist of the early nineteenth century, and from John Stuart Mill's development of that theory. Ricardo, whose theory of value—that only living labour produced value—was heavily drawn upon and developed by Marx in *Das Kapital*, argued that rent was the result of the general advance in civilization. It ought not, therefore, simply to enrich landlords, whose claim to it merely arose from the accident that they owned land which had been increased in value by the general progress. Mill, developing this theory in its political application, argued that because rent was the effect of a natural monopoly and not of any exertion on the part of its possessor, it should properly be appropriated by the State through a special tax on land values, the proceeds of which should be used for the benefit of society as a whole.

The Fabians applied this reasoning to all forms of capital and not merely to capital in land. In a brilliant series of Fabian tracts they argued that, just as it was true that the course of national development increased the value of some land greatly in excess of the increase in the value of other land and there was no just reason why this consequence of social activity should benefit merely the owner of the land thus accidentally enriched, so it was equally true that the return on capital invested in some industrial developments as compared with others was enormously swollen by social causes. The rewards received over and above the average by the investors of capital in such enterprises—the differential rent—was the result, not of their own efforts, but of the social effort. It ought, therefore, to be used for the good of society as a whole, partly through taxation and partly by the social ownership and management of such industries, either municipally or nationally.

They saw the economic struggle not as the Marxists did as a plain struggle between the working-classes on one side and the whole of the capitalist class and its managers and officials, the bourgeoisie, on the other, but one in which the interests of the great mass of the nation, the managers and technicians and professional workers no less than the manual workers, were opposed by appropriators of differential rent, whether their rent came from land or from industrial capital. The conflict, to state it in the phrase which was later to express the nature and width of the Labour Party's appeal, was between "all workers whether by hand or brain"—the inventors, the scientists, the research workers, the administrators no less than the manual workers—and those who acquired wealth merely by the investment of capital without themselves making any social effort of body or mind.

They did not argue from this—although Shaw himself later did—that absolute equality of income was either necessary or desirable to socialism. They took the realist view that so long as the social conscience was insufficiently developed for men and women to be expected to work for the benefit of society as a whole without regard to the degree of personal reward from their work, it was necessary that there should be exceptional rewards for exceptional talent or exceptional effort. But they argued that reward should be related to talent and effort—to social usefulness—and that the mere possession of capital did not entitle its possessor to receive a large reward without talent or effort. It was, therefore, the business of the modern state, through its central and municipal instruments, to see that all those performing useful social service by work should be guaranteed the essentials of a civilized existence, including the educational and other facilities which would enable the most talented and the most active to receive a fair rent for ability over and above the average.

The aims and methods of the Fabians in the light of their reading of the economic, political and social facts of the time were well set out in a report made by the Fabian Society to the International Socialist and Trades Union Congress held in London in 1896. In this they repudiated the idea of revolutionary socialism and affirmed their belief in the achievement of socialism by democratic and constitutional means and by the control of administration by the freely elected representatives of the people. By socialism they stated they meant the appropriation of all forms of economic rent, whether of land or capital, by the nation as a whole and the organization of the essential industries of the country by public authorities, and they considered that the democratic machinery of government, central and local, which then existed in Britain, made it possible to do this by constitutional means if the people could be persuaded to use the political power they possessed.

They were, they said, not interested in the class-war as such, but in appealing to men and women of all classes who wished to remedy the evils of society. The first purpose of the Society was, therefore, to arouse the social conscience of all men and women of goodwill by social investigations which would make the public more aware of existing social evils and would show the practical means by which those evils could be remedied. In doing so it sought to permeate all bodies, and not only specifically Socialist ones, with its ideas. Its members worked with and through Conservative and Liberal groups as well as Socialist and Labour ones, and were urged not to concentrate their interest and activity simply on national policies and national government, but on county, town, district and parish councils and boards of guardians.

It is only necessary thus to state the economic, political and social theories on which the Fabian method was founded, and the practical means by which that method was applied to political life to see the immense influence which the Fabian ideas have had in shaping modern British socialism and on the conceptions which, in some part, govern all political parties in this country today. In the half-century since the Labour Party began, Fabianism has been far and away the most potent and constructive intellectual influence in its domestic policy. Moreover, this influence has been cumulative.

More than half a century after the Fabian Society first enunciated the principles and objectives of democratic Socialist policy as it saw them, the economic and social reform policies of the Labour Government are directly derived from them and the impact of the Fabian idea upon public affairs is greater than at any time in its life.

That is a remarkable achievement. But it is not the only Fabian achievement. Fabianism provided a training in leadership which has proved of incalculable advantage to Labour. It did so in two ways. First, by its advocacy of membership of local authorities. The municipal authorities in the last half-century or so have provided not only the agencies through which many important social reforms have been made effective, but also a training ground for parliamentary leadership, the full extent of which can only be gauged when one examines the records of the present national leaders of the Labour Party and finds how high a proportion of them spent their political apprenticeship in local government.

Secondly, the Fabian Tracts, the Fabian Essays and the Fabian Lectures provided exactly the kind of intellectual discipline that was needed for a party many of whose most prominent personalities had had little formal educational training. These new leaders of Labour first learnt their business of leadership in the hard practical school of working-class and trade-union organization. The Fabian publications and lectures provided them with the theoretical equipment and the intellectual discipline necessary to use that practical experience to the full.

The Fabian Society was thus a potent factor in creating a new ruling class better equipped for the complex business of administering a modern society than most of the old ruling class had ever been. And at the same time it helped to create in the professions, among business technicians and in public administration a receptiveness to, and an understanding of, the democratic Socialist method which has been of enormous advantage in assisting a smooth transition to socialism.

All this was accomplished by a society whose membership during the most active and creative period of its life never numbered more than a few hundreds, and which was—despite that legendary house-painter—almost entirely middle-class in its origins.

How was this miracle accomplished? In part, of course, it was due to the happy fortune of the leadership of the Webbs and of Shaw, without whom the Fabian Society, although it might have been a useful ally of socialism, would never have developed the approach to public affairs which enabled it to exercise the decisive influence it did. But it was due also to the discipline and homogeneity of the Fabians as a whole—a discipline greater than that of any party other than that of the Bolshevists in Russia. But it was of a very different kind from that of the Bolshevists. It was a discipline accepted not from an executive but developed out of discussion among equals—a homogeneity which was functional not social, although the fact that practically all the Fabians were middle-class seemed often to the outsider to give it a social flavour.

The Fabian Society, as Shaw has said, met for the most part "in middle-class drawing-rooms where a labourer would have been unbearably uncomfortable." But his discomfort would, in fact, have arisen not so much from the differences in social background between himself and the others as from differences in intellectual background. He would have been safe from snubs because he did not know how to use a fork or handle a teacup; he would not have been safe from them if he had shown himself, as he probably would at that time, unable to use a Blue Book or handle a complicated economic argument.

The Fabian Society was, to use Max Beer's phrase in his *History of British Socialism*, an "institute of social engineering," and it required from all who joined it the necessary educational and intellectual training to undertake the work of such an institute. It was inevitable, therefore, that in the conditions of the late nineteenth century it should draw in the main upon the middle-classes who alone possessed the equipment necessary for its purposes. But it selected carefully. Those who wished to join were scrutinized individually by the executive committee, and none who failed to reach the exacting standards set, both in intellectual competence and in willingness to devote a great deal of time to the work of the Society, were admitted. It was not interested in people who merely wanted to participate in an interesting and lively discussion group; they must be prepared to work; they must, as Shaw said, positively prefer spending two or three nights a week in acquiring and dispensing information to going to the theatre or drinking or even sweethearting.

Yet this social and intellectual homogeneity had its drawbacks as well as its advantages. Although the Fabian Society, after a false start, came very rapidly to an intellectual understanding of the importance of the trade unions and of the working-class movement, its members had little emotional understanding of the real sources of strength in that movement. Convinced that social reform and ultimately socialism could be secured by the permeation of all classes, they underestimated the resistance of privileged groups to fundamental changes in the social and economic structure. And for a long time they failed fully to realize that those changes could, and would in fact, only be carried out by a movement based on the organization of the working-classes.

Because, under the impact of a developing social conscience the then ruling class was ready to accept what Joseph Chamberlain described as "the gospel of ransom"—the payment in social services and improved working conditions of the sum necessary to avoid the danger of revolution—they sometimes too readily assumed that it would voluntarily abandon the central positions of power. Because they saw clearly that much of Marx's thesis had been made out of date by the development of parliamentary democracy, they did not always give due weight to what was true in that thesis—that the working-classes were an oppressed class whose subordinate position in society would only be ended if they themselves combined to alter it, and that the very existence of this oppressed class itself offered both the necessity and the opportunity to bring about a fundamental change in the structure of society.

They saw, as Marx did not, that the interests of the working-classes and the middle-classes did not necessarily conflict but could be made complementary, and that an alliance between them was both desirable and possible. They did not perhaps fully appreciate that, although the working-classes could find valuable allies among the middle-classes, the upsurge of popular feeling and action that alone could transform society must come from the working-classes themselves, and that they must bear the brunt of the struggle and provide socialism with the large battalions necessary to success.

And because of their intellectual and functional approach to the problems of society, their doctrines, and perhaps even more their methods, were a little cold. They wanted a just and an efficient society. They believed that it could be achieved democratically—and they were right. But they often seemed more interested in efficiency than in democracy and not to understand that although men and women want a just society, warmth and humanity and comradeship and love are no less necessary to human happiness. They disliked muddle; they did not easily accept the fact that men may prefer a muddle that they make for themselves to the neatest of systems made for them by others.

The modern Labour Party as we know it would not have existed without the Fabian Society. But the Fabian Society alone could not have created it. That required the industrial and political organization of the workers in the new trade unionism, and it required, no less, the warmth, the humanity, the moral fervour of the Independent Labour Party.

The scientific method of the Webbs, the iconoclastic, gay and arrogant logic of Shaw, needed the broad sweep of Keir Hardie's humanity, his intuitive understanding of the lives and emotions of his fellows, his moral passion and his staunch and rock-like character to give to Socialist doctrine the depth, the warmth, the passion which would turn it from a scientific method into a crusade.

And it needed also, if it was to become a doctrine drawing upon all the rich resources of the British character and answering the emotional as well as the intellectual needs of the people, the sheer fun and gaiety, the jollity, the sense of comradeship and adventure, the touch of eccentricity even, that Robert Blatchford and the Clarion Scouts could bring.

The Fabians gave modern British socialism its doctrine. The new trade unionism gave it the organized working-class movement which was necessary to success. By his fusing of the two, by his intuitive understanding that socialism could not advance without the trade-union movement and his almost instinctive knowledge of the amount of Socialist policy that the trade unions could be brought at any one time to accept, Keir Hardie, more than any other single man, made the Labour Party possible. Without him there might have been an independent Socialist party or an independent trade-union party—but certainly not a Labour Party.

Hardie was not a particularly clever man. He was not in any formal sense an educated man; he could not even sign his own name until after he was seventeen. Nor was he a great administrator or parliamentary leader. He was a prophet. He was, as Ramsay MacDonald wrote of him: "the Moses who led the children of labour in this country out of bondage—out of bondage, not into Canaan, for that was to be a longer job." In this larger job he had less part. Nor, indeed, had he much aptitude for it, so that, although his active political life continued nearly until 1915 when he died, worn out with toil and broken in heart by war, in a sense his true life work came to an end when the Labour Party was born.

He was a visionary who could give others the eyes to see and the ears to hearken, he was a man of the common people who could speak to the heart of all people, among the pioneers he was the chief of all. In the annals of the Labour Party, where are enrolled the names of many men more brilliant than he, his is, and will remain, the most honoured name. In the memory of the pioneers his is the most loved memory. Among all those who contributed in some measure to the birth of Labour his name stands pre-eminent.

"He is," wrote a contemporary in a weekly newspaper in 1894, the year after the formation of the Independent Labour Party, "above all things a spiritual and yet a simple, practical man. Not tall, squarely built, hard-headed, well-bodied and well-set-up, he is obviously a working man. His head is of the high moral type with a finely developed forehead denoting perception and reason of the kind called common sense. His brown hair is worn long and curling somewhat like the 'glory' round the head of a saint in a painted window and he goes unshaved . . . one needs to be near him to perceive the particularly deep, straight and steady gaze of the clear hazel eyes, which is notable. Altogether one judges him, by appearances only, to be a close-knit, kindly and resolute man, all of which his performance in life bears out."

And Cunninghame Graham, describing him as he was six or seven years before this, wrote:

"At first sight he struck you as a remarkable man. There was an air of great benevolence about him, but his face showed the kind of appearance of one who has worked hard and suffered possibly from under-nourishment in his youth. . . . His voice was high-pitched but sonorous and very far-carrying at that time. He never used notes and I think never prepared a speech, leaving all to the inspiration of the moment. . . . His chief merits as a speaker were, in my opinion, his homeliness, directness and sincerity; and his demerits were a tendency to redundancy and length and a total lack of humour, very rare in an Ayrshire Scot. This was to me curious, as he had a considerable vein of pathos. He always opened his speeches in those days with 'Men' and finished with 'Now, men.' . . . He was an extremely abstemious eater and in the long peregrinations about the mining villages of Lanarkshire and Ayrshire when I was a young unknown M.P. and he an equally unknown miners' leader, in rain and wind and now and then in snow, an oatcake, a scone, a bit of kebbuck of cheese always contented him. He would then sit down by the fireside in the cottage in the mining row and light up his corn-cob pipe and talk of the future of the Labour Party, which in those days seemed to the miners a mere fairy tale. Now and then I have seen him take the baby from the miner's wife and dandle it on his knee whilst she prepared tea."

It was this simple, abstemious, prophetic man, and those who gathered around him, who gave to the new Labour movement its spiritual significance and its soul. He was born in a one-room cottage with a thatched roof and mud floor in the mining village of Laighbrannock, near Holytown, Lanarkshire, on 15 August, 1856. His father was a ship's carpenter, his mother a farm servant, and he was the eldest of nine children. There was radicalism in his blood; one of his ancestors, Andrew Hardie, had been hanged only thirty-six years before after the Bonnymuir riot of 1820, when a handful of miners of whom he was one were provoked by *agents provocateurs* employed by Lord Sidmouth to take up arms in a desperate protest against the harsh conditions of their life. His grandfather died of cholera under terrible conditions of poverty. Both his parents were proud, independent people, free-thinkers later when the hypocrisy of so many of those prominent in the Kirk turned their stomachs against religion. They read books which those who regarded the poor as scarcely human would have been surprised to find in a one-room hovel in a miners' row, *Pilgrim's Progress* and Paine's *Age of Reason*, the poems of Burns. Over the fire in the evening his mother used to recite from memory the ballads of the Border.

When Hardie was six the family moved to Glasgow so that his father could try to get a shore job in the shipyards. He got one in Napier's yard, but after a brief period had an accident and was laid up for many weeks. With the wage-earner ill no income came in; there was no accident insurance or sickness benefit in those days. The family got deeply in debt. Hardly had the father recovered and gone back to work than there was a strike at the docks. The family had to sell pieces of furniture to live, and Keir Hardie, like many other working-class children in that great period of Victorian prosperity, had to become a bread-winner at the age of seven. He had various jobs as a messenger boy at 2s. and then 3s. a week for a 12½-hour day. Then he was taken on when eight years old in Thompson's yard as a rivet heater. He was paid 4s. 6d. a week, but when several boys were killed in fatal accidents with the white-hot rivets his mother became frightened and took him away. He became a baker's boy again. That was his job when his father was thrown out of work once more in the great Clyde lock-out of 1866. The Union funds were small. Strike pay fell to 2s. and then 1s. 6d. a week as the lock-out went on. That and Keir Hardie's 4s. 6d. was the total family income to keep a family of eleven.

During the twelve months or so while his father was in regular work it had been possible to accumulate a few household belongings. Now, one by one, all but the barest essentials were sold to buy food. There was fever in the house and the boy next in age to Keir died of it a little later. His mother was with child and was near her time and she, too, was ill.

Keir Hardie was nine years old. "The outlook was black," he wrote, looking back later upon that time and telling a story which is best repeated in his own words:

"The outlook was black, but there was worse to come and the form it took made it not only a turning point in my life, but also in my outlook upon man and things. I had reached the age at which I understood the tragedy of poverty and had a sense of responsibility to those at home far beyond my years. I knew that, despite the brave way in which my mother was facing the situation, she was feeling the burden almost too great for her to bear, and on more than one occasion I had caught her crying by herself.

"One winter morning I turned up late at the baker's shop where I was employed and was told I had to go upstairs to see the master. I was kept waiting outside the door of the dining-room while he said grace—he was noted for religious zeal—and on being admitted found the master and his family seated round a large table. He was serving out bacon and eggs while his wife was pouring coffee from a glass infuser which at once—shame-faced and terrified as I was—attracted my attention. I had never before seen such a beautiful thing. The master read me a lecture before the assembled family on the sin of slothfulness, and added that though he would forgive me that once, if I sinned again by being late I should be instantly dismissed, and so sent me to begin work.

"But the injustice of the thing was burning hot within me, all the more that I could not explain why I was late. The fact was that I had not yet tasted food. I had been up most of the night tending my ailing brother, and had risen betimes in the morning but had been made late by assisting my mother in various ways before starting. The work itself was heavy and lasted from seven in the morning until closing time.

"Two mornings afterwards, a Friday, I was again a few minutes late from the same cause and was informed on arriving at the shop that I was discharged and my fortnight's wages forfeited by way of punishment. The news stupefied me and finally I burst out crying and begged the shopwoman to intercede with the master for me. The morning was wet and I had been drenched in getting to the shop and must have presented a pitiable sight as I stood at the counter in my wet patched clothes. She spoke with the master through a speaking tube, presumably to the break-fast-room I remembered so well, but he was obdurate, and finally she, out of the goodness of her heart, gave me a piece of bread and advised me to look for another place. For a time I wandered about the streets in the rain, ashamed to go home where there was neither food nor fire and actually discussing whether the best thing was not to go and throw myself in the Clyde and be done with a life that had so little attraction. In the end I went back to the shop and saw the master and explained why I had been late. But it was all in vain. The wages were never paid. But the master continued to be a pillar of the Church and a leading light in the religious life of the city."

That happened to a nine-year-old boy on a New Year's Eve in the days of Victorian prosperity.

Now both the father and the eldest boy were out of work. There was no income coming in. In despair the father went to sea again and Mrs. Hardie and her children went to Newarthill, where her mother lived, near where Keir had been born. When he was ten work was found for him as a trapper in the pit. His work was underground, he had to stay by himself quite alone for ten hours each day opening and closing a door which kept the air supply for the men in the required direction. The only noise to break the underground silence was the whistling of the air as it tried to escape.

From being a trapper he was promoted to being a pony driver. For many years he never saw the winter sun, for he went down the pit at six in the morning and when he came up the daylight had ended. Such an experience, as he said, does not develop the sunny side of one's nature. When he was twelve he was entombed in the mine during a colliery accident. Many years later, in the simple straightforward way that was his wont and that was so much a part of his character, he told the story in the *Labour Leader*.

"I would be about twelve at the time, and was a pony driver. We were working at nights, and some thirty men were employed, I being the only boy. It was dreary work. The pit was very old and very wet. To this day the dreary, monotonous drip, drip, drip of the water on every side is quite fresh in my ears. My pony was a little shaggy Highlander, appropriately named Donald—strong and obstinate, like the race among whom he had been reared. We were great friends, and drank cold tea from the same tin flask, sip about. I have to confess that betimes his old reiving propensities overcame his loyalty, and on these occasions, should opportunity occur, he would steal the tea-flask from where it was kept, extract the cork, and empty it of its contents with,

I doubt not, all the satisfaction which stolen sweets never failed to afford.

"One night, just after midnight hour, when the weird noises of the pit are always at their height, Donald and I were jogging along, when the voice of Rab Mair, the big, genial fireman, came reverberating out of the gloom, his little lamp shining like a star in the blackness. 'Run into the dook and warn the men to come at once; the shank's closing.' I did not stay on the order of my going. The shank closing! The shank is the shaft by which entrance and egress to the pit is obtained. It was the only outlet. Should it close in we were entombed, and what that might mean I did not care to think. In a very short time all the men were at the pit bottom, only to find that already they were too late. We were seventy fathoms from the daisies, and the weary rocks, tired of hanging in mid-air, seemed bent on settling down into some semblance of solidarity. For once in a way the drip of water could not be heard. The timber props were creaking and bursting all around us; whilst the strong rocks were groaning and cracking and roaring as they were settling down. As man after man rushed to the bottom breathless and alarmed, they were met with the news that already the cage, by which men and materials are taken to the surface, was 'stuck in the shank.' The sides of the shaft had so far come together that the cage had no longer a free passage and was held fast some fathoms above us. We were prisoners.

"I can recall every detail of the scene. The men gathered in groups, each with his little lamp on his bonnet, their blackened, serious faces, discussing what should be done. The roaring and crackling, as if of artillery, went on overhead, and gloom began to settle on every countenance. Some of the more susceptible were crying, and I remember two by themselves who were praying and crossing themselves. Rab Mair remained cool and strong, and did his best to keep up the spirits of his fellow-prisoners. By and by I began to feel sleepy, and made my way to the stables, whither Donald had already gone. By this time it was evident the worst of the crisis was over; the noise overhead was subsiding and the drip of the water was again to be heard. But the shaft was closed. We were prisoners indeed. After cleaning Donald down, I gave him a feed of corn, put some hay in his manger, and rolling myself in this, kissed him, as was our wont, and then went off to sleep. A boy of twelve will sleep when there is nothing to do, even if he be cooped in a trap. How long I slept I have no means now of knowing. It was Rab Mair's voice—swearing, if the truth must be told—and some vigorous punches from his fist which brought me back to consciousness.

"The engineman, on finding the cages stuck fast in the shaft, and hearing the signals from below, knew there was something wrong, and raised an alarm. In a short time the news spread, and soon the bulk of the people were at the pit, my mother among the rest. Volunteers were plentiful, and soon some brave fellows had been lowered by an improvised kettle into the shaft, where they soon discovered what was amiss. Cold chisels, picks and saws were requisitioned, and the imprisoned cage cut free and allowed to drop in pieces to the bottom, after which the kettle —a bucket used by pit sinkers, and narrower than the cage— was used to bring the imprisoned men to the surface. But where was the trapper? Everyone had seen him in the bottom, and perhaps in the excitement of the moment no one would have missed him had there not been a mother there waiting for him. And so Rab Mair and two companions had to descend into the depths again and search. For a time their searching was in vain, until Rab bethought him of Donald's crib, and there sure enough I was, sound asleep. Rab pretended to be angry—but he wasn't. I think the reception on the top was the most trying part of the affair. At least, it was the only part when I cried."

In the winter evenings after coming up from the pit Hardie went to night school. His mother had taught him to read and he read much, particularly the Bible which powerfully influenced his speaking and writing style throughout his life. Now he learned to write. At his mother's instigation, too, he learned shorthand and through her also he joined the Good Templars, the Temperance movement which was then establishing itself in the Scottish villages. His mother and father, in whom the iron of their experiences in Glasgow had bitten deep, had by now become strong radicals. Keir Hardie shared their radicalism but not the contempt for all organized religion that life had taught them. Like many of his comrades in the mines he was a religious man—although not given to dogma. He joined the Evangelical Union founded by Dr. James Morrison, who had been expelled from the United Presbyterian Church for heresy because he would not accept predestination but believed that salvation depended upon men themselves and that all could be saved if they would.

By the time he was twenty and a coal-hewer, Hardie was a noted local speaker for the Temperance movement and the Evangelical Union, and, in his small way, a public figure in the village of Quarter in the Hamilton district to which the family had moved. When the miners held a protest meeting about their conditions and their wages which had been crushed down to two shillings a day by the owners, they therefore voted him into the chair and asked him to be a member of a deputation to the colliery managers. His friends in the Temperance movement warned him that if he persisted in such a course he would very soon find himself on the wrong side of the bosses. They were right.

One morning early in 1879—that year in which Shaw and Webb met for the first time—he was in the cage descending No. 4 Quarter pit when, half-way down, the cage stopped and then moved to the surface again. At the top the colliery manager was waiting for him. He was ordered to get off the company's grounds at once and told his tools would be sent home.

"We'll hae nae damned Hardies in this pit," said the manager, and proceeded to sack Keir Hardie's two younger brothers as well.

The other colliery managers were informed and the Hardie family was boycotted throughout the Lanarkshire coalfield as a lesson to any other men who might feel like standing up for themselves and their fellows.

Stage by stage, from the day when as a boy of nine, wet through and hungry, he had been dismissed for being a few minutes late because of nursing his dying brother, Hardie had been taught, not by economic theory, but by harsh economic reality what was the position of the worker in society. The Labour agitator was born.

From thenceforward Hardie's whole life was devoted to the cause of Labour. The family moved to Low Waters, near the Cadzow

Collieries. There, out of their small savings, his mother set up a grocery shop for the colliers and he opened a tobacconist's and stationer's near-by. With the help of the shorthand he had learned at night-school he managed also to get himself appointed local correspondent of the *Glasgow Weekly Mail*. The family was used to living meagrely. With the income from these sources they had enough. Hardie set about what seemed the impossible task of organizing the miners.

Again and again the organization he built up was broken, again and again men striking against intolerable conditions were driven back to work by the hunger of their women and children. At a conference of miners at Dunfermline, Hardie was elected National Secretary of the Scottish Miners—but there was no Miners' Federation for him to be secretary of: it was a hope, a distant and desperate hope, not a reality. He married a girl he had first met in the Temperance movement, Lillie Wilson, who thereafter gave him comfort and sustenance in all his struggles. In 1880 the two of them moved to a tiny two-roomed cottage in Cumnock in Ayrshire so that Hardie could answer a call from the miners of Ayrshire to help them to build a union. It took him nearly a year to build an organization. When that was done the Ayrshire miners put up a demand for a 10 per cent increase in wages. It was refused. There was no alternative but to strike, for if the union accepted the refusal without fight it would be broken before it had well started.

Yet a strike with few funds was a dangerous enterprise. All over the county Hardie addressed mass meetings of the men, putting to them the question: "To strike or not?" And nobody could be sure of how the answer would go. For men had to think of their wives and children before deciding.

William Stewart, Hardie's friend and biographer, tells what happened:

"On the Saturday, at the end of the rows and on the quoitury grounds, the talk was: 'Will there be a strike?' Nobody knew. On the Sunday coming home from the Kirk the crack was the same: 'Will there be a strike?' On Sunday night they laid out their pit clothes as usual, ready for work as usual, but for ten long weeks they had no use for pit clothes. On Monday, long before dawn, there was a stir on the Ayrshire roads.

"At two in the morning the Annbank brass band came playing through Trabboch village, and every miner, young and old, jumped out of bed and fell in behind. Away up towards Auchinleck they went marching, their numbers increasing with every mile of the road. On through Damconner and Cronberry and Lugar and Muirkirk, right on to Glenbuck by Aird's Moss where the Covenanter Martyrs sleep, then down into Cumnock, at least five thousand strong. Never did magic muster such an army of the morning. . . . Over in the Kilmarnock district similar scenes were being enacted. The bands went marching from colliery to colliery and

> *The rising sun ower Galston Muir*
> *Wi' glorious light was glinting*

upon processions of colliers on all the roads round about Galston village and Hurlford and Crookedholm and Riccanton, making, as by one common impulse, towards Craigie Hill which had not witnessed such a mustering of determined men since the days of William Wallace.

"Ere nightfall a miracle had been accomplished. For the first time in its history there was a stoppage nearly complete in the Ayrshire mining industry."

The strike lasted all that summer. Then the winter came as the ally of the coal-owners. Boots and clothes and food were needed for the children. For the sake of the children the men went back to work. But they went back as they came out, all together, as a group, their solidarity unbroken, their Union unimpaired. And within a month the coal-owners, thoroughly frightened by this new spirit among the men, voluntarily advanced wages, a thing that had never happened before in the mining industry.

Hardie at this time was politically a Liberal. In addition to his work for the miners he was editor of the *Cumnock News*, an offshoot of the *Ardrossan and Saltcoats Herald*, owned by a Liberal of great independence and character, Mr. Arthur Guthrie, who had, what many at that time lacked, the courage to stand up against the Bute, the Eglinton and the Dundonald landowning interests and the

Bairds and the other coal-mining magnates. The miners had no parliamentary votes. Because for the most part they lived not in towns but in scattered mining villages, they had not been given the franchise in the Reform Act of 1867 when the Tory landowning interests, while accepting Disraeli's extension of the vote to the working-classes in the towns, had successfully defended their own privileged position in the country areas.

What the miners wanted politically was the vote, legislation for an eight-hour day, an improved safety code underground and some working-class M.P.s who understood their needs and would press them in Parliament. They still hoped that they could get these things from the Liberals who, drawing, as they did, so much of their strength in the country from the chapels and the Temperance societies, naturally recruited into their ranks most of the earnest and thoughtful among the mining community.

In 1884 they got the vote—it was impossible for the landowning interests to stand out any longer against reforms which the Act of 1867 had made inevitable. But they got nothing else from the Liberals; not even—which would have seemed the barest political common sense on the part of the Liberal Party and might well have delayed the formation of an independent Labour Party for many years—any sympathy for the proposal that some working-class candidates should be adopted.

And so Hardie, finding the Liberals opposing every political demand the miners made, began to think more and more in terms of an independent Labour Party. He was stimulated in his political thinking by two things. One was a visit to Ayrshire by Henry George, whose panacea for all social ills, a single tax on land, he could not accept as all-sufficient, but who stirred his reforming passion and in discussions with whom he began to evolve his own political philosophy. The second was a visit he paid to London in 1887 as secretary of the Ayrshire Miners' Union, by which he was now paid £75 a year, and of the embryonic Scottish Miners' Federation. There he met a number of leading Socialists, including Eleanor Marx-Aveling—who by this time had quarrelled with Hyndman—and Marx's collaborator, Friedrich Engels, both of whom helped to convince him of the need for an independent Labour Party with close contact with the trade unions.

He returned to Scotland and, in his paper, *The Miner*, which he had just founded, began to criticize the policy of Lib-Lab leaders who still dominated the trade-union movement. At demonstrations of Ayrshire miners on Irvine Moor and Craigie Hill he got a resolution adopted "that in the opinion of this meeting the time has come for the formation of a Labour Party in the House of Commons, and we hereby agree to assist in returning one or more members to represent the miners of Scotland at the first available opportunity." Shortly afterwards he was adopted as miners' candidate for North Ayrshire.

He was busy also as secretary of the newly formed Scottish Miners' Federation, for whom he travelled six thousand miles all over Scotland. The first annual report of the Federation—which stated that the average earnings of Scottish miners were still only 12s. a week—concludes with a characteristic Hardie exhortation: "Ours is no old-fashioned sixpence-a-day agitation. We aim at the complete emancipation of the worker from the thraldom of wagedom. Co-operative production under State management should be our goal, as never, until this is obtained, can we hope for better times for working people."

That autumn he attended the Trades Union Congress as a miners' delegate. He leapt to the front of trade-union controversy by delivering a great attack on Henry Broadhurst, the secretary of the T.U.C., who was a Liberal M.P. and had held junior office as Under-Secretary at the Home Office in Gladstone's short-lived administration of 1880—the first working man ever to hold Government office. Hardie attacked Broadhurst and other Lib-Lab leaders for their failure to press working-class claims and for supporting at the elections Liberals who were "sweating" employers. He got little support from the Congress. But the battle for an independent Labour Party was now on.

The March of the following year, 1888, it received a new impetus. Hardie was invited to fight a bye-election in mid-Lanark as an independent Labour candidate. The mid-Lanark Liberal Association had refused to consider him, although he was still a member of the Liberal Party and ready to support Liberal policy in general. The Association could not, however, stomach a miner as its candidate and preferred a young Welsh lawyer, J. W. Phillips, later Viscount St. Davids, whose son—thus does time bring its changes—is now a Labour peer.

In the middle of the campaign there arrived on the scene, as Gladstone's special emissary, Sir George Trevelyan—whose son, to carry the story of changing times a little farther, was also to join the Labour Party and become President of the Board of Education in the first Labour Government—and Schnadhorst, the chief Liberal organizer. They had an offer to make to Hardie. They had already made it to T. R. Threlfall, secretary of the Labour Electoral Committee, which had been formed by the T.U.C. two years earlier to further working-class representation, and Threlfall had accepted it whole-heartedly. It was that Hardie should retire from the contest and that, in return for his doing so, the Liberals would find him a seat at the General Election, pay his election expenses and give him a salary of £300 a year when he became an M.P. Much to the Liberals' surprise Hardie refused. They could not understand why a working man should find so generous an offer insulting. When Threlfall excitedly told him that he had fixed everything up and that he must stand down, Hardie lost his temper and chased him from the room.

That incident marked the end of any further possibility of an alliance between Hardie and the Liberals or any healing of the breach between himself and the Lib-Labs. The election was fought to a conclusion. Hardie, with no real organization behind him, came at the bottom of the poll. The Liberal won.

But a flame of political independence had been lit and three weeks later, on 19 May, 1888, Hardie and twenty-six others met in Glasgow. The chair was taken by John Murdoch, a Highland peasant, and, like Robert Burns, a one-time excise man who in his journeyings in the wild northern countryside and the still wilder islands, mostly on foot, had made himself the leader of the crofters in their fight against the landlords who oppressed and evicted them. Hardie explained that they were met together to form a Labour Party for Scotland, and after discussion it was decided to call a larger conference. Three months later, in the Waterloo Rooms, Glasgow, this conference met.

R. B. Cunninghame Graham, the Scottish aristocrat and landowner, who cared nothing for the opinions of his fellow lairds and who had been one of the heroes of the Trafalgar Square riots, presided. A Scottish Labour Party was there and then founded with Cunninghame Graham as its president, J. Shaw Maxwell as its chairman and Keir Hardie as its secretary. Its programme included the "State acquisition of the railways and all other means of transport" and a National Banking System.

From that meeting, from the propaganda work that flowed from it and from the inspiration that it gave to the launching of similar Labour bodies across the border, stems the founding of the Independent Labour Party, the I.L.P., five years later.

But before then Hardie himself was to achieve an even wider fame and was to become a leader whose vision inspired men and women in every part of Britain. He turned his paper, *The Miner*, into the *Labour Leader*, and made it the mouthpiece of the movement for a national independent Labour Party. He attended the Paris Conference called by the Continental Marxist parties at which the Second International was formed—William Morris and Cunninghame Graham were his fellow delegates from Britain—and although he never became a Marxist, was confirmed in his Socialist faith and accepted wholly the belief that working-class unity could form a permanent bulwark against war. He continued his campaign at the Trades Union Congress. Although he did not succeed in converting the Congress to socialism, he succeeded with the help of John Burns, Ben Tillett and other leaders of the new trade unionism in carrying a resolution in favour of a legal eight-hour day and forcing the resignation of Broadhurst from the secretaryship.

And in 1892 he was elected M.P. for West Ham at the General Election, which also brought John Burns into Parliament for Battersea and James Havelock Wilson, the seamen's leader, for Middlesbrough. All three had been returned as independent Labour M.P.s. But Burns, once much farther to the Left than Hardie ever was, was already quarrelling with most of his fellow-Socialists and turning towards the Liberals whom he had previously attacked so ferociously, and Havelock Wilson, a trade-union organizer first and a politician last, became less and less interested in political Labour. Hardie had to carry the banner of socialism alone. He was quite prepared to do so.

He arrived at the House of Commons in a two-horse brake with a trumpeter on the box, not so much because he himself enjoyed dramatic arrivals as because his constituents in West Ham wanted to convey him there in style, and being, as William Stewart his biographer says, a natural gentleman he accepted their company and their equipage in the spirit in which it was offered. As he also arrived in a cloth cap and a tweed jacket, his customary wear at the time, although the dictates of custom, so much stronger than any written rules, laid it down that a top-hat and a frock-coat were the only proper wear for a member of the best club in London, he created a sensation of horror that for a time almost drove from the main pages of the newspapers the discussion as to whether Rosebery or Harcourt would succeed Gladstone as Prime Minister.

Hardie did not stop at shocking the House of Commons by his unconventional attire. For him the House of Commons was not a club but a platform from which the wrongs of the poor and oppressed could be forced upon the attention of the people. He at once moved an Amendment to the Address demanding an autumn session to consider measures "designed to improve the condition of the people" and to help the unemployed and restore their right to work. He was ruled out of order. Later when, after adjourning from August to February, Parliament had returned to its labours, he became the centre of a still greater parliamentary sensation.

On 23 June the Duchess of York gave birth to a child. On that same day there was a colliery disaster at Cilfynydd in South Wales in which 260 men and boys lost their lives. On the following day, 25 June, M. Carnot, the French President, was assassinated. On 25 June Sir William Harcourt moved a vote of condolence with the French people and on 28 June the same Minister moved an address of congratulation to the Queen on the birth of the Duchess of York's baby.

When Harcourt moved the vote of condolence with the French people Hardie at once rose to ask whether the Government proposed to move a similar vote of sympathy with the relatives of the 260 dead miners.

"Oh no," said Harcourt, in an offhand tone of voice. "No. I can dispose of that quite easily now by saying that the House does sympathize with these poor people."

This reply and the tone of voice in which it was given stung Hardie to passionate fury. In that offhand tone, that careless dismissal of the relatives of 260 dead miners as not warranting the time of Parliament, he heard the voice of all those who were well fed and comfortable because miners were driven underground at 12s. or so a week, the voice of all those who had fought his demands for a safety-code in the mines, the voice of privilege everywhere with its contempt for the workers. When the congratulatory address to the Queen came up he moved an amendment that the Queen should be asked to express her sympathy with the victims of the Cilfynydd disaster and that the House itself should express its detestation of a system which made the periodic sacrifice of miners' lives inevitable.

This was an insult to the Royal Family. The whole House of Commons rose shouting and screaming at him in an indescribable hysteria of anger. "In all my life," wrote a reporter in the *West Ham Herald*, "I have never witnessed a scene like this. They howled and yelled and screamed. But he stood his ground." In the newspapers the following day he was denounced as a dangerous agitator and a notoriety-hunting vulgarian who had insulted the Queen in order to get personal publicity. In the House of Commons he was ostracized by nearly all members.

But he stood his ground. He carried on his campaigns for the unemployed, for dockers on strike in Hull where the Government sent soldiers and gunboats, for better factory-inspection, for every measure that would improve the condition of the working-classes. And all that time—for there were no salaries for M.P.s then—he was keeping himself and his family by odd bits of journalism. He was never able to send home to Mrs. Hardie and the children more than 25s. a week.

At the General Election in 1895 he lost his seat. He no longer had a national platform in the House of Commons. That did not matter. Now he became a national propagandist travelling from end to end of the country addressing thousands of meetings, devoting almost every minute of his long working day—save for one short trip to America—to the service of the I.L.P. and the cause of a great independent Labour Party.

The I.L.P. came into being six months after Hardie's election to Parliament. Not Hardie alone had fought and campaigned for

100

it. There had been others, chief among them in the influence they were able to exercise, Joseph Burgess, who owned and edited a paper called *The Workman's Times*, which consistently urged in local editions published in many parts of the country the formation of independent Labour societies and clubs, and Robert Blatchford, whose *Clarion* was winning converts to socialism on a scale hitherto undreamed of.

But Hardie, although not the only begetter of independent Labour, was the one chiefly responsible, and it was he who presided over the conference of the 121 delegates from all parts of England and Scotland and from all manner of Labour clubs and Socialist societies, which met in the Labour Institute, Bradford, on 13 and 14 January, 1893.

Shaw was there (to give the new Party his blessing, but to make it clear that the Fabian Society had no intention of sinking its identity in it), Blatchford was there, Ben Tillett, Robert Smillie—who had followed Hardie in the organization of the Scottish miners—Bruce Glasier, James Sexton, F. W. Jowett and many others whose names were widely known and were to become much more so in the future. Ramsay MacDonald and Philip Snowden, the most famous of all its leaders in later days, did not, however, join until later. MacDonald, as secretary of the London Committee of the Scottish Home Rule Association, had had a good deal of contact with Hardie and had supported him in the Lanark election. But he still hoped that it would be possible to get the reforms he wanted by working with the Liberals and did not lose that hope and join the I.L.P. until eighteen months later. Philip Snowden was still quite unknown, an invalid living in the little Yorkshire village of Cowling. He came into the I.L.P. two years after its formation.

There was from the start no doubt about the I.L.P.'s socialism. By a large majority the conference voted in favour of resolutions that the object of the new Party should be "to secure the collective and communal ownership of all means of production, distribution and exchange," and that it should stand for "representation of the people in the House of Commons by men in favour of the object of the Party and rigidly pledged to its policy," and should work for "the federation of all organizations in Great Britain and Ireland seeking to realize the object of the Party by the Independent representation of Labour in all legislative, governing and administrative bodies."

It is perhaps difficult for those of a later generation to understand the impact which the I.L.P. in those early days under Hardie's leadership had upon the life of many thousands of people in Britain, an impact far greater than its actual membership or the vote it was able to muster at elections showed—for it appealed particularly to the young who had no votes. But not only the young. Men and women of all ages and all classes came under its spell. It was to them much more than a political party.

"The Sunday meetings of the I.L.P. held in a thousand halls," writes Lord Snell, one of its earliest propagandists, in his autobiography, "suggested religious revival meetings rather than political demonstrations. The fervour of the great audiences that assembled in centres like Glasgow, Bradford, Leeds, Huddersfield, Birmingham and Bristol was quite without precedent in British political history. Men who had grown old in years had their youthful enthusiasms renewed under the glow and warmth of a new spiritual fellowship. They were born again: they joyfully walked many miles to listen to a favourite speaker; they sang Labour hymns; and they gave to the new social faith an intensity of devotion which lifted it far above the older political organizations of the day. The women members of the movement were self-sacrificing beyond all experience. . . . The children also played their part; they distributed leaflets, sold pamphlets and journals and performed other duties with exemplary zeal."

And he continues in tones shared by all who took part in those days: "No purely selfish movement could have aroused and sustained an enthusiasm of the kind which then existed. The men and women who were its members and workers were not moved by envy of those who were richer than themselves; they were in the grip of a new and compelling faith. It appealed to the emotional side of their natures and they became in imagination citizens of a new and better world. The ideal of a co-operative commonwealth, the possibility of creating a social environment in which men would live 'with the light of knowledge in their eyes,' released in them hidden stores of moral energy."

And Philip Snowden, who in the days when he first joined the I.L.P. never for ten years travelled less than a hundred miles a week speaking at meetings in little halls and in market places, wherever a few people or a great crowd could be gathered to listen to the Socialist gospel, tells how:

"Working men who had toiled all day at arduous work went out at nights into the streets to preach in their simple way the new gospel of emancipation. Men who had never before attempted public speaking were given courage and the gift of effective oratory by the new passion for social justice which consumed them. The movement was something new in politics. It was politics inspired by idealism and religious fervour. Vocal unions were formed which accompanied cycling corps into the country at week-ends and audiences were gathered on village greens by the singing of choirs; then short and simple addresses on socialism were given. On their country jaunts the cyclists distributed leaflets and pasted slips on gates, and sometimes stuck them on cows, bearing such slogans as 'Socialism the Hope of the World' and 'Workers of the World Unite'."

All was grist that came to the I.L.P.'s mill in those days. Anyone who, if he could not make a public speech, could sing a song or play a fiddle and say a few words in between was pressed into service. And those who could not talk on politics or economics talked on what they could. Jim Connell, who wrote the "The Red Flag," a big, broad-shouldered Irishman with an enormous moustache who was over six feet in height and always wore an Inverness cloak, a big-brimmed slouch hat and a large red scarf, had been a famous poacher in his day, so he gave a lecture on "The Game Laws." To this, when anyone would let him, he added an erudite discourse on Evolution under the title of "From Protoplasm to Man"—so erudite indeed that he was never known in the course of a two hours' talk to get beyond the introduction.

The I.L.P. was a political movement, but it embraced much more than politics. It was a great energizing influence in education, it created among its members an enthusiasm for art and literature and music and knowledge of many things, because those who inspired it believed passionately not simply in economic reform but in the good life for all. Although it was rooted in the working-classes it was much more than a class movement. It attracted to itself, by the ethical and humanitarian nature of its appeal, many of the middle and professional classes and drew deeply upon the religious and especially the nonconformist spirit of the British people. It made little contribution to the theoretical content of Socialist philosophy. For its theories and its detailed facts it drew mainly upon the Fabian Society, but it translated Fabian theories into the broad, simple, human and moral terms that ordinary men and women could understand.

Keir Hardie himself tirelessly journeyed up and down the country. But he was not alone. Bruce Glasier, Mrs. Bruce Glasier, Tom Mann, F. W. Jowett, Enid Stacy, Caroline Martyn—these last two, like Mrs. Bruce Glasier, young university women who had abandoned everything to work full time for the I.L.P. which could offer them nothing but hardship—Mary Macarthur, Margaret Bondfield, Mrs. Pankhurst, J. R. Clynes, Ben Turner, Bob Smillie, James Sexton, Willie Anderson, Dick Wallhead, Ramsay MacDonald, Philip Snowden, and many others took up the fight, always putting before their audiences something that was more than just an economic creed—that was a new faith, a vision of a new world.

Hardie himself never lost sight of the fact that the I.L.P. was only a stage on the way. He knew from the first, and experience year by year confirmed it—for, despite the enthusiasm, membership of the I.L.P. in those years stayed obstinately round the 21,000 level—that the only effective way to a politically powerful Labour Party in Britain was an alliance between the Socialists and the trade unions even although that might, for the time being, require the Socialists to accept a much less radical programme than they believed in. He knew the opposition of the old trade unionists to any such alliance, but he knew also the ferment that the new unionism was bringing to the whole trade-union movement and that events were on his side.

He could talk to local trade-union leaders in terms that they understood. He was of them. He spoke—it was his natural tongue—in the phraseology of the Bible and *Pilgrim's Progress*. He talked not of economic man, but of moral man in the kind of terms that fell familiarly upon the ears of men most of whom had found their first pathway to wider horizons in the chapels, the Temperance halls and the Brotherhood meetings, and whose radicalism was linked closely with their staunch nonconformity.

He, and those who worked with him in the I.L.P., made of socialism something that far transcended the materialistic creed of the Marxian Socialists. By so doing they made possible that alliance with the organized industrial workers through which alone a genuine Labour Party could come into being.

But although the leaders of the I.L.P. were a diverse and remarkable group of men and women, who served it with extraordinary courage and energy, it was not only from the quality of its leadership that the influence the I.L.P. was able to exercise upon the social and political life of the times derived. It came from the burning faith of the thousands of ordinary men and women who gave to it their selfless devotion.

Philip Snowden tells of a working man in Bradford, Johnny Coe, who said to him: "I've read about these old martyrs who went to the stake for their religion. I used to have my doubts about that, but since I became converted to socialism I can understand it. I'd be willing to go to the stake for my socialism." There were many thousands of Johnny Coe's in the I.L.P.

Their vision of socialism was the same as that of Bruce Glasier when he wrote in *The Meaning of Socialism*:

"It is from the prophets, apostles and saints, the religious mystics and heretics, rather than from statesmen, economists and political reformers, that the Socialist movement derives its example and ideals. . . . Socialism means not only the socialization of wealth, not only the socialization of the means of production and distribution, but of our lives, our hearts—ourselves. Socialism, when finally resolved, consists not in getting at all, but in giving; not in being served, but in serving."

It was that spirit that made the early I.L.P. and it was that spirit when harnessed to the intellectual integrity of the Fabians and the practical idealism and economic experience of the trade unions that made the Labour Party.

"We want no Karl Marx and surplus values and that sort of stuff," Johnny Coe used to tell speakers. "Tha' make it simple."

And make it simple they did. In this they were helped, to a degree impossible to overestimate, by Robert Blatchford and the *Clarion*.

Blatchford had a genius, never equalled before or since, for simple, appealing and exciting exposition of Socialist principles. His own conversion to socialism, according to his own account, was due to a pamphlet signed by Hyndman and William Morris, but he had none of Hyndman's Marxist views. He took much more after Morris—the Morris who, when asked at a public meeting, "Does Comrade Morris accept Marx's theory of value?" replied, "I am asked if I believe in Marx's theory of value. To speak quite frankly, I do not know what Marx's theory of value is and I'm damned if I want to know." And he would have agreed with Morris when he went on to add: "Truth to say, political economy is not in my line and much of it appears to be dreary rubbish. It is enough political economy for me to know that the idle-class is rich and the working-class is poor and that the rich are rich because they rob the poor. That I know because I see it with my eyes."

By the time he became a Socialist the ex-sergeant of the Dublin Fusiliers, who as a boy had been so poor that he used to be sent by his mother to root in dustbins for old bottles that could be sold to buy coal, had already travelled a good way. He had met Alex M. Thompson, "Dangle," and E. F. Fay, "The Bounder," who were to be, with him, the chief and shining stars of the *Clarion*. After writing a comic column for *Bell's Life* at £4 a week, he had been brought up to Manchester by Edward Hulton, the owner of the *Sunday Chronicle*, to write a weekly column signed "Nunquam."

That column made him one of the most popular journalists of the day, with a salary of, for those days, the very high amount of £1,000 a year. But neither money nor comfort could stop Blatchford from seeing with his eyes and, when he saw robbery, calling it such.

In a series of articles he exposed conditions in the slums of Ancoats in Manchester. Then, being converted to socialism by what he had seen and what he had read, he announced his conversion in the *Sunday Chronicle* and proceeded to become a raging, tearing propagandist for the faith that was in him. Hulton intervened. "No socialism in my paper," he said. "Then no 'Nunquam'," said Blatchford, and with Alex M. Thompson, Fay, and his brother Montague Blatchford, walked out.

They had practically no money, for although they had had good salaries they had all been living up to their means and Blatchford had just lost whatever savings he had in backing a comic opera that failed. But that did not matter. Principles came first.

Joined by a clerk of the same sort of stuff, R. B. Suthers, and an advertisement canvasser, Tom Wilkinson, they gathered together and decided they would start a Socialist weekly paper. "What shall we call it?" said Fay. His own idea of a good title was *The Perisher*.

"Let's call it *The Champion*, said Thompson.

"Haw," said Fay, mishearing. "That's it. *Clarion*."

And so *Clarion* it was. Between them they raised £400 on their insurance policies. A then unknown actor friend of Alex Thompson's, Robert Courtneidge, lent them another £100 free of interest. With this they set to work. At first they could not find anyone to print for them. All the printers they approached regarded it as too dubious a commercial risk to touch. But at last the *Co-operative News* printers agreed. Then they had to get paper. Again a friend of Thompson's came to the rescue. But the paper when it arrived was inferior stuff, loaded with china clay which stuck to the cylinders of the printing press, so that large numbers of copies were almost unreadable, and the advertisers whom Tom Wilkinson had canvassed cancelled their contracts when they saw it.

But "Nunquam" was a name the people of the north of England knew and liked. They wanted to hear what he had to say and, despite the sorry condition of the first issue, nearly forty thousand people bought it. Thereafter it sold regularly thirty-five thousand copies a week, and "Nunquam," "Dangle" and "The Bounder" became household names all over England. When in 1894 Blatchford started to write *Merrie England*, his view of what England could become, written as a serial in simple, homely words to "Dear John Smith," the circulation of the *Clarion* rose to nearly one hundred thousand, an altogether phenomenal figure for a Socialist paper in those days. Reprinted, at first as a shilling book and then as a penny one, *Merrie England* itself sold three-quarters of a million copies in a year. It was translated into eight languages and in a pirated edition in America sold not far short of another million.

Fifty-six years later, still hale and hearty at the age of eighty-nine, Blatchford, in an introduction to a book of his essays and short stories, *What's All This?*, wrote: "I have been an Englishman for close on ninety years and I think I understand the average Briton. I am myself an average Briton." And then he catalogued some of the things he loved: "The sliding landscape seen from the window of a train, the village street one glimpses, with unknown people walking, a passing band with the tramp of soldiers marching, an orator on his soap box tinkering at the 'sorry scheme of things.' . . . The common people who are so uncommon. The women and men we meet, the jolly nobodies; they who feed us and clothe us, nurse us, doctor us, sing for us, play for us, knit our stockings, cut our hair, dance with us, make love to us, marry us, tease us, please us, give us our medicine, cry over us, bury us and forget us."

And he gave as his choice of an epitaph this verse from Henry Baerlein's translation of *The Diwan of Abu 'l-Ala:*

> *"If I have harboured love within my breast*
> *'Twas for my comrades of the dusty day,*
> *Who with me watched the loitering stars at play,*
> *Who bore the burden of the same unrest."*

It was because he was in truth an average Englishman and because he loved every shade and facet of life, because he most passionately wanted everyone to be happy, as he was himself, and so much hated cruelty and injustice, and because he wrote as he felt, not for people who understood politics and economics or had read history, but for ordinary people who could see for themselves if only he pointed the way, and, when they saw, would say with him that poverty was wicked and injustice cruel, that he was one of the greatest Socialist propagandists of all time.

Those who formed with him the great *Clarion* team, Alex M. Thompson, Montague Blatchford, R. B. Suthers, the huge Fay, six-foot-two, bearded, wearing an immense great-coat and a hat on the back of his head, with a great bamboo cane under his arm, who said that the only doctor's prescription he ever took any notice of was, "Take a long time over your meals—and eat very fast," were all men of the same kind—boisterous, human and tempestuous men who loved life and people and could communicate their love.

They made the *Clarion* into a Socialist paper unlike any Socialist paper there has been before and since, and they made its readers into a great family, "The *Clarion* Fellowship," which really was a fellowship and which did really raise the clarion call of socialism wherever its members met—a clear call, a great call, but one that sounded a note that men could laugh to and dance to as well as fight to, and in which even while they laughed they found inspiration to work and struggle and labour for a better world ahead.

And so, although later the *Clarion* fell in influence as Blatchford —always the soldier as well as the Socialist—preached of the need for armed preparation against Germany and thus quarrelled with the pacifist spirit that was so strong a part of the I.L.P., and hailed science as heralding the end of all religion and thus mortally offended the nonconformists, and although neither he nor the *Clarion* ever fitted easily into any party organization but remained individualists going their own cheerful way—the *Clarion* has its place, and it is a great one, among the pioneers who made the Labour Party possible.

Hyndman and the Social Democrats, Morris and the Socialist League, Stewart Headlam and the Christian Socialists, Shaw and the Webbs and the Fabians, Blatchford and the *Clarion*, Keir Hardie and the I.L.P., Burns and Tillett and the other leaders of the new trade unionism—all these and many more had their part.

That meeting in the Memorial Hall was not colourful and dramatic—but it had behind it the drama, the excitement, the humanity, and the humour, of all these and the many thousands who had laboured with them. They had made it possible. And in doing so they had given it roots that went deep into the soil of the British character and that were to grow ever stronger with the years.

CHAPTER IV

THE ROOTS IN HISTORY

IT WAS the coming together of all those social, economic and political movements of opinion described in the two previous chapters, as the nineteenth century, with all its triumphs of production and invention, its naked exploitation of the unorganized masses, its great advances in political freedom, its awakening social conscience, its genuine idealism and its confident and ruthless imperialism, moved to its close, that brought the Labour Party into being.

And it was the convergence at the very close of the century of the economic struggles of the new trade unionism, the moral and political idealisms of the I.L.P., and the intellectual subtlety and self-confidence of the Fabians that gave the new party its constitution and form.

But when one appreciates this one still cannot understand the true significance of that quiet and undramatic meeting in the Memorial Hall, one cannot give the decisions there taken their true historical value nor understand how remarkable and how decisive a stage in the slow advance of the common people to political freedom and social justice those dry and superficially unexciting resolutions marked, unless one looks even farther back.

When those hundred and twenty-nine delegates met on that February morning in the first year of the new century they came to their meeting-place as the legatees of a struggle that had begun many centuries before. They were the heirs of men and women who had fought in every century and who again and again had been defeated and again and again had reformed their forces and gained a precarious vantage from which it was possible to press on.

Sometimes the main emphasis of the struggle had been economic; the battle for industrial freedom, for the right to organize, for a fair share of the products of labour; sometimes the main emphasis had been political; for the right to vote and to participate in the government of the country, for freedom of speech and the written word and of political assembly. The story which those delegates were carrying forward into the new century was one of the great stories of the world: the story of a struggle in which, although the main armies had always come from the poor and the disinherited, from the peasants and the town and country labourers, there had also always been found some others even among the safe and privileged who were ready to step into the ranks beside them and fight shoulder to shoulder with them; a story which, although stained throughout its history by oppression and cruelty and the blood of martyrs, was lit by an idealism whose flame was never dimmed. And throughout it, as a theme that had recurred over and over again, often defeated but never destroyed, had been the vision of a Socialist commonwealth.

The history of socialism in Britain goes back through the soil of the centuries to the early peasants' revolts against the enclosure of the common lands, to the Christian communism of John Wyclif, to John Ball, the hedge priest, who asked:

> *"When Adam dalf and Eve span*
> *Who was then the gentleman?"*

and who preached: "My good people, things cannot go well in England, nor ever will, until all goods are held in common, and until there will be neither serfs nor gentlemen and we shall all be equal," and who, like so many who were to follow him, died on the gallows, being hanged at St. Albans as a lesson to all, whether they be priests or laymen, who should ask disturbing questions.

The history moves to Jack Cade and the revolt of the Kentish peasants, to the rising of the Cornishmen and to that imperishable document of the early Socialist ideal, More's *Utopia*. It becomes vocal again in the voice of Milton's republicanism, in the demands of the Levellers in the war between Parliament and King, in those of the Diggers who started to dig the enclosed lands, and in the *Ideal Commonwealth* of Gerard Winstanley—it is a thread that runs unbroken through British history.

At first its voice was that of the dispossessed peasants and when it flared into action it took the form of agrarian revolts, but when it found its interpreters, as in More's *Utopia* and less memorably in Winstanley's writings, it expressed a conception of the good life that embraced the whole community.

With the economic revolution of the eighteenth century it took on a harsher note as the new inventions of Watt and Hargreaves and others destroyed the livelihood of the old craftsmen, as the advance of industrial capitalism herded the workers, men and women and children alike, into the factories and the fetid slums, and as the Enclosure Acts in the rural areas turned the small yeomen farmers and cottagers into landless labourers and paupers. The struggle of the common people for liberty found its voice then in the writings of Tom Paine and William Cobbett, himself no Socialist but a great individualist and radical, its economic justification, at any rate in part, in the writings of Locke and Ricardo and their disciples, its moral and ethical message in those of William Godwin, Samuel Taylor Coleridge, Southey and the young Wordsworth, and in William Blake's vision of an England whose dark satanic mills should give place to a green and pleasant land in which men should be happy and free. Its challenge to revolt it found in the fire and thunder of the French Revolution, although in Britain that challenge was never fully taken up.

There are many threads in that story—that unbroken tradition of the struggle for social justice and the rights of common people which has so coloured the pattern of British history and has brought to its service so many men and women of widely differing talents and widely varying backgrounds.

But always the battle persisted, now agrarian, now industrial, now political, and always the forces of reaction and repression were mobilized by the powerful and the privileged to crush those who sought to give to ordinary men and women a larger share of the products of the wealth they produced and a voice in the affairs of the nation of which they formed the largest part.

Those forces were used to crush the first of the political societies of the working-class, the London Corresponding Society which, on its foundation in 1792 under the inspiration of a Scottish shoemaker, Thomas Hardy, and a London journalist and poet, John Thelwall, sought for the first time to promote independent political action among the working-classes and whose leaders were charged with high treason because they did so.

Organizations, repression, the challenge to repression, the pattern continues so that the voice of John Thelwall—charged with treason because he sought to link working-class societies for the discussion of political ideas—rings across a century and a half with the authentic voice of modern social democracy:

"It is property we are told that ought to be represented because by property government is supported. What? Does property man the Navy or fill the ranks of the Army? Let us not deceive ourselves! Property is nothing but human labour. The most inestimable of all property is the sweat of the poor man's brow; the property from which all other is derived and without which grandeur must starve in the midst of supposed abundance. And shall they who possess this inestimable property be told they have no rights, because they have nothing to defend? . . . No! Man and not movables is the object of just legislation. All, therefore, ought to be consulted where all are concerned, for not less than the whole ought to decide the fate of the whole."

The London Corresponding Society was proscribed. To aid the work of suppression, the Habeas Corpus Act—the foundation of British liberties—was suspended and men arrested and imprisoned without trial. The Corresponding Act was passed making it illegal for political groups in the country to communicate with each other. The Combination Laws were passed making it illegal for workers in any trade to organize themselves together. But the struggle went on.

As the development of industrial capitalism and the depressions that followed the Napoleonic wars forced the workers into a deeper subjection, the struggle for freedom drew to itself greater numbers and was suppressed with greater violence. Again in 1817 the Habeas Corpus Act was suspended and again the response and the challenge came from the workers. This time it came particularly from those of the North and Midlands, who organized great meetings to demand reform, culminating in a concourse of eighty thousand people on St. Peter's Field in Manchester.

"It was deemed expedient," wrote Samuel Bamford, the silk weaver, of Middleton in Lancashire, whose writings on the struggles of the workers throw a remarkable light on the courage and dignity of poor men fighting for freedom:

"It was deemed expedient that this meeting should be as morally effective as possible and that it should exhibit a spectacle such as had never before been witnessed in England. We had frequently been taunted by the Press with our ragged dirty appearance at these assemblages; with the confusion of our proceedings, and the mob-like crowds in which our numbers were mustered; and we determined that, for once at least, these reflections should not be deserved—that we would disarm the bitterness of our political opponents by a display of cleanliness, sobriety and decorum such as we never before had exhibited. In short we would deserve their respect by showing that we respected ourselves, and knew how to exercise our rights of meeting, as it were well Englishmen always should do—in a spirit of sober thoughtfulness; respectful at the same time, to the opinions of others."

And so the contingents set out to what was to be the massacre of Peterloo.

"At our head," writes Bamford of the Middleton column, "were a hundred or two women, mostly young wives, and my own was amongst them. A hundred or two of our handsomest girls—sweethearts to the lads who were with us—danced to the music and sang snatches of popular songs. . . . Thus, accompanied by our friends and our dearest and most tender connexions we went slowly towards Manchester."

All weapons, whether of offence or defence, had been prohibited by the committee organizing the demonstration. The marchers had drilled beforehand the better to maintain order and discipline.

The columns met in orderly fashion in St. Peter's Field and took up their places to listen soberly to the speakers. Hunt, "Orator Hunt," a great Reformist leader of that day, mounted the stage, took off his hat and began to speak to the people.

"A noise and strange murmur arose towards the church," says Bamford. "Some persons said it was the Blackburn people coming; and I stood on tiptoe, and looked in the direction whence the noise proceeded, and saw a party of cavalry, in blue and white

114

uniform, come trotting, sword in hand, round the corner of a garden wall and to the front of a row of new houses, where they reined up in a line.

"When the people in the crowd saw them they waved and gave a shout of goodwill. The cavalry shouted in reply and then waved their sabres over their heads; and then, slackening rein, and striking spur into their steeds, they dashed forward and began cutting the people. 'Stand fast,' I said, 'they are riding upon us, stand fast.' And there was a general cry in our quarter of 'stand fast.' The cavalry were in confusion: they evidently could not, with all the weight of man and horse, penetrate that compact mass of human beings; and their sabres were plied to hew a way through naked held-up hands and defenceless heads; and then chopped limbs and wounded gaping skulls were seen; and groans and cries were mingled with the din of that horrid confusion. 'Ah! Ah!' 'For shame! For shame!' was shouted and then 'Break! Break! They are killing them in front and they cannot get away'; and there was a general cry of 'Break, break.' For a moment the crowd held back as in a pause; then there was a rush, heavy and restless as a headlong sea; and a sound like low thunder with screams and prayers and imprecations from the crowd, moiled and sabre-doomed, who could not escape."

Thus were those men and women of the working-classes, who had assembled peaceably by the side of St. Peter's Church, shown the peril of raising their voices to ask for any improvement in their condition or that they should be given some voice in the choice of those who governed them. Eleven were killed, more than four hundred, including at least a hundred women, were badly wounded. Hunt, Bamford and other leaders were arrested and imprisoned, and Cobbett was forced to flee temporarily to America.

All meetings of more than fifty persons were made illegal, all marches and processions were banned. Any writer, publisher or bookseller who dared to write, print, publish or sell anything which might "bring into contempt the Government or Constitution as by law established" was made liable to transportation. Newspapers and pamphlets were taxed that they should be too dear for the masses.

No crack it seemed, remained unstopped through which the

pernicious light thrown by the lamps of those who fought for reform might be seen, and by its flicker raise to hope and to action the mass of those who worked. But the struggle went on.

The London Corresponding Society had been broken and suppressed more than twenty years before, but its ideas continued. They found a home in the ranks of the Spencean Philanthropists, a group inspired by an ex-schoolmaster, Thomas Spence, a Socialist and apostle of land nationalization.

Active among this group—a living evidence of a continuity repression could not shatter—was Thomas Evans, a traces-maker, who had previously been secretary of the London Corresponding Society itself and who like the other leaders of that Society had been arrested and kept in prison without trial for three years before their Society was finally suppressed. And also of their number was one who was to pay an even higher price for opposition to tyranny— Arthur Thistlewood.

In 1816 the leaders of the Spencean Philanthropists—the pattern hardly varies at all—were arrested for high treason, the high treason of talking of political reform and of persuading men and women to discuss Socialist ideas. But this time they were lucky. Their counsel was able to show that the chief witness for the Crown was a hired Government spy of notorious character. This threw such disrepute on the whole case for the Crown that the arrested men were acquitted. Thus defeated by the courts, the Government immediately brought in and carried a Bill suppressing all associations known as Spenceans.

Four years later, Thistlewood, after being in prison for twelve months for "defaming" Lord Sidmouth, the Minister primarily responsible for the "Gagging Acts" and for the employment of Government spies and *agents provocateurs* to concoct evidence against Socialists and reformers, was again arrested on the evidence of a Home Office spy named Edwards and charged with four others with plotting at a house in Cato Street off the Edgware Road to murder the Cabinet while at dinner.

It was shown at the trial that Thistlewood and his companions, who had been made desperate by oppression and had been deeply stirred by the Peterloo massacre, had nevertheless only been persuaded with difficulty and at the constant instigation of Edwards to contemplate and discuss such an attempt and had rejected even more violent proposals to which Edwards had tried to persuade them. But Thistlewood was not allowed to call any witnesses and was condemned. He addressed the Court:

"With respect to the immorality of our project," he said, "I will just observe that the assassination of a tyrant has always been deemed a meritorious action. If the laws are not strong enough to prevent them murdering the community it becomes the duty of every member of that community to rid his country of its oppressors. . . . Albion is still in the chains of slavery. I quit it without regret."

On 1 May, 1820, he and his companions were publicly executed on the gallows at Newgate. He walked to the scaffold, says Cobbett's *Political Register*, with a composed countenance and bowed to the people. "I desire all to remember that I die in the cause of liberty and that my last breath is given in that cause," he said. Of his companions one said: "My poor wife," a second prayed, a third sang: "Oh give me death or liberty," and seeing a newspaper reporter taking notes said: "I die an enemy to tyrants. Write down that, sir"; a fourth, seeing the soldiers, said: "What! Dare they not execute us without the aid of the army?"

"The people," says the *Political Register*, "testified by hissing, groaning and by crying out, 'Murder, murder, murder'."

And still the struggle went on. And now the vengeance of the Tory Government against those who demanded political reform and social justice moved northwards, where workers fighting for political freedom sought to use the weapon of industrial action in their political cause.

In Glasgow and near by, sixty thousand workers went on strike in response to a proclamation from "The Committee for Organization of a Provisional Government" calling upon them to close the factories and workshops and cease work until equality of political rights was granted. At Bonnymuir the strikers clashed with the military, and Andrew Hardie, a forebear of Keir Hardie, and another miner, Baird, were taken prisoner for resisting an escort of cavalry.

They were imprisoned and tried in Stirling Castle, and were condemned to be hanged and afterwards beheaded.

"Whilst Baird was addressing the spectators," Carlile's *Republican* reports, "Hardie sat himself down with perfect composure on the block prepared for the decapitation and, when Baird had finished his address, he arose in turn and began to address the spectators, just as if he had been conducting the business of a public meeting. The Sheriff or his deputy tapped him on the shoulder and bade him say something about religion. Hardie was not to be alarmed but shortened his address by saying: 'I die a martyr to the cause of liberty, truth and justice.' This expression drew forth from the spectators as enthusiastic a cheer as if it had been a public meeting for petition and remonstrance. . . . Thus died two brave men whose zeal for liberty was their only crime."

That was in April, 1820. Half a century later the descendant of Andrew Hardie was to take up that same cause of "liberty, truth and justice" in those same mining villages. Although men might be murdered, the cause for which they died could not be.

It found instead at this moment a new voice in the passion and indignation of Shelley in *Queen Mab* and *Prometheus Unbound*, the challenge of genius to the tyranny of the men of privilege who had fought freedom at Peterloo and Bonnymuir.

And ten years later it flared again into action in the "last labourers' revolt." Over all the southern countryside of Kent, Surrey, Sussex, Dorset, Gloucestershire, Hampshire, Wiltshire, Oxfordshire, the agricultural labourers rose to demand a wage of half a crown a day, a reduction of tithes and rents, and political emancipation, and were beaten down under the hammer-blows of reaction as throughout the centuries the protest of the dispossessed peasants had been beaten down again and again.

The agricultural labourers who thus protested against the starvation to which they and their families were being forced, and who dared to demand those political rights that should be common to all men, were orderly and dignified.

"Divested of its objectional character, as a dangerous precedent," wrote the reporter sent by *The Times* to describe the outbreak in Sussex, "the conduct of the peasantry has been admirable. . . . Each parish, generally speaking, has risen *per se*; in many places their proceedings have been managed with astonishing coolness and regularity; there has been little of the ordinary effervescence displayed on similar occasions: a deputation of two or more of the latter produce a written statement, well drawn up, which the farmers are required to sign; the spokesman, sometimes a Dissenting or Methodist teacher, fulfils his office with great propriety and temper."

But this propriety and temper did not save them any more than it had saved those others who had been ridden down at Peterloo or hanged at Bonnymuir. The military were sent into action, wholesale arrests made and special Commissions set up at Winchester, Salisbury, Dorchester, Reading and Aylesbury to try rioters for offences which were rarely more serious than unlawful assembly or at the worst damage to property without loss of life, but for which nine men were hanged, 457 transported and the same number imprisoned for long terms. The villages, in which so often from the days of the first peasant risings freedom had flamed and been beaten down, were forced into a sullen torpor of subjection from which they did not rouse themselves for many years.

Flushed with triumph the Whig Government now sought to silence the most powerful voice of protest by arresting Cobbett.

But here they had a man of a different metal from the ill-educated agricultural workers to deal with and one who had the ear of the country. In his blistering defence Cobbett called witnesses to prove that imprisoned rioters had been threatened with death unless they would come forward and testify that he had incited them to violence and told they would be given a free pardon if they would make the testimony the Government required.

He was acquitted. His voice remained to rally men once more in the battle for parliamentary reform, although he could do nothing to save those transported for life because they had dared to demand a wage of half a crown a day.

Now the demand for parliamentary reform was at full flood. And now even oppression could not stay it, for it had behind it not only the voice of "Socialist and Radical agitators" and the ill-organized manual workers of town and country against whom the soldiers could be sent and the weapons of hanging and transportation be used, but the full force of the new and powerful groups of industrial employers, the middle-classes. They were no longer prepared to tolerate a situation in which great cities like Manchester, Birmingham and Leeds had no independent parliamentary representation, while tiny villages and even single derelict cottages in the private ownership of great landlords had the right to return members.

To their demands were added the reasoned arguments of Bentham and Hume and the two Mills, the restless vigour of Cobbett, whose writings had the power to rouse thousands, and the political skill of a breeches-maker of Charing Cross, Francis Place, who—how the thread moves on without a break—had been converted to radical socialism by membership of the London Corresponding Society many years earlier.

Place, the son of a bailiff of Marshalsea Prison and keeper of a "sponging house," a private debtors' prison, had been reared in the slums of London and had bade fair in his youth to develop into a near-criminal. But he reformed on his marriage and succeeded after much struggle in making himself into a master breeches-maker with his own shop. Through much reading and discussion and through his membership of the London Corresponding Society until it was suppressed he became a skilled and active politician.

Place was a man of great natural talent. He was a close friend of James Mill and of Bentham and much impressed both of them by his practical abilities. He had, moreover, to a degree unequalled until the advent of the Webbs, a truly remarkable capacity for handling committees, for persuading men of influence to accept policies he drafted for them and for infiltrating into the most unlikely quarters. He was a reformer, but he was what at that moment was perhaps needed more than anything else, a reformer who was also a great organizer and a political strategist of genius. Ten years prior to the introduction of the first Reform Bill he had—almost by his own efforts and through his skilful briefing of a worthy but rather dull radical M.P., Joseph Hume—succeeded in getting the Combination Act repealed before any of its supporters realized what was afoot.

Now his abilities and the resolution of the political reformers were to be put to even greater test. In March, 1831, a Whig Ministry headed by Lord Grey at last introduced a bill which seemed to many the culmination of the long campaign for parliamentary reform. The bill went much farther than many had expected. It abolished most of the rotten boroughs, it gave parliamentary representation to the new industrial towns and it proposed a drastic redistribution of seats. It did not include universal suffrage and the secret ballot, and although it raised the number of the electorate from 440,000 to over 650,000—out of a total population of 14,000,000—it did not give any political power to the workers, although by giving votes to the middle-classes it made possible the development of a new radicalism. To many, although not all, of the reformers and the leaders of the working-class movement it seemed as though they were on the eve of triumph.

The bill was carried by a majority of one, amid scenes of wild enthusiasm among the supporters and dismay and horror on the part of its opponents.

"And the jaw of Peel fell," wrote Macaulay, "and the face of Twiss was as the face of a damned soul; and Herries looked like Judas taking off his necktie for the last operation. We shook hands and clapped one another on the back and went out laughing, crying and huzzaing into the lobby."

A few days later, however, the Government was defeated in Committee. It resigned and went to the country. It was returned with a majority of over a hundred pledged to reform. The bill was introduced again and passed. It was sent to the Tory-dominated House of Lords. The Lords immediately rejected it.

All over the country the people gave their answer to the Lords. At Birmingham a meeting attended by one hundred and fifty thousand people passed a resolution that no taxes should be paid until the bill was passed. At Nottingham the Castle was seized and burnt down. At Bristol the Mansion House and Bishop's Palace were set on fire. Cobbett, who at the beginning had opposed the bill because it did not go far enough, now in view of the attitude of the Lords swung the immense following of his weekly *Political Register* behind the demand for "the Bill, the whole Bill, and nothing but the Bill."

It was at this stage that Francis Place, the breeches-maker who had made himself a master of political strategy, played a decisive part. He worked furiously to persuade the Whig administration to stand firm despite the fears that rioting had, as always, engendered in those in office. At the same time he formed the National Political

Union which linked reform associations throughout the country and gave him control of agencies of agitation and political revolt in every part of the country.

The Grey Ministry brought forward a third Reform Bill. Again it was passed by the Commons with a large majority. Again the Lords rejected it. The Government asked the King to create sufficient peers to pass it. The King refused and called upon the Duke of Wellington to form a Ministry and govern by martial law if need be.

Place and the reformers had their answer. It was not in great demonstrations which could be crushed by a sabre charge. Place and his fellow reformers had learnt from the past. Now what they planned was a national breakdown with which no military force could cope. Place had all his plans and the necessary measures for their execution prepared. They included separate agitations and uprisings in every part of the country for the purpose of engaging the military and preventing reinforcements being sent from any one part of the country to another. At the same time there was to be a run on the banks—"To Beat The Duke Go For Gold" read the placards Place had printed in preparation—trade everywhere was to be brought to a standstill.

With the confidence of one who knows he holds the winning cards, Place informed the new Cabinet of what was arranged and asked them to consider whether any military or other force they could command could hope to handle such a situation. The victor of Waterloo was a die-hard and a reactionary, but he knew, none better, what soldiers could do and what they could not. Faced by the revolutionary temper of the country and afraid of the consequence of a run on the banks and financial panic he advised the King to recall Earl Grey.

The Reform Bill was passed. The long battle was won. And the workers awakened from the triumph in which they had played so large a part to find—as was so often to be their lot until at last they learned how to forge a political party that should truly represent them—that it held little for them.

The men who were returned to Parliament as a result of the Reform Bill were in the main representatives of the new middle-classes of industrial capitalism, not of the workers. Those few who, like Cobbett, wanted more than this were lonely voices without influence in the new Parliament in which they found themselves. The majority were no less hostile than had been the old to the claim of the workers and shared the same view of them as a helot class. A Poor Law Act, which denied all relief to the "able-bodied poor" outside the workhouse and separated husbands, wives and children as though the commonest human feelings were not possessed by those who were unemployed, soon showed how far reform had gone.

Yet the struggle for parliamentary reform had not been altogether fruitless. Nor was the gain so small as it first seemed to those who had expected so much. The reformed Parliament introduced the first Factory Acts, it initiated popular education on a national scale, it abolished slavery in the British Colonies. Above all it altered the political balance between Commons, Lords and Crown and provided the mass basis for a new Liberal Party which, although essentially middle-class, was also to become the instrument of far-ranging reforms.

These fruits lay ahead. For the moment it seemed to the workers that they had gained nothing. And, indeed, although time was to show that the gain was greater than it at first seemed, it was now only too clear that only by their own efforts could the workers obtain the economic and political freedom that was their right. Because until now the new middle-classes had been as much without parliamentary representation as the working-classes, the economic antagonism between them had been masked by their joint interest in political reform. They had fought as allies in the parliamentary field. The rewards of political victory had fallen to one of the allies, but had been withheld from the other; the usefulness of the alliance to the middle-classes was past—their economic antagonism to the workers remained.

In new ways and in new forms the struggle had to be renewed.

It moved now from the political to the economic field. The failure of the hopes they had centred in parliamentary reform—and the refusal of the reformed Parliament to remove immediately such penal legislation as the Corresponding Act—convinced the workers that only by direct industrial action could their hopes be achieved. The struggle went on.

It found now its leader and its inspiration in Robert Owen, the factory owner who, by his own successful efforts at co-operation

123

with his employees, had become convinced of both the moral and practical case for co-operative socialism. Owen was inspired by a great vision, a vision of socialism which he at first believed others among the employing classes could be persuaded to accept—only to find very soon that they were interested in his ideas only when they promised larger profits.

Now in their political disillusion the workers' leaders turned to him for guidance. Under the stimulus of his organizing zeal and passionate vision of a new society in which the producers of wealth should own the wealth they produced, the conception of great co-operative unions spread like wild-fire. The Union of Operative Builders led the way with the formation of the National Guild of Builders to undertake building all over the country and substitute co-operation for competition and money economy.

The National Guild of Builders was followed in February, 1834, by the Grand National Consolidated Trade Union, whose purpose it was to bring all workers into a single body which, by itself engaging in production and opening co-operative stores, would "enable the working classes to secure, protect and establish the rights of industry." Within a few months it had more than a million members, and branches were being started all over the country.

It was a utopian movement—a movement of men who misjudged the difficulties they faced and the implacable opposition they would meet from all those who held the existing reins of power. And because it was such and because its leaders had altogether underestimated the hatred of the privileged for the Socialist principles it sought peacefully to establish, the movement crumbled and was shattered when the Whig Government and the Whig employers gathered their forces and struck. Wherever the Grand National Consolidated Trades Union appealed to the workers, employers brought their economic power into play. Throughout the north of England there were extensive lock-outs of workers by employers; all those who refused to sign a paper renouncing membership of the trade union were refused re-employment.

In Tolpuddle, in Dorset, the law was brought into action to reinforce by its example the economic lesson. Six agricultural labourers who tried to form a branch of the Grand National Trades Union were arrested and sentenced to seven years' transportation.

Again there was defeat and again the struggle was renewed.

It returned to a political form—but to a more organized political form than previously—in the great movement of the Chartists which, led in London by William Lovett, a cabinet-maker, in the North by Feargus O'Connor, the son of an Irish landowner and radical M.P. in the reformed Parliament, and in the Midlands by another Irishman, a lawyer, James Bronterre O'Brien—seemed for a time in the years between 1837 and 1847 likely to develop into a great political revolutionary movement with the *Northern Star*, the *Poor Man's Guardian* and the *Midland Representative* as its voices in the Press.

Many movements and many ideas, from those who believed in revolutionary action to those who put their faith in moral persuasion, fed the Chartist movement. Industrial depression swelled its ranks. And in the People's Charter, drafted by Lovett and published on 8 May, 1838, it expressed the desires and demands of the workers in a form which stirred the imagination of hundreds of thousands. As it grew and developed it became increasingly Socialist in its outlook—for now the lesson was being learned that not by political action alone, nor by industrial action alone, but only by a Socialist conception linking the two, could labour's true aims be achieved.

At last on 14 June, 1839, after scenes of great excitement in all parts of the country, the great Chartist Petition was presented to Parliament. It contained 1,250,000 signatures, nearly twice the number of parliamentary voters.

It demanded universal suffrage, the secret ballot, annual Parliaments, payment of Members and the abolition of the property qualification for Members.

It declared: "Your petitioners dwell in a land whose merchants are noted for enterprise, whose manufacturers are very skilful and where workmen are proverbial for industry. The land itself is goodly, the soil is rich, the temperature wholesome; it is abundantly furnished with the materials of commerce and trade. . . .

"Yet with all these elements of natural prosperity and with every disposition and capacity to take advantage of them we find ourselves overwhelmed with public and private suffering . . .

our traders are trembling on the verge of bankruptcy; our workmen are starving; capital brings no profit and labour no remuneration, the home of the artificer is desolate and the warehouse of the pawn-broker is full. . . . The good of a party has been advanced to sacrifice the good of the nation; the few have governed for the interest of the few, while the interests of the many have been neglected or insolently and tyrannously trampled upon.

"It was the fond expectation of the people that a remedy for the greater part if not the whole of their grievances would be found in the Reform Act of 1832. . . . They have been bitterly and basely deceived. . . . The Reform Act has effected a transfer to power from one dominant party to another and left the people as helpless as before. . . .

"We come before your honourable House, to tell you in all humility that this state of affairs must not be permitted to continue . . . that the capital of the master must no longer be deprived of its due return; that the labour of the workman must no longer be deprived of its due reward; that the laws which make food dear, money scarce, labour cheap must be abolished . . . that the good of the many must be made the sole end, as it is the legitimate end of government. . . .

"We perform the duties of free men, we must have the rights of free men."

But these rights were still to be denied. The Petition was debated in Parliament. It was rejected by 237 votes to 48.

There were riots and strikes in protest. Lovett and other leaders were arrested. The National Convention of the Chartists met to consider what should next be done. Some, O'Connor amongst them, wanted to call a general strike—a sacred month of rest— to demonstrate the firmness of the people's will. But there were no funds to finance it, nor were any but a few of the more extreme ready for the possibility of the civil war that such action might bring. It was decided instead to make a moral demonstration of one day's stoppage of work.

But the fires of revolt that had been lit by the rejection of the Petition could not altogether be put out. In Wales, Chartists, believing that others would rise to support them, marched, a thousand strong, to Newport, where one of their leaders lay imprisoned. Some of them carried ancient muskets, most of them staves. They marched in three columns, singing the Chartist song:

> *Then rise my boys and fight the foe,*
> *Your arms are truth and reason;*
> *We'll let the Whigs and Tories know*
> *That union is not treason.*

> *Ye lords, oppose us if you can,*
> *Your own doom you seek after;*
> *With or without you we will stand*
> *Until we gain the Charter.*

They were men of all kinds and trades and ages. Many of them were scarcely more than boys. There was one of eighteen, George Shell, who before he set out wrote this letter to his parents:

Pontypool, Sunday Night,
3 November, 1839.

Dear Parents,

I hope this will find you well, as I am myself at this present. I shall this night be engaged in a glorious struggle for freedom, and should it please God to spare my life I shall see you soon, but if not grieve not for me, I shall have fell in a noble cause. My tools are at Mr. Cecil's and likewise my clothes. Farewell.

Yours truly,
George Shell.

They marched to the Westgate Hotel, in the centre of Newport, where the magistrate lodged, and there halted and called for the liberation of the prisoner. In answer soldiers stationed at the windows of the hotel opened fire. Ten of the Chartists, including George Shell, were killed, fifty were wounded and were left lying in the square.

There were immediate arrests and seven of the leaders were condemned to death, although later in the face of public feeling this was commuted to transportation.

All over the country now the arrests grew, and great numbers of Chartists were convicted on the familiar charge of high treason and transported or imprisoned. Their families would have been left to starve if the Chartists themselves had not raised funds to support them.

Yet still the movement grew. As those leaders who had received only short sentences were released they embarked on pilgrimages throughout the country exhorting men to new efforts.

In May, 1842, a second petition was presented to Parliament. This time it was signed by over 3,315,000 men; not a single industrial locality in Britain was unrepresented. It was couched, this time, in sharper and more revolutionary terms than the first, and again it put forward the demand for universal suffrage and for the other parts of the Charter. Again it was debated—and again it was rejected—by 287 votes to 49.

And again the workers, driven desperate by the rejection of their political claims and the miserable conditions to which industrial depression and low wages had brought them, used the only weapon available to them and struck work. The strikers marched from town to town calling out the workers. Soon there was not a mill chimney smoking in the whole city of Manchester. The whole of the commercial and industrial centres of the Midlands and the North seemed on the verge of insurrection. Again the prospect of a general strike seemed at hand. But O'Connor and the other leaders hesitated—perhaps because they had no funds, perhaps because again they feared the consequences that a general strike might bring. They gave no word and gradually the strikes were broken.

The Government ordered wholesale arrests. At least fifteen hundred were taken, many hundreds were sentenced to imprisonment, nearly eighty were transported to the convict settlements in Australia.

And still the movement did not die. It took a new turn in the establishment of a great Chartist Co-operative Land Association, in which men should find freedom from the slavery of the factories and live on co-operatively owned small holdings while they continued the struggle for the Charter: an inn, "The Land of Liberty," still stands among the neat villas of Heronsgate, near Rickmansworth in Hertfordshire, to mark where one such enterprise began. The land scheme failed, but the work for the Charter continued.

PETERLOO, 1819

A crowd of working people, gathered in Manchester to demand political reform, was charged by troops who caused over four hundred casualties.

COMMEMORATION OF "BLOODY SUNDAY," 1887

Labour demonstrations were frequently met by force in the 'eighties.

But it was doomed—this time as much by the incapacity of its leaders as the oppressive measures of the Government.

It suffered its death blow on 10 April, 1848, when a vast demonstration on Kennington Common, which O'Connor had pledged himself to lead to Parliament, was dispersed in face of a show of force by the police and military, who had been put for the purpose under the command of the aged Duke of Wellington. A fourth petition which O'Connor claimed had nearly six million signatures was presented to Parliament and found to have less than two million, of which, in striking contrast to the previous petitions, a large number were fraudulent.

For many years from its first beginnings Chartism had mobilized the hopes of the workers. It represented at its peak a genuine struggle to achieve, not political equality alone, but a true co-operative Commonwealth. It was defeated in part by the incompetence and irrationality of many of its leaders, in part by economic depression and the blows of police and military. Yet it had accomplished much, Even while Parliament rejected the Chartist demands it was forced to take notice of the desperate mood of the workers and give to their condition a consideration it would not otherwise have bothered to do. Hence the period of Chartism is also the period of the first law to protect women and children in the mines, of the Ten Hours' Act, which prevented juvenile labour being employed for longer than that period at a time, of the reduction of the newspaper tax, of the ending of the Corn Laws and the abolition of the Corresponding Acts, of the start of the Co-operative movement by the Rochdale Pioneers.

The workers were still far from the achievement of which they had dreamed, but they had accomplished more than they reckoned in the bitterness of defeat.

And now the struggle, which after every reverse renewed itself, took on a new form. It became at once less wide and more practical. The vision which had in some part inspired both Owenites and Chartists of a sudden sweeping away of the old, of the establishment almost overnight of a new order, either by a great all-embracing co-operative union or by the triumph of a Charter which should reform the political system at one blow, faded—and with it there went the possibility of, and the desire for, a revolutionary movement of the working-classes that should seize power and exercise it by non-parliamentary means.

The faith in a short cut perished. It did not, of course, end abruptly, existing one day and not the next, nor did it come to an end wholly or even primarily as a consequence of deliberate political judgment. It was influenced and shaped by the immense growth in the trade and commerce of Britain in the third quarter of the nineteenth century and by the fact that, although the major benefits of Britain's position as the workshop of the world went to the factory-owners and manufacturers, there was enough to offer the possibility of advance to large numbers of the working-classes and more particularly to the most energetic and best organized among them.

Advance—but not by one sweeping headlong rush in the fire and fury of civil struggle. Instead by the slow development of co-operative, trade-union, and to a lesser extent political, agencies which would consolidate after every advance and which above all would deal with practical issues.

This, therefore, was the period of the development of the co-operative societies and the building up of trade unions which were concerned much more to establish standards of wages and conditions within their own trades and to accumulate Friendly Society funds for the benefit of their members than to lead a general working-class movement.

As the old division between the Tories and the Whigs altered with the economic and social movement of the times to the new division between the Conservatives and the Liberals, and as the demand for a second and more radical Reform Bill took shape and gathered strength under the advocacy of John Bright's National Reform Union and its trade-union allies and rivals in the National Reform League the skilled workers, at least, could feel that liberalism offered a genuine promise.

The political philosophy of John Stuart Mill in his *Essay On Liberty*, the moral energy and reforming zeal of Gladstone—these it was which now seemed to offer the most hope, not only of the material advancement of Labour, but of the achievement of the great ideals of liberty and comradeship which had inspired the struggles that had gone before. And, indeed, great reforms were truly on the march. It was a period when it was not altogether utopian to believe that the social forces which, as Gladstone declared, "move onwards in their might and majesty," on the side of liberalism, might advance with scarce an interruption to ever new triumphs.

This new movement of Labour allied itself to the Liberal cause and might well, if the Liberals in the last quarter of the century had maintained the promise of the previous twenty-five years or had been willing to anticipate by some years the social reform policies of the early Lloyd George, have become wholly absorbed in the Liberal Party and have transformed it instead of helping to destroy it. It was international as well as domestic in its aspirations. But it was the internationalism of liberalism that it shared, not that of the Communist Manifesto and the International Working Men's Association of Karl Marx.

The impact of that great historical document upon working-class thought in Britain was nevertheless, as elsewhere, profound and pervasive. That it helped to make many aware both of the materialistic basis of many of the great historic developments of the past and of the historical mission of the working-classes to forge the instruments that should, in the fullness of time, bring a truly classless society, cannot be doubted.

But it was received in Britain by a working-class whose political philosophy had been profoundly affected not only by the idealist socialism that had run as a constant thread through so many of the struggles of the past, but also by the Liberal idea of liberty and the political importance of the individual, and by the moral ideas of the nonconformists with their emphasis on the individual conscience and the individual responsibility. Marxism became, therefore, not the sole and dominating influence in British as it did in so much of Continental socialism, but simply one influence among the many that went to shape the thought of British Labour.

When the working people of London turned out a million or more strong to welcome Garibaldi, the Italian liberator, the address presented to him on their behalf by the "Working Men of Great Britain's Metropolis" said:

"Your name is to us a household word, the symbol of liberty, associated with lofty daring, bold enterprise and unselfish devotion to the cause of human progress; for your noble deeds we thank, love and welcome you; and, in the name, the sacred name, of that liberty for which you have fought, bled and won for the oppressed peoples, we give you a place, the first place, in our hearts."

It was an internationalism inspired by that faith in "the sacred name of liberty" which inspired the working-class movement, not one inspired by a materialist notion of the international class war.

In that third quarter of the nineteenth century Labour consolidated and strengthened itself. Industrially the great new Amalgamated Societies were formed and in 1868 the first Trades Union Congress held. From its small beginning in Toad Lane, Rochdale, in 1844, when twenty-eight pioneers, half of them Owenite Socialists, opened a shop with a trading capital of £28, the Co-operative movement flourished and spread until by 1863, with the formation of the Co-operative Wholesale Society, it became a great national organization. Politically, with the Reform Act, it became possible to put forward at least some working-men candidates for Parliament with a hope of success. The London Working Men's Association and the Labour Representation League were formed to do so. Their success was not large, but two miners, Alexander Macdonald and Thomas Burt, were returned at the 1874 General Election out of thirteen candidates put up.

It was a period of Liberal-Labour alliance in a typically Victorian compact directed to bring some of the advantages of an expanding industrial capitalism to those among the working-classes who were properly respectable and hard-working. It had results in the development of improved labour laws, the establishment of conciliation boards, and the first beginnings of "municipal socialism" under the radical urge of Joseph Chamberlain, then still a Liberal in Birmingham.

But by 1875 the lustre of liberalism had begun to fade, and the hopes it had engendered grew dim. Free trade, the paramount instrument of Liberal economic philosophy, had failed to produce prosperity for all, economic depression began as always to claim its first victims among the workers, widespread strikes in the mining, manufacturing and agricultural areas—where Joseph Arch roused the farm-workers from the sullen apathy that had possessed them since the crushing of "the last labourers' revolt"—heralded the end of the period of social calm. Politically, it became ever more clear that the Liberal Party had no intention, in its relations with Labour, of moving forward from a paternalism which, although it might accept one or two working-class M.P.s as an interesting manifestation of social progress, had no intention of allowing any claim for political independence, still less for political equality. And economically the vast mass of the workers remained almost unaffected even by the small advances secured by the skilled minority of their number.

Once again the struggle had to be renewed, once again new weapons had to be found. They were forged in the brief insurrectionism of the period of the Trafalgar Square riots, in the stirring of the unorganized masses that created the new trade unionism, in the moral indignation of the Christian Socialists, the crusading zeal of the I.L.P., and in the intellectual creativeness of the Fabians. And this time—at long last—the struggle succeeded. For the first time, there was created an instrument exactly suited to the task before it, a political organization capable of fusing the forces within the Labour movement and giving them a coherence and a power such as they had never before possessed.

The delegates to the Labour Representation Conference in February, 1900, passed a vote of thanks to their chairman and went out from the Memorial Hall into Farringdon Street and Fleet Street where the newsboys were crying the latest news of the Boer War. The meeting had created no public stir, but those who attended it were of the company of a great army that had fought throughout the centuries. They had talked and debated and their words had fallen into place in a sequence that stretched back in an unbroken line to John Ball and beyond.

They had at last succeeded in forging a weapon which would not be broken by crisis or shattered by assault. They went out into a new century: the century in which Labour was to come into its inheritance.

PART TWO

THE YEARS OF GROWTH

CHAPTER V

THE TRADE UNIONS MAKE UP
THEIR MINDS

ON THE face of things, it would hardly have been possible to choose a less auspicious moment to found a new political party than that February in 1900 when the Labour Representation Committee was born.

The Memorial Hall Conference was to prove the culmination of the centuries-old struggle of the working-classes towards political independence, but not only was it unrecognized as such at the time by the overwhelming majority of the working-classes themselves, but it came at a period of intense political reaction when all those with a radical viewpoint were doomed to unpopularity and to public vilification.

The South African War was at its height and already the Independent Labour Party by its opposition to the war had made itself, along with a body of anti-war Liberals, the most unpopular political group in the country.

Five weeks before the outbreak of war the National Administrative Council of the I.L.P., meeting at Blackburn, had defined their attitude to the coming war with a clarity that left no room for misunderstanding. It was one which expressed the attitude of most Socialists, and many radical Liberals, but not of the majority of the trade unionists with whom Keir Hardie and the I.L.P. were seeking to combine and not, oddly enough, of the Fabian Society nor, less oddly, of Robert Blatchford and the leaders of the *Clarion*.

The Fabian Society, immersed in social science and in the possibilities of an advance towards a social security state through the permeation of municipal authorities and the older political parties, was not very interested in the Boer War. It never entirely made up its mind on the issues involved in it and never fully defined its policy towards it. It was not at that stage much interested in imperialism.

As for Robert Blatchford and his *Clarion* colleagues, they were pro-war. Blatchford, an old sergeant of the Royal Dublin Fusiliers, reacted emotionally to the war as a professional soldier might be expected to, and carried the *Clarion* with him into an imperialistic phase which lost it many readers. The trade unions as such had no particular policy either way. Although at the T.U.C. Conference in 1900 an anti-war resolution was carried, it was carried by a tiny majority only. Very many of the rank-and-file members of the trade-union movement shared the popular feeling and sang jingo songs with the best. Only the S.D.F. among the groups that converged to form the Labour Representation Committee fully shared the anti-war opinions of the I.L.P.

The I.L.P. had no doubts at all. At the Blackburn meeting the National Administrative Council, which included Keir Hardie, Bruce Glasier, Philip Snowden and Ramsay MacDonald, expressed its uncompromising opposition to the Government's policy.

"The National Administrative Council of the I.L.P.," it declared, "protests against the manner in which the Government, by the tenor of their dispatches and their warlike preparations, have made a peaceful settlement difficult with the Transvaal Republic.

"The policy of the Government can be explained only on the supposition that their intention has been to provoke a war of conquest to secure complete control in the interests of unscrupulous exploiters.

"A war of aggression is, under any circumstances, an outrage on the moral sense of a civilized community and in the present instance particularly so, considering the sordid character of the real objects aimed at.

"It is especially humiliating to the democratic instincts of this country that an ulterior and unworthy motive should be hidden under pretence of broadening the political liberties of the Uitlanders. Even if the admitted grievances of the Uitlanders were the real reason of the threatened hostilities, war would be an extreme course quite uncalled-for.

"We also protest against the action of the Press and the bulk of the leading politicians in strengthening the criminal conduct of the Government by misleading the public and rousing the passion for war, and we express the hope that it may not yet be too late for the manhood of the nation to prevent this outrage upon the conscience of our common humanity."

"Unscrupulous exploiters" . . . "outrage on the moral sense" . . . "sordid" . . . "humiliating" . . . "criminal," these were not the kind of words to make those who uttered them popular with a public opinion that was soon to rise to a crescendo of war hysteria and intolerance in which Keir Hardie and other Socialist leaders, along with Liberals like John Morley, Lloyd George and James Bryce, were to be drenched with the most bitter abuse from those who held that to think while war was on was the grossest treachery.

Yet in this manifesto and in Keir Hardie's later declaration that "modern imperialism is to the Socialist simply capitalism in its most predatory and militant phase," the early I.L.P. leaders expressed principles which, although they had a temporary unpopularity, were in the end to rally to the cause of socialism great numbers of devoted and public-spirited men and women, and give to the Socialist cause in Britain a humanitarian and internationalist vision that was indelibly to stamp all its policies and propaganda.

Yet, when the Labour Representation Conference met in the Memorial Hall, this forthright opposition to the great tide of patriotic and imperialist emotion that was sweeping the country could not help but seem to stand as another barrier to success.

The new party had only been in existence a few months when it had the opportunity—indeed the obligation—to try out its strength at a General Election. The Conservative Government decided to go to the country for a mandate to fight the war to a successful conclusion. Amidst mounting war feeling in 1900 the Khaki Election was foisted on the nation.

The Labour Representation Committee was altogether unprepared to enter such a contest at the very beginning of its career. Even those trade unions which had joined it were not by any means ready to put candidates in the field. It had no independent funds. Working-class opinion was, like all other opinion at the time, rent by the conflict between the minority who opposed the war and the vast majority who supported it. The Fabian Society was a research organization, not a campaigning body. The S.D.F. had hardly any funds and had already lost most of those among its early members who might have proved suitable Labour candidates. The I.L.P. itself could contribute only enthusiasm, much temporary public unpopularity, and a very little money.

Nevertheless, the Labour Representation Committee put fifteen candidates in the field, among them Keir Hardie, Philip Snowden, Fred Brocklehurst, F. W. Jowett, Ramsay MacDonald, Will Thorne, George Lansbury and Richard Bell. Keir Hardie stood for two constituencies, Merthyr and Preston, so that sixteen constituencies in all were contested. Of these fifteen candidates sponsored by the Labour Representation Committee only two, Keir Hardie at Merthyr (he came bottom of the poll at Preston) and Richard Bell at Derby, were successful. In Lancashire and Yorkshire, where the I.L.P. was believed to be particularly strong, it had no success. And although John Burns was also sent back to Parliament for Battersea it was as a Lib-Lab, not a Labour man.

The return of two candidates could hardly be regarded as an electoral triumph. It was even smaller in reality than in appearance. For although Richard Bell, the Secretary of the Amalgamated Society of Railway Servants, was nominally a supporter of an independent Labour Party and was, indeed, the first treasurer of the Labour Representation Committee, he was, in fact, much more a Liberal than a Socialist or a Labour man, acted as such in Parliament and within three years severed his connexion altogether with the new party.

Thus all that the Labour Representation Committee succeeded in achieving in the first General Election to which it committed its infant forces was to secure the return of a "One Man Party" to the House of Commons—although if it was to be represented by one man none better than Hardie could possibly have been found.

There were, it is true, other M.P.s besides Hardie and Bell who could properly be regarded as trade-union or working-class representatives, although they were not directly connected with the Labour Representation Committee. These were John Burns and two other Lib-Lab representatives—Henry Broadhurst, who won at Leicester, where Ramsay MacDonald, fighting as an L.R.C. candidate, came at the bottom of the poll, and W. R. Cremer—and five miners' M.P.s, William Abraham, Thomas Burt, Charles Fenwick, Ben Pickard, and John Wilson. But they would have little to do with Hardie and never acted with him as members of a parliamentary group.

Indeed, the lack of faith of the majority of trade unionists in the new Labour alliance was shown, not only by the refusal of the miners to have anything to do with it, but by the fact that at Leicester Henry Broadhurst, the former Secretary of the T.U.C. Parliamentary Committee, and Ramsay MacDonald, the Secretary of the Labour Representation Committee, fought each other, while W. C. Steadman, who had presided at the Memorial Hall Conference, nevertheless fought at Stepney as a Lib-Lab, not as a Labour Representation Committee candidate.

It might well have seemed, therefore, that not only had the concept of a great alliance between Socialists and trade unionists to form a genuine Labour Party fizzled out almost at birth, as so many previous efforts to mobilize Socialist and working-class opinion politically had done, but that the propaganda campaigns conducted by the I.L.P. with such fire and enthusiasm throughout the country had failed to make any real impact upon political opinion.

Such a judgment, as the next few years were to show, would have been mistaken, although it remained true for many years that the Independent Labour Party created more enthusiasm in the country than was ever reflected in votes when an election came.

The following year, however, the political apathy of the trade unions was sharply ended by a legal decision which threatened their whole effective existence as industrial organizations.

It is significant and not altogether out of character that it was a severely practical issue, rather than the appeal of a philosophical and ideological conception of society, that brought the trade unions to a livelier sense of the importance of political action and a truer understanding of the value of the instrument that lay to their hand in the Labour Representation Committee.

The Labour Representation Committee had seemed at first likely to remain a gesture rather than a fighting reality. It was there as a concrete but not very substantial indication of trade-union and Socialist goodwill towards each other and of their common interest in establishing an independent Labour movement.

But even those trade unions which affiliated to it took a benevolent rather than an urgent practical interest in it and the majority remained largely unaffected in their practical political outlook by its existence.

As the Khaki Election had shown, the awakened political conscience of the trade unions—of which there had been so much talk—and the Socialist ferment throughout the countryside—of which there had been so many rumours—seemed unlikely for some time, if ever, to reach either a size or an effectiveness of expression that need trouble the older parties. There had been earnest, well-meaning and eager efforts to forge industrial labour into a political force before. They had achieved little. In the first year or so after its formation it seemed probable that the Labour Representation Committee would make no more permanent impact upon the political history of the nation than those others had done, despite Keir Hardie's passionate advocacy and crusading zeal, Ramsay MacDonald's hard, intelligent work on organization, the enthusiasm of some trade unionists and the intellectual ammunition offered to the new organization by the Fabian Society.

This situation was altered dramatically by a legal decision of the House of Lords: the Taff Vale decision of 1901. And, because it already existed as an instrument of Socialist and trade-union alliance for political purposes, the Labour Representation Committee was able to seize the opportunity thus provided and turn the anger of the trade unions against the Lords' decision into channels wider and politically more constructive than would otherwise have been the case.

The issue which was to prove of such historic significance in the development of the Labour Party—was indeed to make a genuine and effective Labour Party possible within five years instead of, as otherwise might well have been the case, taking a decade or longer—arose in this way.

Railway workers employed by the Taff Vale Railway Company came out on strike. At first the strike was unauthorized by the union. At an early stage it was, however, recognized by the Amalgamated Society of Railway Servants. Thereafter it proceeded along the normal course followed by many industrial disputes between trade unions and employers before it. There was no special circumstance about the dispute which seemed likely to mark it out as singular or to give it the character of an event from which political consequences of the highest importance were to flow. But for the character of a Mr. Beasley, the General Manager of the Taff Vale Company, it would have had no place in history. But Mr. Beasley was distinguished by a great stubbornness of character and judgment and because of this he was to become, what he certainly had no desire to be, one of the most powerful if unconscious of the agents responsible for creating a powerful Labour Party.

Beasley, who was both a determined and a self-opinionated man, conceived the idea during the progress of the strike of suing the men's union for losses to the company arising out of their action in supporting and financing a strike of its employees. He went to the company's lawyers and put the idea up to them. They advised him to abandon the notion. They informed him that he had no case and that the union had merely been carrying out a recognized and well-established trade-union function—indeed one of the primary functions for which the trade unions existed—and one legalized by an Act passed thirty years earlier.

But Beasley was not to be advised. Despite the attitude of his lawyers he lodged his suit. He lost it and thereafter proceeded to carry it through successive courts right up to the House of Lords. The House of Lords, to the amazement of most informed opinion and the consternation of every trade union in the country, gave judgment in Beasley's favour. The Amalgamated Society of Railway Servants was ordered to pay damages of £23,000 to the Taff Vale Railway Company and meet legal costs amounting to an even larger sum.

This decision struck at the whole foundation of trade-union status as it was commonly believed to have been established by

140

two Acts: the Trade Union Act of 1871 and the Conspiracy and Protection of Property Act of 1875. Under these Acts the trade unions had believed themselves to be legally entitled to support their members in industrial disputes and to be free from any legal claim upon their funds as a result of such disputes. The Act of 1871 had deliberately refrained from giving a trade union the legal status of a corporate body. By so doing it had, in the belief of employers as well as trade unions, made it impossible for a trade union to be sued for damages.

The Law Lords now ruled otherwise. They ruled that a civil action could be brought against a trade union and that it could be sued for damages arising out of the actions of its officers or servants during a trade dispute and be restrained by an injunction from authorizing or committing any action which might be held by the courts to be wrongful. As a result of this decision no union whose members were involved in a trade dispute could any longer be regarded as safe from an action for damages that might completely denude it of funds, even those funds maintained for Friendly Society purposes. Such an action might, moreover, be brought against it even although strike action had been taken by a local branch in defiance of the executive's decision.

There had been other legal decisions, particularly on picketing, in the immediately previous years which had seriously narrowed the rights trade unions had believed themselves to possess for more than a quarter of a century. These cases had seemed to indicate an increasingly anti-trade-union temper on the part of the Courts and had created disquiet. But the Taff Vale decision went much further than anything previously feared. It undermined at one stroke the whole system of collective bargaining upon which trade unionism depended, and made the effective carrying out of the main purpose for which trade unions were established impossible.

In the minds of most trade-union leaders and Socialists, as they studied this judgment and considered its full implications, there was little doubt that, although it might be claimed that the Lords' decision was legally justified on a strict, if hitherto unthought of, interpretation of the Act of 1871, in fact it was inspired by political motives—the determination of those in power to curb the growing strength of the trade unions and to strike back at the militant

141

industrial activity which had followed the successful mass strikes of the late 1880s and the 1890s. It was equally clear that there was only one answer—to get the law changed.

The case for political and parliamentary action by the trade unions now took on sharper urgency. It was no longer simply a question of trade-union and labour representation in Parliament to fight the cause of the social advancement of the workers, but of a political battle for the very survival of trade unionism as an effective force. On this issue trade unionists of all shades of opinion could see eye to eye.

But although the Taff Vale decision brought with it an immediate trade-union awareness of the need for political action which at first sight boded well for the Labour Representation Committee, it also brought with it a danger which those who were fighting for the establishment of a genuine Labour Party were quick to perceive. This was the danger that trade-union political activity would take the form not of support for Labour candidates as such, but of a decision to run candidates specifically nominated to represent the interests of the particular trade-union group to which they belonged.

This was already the case with the miners' M.P.s, and the first result of the Taff Vale ruling was to confirm the miners in their attitude. They reaffirmed their decision not to affiliate to the Labour Representation Committee, but to organize parliamentary representation through the Political Committee of their own Miners' Federation and to institute a political fund for the return and maintenance of miners' representatives.

Other trade unions began to adopt a similar course. They were for the most part, however, tactically in a less strong position than the miners to achieve parliamentary representation by such methods. The mining constituencies were inhabited almost exclusively by miners. If the miners themselves voted for a candidate put up by their union he was, in most of the coal areas, certain to be returned. That was not the case elsewhere. In most of the other constituencies trade-union candidates must, for the most part, depend for success upon the support not only of fellow members of their own trade union but of many other voters whose interest a purely sectional appeal was hardly like to win.

Nevertheless, in the mood engendered by the Taff Vale decision, there was a real danger that the conception of a Labour Party which would represent not simply sectional trade-union interests but the interests of all those who were striving for a more just and economically sound social system would be swamped by the idea of M.P.s elected simply to act as members of a trade-union pressure-group.

The Labour Representation Committee sought to meet this danger at its annual conference at Birmingham in 1902.

Already, when the conference met, the political excitement caused by the Taff Vale decision had had some effect. In twelve months the affiliated membership of the committee had risen from 375,931 to 469,311, the number of trade unions affiliated from 41 to 65 and the number of trades councils from 7 to 21. But the majority of the unions newly affiliated were small; the only sizable ones were the Postmen's with 24,000 members, the Masons' with 20,000, the Plasterers' with 11,000 and the North Yorkshire Miners' with 7,500. None of the others had more than 4,000 members, and several of them, like the Zinc Workers' with 104 members and the Willyers' and Fettlers' with 200, had only a hundred or two.

Moreover, the weakness of the Labour Representation Committee had been demonstrated only a few weeks earlier during a bye-election in Dewsbury. Here, despite the fact that the Committee already had a candidate in the field, the Social Democratic Federation, which had withdrawn from affiliation a few months earlier because the L.R.C. was insufficiently Socialist and Marxist for it, put up its own candidate, Harry Quelch. And it finally forced the withdrawal of the candidate sponsored by the Labour Representation Committee although he had the support of the local I.L.P.

It was clearly essential, if the idea of a Labour Party was to survive, that the committee should somehow acquire new authority and be accepted not merely as an advisory body whose advice could be taken or rejected at will, but as the central organization for sponsoring Labour candidates.

Pete Curran of the Gasworkers', which with a membership of 45,000 was the second largest of the unions affiliated to the committee, and who was himself an I.L.P. pioneer, therefore moved that the conference should instruct the committee to consider ways and means of raising funds to meet the expenses of those candidates sponsored by it and of maintaining those returned to Parliament.

It was essential, he said, for the committee to be more than advisory. They must oppose the idea of sectional labour representation—"miners' members and bricklayers' members"—and have candidates who would be recognized as representatives of British labour as a whole.

"If we are ever to have a Labour group working together in the House of Commons," he declared, "we must send them there as representatives of all labour interests and they must be supported not from the fund of one union but from the joint funds of all unions."

His motion was seconded by Richard Bell on behalf of the Railway Servants', the largest union affiliated and the one directly affected by the Taff Vale decision. He, too, urged that the time had come to place political finance on a general basis, so that those sent to Parliament should be not merely the representatives of one society but of the whole Labour movement, and appealed particularly to the miners not to confine their political activities to their own union. James Sexton carried the proposal further by moving that the Committee should send its scheme to all trade unionists and ask for their support.

The joint Curran-Sexton proposal was carried, but the discussion which took place first is interesting as evidence of the divided views as to the function of Labour members that still prevailed. The Postmen's delegate, for example, informed the conference with great emphasis that his union intended to run its own candidate, since they believed that it was necessary to have men returned with special knowledge of various trades. A delegate of the Railway Workers', however, taking a wider view, said that his union believed that Labour members were needed not only to get trade-union legislation considered, but also much general legislation, such as old age pensions.

When it was finally agreed that the committee should draw up plans to further the central sponsorship of Labour candidates and provide them with the necessary funds, the second great step towards the establishment of a genuine Labour Party had been taken. The first had been made when the Labour Representation Committee itself was formed two years previously. Now it had been recognized that in order to make that committee effective it must be given the authority and the money to build a parliamentary party that should be truly representative of all the interests of labour.

The conference was not yet ready to agree on a definite programme—it was certainly not yet ready to agree on a Socialist programme and was not to be so for many years. The fight to make the Party something more than a narrow trade-union group was not yet over—indeed, resolutions proposing the exclusion of the Socialist societies, the restriction of membership to trade unions and of labour representation in Parliament to working trade unionists, were to be brought before the conference periodically for some years, although fortunately they were always to be defeated. Nor were the trade unions by any means all yet convinced that politically they should sink their identities in a broadly based Labour Party instead of devoting themselves to securing parliamentary representation for their particular trade interests—indeed, not until 1909 were the miners to give up their policy of parliamentary exclusiveness and join the Labour Party.

Nevertheless, the choice had been made: the constitutional steps had been taken which alone could convert this loose political alliance of Socialist societies and trade unions into a genuine Labour Party.

Those who made the decision had perhaps for the most part no great ambitions for the party they were establishing. They were still thinking mainly in terms of a small group of Labour M.P.s able to exercise parliamentary influence on the greater parties, not of a Labour Party which should be able to form the Government of the country. Indeed, when at the end of this Birmingham Conference the delegates visited Bournville at the invitation of Mr. and Mrs. Cadbury—both leaders of social reform who had shown their friendliness to Labour's aspirations in many ways—and heard Mr. Cadbury declare that he would be glad to see even as many as fifty Labour M.P.s in the House of Commons, there were probably few who took exception to such a target as altogether too modest.

Nevertheless, they had just taken decisions that were to help to bring a Labour Government into office within a quarter of a century and into power within half a century.

The first results were seen at the following year's conference at Newcastle when the scheme which the committee had been instructed to draw up was approved. It was agreed by a great majority that each affiliated body should be required to contribute one penny per year for each of its members to form a parliamentary fund to assist candidates in fighting elections and give those who were successful in getting into Parliament a maintenance payment of £200 a year. Ramsay MacDonald, the secretary, was, moreover, able to report that more than seventy trade unions had already agreed to support the scheme. It was also agreed that candidates should be required to give a pledge to abide by the majority decisions of the Labour Representation Committee group in Parliament or resign their seats, and should undertake not to associate with other parties.

Now indeed the committee was beginning to take the shape of a genuine political party.

Moreover, the conference itself looked more like the annual gathering of a party of strength and influence than it ever had before. It is true that the Social Democratic Federation was no longer there, but that was perhaps more gain than loss, for the leaders of the S.D.F. had little sympathy with the idea of a democratic Labour Party, and, when not quarrelling among themselves, were a potent source of disagreement with the trade unions which alone could give the Party the numerical foundation it required.

But the total membership had nearly doubled, rising from 469,311 to 861,150, an increase of nearly eighty-four per cent, and the number of trade unions affiliated had grown from 65 to 127—three times as many as those affiliated when the committee began. Moreover, the new members included trade-union giants like the Textile Workers' of Lancashire with over 100,000 members, the Amalgamated Society of Engineers (who had been represented at the Memorial Hall meeting but had taken no action to affiliate to the new body until now) with 84,000 members, the Carpenters' with 62,000 members and the Boilermakers' with nearly 50,000. The Taff Vale decision and the Labour Representation Committee's reaction to it was beginning to have its full effect.

In addition to these giants there were many medium-sized unions of considerable importance—among them, and to be noted particularly because of the man it sent as leader of its delegation, the Friendly Society of Ironfounders. Its representative was Arthur Henderson, who more than any single man was to be responsible for making the Labour Party the most effective political organization in the country and who was later to be justly described by a famous political opponent, Lloyd George, as the greatest political organizer in Britain. Henderson spoke at this, his first conference, typically urging that the levy for the parliamentary fund should be 4d. for every member of affiliated organizations per year instead of a penny, as a penny would be insufficient to establish an effective fighting fund.

He was defeated on that point but was elected treasurer of the committee, and in that capacity began an association with MacDonald, the secretary, which was to have an effect upon the future fortunes of the Labour Party of the highest importance.

At this conference also there was for the first time one woman among the nearly 250 delegates. She was Miss I. O. Ford of Leeds, a member of the I.L.P. She was perhaps a little lonely among so many men, but she was making history: she was blazing a trail along which many women were to come in the years ahead, bringing their knowledge and experience to help in the shaping of Labour policy.

She, no less than the new trade-union members crowding the Co-operative Hall in Newcastle where the conference was held, was a sign and a portent. The Labour Party was growing up.

CHAPTER VI

THE FIRST VICTORY

Six years almost to the day from that first meeting in the Memorial Hall, Farringdon Street, when the decision was taken from which so much of modern political history has derived, the delegates to the Annual Conference of the Labour Representation Committee met again in this same hall.

On that earlier occasion 129 delegates, representing some sixty-seven trade unions—most of them small, many of them apathetic to the idea of a political Labour Party, several of them unwilling, as was soon to be seen when the question of affiliation arose, to link themselves with the new project—had met the delegates of three Socialist societies to discuss and finally, with some reservations, to approve a project which only the most determined and enthusiastic among them expected to have any immediate practical results. They had met, held their conference and dispersed with scarcely a ripple of public interest in what they were doing or what its consequences might be.

Vastly different was the situation on this February day six years later. Now crowding the long tables running down the hall at right angles to the platform were delegates from every important trade union in the country with the single exception of the Miners' Federation—although the miners of Lancashire and Cheshire and of Cleveland and of North Yorkshire were represented.

At that first meeting only a baker's dozen of the trade unions represented had had more than 30,000 members each, and of these only nine had joined the new alliance. Now there were nearly thirty with more than that number of members and five with 50,000 or more. Nor had the little unions like the Bookedge Gilders, with fifty-seven members, and the quaintly named Pen and Pocket Blade Forgers' Protection Society, with seventy-four, been squeezed out.

The 363 delegates were able to speak for at least 900,000 organized workers and Socialists. And, most significant of all, among these delegates there were seventeen Labour M.P.s, part of a group of twenty-nine Labour M.P.s returned to Parliament at the General Election only just held.

Moreover, the Labour Party, as it now was in fact and was at this Conference to become in name also, had become, instead of an unimportant political group of little interest to anyone outside it, the most discussed political movement in the country. The newspapers and political clubs which six years previously had not bothered to take any note of its existence were now anxiously debating the probable future consequence of its success. So much so that W. T. Stead devoted one whole number of his *Review of Reviews* to the new Labour members, and Mr. Balfour, writing on the morrow of his own crushing political defeat, commented: "We have here to do with something much more important than the swing of the pendulum or all the squabbles about Free Trade and Fiscal Reform. We are face to face (no doubt in milder form) with the Socialist difficulties that loom large on the Continent. Unless I am greatly mistaken, the election of 1906 inaugurates a new era."

The Labour Representation Committee had put fifty candidates into the field at the General Election and had raised its parliamentary strength at one bound from four members: Keir Hardie, David Shackleton, Will Crooks and Arthur Henderson, the last three having been returned at bye-elections, to twenty-nine. Moreover, in the fifty constituencies in which it fought it had polled more than 323,000 votes, thirty-nine per cent of the total cast. Of the twenty-nine successful candidates sixteen had been returned for constituencies in which a Labour candidate had never previously fought. In the case of all but one of the others the Labour vote had been dramatically increased; in some cases by two, three or four times.

Nor was this all. In addition to the twenty-nine independent Labour members returned there were also twenty-five Lib-Labs, of whom thirteen were miners' M.P.s who could be relied upon to vote with the independent Labour M.P.s on most issues (one of them joined the Labour Party immediately after his election). So, indeed, could most although not all of the other Lib-Labs. Moreover, the Labour vote had exercised considerable influence in a great many constituencies in which no Labour candidate had fought. So much so indeed that a majority of the Liberal M.P.s returned were pledged to support Labour's demands for early legislation to reverse the Taff Vale judgment.

The return of twenty-nine Labour M.P.s was in itself a triumph. What made it even more significant was the fact that twenty-two of these M.P.s were convinced and active Socialists concerned to advance a distinctive Labour policy over a wide field of public affairs, and not simply to confine themselves to defending trade-union interests, important though they recognized these to be. This first Parliamentary Labour Party was indeed a remarkable body. Keir Hardie, Ramsay MacDonald, Arthur Henderson, Philip Snowden, David Shackleton, F. W. Jowett, G. N. Barnes, J. R. Clynes, G. H. Roberts, Will Crooks, Will Thorne—men who were to play a notable part in the political history of Britain during the next quarter of a century or more—were all members of it.

Well might the Annual Report put before this second Memorial Hall Conference jubilantly declare:

"Six years of organization, of propaganda, of preparation have not been wasted. . . . Suddenly politicians of all parties realize that a new factor in politics has appeared; that organized labour as a political force is already a menace to the easy-going gentlemen of the old school who have slumbered for so long on the green benches of St. Stephen's. Everybody is asking, 'What does it all mean? What does the Labour Party want? What will it do?'"

Well might it propose also that the name should now be changed from the Labour Representation Committee to the Labour Party and add, in another section of the report:

"A Labour Party now sits in the House of Commons and our success at the polls has been regarded as the most significant event of the Election. We have won national recognition and for the time being the fate of our Movement has to be decided, not only on the platform, but also on the floor of the House of Commons."

And well might Arthur Henderson, not a man ever given to

oratorical fancies or political exaggerations, declare in his opening speech to the conference over which he presided:

"The wage-earners have at last declared in favour of definite, united independent political action, and we this morning can rejoice in an electoral triumph which, having regard to all the circumstances, can safely be pronounced as phenomenal. We can congratulate ourselves today that a real live independent Labour Party, with its own chairman, its own deputy chairman and its own whips, is now an accomplished fact in British politics."

The delegates—among whom there were now five women, Miss Margaret Bondfield being one and Mrs. Margaret MacDonald another—cheered this statement loudly. But they reserved the biggest cheer of all for Henderson's reference to the "experienced and loyal social reformer," under whose leadership Labour's forces in Parliament were marshalled. There was no one in that hall who did not know the debt their movement owed to Keir Hardie.

And, indeed, Keir Hardie, and those with him who had staunchly held in the face of many disappointments that the best hope of an effective Labour Party lay in an alliance between Socialists and trade unionists, might well, as they looked at that crowded conference and considered the election results, have felt that their strategy was producing results even more quickly than they had ever had reason to hope. Not only had the alliance secured within a remarkably short time the return of a properly organized Parliamentary Labour Party of twenty-nine members, or thirty with the new miner recruit, but the Independent Labour Party itself, although it accounted for not much more than one-sixtieth of the total affiliated membership of the Labour Representation Committee, had nominated six of the successful candidates. Another six among the successful nominees of the trade unions were members of it.

The Social Democratic Federation, which had preferred to break with the Labour Representation Committee and crusade alone for its own brand of socialism, had put, either directly or in association with other small independent Socialist bodies, thirteen candidates into the field. Not one of them had been returned. Almost without exception they had come bottom of the poll and the total number of votes they had been able to secure was only 24,473.

The Labour Representation Committee had commanded almost fourteen times this number—Keir Hardie and Ramsay MacDonald between them mustered more votes than the entire S.D.F. contingent. The practical case for the policy Keir Hardie had consistently urged and the S.D.F. had rejected did not seem any longer in doubt.

Nor were the parliamentary victories the only grounds for satisfaction. The new Labour alliance had also made solid and substantial progress in the municipalities. Some thirty of the delegates to the second Memorial Hall Conference were themselves aldermen or councillors, and they were only a small minority of the Labour men and women who had secured representation on local government bodies. Indeed, the Report presented to the Conference was able to state that, as a result of the application to municipal work of the methods adopted in parliamentary elections, the municipal gains secured by the local Labour Representation Committees in the last municipal elections had exceeded those of either the Liberal or Conservative Parties. All over the country, in cities and towns and villages, Labour men and women were putting into practice that training in "gas and water socialism" which the Fabian Society had advocated and the I.L.P. had preached.

The tradition of municipal activity which was in the future to provide the Labour Party with so great an opportunity to improve the conditions of the people and give so many of its leaders their first schooling in public affairs had successfully begun.

The Labour Party, as it was henceforth to be called, had indeed gained such a lodgment in the national and local political system as would have seemed quite impossible even a few years earlier.

It had now a considerable organization in the country built up on lines laid down by Arthur Henderson, who brought to the task not only immense natural administrative ability but much previous experience gained as a Liberal election agent before he had realized that the only real hope of the kind of policies he wanted lay in a Labour Party. It had begun to develop that service of propaganda literature which was to be one of the most characteristic and successful features of Labour activity and in the year just ended had sold over 4,400,000 leaflets, nearly eight times as many as in the year before. It had been active not only in domestic but also in international affairs, had taken part in a National Peace Conference to urge the employment of methods of arbitration to settle differences between nations and had raised a fund to help the families of Russian workers killed in the massacres of St. Petersburg when troops had been ordered to shoot down strikers.

It could now by every standard regard itself as a genuine independent political party, with its own growing organization and its own representation in the House of Commons.

Yet although this success had been largely due to the zeal and propaganda of Socialists, and although the majority of the new M.P.s were themselves Socialists, it would be a complete misjudgment to regard the success as a Socialist success or the Labour Party as, at that time, a Socialist party.

It is one of the ironies of the period that although the impact of the Fabian philosophy and the I.L.P. crusading spirit upon the political and social life of the community and upon the outlook of the Labour movement had been immense, the actual membership of the Socialist societies remained amazingly and disappointingly small.

The Fabian Society, it is true, had never had any ambitions for a large membership. Even so its membership total of 784 in 1906— as against 861 at the first conference in 1900—hardly suggested that it was gaining many adherents even among the intellectually able to whom it specifically appealed. Its ideas had permeated into many corners where the name Fabian was hardly known. Its actual membership was not increasing.

The Independent Labour Party, unlike the Fabian Society, had always desired and sought a widespread membership. Yet in thirteen years of crusading life it had only succeeded in attracting sixty thousand members, and in the six years since the first Memorial Hall meeting—six years which had brought so radical a change in the fortunes of the Labour movement as a whole—its membership had only increased by three thousand. With the *Clarion* movement, which was still active, although it had never quite recovered the first fine careless rapture that had distinguished it before Blatchford's support of the Boer War, it had carried the gospel of socialism the length and breadth of the country and particularly of the north of England.

They had stirred the hearts and minds of men and women, but in the main their influence had been to make people ready to work for a moderate Labour Party rather than themselves to become active Socialists and members of a Socialist society. Much of their activity had not done even this. Instead it had simply created a ferment which had no particular political direction. It had spread a dissatisfaction with conditions and a longing for a better society. But many who had been influenced by it were apparently not ready to submit to the disciplines of the political life or accept the obligations of the practical reformer.

Nor had the Labour Party won its electoral victories on a Socialist programme. It had fought primarily on an appeal to trade unionists to combine to secure the essential constitutional rights needed for industrial organization which had been challenged by the Taff Vale judgment. With this appeal there had been combined a strictly social reform programme of slum clearance, old age pensions and taxation of land values.

The purpose of the campaign had been to mobilize the trade-union vote. Labour candidates, however strong their own Socialist views might be, had been careful not to advocate any permanent changes in the social order which might lose any part of that vote.

Moreover, although they had fought as an independent party, they had conducted many of their campaigns in close harmony with the Liberals. Twenty-four of their successful candidates had had to fight only against Conservative opponents, the Liberals abstaining from putting up candidates who might have split the progressive vote. In Lancashire and Cheshire, the area in which the biggest single group of victories was won, all the thirteen successful Labour candidates were returned as a result of an alliance of Labour and Liberal voters.

This was not equally true elsewhere. In many constituencies Labour and Liberal candidates did fight each other, and in Scotland all the four Labour Representation Committee candidates as well as five put up by the Scottish Workers' Representation Committee in mining constituencies had to fight Liberals as well as Conservatives.

Nevertheless, although there was no national agreement and in many constituencies local feeling stood in the way of even a loose alliance, the Labour successes were to no small extent due to the fact that the programme on which they fought was of a kind which many Liberals could support.

And it was, of course, even more due to the fact that on the issue which had precipitated the election and which dominated it above all others—the issue of Free Trade or Protection—Labour saw eye-to-eye with the Liberals. They were both equally opposed to the Tariff Reform policy of Joseph Chamberlain, which had brought the Balfour Government down and equally determined to bring to an end the reign of conservatism. And they were of like mind also on the question of Home Rule for Ireland, the issue which, after Free Trade, was most prominent in the election.

The twenty-nine Labour M.P.s, no less than the twenty-five Lib-Labs, therefore, owed their success in no small part to the tide of Liberalism which was sweeping the country. Even before the General Election, bye-elections losses had reduced the majority o 134 over all other parties with which the Tories had been returned in 1900, to 74.

At the election itself the combined Conservative and Liberal Unionist forces in Parliament were cut from 392 to 158, and Campbell-Bannerman was returned to power with a majority of 130 over all other parties—a majority which was, moreover, for all practical purposes even greater than this, as on most issues Campbell-Bannerman could depend on the support both of Labour and of the eighty-three Irish Nationalist members against the Tories.

It was a tide with which the new Labour Party could swim without any straining of conscience. It was true that, as Arthur Henderson declared in his opening address at the Memorial Hall Conference, the Labour Party owed no more formal allegiance to the new Government than it had to the old; its attitude towards it was the same: "To support it when possible and to oppose it when it is necessary."

Nevertheless, the 1906 election heralded the beginning of an era of social reform which Labour could support with conviction, although it might urge that it ought to be carried much farther than the Liberals were yet prepared to go. It was an era which included the Trade Disputes Act, a Workmen's Compensation Act which gave protection to six million workers formerly unprotected, an increase in death duties, reform in income-tax scales, the establish-

155

ment of school medical inspection and of measures to provide school meals for necessitous children, old age pensions, the Coal Mines Eight Hours Act, a new Education Act, a Trade Boards Act instituting a legal minimum wage in sweated trades, the setting up of Labour Exchanges and, finally, the famous Lloyd George Budget of 1909.

The ferment of a new social conscience, which had helped to bring the Labour Party into being and which it had helped to mobilize, was now at last having its tremendous impact upon Liberalism. It reawakened within the Liberal ranks that radical tradition and that consciousness of a social mission which had always been the truest part of the Liberal heritage. Ten or fifteen years earlier such an awakening might well have enabled Liberalism to absorb within itself the emergent Labour movement. Now it was too late—even although John Burns, the one-time leader of the great dock strike and hero of the Trafalgar Square riots, sat now in Campbell-Bannerman's administration as President of the Local Government Board, "the first of the ancient lowly to reach the position of Cabinet Minister."

"Bravo, Sir Henry! Bravo!" said John Burns, wholly true to character, when Campbell-Bannerman offered him the post. "This is the most popular thing you have done yet."

That was true and it was not least true among the Labour members who, despite differences of opinion, had an affection for Burns because of the part he had played in their movement in the past and saw in his appointment—even although he did not prove very successful in it—a symbol of the political importance the working-classes had now at last acquired. But Burns was no longer a Labour man and his appointment to the Cabinet could not affect the course of Labour history nor that of the Liberal Party, as the future was to show.

The Liberal administration did not proceed along its path of reform without some hesitations, nor were all its members so enthusiastic for social legislation as were Lloyd George and, in those days, Winston Churchill. Nevertheless, it made a vast advance which permanently altered the pattern of British life and was responsible for a body of legislation designed to improve the condition of the people unequalled by any Government until the

Labour Government of 1945. It was, as it proved, the climax of Liberalism, but it was a climax which did it honour.

Yet its first reform measure, the Trade Disputes Act, was only made into a satisfactory measure by the political skill and determination of the new Labour Party. Without the thirty Labour M.P.s not all the pledges given by Liberal candidates would have produced the complete reversal of the Taff Vale judgment which was essential if trade unionism was to be able to advance by constitutional means along the path which the economic developments of the time required.

The Liberal Government's own Trade Disputes Bill proved when it was presented to the House to be almost wholly unsatisfactory. While it went some way towards allowing peaceful picketing and to establishing that an act done in combination should not be illegal if it would not have been so if done by a single person, it left the Courts to decide which acts were wrongful in the eyes of the law and under what circumstances they should be regarded as being done with the authority of a union and it still left trade-union funds open to claims for damages.

Fortune favoured the Labour Party in their demand for more radical action. By the luck of the ballot they secured the right to introduce a Private Member's Bill at the very beginning of the session, and at once took the opportunity to bring forward a Trade Disputes Bill of their own. This, after consultation with a special conference representing the entire trade-union movement, embodied proposals which were to provide the legal foundation for all subsequent trade-union development and which were to free them from the threat of civil claims upon their funds in consequence of trade disputes.

When the debate on this Private Member's Bill took place it became clear that a large number of Liberal members had given pledges at the General Election that would make it very difficult for them to vote against the Labour Party's proposals, even although they ran counter in vital respects to those contained in the Liberal Government's own bill.

Thereupon, Sir Henry Campbell-Bannerman took the unprecedented step, during the course of the debate, of announcing, without any prior consultation with his Cabinet, that the Government would accept the Labour Party's bill in place of its own and make it a Government measure.

The battle for trade-union rights was won. The possibility of any further Taff Vale decision was ended. The Labour Party had shown at the very opening of the new session and in the most emphatic way the advantages that the trade unions had gained from the establishment of an independent political party. In the next few weeks Labour had other triumphs. It succeeded in forcing the Government to accept an amendment widening the scope of the Workmen's Compensation Bill, and it got its own Education (Provision of Meals) Bill passed into law with Government support, thus carrying out a demand put forward by a Labour Conference more than a year before when it had been shown that between fifteen and sixteen per cent of the children in schools were so underfed as to be unable to benefit by education.

In this first session the Labour Party could feel that it had made a substantial beginning. All seemed set for its further advance.

Yet before long it was to be faced with a growing disillusionment. There was no easy pathway forward.

CHAPTER VII

POLITICAL ADVANCE
AND POLITICAL DISILLUSIONMENT

IN July, 1907, eighteen months after the triumphant return of the first real Parliamentary Labour Party, a bye-election was held in the Colne Valley Division of Yorkshire.

The result of that bye-election stirred the whole country and caused many a respectable middle-class gentleman to prophesy with a shudder that revolution was on the march. Yet, despite the immediate excitement, it made no settled impact upon the history of the Labour Party. The young man who, because of it, shot suddenly like a meteor across the political sky, causing exhilaration or consternation according to the hopes or fears of the observer, burned himself out like a meteor within a few years and in the end disappeared altogether, leaving behind him one of the unsolved personal mysteries of British political life.

But it lights so vividly a conflict that troubled the Labour Party at this stage—a conflict that has indeed troubled it again and again during its history—and symbolizes so clearly the clash inherent in all progressive movements betweeen those who must concern themselves with the business of constitutional advance and march forward step by practical step, consolidating what they have gained, and those who believe, or wish to believe, that if only the trumpet of revolution is loud enough the walls of the citadel of privilege will fall of their own accord, that it takes on both a particular and even, in some sense, a timeless significance. Unimportant itself when the whole march of events is considered, it provides a focus for much that is of permanent importance.

Moreover, there was a moment, even although only a brief one, when some of the consequences that followed upon it seemed likely to split the I.L.P. and rob it of its future influence on the course of Labour history.

The Labour Party had established itself. It had now the support of most trade unions, and very soon, when the Miners' Federation with its 550,000 members affiliated, was to have the support of practically all. It had established early in 1906 a Women's Labour League to obtain direct Labour representation for women in Parliament and on all local bodies and had admitted many women members.

After some years in which its office had been simply a room in Ramsay MacDonald's flat in Lincoln's Inn Fields, it had offices of its own efficiently run by the assistant secretary, Jim Middleton, who had come down from Cumberland in 1903 to give his ability to the Party for a mere £75 a year, and to whose tireless and completely disinterested labours the Party was to owe an increasingly great debt as the years passed. It was shortly to appoint a national election agent, Arthur Peters.

Its total affiliated membership was now well over a million. The Socialist societies also were gaining new recruits at a much more rapid rate than formerly—the I.L.P. had passed the 20,000 level and was before long to reach its pre-war peak of 28,000 members. Even the Fabian Society had passed the 1,200 mark and was climbing rapidly to over 3,000.

In Parliament the Party could point to solid achievements.

But the shadow of its secondary position to the Liberals lay over it. It could claim that it had a part in such social reform measures as were passed: it could even claim that some of them were much better than they would otherwise have been because of the pressure it had been able to exercise. But inevitably the main credit for any achievements went to the Liberal Party.

Moreover, almost unavoidably the character of Labour propaganda had changed with the advent of a compact and sizable group of Labour members to Parliament. It dealt now primarily with current political issues—it was concerned with the practical questions of the day rather than with that sweeping vision of a Socialist commonwealth in which all men should be as brothers that had previously been the inspiration of its most challenging appeal.

Finally, although the Liberal Party was prepared to do much in the way of social reform of which the Labour Party could approve, it was not prepared to deal with the basic human and economic causes of unemployment.

SIDNEY WEBB   ROBERT BLATCHFORD

MARGARET BONDFIELD   PHILIP SNOWDEN

Distinguished figures of the Labour Movement in 1910.

VOTES FOR WOMEN

The funeral of the suffragette who threw herself under the King's horse in the Derby of 1913. Labour was divided on the "militant" issue.

Keir Hardie, when he was fighting a lone battle in the House of Commons, had earned for himself the title of "Member for the Unemployed." The Labour Group, now that it was not one but thirty, found itself unable to do much more for the unemployed than he had. Moreover, it had commitments, even although of an intangible character, towards a Liberal government such as he had never had towards a Conservative government. These commitments were increased by the fact that the Liberal Party had to meet the opposition of the House of Lords on every major measure of social reform. In that struggle Labour was bound to ally itself with liberalism even when liberalism was not as bold or as fundamental as it wished.

The Labour Party was thus faced with the problem that faces all political parties that have some chance of influencing legislation and achieving concrete results however small: the need to move onwards from denunciation without losing in the process the fire and enthusiasm that sustained it earlier.

For fire and enthusiasm, for the Socialist vision untrammelled by practical political considerations of the immediately possible, there was still a great hunger among many. It was that hunger that was satisfied at the Colne Valley election. And if the diet offered was words, it was on words, on emotion and passion and vision that those who were hungry could most easily satisfy themselves.

Colne Valley was a Liberal stronghold, and when there was a bye-election in July, 1907, both a Liberal and a Conservative presented themselves to the electors.

There had been no Labour candidate at the two previous elections, since it had not been felt that a Labour candidate had much chance. At this bye-election the Labour Party and the National Council of the I.L.P. felt, however, that a candidate should be put in the field. They went through the list of well-established members of the I.L.P. who were on the Labour Party's list of endorsed candidates to find someone of sufficient political experience and reputation to undertake with credit what might well prove a difficult task.·

While they were considering whom to put up, however, the local branch of the I.L.P. suddenly decided, without seeking the approval of the I.L.P. National Council—indeed, in the teeth of its opposition—and without applying for Labour Party endorsement, to put up a candidate of its own choice: a young man of twenty-five, Victor Grayson.

Grayson had been an apprentice engineer, but had early shown great powers as a popular speaker. These powers had attracted the attention of leaders of the Unitarian Church of which he was a member and they had provided the funds to send him to Manchester University to train for the Unitarian Ministry. Arrived there his gifts of passionate advocacy soon found other causes to spend themselves on than Unitarianism. He was caught up in the I.L.P. and Socialist movement and, above all, in the plight of the Manchester unemployed. He became their leader, able to stir the emotions of great crowds by his oratory and by the youthful and engaging personality to which it was allied.

It was this young man whom the Colne Valley branch of the I.L.P. invited to fight the bye-election. Despite the opposition of official Labour, which favoured an older and more experienced man, he agreed to do so.

He stood as a Socialist and non-official Labour candidate and he stirred the people of the Colne Valley to such a pitch of enthusiasm with his angry and passionate denunciation of the world as it was and his glowing vision of what it could be that the news of the election fight, and of the young man who was carrying the torch of a new crusade into every corner of the constituency, spread over the whole country. The result was awaited with an eager and, in many cases, an anxious expectancy far exceeding that commonly centred on a single bye-election.

When the poll was over it was found that Grayson had beaten both his Liberal and Conservative opponents and carried an industrial constituency with an appeal for socialism of the most undiluted kind.

He had answered the longing for colour and drama that commanded the emotions of so many of those who found it difficult to adjust themselves to the responsibilities and frustrations of the political life upon which the Labour Party was now of necessity embarked. He was, as everyone who ever heard him speak confirms, a magnificent and inspiring mob orator with a most attractive and friendly personality. It seemed to many when the election

162

result was known that Grayson was the first portent of a revolution.

But he was a propagandist, not a politician. His success went to his head. What had been an attractive strain of youthful egotism developed under the pressure of flattery, much of which was far from disinterested, into an obstinate refusal to consider any opinion but his own.

He was not a success in the House of Commons. Nor was he willing to work with the other Labour members there or for the Parliamentary Party. He regarded himself as the only Socialist among them and was contemptuous even of those like Keir Hardie who had been pioneers before he was born.

But although he made no real impact on the House of Commons, and was suspended for challenging the Speaker's ruling on a motion to deal with unemployment in circumstances that cast much doubt on his sincerity, he remained immensely popular in the country. Invitations to speak at great meetings showered upon him. Everywhere he appeared he was able to command large audiences and stir them to a mood of political revivalism.

He provided an answer, even although an intemperate and unbalanced one, to that need to feel a part not simply of a new political party but of a great social crusade that is so much a part of socialism. It was that spirit which had given socialism its strength in the early pioneering days of Keir Hardie, the I.L.P. and the *Clarion* vans, and which now, in the transition to the practical problems of current politics and the parliamentary struggle, seemed to be missing.

Behind the scenes, Arthur Henderson, with a clearer if more pedestrian vision of what was needed to make Labour into an effective political force and to bring reality to the Socialist dream, was working with tireless energy to improve the Party's organization.

"Whenever a vacancy occurs," he told the annual conference, "the executive is asked to respond to the enthusiasm of Labour electors, and asked to respond without an atom of the organization that is absolutely essential to successful electioneering. We have delayed far too long. The longer we delay the more we shall suffer."

To that task of organization he and Jim Middleton, with Arthur

Peters as national agent and Scott Lindsay as assistant in the Whip's Department at the House, devoted themselves with the single-minded loyalty that most people are capable of bringing only to their personal relationships.

But those outside saw for the moment little of the result of their efforts—they were building for the future and the hunger was for a messiah of the moment. That hunger was the greater because, as the relatively prosperous trading conditions of 1906 and 1907 began to worsen, trade depression and unemployment grew and the anger and frustration of the poor and dispossessed mounted. Parliamentary action seemed ineffective to meet the deeper miseries of the time. "Is the Parliamentary Party a Failure?" asked Ben Tillett in an angry pamphlet which picked out Henderson, Shackleton and Snowden for particular vilification because they had supported Liberals on temperance problems. The more active and militant trade unionists began to talk again of direct action as the only hope of the workers. And behind all this, explaining it and feeding it, was a sense of disappointment at what had so far been achieved by political action—that old, old problem of reconciling the possible with the ideal.

Grayson was the figure around whom much of this feeling centred. He was, and that is his real historical importance, a symbol of the frustrations, the discontents, the disillusionments, the difficulties of emotional readjustment that are inevitable when a crusade becomes part of the machinery of government. Although he himself was soon to disappear from the political scene, burnt out by his own success and the temptations that accompanied it, the mood of which he was the manifestation was to remain and was to reappear again and again in the history of the Labour Party. It was to provide it with some of its strength, its restless and passionate refusal to give up its vision and accept a limited administrative achievement in its place, but it was also to provide it with some of its weakness, the recurring suspicion of leaders struggling with the hard and often intractable problems of politics and faced sometimes with the necessities of compromise if anything at all is to be achieved.

Yet, if Grayson was in the beginning a symbol of the passionate desire of many thousands of ordinary men and women that the vision of a new commonwealth should not be lost in the day-to-day business of parliamentary committees and party organization, he became in the end, as often happens with visionaries, a potential agent of disruption threatening the hope of any general Socialist advance. He had proved himself impossible as a colleague in the Parliamentary Labour Party—now he became increasingly impossible as a Labour speaker on public platforms.

The climax came when he and Hyndman, with whom he was now associated, refused to appear on the same platform with Keir Hardie at a great *Clarion* van meeting at the Holborn Hall and Hardie was thereupon asked by the organizers to stand down. Behind this was not only Grayson's personal vanity and dislike of Hardie, but a notion shared by Hyndman, Grayson and to some extent Blatchford—who from the first had stood outside the Labour Representation Committee because he felt that an alliance with the trade unions meant a compromising of Socialist principles—that it might be possible to start a new Socialist Party. This they thought could be based upon the Clarion Fellowship and the Clarion Scouts, together with such members of the I.L.P. as could be attracted away from its ranks in this period of political—or, more correctly, propaganda—frustration.

The answer of the I.L.P. executive was to include in its report to the I.L.P. Conference at Edinburgh in 1909 a statement that it was not possible for it any longer to arrange meetings for Grayson. When the report came up before the conference, Grayson rose and proposed that this paragraph should be "referred back," that is, deleted. This was carried by 217 votes to 194. A majority of the conference was, it appeared, prepared to endorse Grayson's attitude even although it had just previously defeated by 378 votes to 8 a proposal that the I.L.P. should sever itself from the Labour Party, affirmed by 352 votes to 64 that no salary should be paid to Members of Parliament who refused to sign the Labour Party Constitution—which was one of the charges against Grayson—and had just re-elected Hardie to the National Executive by a huge majority, putting him, as always, at the top of the poll. This was an evidence of muddled inconsistency not unique in Party Conferences when personal issues arise.

Thereupon Hardie, MacDonald, Snowden and Bruce Glasier, taking the only course open to them to force the I.L.P. members to realize where their support of Grayson was leading, resigned in a body from the National Administrative Council of the I.L.P. They were not, they declared, willing to associate themselves with the growth of an impossibilist and disruptive spirit within the Party which threatened the whole consolidation of the working-class movement.

Immediately the conference, which had been swayed by emotion, not reason, in its support of Grayson, passed, with only ten dissentients, a resolution expressing its "emphatic endorsement" of the past policy of the National Administrative Council and its "emphatic confidence, personal and political," in Keir Hardie, MacDonald, Snowden and Bruce Glasier, and earnestly requesting them to withdraw their resignations.

This the four refused to do. They were determined to drive the lesson of the Grayson movement home to the I.L.P. branches to whom the delegates were required to report.

As they left the council it no doubt seemed to some of Grayson's supporters that he had won. In fact, his influence from that moment declined. At the General Election in 1910 he was defeated in the Colne Valley, although only by a narrow margin, and this defeat, combined with his own increasing irresponsibility, brought a sharp decline in his popularity in the country.

For a few years he made a precarious living as a paid speaker at public meetings, but it soon became evident even to himself that a career in British politics which had opened sensationally, and might, if he had been able to harness to his great gifts of oratory and his early idealism an ability to co-operate with others who sincerely sought the same ends, have been a magnificent one, was ended. With money subscribed by friends he sailed to Australia, hoping to make a new start in the Labour movement there. He failed to do so and moved to New Zealand, where he got into some sort of trouble. From this he extricated himself by enlisting in the New Zealand Forces on the outbreak of war.

He had lived hard and roisterously and shortly after being sent overseas to England broke down in health, was sent to a military hospital and eventually discharged. From hospital a few days before his discharge he wrote to a friend in Colne Valley asking if he could come and stay with him for a few weeks. Perhaps he had in mind some attempt to win his way back into political life. That will never be known. The friend wrote back saying that he would be delighted to have him. The train on which he was to arrive was met. He was not on it. From that day onwards no trace of him can be found.

When Philip Snowden became Labour candidate for Colne Valley he wrote, as he records in his autobiography, to the New Zealand authorities to try to trace him. He was informed that he had been in receipt of a war disability allowance, but that no reply had been received to a letter to his last known address, in December, 1920, asking him to appear for medical re-examination. His disability allowance had not been claimed and all subsequent inquiries had had no response.

He was then only thirty-eight, at what should have been the height of his political powers. In the country which only a few years earlier had rung with his name and where his appearance and speech had been known to many hundreds of thousands he disappeared from all public knowledge without a sign. What happened to him is one of the unsolved mysteries of our political life.

Given a little more stability and balance, a little more willingness to work with others, a little more readiness to reconcile the possible with the ideal, he might have been one of the Labour Party's great leaders and have played a noble part in the forward march of British socialism.

As it is he remains a legend—a legend of which he was himself the victim in his own political lifetime, but one which has warmed the imaginations of many and which has its importance in the record of the Labour Party because it expresses something permanent in its character. He was of the prophets and agitators and, although in his case prophecy changed too quickly to irresponsibility and agitation to indiscriminate denunciation and his great talents ran away into the sand of a personal tragedy, the prophets and agitators are a part of the history of socialism. They will always have their place within the ranks of a party which needs irritants as well as administrators, visionaries as well as statesmen, if it is to be true to the spirit within it.

Although the support for Grayson was an extreme example of the feeling of frustration which had come over the Party at this stage, others more important were conscious of the same *malaise*.

Keir Hardie himself suffered from it. He was not a success as parliamentary leader and he knew it. He, too, was of the prophets and agitators, although on an infinitely grander scale than Grayson. He had none of that accommodating spirit which is necessary in a party leader, who must enter into many discussions and arrangements with his opponents, and from the first he left most of this to Arthur Henderson, who was Chief Whip.

"Nature," he wrote, "never intended me to occupy an official position. I think I have shown you I can be a pioneer but I am not guided so much by a consideration of policy or by thinking out a long sequence of events as by intuition and inspiration." But it was not only that he was not personally adapted to the duties of parliamentary leadership—the *malaise* went deeper. He was deeply disturbed by what he regarded as the subservient position to the Liberals that the Labour Party seemed to be accepting—the more so as many of the trade-union members of the Party, who had never pretended to be Socialists and were only concerned to safeguard trade-union interests and secure a little mild social reform, seemed very well satisfied with this position.

Towards the end of 1907 he made it clear that he did not wish to seek nomination for a further term and, writing to Philip Snowden, expressed his disillusionment in the frankest terms.

"My strongest reason for desiring to get out of the Chair," he wrote, " is that I may be free to speak out occasionally. In the last session the Party has practically dropped out of public notice. The comic papers and the cartoonists are ignoring us—a fatal sign! The tendency evidently is to work in close and cordial harmony with the Government and if this policy be persisted in we shall lose our identity and be wiped out along with the Liberals and we should richly deserve our fate. By another session those of us in the Party who are Socialists and who believe in fighting will have to get together occasionally on our own account and if we cannot drag the Party with us we will 'gang oor ain gait.' "

On parliamentary ability the obvious successor to Hardie as leader was MacDonald. Not only had he done more than any man other than Hardie to build the Party in the first years of the Labour Representation Committee, but he had shown himself the most adroit and commanding of its parliamentary debaters and one, moreover, who could attract and inspire large audiences in the country. He had an ability and a presence which would have taken him quickly to the front rank in any party.

But he was not wholly popular with the trade-union group, who alternated between suspecting him of being too Socialist and of being not Labour enough. And he himself was suffering from something of the same *malaise* as Hardie, although not altogether for the same reasons. He found it increasingly difficult, he told his friends, to work with "class-conscious trade unionists," and wondered whether he and the other I.L.P. Socialists "should not cut the painter and seek refuge anywhere except in this distracted little whirlpool of conflicting eddies."

Nor were things going well with the Labour Party in the country. It fought a number of bye-elections, but had no success in any of them, polling in several important ones, indeed, many fewer votes than it had in the General Election.

It held special conferences on unemployment and old age pensions, but was unable to secure much practical remedy for the ills it attacked. And, economically, it was becoming clear that, despite the industrial achievements of the decade, despite some advances in social reform and despite the emergence of a political Labour Party, the position of the workers as a whole had not improved. Indeed, their share of the national wealth since the opening of the new century had, as Board of Trade statistics showed, declined.

Throughout this time there had been a steady increase in prices with the result that, in the first ten years of the century, the purchasing power of the pound dropped to only 17s. All over the country, while the rich had become richer, the poor had become poorer. Industrial capitalism was marching forward with giant strides, producing ever greater combinations of capital, driving the small man out of business in industry, in commerce and in shop-keeping; producing a new class of the industrially rich whose wealth, expenditure and high standard of life was the wonder of the world— but leaving the immense majority of the industrial workers worse off than before as they struggled to buy food and clothes and pay rents, all of which were becoming more expensive, out of wages that did not rise—or rose only by a tiny fraction.

Between the years 1900 and 1911 wages in the five principal industries, building, mining, engineering, textiles and agriculture, rose only by 0·31 per cent. But the London retail prices of food rose by 9·3 per cent.

When the Board of Trade published, in 1913, the results of an enquiry into the earnings of workpeople it was found that the highest recorded annual wage, that in the iron and steel industry, was only £82. In the cotton trade it was only £48, in wool £40, in the industries making biscuits, hosiery and paper £38, in the linen industry £29. Moreover, these were maximum wages obtained by the most highly organized workers. Although the average annual earnings in the building industry were £68, half the labourers employed were getting less than 25s. a week even when fully employed. In the cotton trade nearly a quarter of the workers were only earning 15s. a week and over sixty per cent of those in the woollen and worsted trades were at the same starvation level. The average wage of railway workers was 26s. a week, and even in the highly skilled engineering and shipbuilding industries forty per cent of the workers earned less than 30s. a week.

Facts like these, when compared with the rising profits of industry and the stories of wealth and extravagance among a few that the popular newspapers daily published for the pleasure and titillation of their readers, made Socialists. But they tended now to make Socialists who had lost faith in parliamentary action and who were beginning to think that a political Labour Party, although it might succeed in prodding the Liberals to provide meals for hungry school children or pensions of 5s. a week for those over seventy, could do nothing radically to alter and improve the state of society.

Men and women were being driven to think economically by the harsh impact of economic events upon their lives. They had voted for Free Trade—Free Trade had enabled the wealthy to grow still richer but had brought no improvement to the poor. They had returned a Labour Party which had secured legal freedom for the trade unions—but the constitutional progress of the trade unions had brought no amendment in the economic structure of society. They had voted for social reform and some social reform there had been, but the basic differences between rich and poor, between those who worked and those who took the profit, remained unaltered.

The idea of syndicalism, of revolutionary industrial action, grew and with it the number of strikes. But it was not only in its revolutionary context or even in its industrial context that the idea of direct action increased in popularity. There were many who began to feel that the obstacles that faced Labour in its desire to achieve a more just society were so deeply rooted in the economic system, and would prove so impervious to any kind of reform through political means—certainly political means of a kind any Liberal Government was likely to allow itself to be persuaded to adopt as a result of Labour parliamentary pressure—that those who wished to bring socialism into being would do better to concentrate their activities mainly on industrial and economic changes.

This movement found much of its intellectual content in the pages of the *New Age*, founded in 1907 and edited by a brilliant writer and editor, A. R. Orage, who later became an advocate of Social Credit as a means to solve economic ills. Orage gathered around him a team of brilliant and independently minded people who, for a time, greatly influenced the political attitude of many intellectual Socialists. In the columns of the *New Age*, G. D. H. Cole, S. G. Hobson, Arthur J. Penty and William Mellor expounded with great force and lucidity the idea of a Guild Socialism which should replace the political Socialist conception of national control and ownership of the principal instruments of production and distribution through parliamentary means, by the conception of an economic socialism or industrial democracy in which the trade unions themselves should be organized to make possible the management of industries by the workers.

Whether it took the form of syndicalism on a Continental and Marxian model, or on the British model of Guild Socialism in which great importance was given to the state as representing the consumers' interests and the remedy to the ills that beset the workers as producers was found in workers' control of industry, the tide of active Socialist and militant trade-union thought seemed to be turning increasingly against the belief in parliamentary action as the main instrument and in social reform as a means to socialism.

It was not, of course, entirely running in that direction. The Fabians, with their advocacy of social reform policies, were still active. In 1909, through the Minority Report to the Royal Commission on the Poor Laws delivered by Beatrice Webb and written by Sidney Webb, and through the National Campaign which they launched to arouse public support for the social security measures put forward in that report, Fabianism made a tremendous impact upon national thinking.

Moreover, the much milder Majority Report of the Royal Commission was itself so condemnatory of the existing Poor Law system and disclosed such extensive poverty and destitution that even those who tried to persuade themselves that the Minority Report was simply propaganda—and of this they could not very easily persuade themselves if they actually read it—were faced with sufficient to trouble the conscience of any honest man and persuade him that Britain in this golden age was still almost as much two nations as in the days when Disraeli coined the phrase.

It is true to say that the ferment of socialism was almost everywhere at work. To the iconoclastic masterpieces of Shaw there had now been added the imaginative humanitarian writing of H. G. Wells to scarify the conventions and prejudices of the middle-class and stir the minds of all who were ready to read and to work and to hope. In the I.L.P. branches, at the recently formed National Labour Colleges and in the lectures and discussions of the Workers' Educational Association, and up and down the length and breadth of the country in the examination of economic and political problems—the search for a solution went on.

The search took many forms, but at that moment it did not seem to take the form of adding strength to the Parliamentary Labour Party.

Perhaps of all the leaders of that small group only Arthur Henderson never faltered in his faith in the ultimate destiny of the Labour Party. To him there was only one possible instrument for the political advance of the workers, and only by political advance could the permanent economic and social betterment of the working-classes be secured and the workers be given their true share in the control of their own and the nation's destinies.

That instrument was, as Keir Hardie had seen many years

earlier, a Labour Party firmly based on an alliance between the trade unions and the Socialists and organized to secure a strong Labour representation in Parliament. Organized. That was the key word for Henderson. Without organization all hopes would run away into nothing but words.

The Party must be organized in the constituencies. With the financial backing of the trade unions and the devoted efforts of all those men and women in the constituencies who were ready—as so many of them had proved—to work without ceasing for the Labour cause, an organization could, he knew, be built incomparably more durable than that any other political party could establish.

But it must be organized. To that task he set himself with selfless devotion, and with his characteristic drive and resolution. In 1908 he accepted the post of successor to Hardie in the parliamentary leadership of the Party. But he had already made up his mind that the parliamentary leader should be MacDonald, and he set himself to persuade his fellow trade unionists that this was so. No personal ambition—although he was not, of course, without ambition—could stand in the way of what was best for the Labour Party. Organization was his job. The Labour Party, despite all the currents of opinion that were running against it, must survive and be given the means to climb to greater strength.

And then, in 1909, there came a new development which seemed for a time as though it might cut away all the foundations upon which the Labour Party so far had been established and upon which it could build for the future—the Osborne judgment.

CHAPTER VIII

LABOUR FACES A NEW CHALLENGE

BY THE Taff Vale judgment the Law Lords had sought—or so it seemed to the politically conscious members of the working-classes—to cripple the workers in their organization for economic ends.

With the Osborne judgment—or so it seemed to the politically conscious members of the working-classes—they sought to cripple the workers in their organization for political ends.

If the Taff Vale judgment had been maintained it would have become impossible for the workers to mobilize their economic power through the only means open to them, their trade unions. They would have been denied the right to make the one economic decision available to them, the decision to withhold their labour in order to force employers to accede to their legitimate demands.

By these means, or so it seemed to them, the ruling-classes had sought to destroy powers which had been accepted as legally belonging to the trade unions for thirty years and the right to exercise which had been the culmination of a struggle going back through the centuries. That attempt had been defeated only because of the political power of the trade unions—a political power made effective in part through pledges extracted from Liberal candidates but primarily through the instrument of the Labour Party. It was this alone which had provided them with the means effectively to state their case in Parliament and get the sort of bill they needed passed into law.

Now, through the Osborne judgment an endeavour was being made to destroy this political power—a political power which had previously been exercised unchallenged for nearly fifty years by many trade unions and was only now challenged because with the formation of the Labour Party it seemed likely at last to find an effective instrument.

The Osborne case thus raised issues of the most fundamental

kind and issues which confronted the organized working-classes with questions of a far-reaching character—questions to which in the opinion of some only a revolutionary answer could be given. At the time and in the context in which the judgment was given it provided not only a severe threat to the political power of the trade unions, but a test of the democratic and constitutional attitude of the workers.

It is in the response to that test and to the general feeling of political frustration which for various reasons coincided with it that the real significance of the Osborne judgment in the history of the Labour Party is to be found.

Although the judgment of the Lords was not given until 21 December, 1909, the Osborne case began eighteen months earlier, in July, 1908. Once again, as in the Taff Vale case, the union involved was the Amalgamated Society of Railway Servants. But on this occasion the case against them was taken not by an employer but by one of their own members, W. V. Osborne.

Osborne, whose name was shortly to echo like a thunderclap throughout the working-class movement and who has secured a permanent place in history, was a foreman porter at Clapham Junction. He had previously enjoyed only such local and restricted fame as came to him from his position as Secretary of the Walthamstow Branch of the Amalgamated Society of Railway Servants. He was a member of the Liberal Party and as such he objected to the funds of his union being used to assist the promotion of parliamentary candidates pledged, if returned, to accept the constitution of the Labour Party and be subject to its whip. His views were not altered by the fact that a very large majority of his fellow members had voted in favour of the society using funds for exactly that purpose. He refused to abide by the majority decision.

He was not fighting an individual battle. He had strong financial backing from interests opposed to the Labour Party. Means were found for him to fight the case right through to the House of Lords. The case was indeed a test case in which political and anti-Labour interests were heavily involved. So far as Osborne himself was concerned, however, it was a genuine and legitimate matter of principle that was at stake. He was a Liberal as well as a trade unionist and he saw no reason why as a trade unionist he should be committed by a majority decision of his union to giving financial support to a political party of which he did not approve.

He was not prepared to accept the trade-union view that political action was an extension of industrial action and that, just as a majority decision must be accepted in the one case, so it must in the other.

This was not the first occasion on which such an issue had arisen. It had arisen previously in 1905, when the Canning Town Lodge of the Plumbers' Society objected to any part of their trade-union dues being used for political purposes on the grounds that the purpose of the union should be industrial only. They lodged an action against the executive of the society. This action was later withdrawn, but, in order to clarify the position, legal advice was then taken by the leaders of the trade-union and Labour movement. They were advised by two eminent lawyers, Sir Edward Clarke and Sir Robert Reid, that parliamentary representation came within the scope of legal trade-union activity. The Chief Registrar of Friendly Societies confirmed this view.

In the Annual Report of the Executive of the Labour Representation Committee to the 1906 Conference, the result of these discussions was given for the guidance of trade unions. They were informed that the Chief Registrar had accepted rules providing for a levy for Labour representation purposes and for payment to the Labour Representation Committee in considering the drafting of a proposed constitution for the Railway Clerks, but that trade unions proposing to make compulsory levies should in the first place pass a rule giving them power to do so. Societies not making a special parliamentary levy could quite properly, it was stated, make payments to the Labour Party out of their general funds.

A model rule sanctioned by the Chief Registrar was included as an appendix to this report for the guidance of trade unions. This contained a clause which set out as among the methods adopted by a Society to further the objects for which it was established: "The securing, or assisting in securing, of legislation for the protection of its trade interests and for the general and material welfare of its members." The position seemed clear: there was no legal obstacle in the way of a trade union taking what political action the majority of its members considered desirable.

176

This, it should be added, merely confirmed what had been accepted trade-union practice for a great number of years—at least since 1894. Many trade unions—notably the miners'—had for a considerable time used funds either to promote their own parliamentary candidates and maintain them when in Parliament or to support Lib-Lab candidates. So long as the candidates financed by trade unions allied themselves to one of the traditional parties there had been no serious objection from anyone. It was only now when trade unions had moved forward from that position to membership of, and financial support for, an independent Labour Party that protests about the illegal and unconstitutional use of trade-union funds to promote the cause of the workers politically as well as industrially began to be heard.

The advice given by Sir Edward Clarke and Sir Robert Reid and the ruling of the Chief Registrar were confirmed by a court decision in 1907, when an action was taken against the South Wales Miners' Federation by one of its members named Steele who objected to contributing to the union's parliamentary fund. His lawyers based their case on the argument that legally a trade union could only undertake acts specified as appropriate to its functions in the Trade Union Acts of 1871 and 1876, and these did not include the promotion of parliamentary candidates. Mr. Justice Darling and Mr. Justice Phillimore, however, gave judgment against this view. They held that the definition of a trade union and its functions in these acts was not intended to be exhaustive or to prevent a trade union from acts not there specified. The position seemed clear. A rapidly increasing number of trade unions affiliated to the Labour Party—in every case on the instructions of a majority of their members.

In July, 1908, however, Mr. Osborne, the Liberal foreman porter of Clapham Junction, entered the lists—the occasion being an alteration in the rules of the Amalgamated Society of Railway Servants requiring candidates sponsored and financed by it to accept the constitution of the Labour Party. In the first engagement he fared no better in his attempt to stop political activities by the union of which he was a member than had Steele in his case against the South Wales Miners' Federation.

Mr. Justice Neville, before whom the case came, considered

himself bound by the earlier decision made by Mr. Justice Darling and Mr. Justice Phillimore. He added that, given the right of trade unions to spend their money in promoting their interests in the House of Commons, how they did so was purely a question of policy with which the Courts could not concern themselves. Osborne's action against the Amalgamated Society of Railway Servants was, therefore, dismissed with costs against him.

The political interests supporting Osborne were, however, determined to carry the matter further. They appealed and the Court of Appeal found in his favour. It did so partly on a legal interpretation of the provisions of the Trade Union Acts of 1871 and 1876 different from that of Mr. Justice Darling and Mr. Justice Phillimore, and partly on the argument that the Trade Disputes Act of 1906 must also be taken into account since it had altered the situation. It went, however, even further than this. Lord Justice Fletcher Moulton, in assenting to the view of the Master of the Rolls, who presided, expressed the opinion that the object of the Parliamentary Fund of the Society was to secure the return of M.P.s pledged to vote in a prescribed manner and that this was contrary to public policy.

The statement that trade-union assistance for candidates pledged to support their own political party, the Labour Party, was "contrary to public policy" helped to convince politically active trade unionists that the real basis of the attack against them was a party one.

The Amalgamated Society of Railway Servants took the case to the House of Lords. And on 21 December, 1909, the House of Lords confirmed the ruling of the Appeal Court. It did so, moreover, in terms which added greatly to the suspicion of trade unionists and Labour men and women that this was, in fact, a political attack on the Labour Party and not simply a matter of legal interpretation of the Trade Union Acts.

Thus Lord Halsbury, a leading Conservative lawyer, stated flatly, but not very precisely, that a union only existed as a legalized combination within the limits of the statute, "whatever those limits are," and that the collection of political contributions "is to my mind manifestly beyond the powers possessed by a trade union." Lord James of Hereford, while he found no legal bar in the Trade

Union Acts to the provision of a fund by a trade union to meet the expenses of a parliamentary member, held that a rule requiring such a member to accept the Labour Whip was "unconstitutional."

Lord Shaw of Dunfermline, acquiescing in this view, said he was not clear in his mind that payment to members of Parliament was *ultra vires*, but said that the requirement that a trade-union member should conform to the decisions and policies of the Labour Party was not "compatible either with the spirit of our parliamentary constitution or with that independence and freedom which has hitherto been held to lie at the basis of the representative government of the United Kingdom."

To most politically active trade unionists this seemed simply to mean that the Law Lords were ready to defend the political independence and freedom of trade unionists to take political action so long as that action followed courses of which the ruling classes of the day approved, but declared it unconstitutional and against the public interests so soon as it took a course of which they did not approve and which might lead to the development of a working-class party which would threaten their domination.

At the Trades Union Congress, James Haslam, M.P., the president, pointed out that from 1894 onwards the funds of trade unions had been used to return and pay members of Parliament and that even those who had taken action against the Railway Servants had for years been content to pay for political representation and had taken no action of any kind until the Labour Party was formed. He made it clear that in no case had any trade union embarked upon political representation without taking a ballot vote of its members and that five to one of the railway workers had been in favour of such a course.

At a special conference, called by the Joint Board of the T.U.C. and the Labour Party, Keir Hardie declared that the whole right of the common people to pay for their own Party was the issue they were fighting.

"If the Labour members were being paid by brewers or landowners, or railway directors, or financiers, to represent their interests in the House of Commons," he said, "no objection would have been taken. It is only because they are being paid to represent an interest which is dangerous to all the other interests that the issue is being forced upon us."

And in its report to the 1910 Annual Conference the executive of the Labour Party completely expressed Labour feeling when it accused the judges of political prejudice and said that judges who from the bench had stated that, in asking its members to work together as a party, the Labour Party was doing something contrary to sound public policy, had themselves been, when members of the House of Commons, "the most faithful and docile servants of their Party Whips who in their parliamentary actions daily violated the principles which they put in operation against the Labour Party from the bench."

The full extent of the blow to the trade unions moreover became even clearer when legal advice was taken as to its implications. It was then found that it could be held to make illegal, not merely parliamentary action by the trade unions, but even support for candidates in municipal elections; that it was not only financial aid for candidates that was *ultra vires*, but any political action of any kind, including, it might well be, the sending of a deputation to a Minister, the discussion of political matters at the Trades Union Congress, participation in local trades councils and a great deal of the educational work on which many trade unions had embarked.

It was indeed an attack upon the trade unions ultimately even more serious and of much wider implications, as Keir Hardie pointed out, than that of the Taff Vale decision. Certainly so long as the law, as now interpreted, remained unaltered, all that long effort to secure the alliance of trade unions and Socialists in a Labour Party that would make possible the constitutional advance of the working-classes and the achievement by lawful and parliamentary means of the ideal of a more just society appeared doomed.

Hard on the heels of the Osborne judgment, legal actions were taken against twenty-two trade unions and injunctions issued against them forbidding them to continue a practice which some of them had been carrying on for over forty years. Twenty of the Labour and trade-union Members of Parliament were affected. This was a beginning. It was difficult to see where the consequences would end.

This threat to the whole future of the Party came at the very moment when organizationally, at any rate, it had reached a record strength. Before the Osborne judgment its membership was 1,486,000. More than 170 trade unions and 155 trades councils and local Labour parties were affiliated to it. Following the Osborne judgment the membership dropped by 56,000 and the number of affiliated trade unions by twenty-one. Moreover, in the first of the two general elections of 1910, forced on the country by the rejection of the Lloyd George Budget of 1909 by the House of Lords, the Labour Party, although now reinforced by the affiliation of the Miners' Federation, lost eight of the seats formerly held by Labour and miners' members. It succeeded, this time, in winning three new ones, but even so its net loss was five. It thus returned with a total strength of forty, of whom seventeen were miners.

This reduction in its strength was, it is true, only partly due to the effects of the Osborne judgment, although the financial effects of that were severe. It was even more due to the fact that the whole election was overshadowed by the Budget crisis in which the Labour Party inevitably appeared merely as the junior partner of the Liberals. Nor were its losses anything like so heavy as those of the Liberals themselves. They lost 124 seats. As for the Lib-Labs, they shrank from twenty-four to seven.

Nevertheless the rising tide of Labour—as it had seemed in 1906—had been halted. It was clear to its leaders that if the Party was to be able to march forward the law as interpreted in the Osborne decision must be changed.

In this determination they were, however, by no means entirely supported by the whole of the Socialist and working-class movement. For, although it might have been anticipated that the whole Labour movement would react unanimously to the Osborne decision as it had to the Taff Vale judgment, this was not the case.

On the contrary, the Osborne judgment fanned the flames of two strong and divergent movements. Both of these were opposed for different reasons to the federation of the trade unions and Socialist societies in a parliamentary alliance—which was the basis of the Labour Party. Coming at the moment when it did, the Osborne decision confronted the infant Party, not merely with the threat of frustration by a legal process, but by disruption from within. It threatened to destroy the foundations of the Labour Party as laid in 1900 because it gave support to, and in part confirmed, movements within the Socialist and working-class movement which were in any event antagonistic to the Labour Party.

On the one hand there were Socialists who regarded the Osborne decision as a blessing in disguise because its result might be to free them from what they regarded as the impediment of the reformist trade unions. On the other hand there were powerful elements within the trade unions who regarded it as a confirmation of their belief that no real working-class progress could be secured by parliamentary means and that direct industrial action was the weapon that should be used. To both these groups, but particularly to the second, the Osborne judgment was a weapon almost as valuable as it was to the Liberals and Conservatives who were fighting the Labour Party for quite other reasons.

The Socialists who supported the first view and whose attitude had been previously expressed in their response to the disruptive appeal of Victor Grayson had come to believe that the original decision to federate politically with the trade unions was a tragic mistake—an obstacle to socialism, not an aid to it. The subservient position of the Labour Party—as they saw it—to the Liberals in the House of Commons; its seeming willingness to act, in the main, as an ally and junior partner of a mildly reformist Liberal Government which rejected any alteration in the basic structure of society —these they saw as due to the numerical and financial domination of the Labour Party by the trade unions. The trade unions were, they considered, still Liberal and reformist at heart and unwilling to allow the new Party to adopt a genuine Socialist policy.

They argued, therefore, that if the Osborne judgment drove the trade unions out of the Labour Party that would in the end be all to the good. Shorn of its reformist fat a new Labour Party would at last have a chance to arise—a Labour Party that would also be a Socialist Party drawing its strength not from the support—at the best passive and at the worst unwilling—of hundreds of thousands of trade unionists who were just as frightened as their masters of a truly Socialist policy, but from convinced and passionate individual Socialists in the constituencies. To them the Osborne judgment gave a chance for a new start. In it the "ruling classes" had shown their hand and their real hatred of working-class political power. The longer it remained effective and the clearer this hatred became, the greater would be the chance of building a genuine Labour Party.

This attitude was a sufficiently serious challenge to the conception of the Labour Party for which Keir Hardie had originally worked and for which MacDonald, Henderson and the other leaders were working now. But an even more serious threat came from syndicalist groups in the trade-union movement—more serious because it represented an attack, not merely on the alleged failure of the Labour Party, from whatever cause, to follow a sufficiently Socialist policy in Parliament, but upon the whole idea of a democratic and constitutional advance to socialism by the exercise of political power in Parliament.

To these groups the moral of the Osborne case, one that they used every means to impress on the workers, was that there was no hope of any advance by parliamentary means. Any such advance would, they declared, always be thwarted by those in power. If other means failed they would always use the judges to serve their purpose as they had done in this case and so often in the past. The workers must recognize that the whole political and legal system was their enemy. They must abandon political and parliamentary methods, which were inevitably doomed to failure and which merely led to a dissipation of working-class strength. They must turn to the surer weapon of industrial action.

This attitude, strikingly parallel in many ways to that which followed the political disillusionment of the workers after the first Reform Act, found its direct expression in widespread strikes throughout 1910 and 1911 involving transport workers, dockers and railwaymen. All these strikes, although they arose from economic causes and particularly from the failure of wages to keep pace with rising prices, were given a political direction.

This political direction was based philosophically on the belief that producers' control over all production and distribution was the correct, indeed the only, way to socialism. The instrument to achieve this was considered to be the general strike, which would bring the trade and industry of the nation to a standstill and thus enable the workers, without whom production and distribution were impossible, to step in and take charge.

It derived partly from ideas which were at work within the

French *syndicats*, or trade unions, and partly from the methods adopted by, indeed almost forced by circumstances upon, militant groups within the American trade-union movement who were fighting employers of a much more ruthless and less constitutionally minded kind than British employers, in conditions which favoured violence on both sides without any check by public opinion. They were the methods of the I.W.W., the famous "Industrial Workers of the World."

The principles that inspired the Industrial Workers of the World, and through them the British syndicalists and their principal leader, Tom Mann, were drafted by the intellectual leader of the American Labour movement, Daniel de Leon, a university lecturer and Marxist who had been convinced by a study of American politics at their most corrupt that advancement for the workers through political means was impossible.

He held that there was no common ground of any kind between the working-class and the employing-class, but that they were and must always be implacable and bitter enemies. The struggle between the two must, therefore, go on until the workers were able through their economic organization to take hold of what they produced and control it in their own interests, thus abolishing the whole employing class. The means to this end lay in industrial action free from alliance with any political party. This could, de Leon believed, only be achieved by the development of labour unions embracing, not simply the workers in one craft, but the whole of the workers in one industry. They would then be in a position to confront the new concentrations of industrial capital with a strength equal to their own. When they struck they would bring a whole industry to a standstill—or, if they acted together in the general strike, all industry. Parliamentary action of any kind by the workers stood, in the I.W.W. view, in the way of such a concentration of labour power. It led to compromises with the political parties of the employing interests and served merely to strengthen the State as the political instrument of the capitalists.

These ideas converged in Britain with the somewhat more theoretical and philosophical conception of syndicalism held by a combined group of French Marxists and anarchists who were active in the *Confédération Générale du Travail*. They were adopted by the Scottish Socialist Labour Party (a small secessionist body from the Social Democratic Federation) and rapidly spread through the trade-union movement, particularly among the transport workers and miners. They provided the main impetus behind the formation of the Plebs League, out of which the National Council of Labour Colleges and with it a widespread system of workers' education from a generally Marxist standpoint came into being. And they found their most vigorous exponent in Tom Mann—one-time leader with John Burns and Ben Tillett of the London dock strike, and like them a powerful open-air orator and leader of crowds.

Mann, like many other men of great talent in aggressive popular leadership, found it difficult to co-operate with anyone for long. He had at first been a member of the S.D.F. Then he moved over to the I.L.P., and for a time became its secretary. He grew disappointed with the I.L.P. and emigrated to Australia, where the I.W.W. influence was strong. He returned to England in 1910. He at once found the mood of many of the industrial workers, embittered by economic distress and disillusioned by the results so far of political action, exactly suited to the ideas he had brought back with him—ideas reinforced by a visit to Paris and talks with leaders of the C.G.T.

The syndicalist movement under his vigorous leadership spread rapidly, taking hold particularly in the coalfields. By November, 1910, it was in a position to hold a conference in Manchester at which sixty thousand workers were represented. Its total strength and influence was much greater than this. A monthly journal, *The Syndicalist*, was launched and a great number of pamphlets and fly-sheets issued. Every effort to promote industrial strife and persuade the workers to refuse the advice of their established trade-union leaders was taken.

With the syndicalist anti-parliamentary threat on one flank, the anti-trade-union Socialist threat on the other, and the Osborne judgment threat facing it ahead, the Labour Party thus moved into difficult and narrow waters in which many hoped to see it wrecked.

Its position was not made easier by a parliamentary situation which forced it to accept an even closer appearance of alliance with the Liberal Government. In the first general election of 1910 the Liberal strength had been reduced from 399 to 275 and the Conservative strength increased from 158 to 273. This meant that the Liberal Government was now dependent for its majority upon Labour and Irish Nationalist votes. Theoretically, this increased the power of the Labour Party to influence Liberal policy and to force a revision of the law as revealed in the Osborne judgment. But, in fact, the session following the election was inevitably dominated by two great issues, the Budget clash with the Lords and Home Rule for Ireland. On neither of these could the Labour Party, without ruining itself in the country, take the risk of turning out a Liberal Government. Nor did it wish to do so. On both of them it was wholeheartedly on the side of the Liberals against the Tories and was entirely committed by its public declarations to the Liberal side.

Nor could it in any event, as the Liberal Government well knew, contemplate a Liberal defeat on any issue when the only alternative was a Conservative Government, to which it was infinitely more opposed. The position of political arbiter which it theoretically enjoyed was, in fact, therefore much more like that of a prisoner who dare not escape from his prison because of the greater perils outside. Moreover, although the strength of the Parliamentary Labour Party was nominally forty, seventeen of these were miners' M.P.s, of whom a fair number, although they had become Labour in name when the Miners' Federation affiliated, had remained in fact what they always had been, reformist Liberals who were quite satisfied with the Liberal Party's general approach to political and social questions.

As for the Liberal Government, it was preoccupied with the constitutional struggle resulting from the Lords' rejection of the Lloyd George Budget and with the search for means permanently to curb the power of the Lords to veto House of Commons legislation. It was unwilling, in such circumstances, to give time to the social reform measures desired by Labour. Still less was it ready to throw into the political arena a controversial bill to restore to the trade unions their political freedom of action.

In their concentration on the constitutional issue at this time the Liberals were, of course, right. Unless the power possessed by the Lords and used by them in dealing with the Lloyd George Budget were curbed no progressive government could ever have any hope of carrying out its programme. For progressives that was the first issue to settle, far exceeding in importance even that created by the Osborne judgment. But it did not help the Labour Party to meet the criticism from both Socialists and Syndicalists that its existence made practically no difference to the political scene.

In April, 1910, the Liberal Government introduced a Parliament Bill designed to curb the Lords' powers. The proposals it embodied were that the Lords should henceforward have no power to reject money bills, that in the case of all other bills the veto power of the Lords should be reduced to one of delay so that if a bill were passed by the House of Commons in three successive sessions it should become law even if rejected by the Lords, and that the life of any Parliament should be restricted to five years. If this bill was to become law it was necessary, however, to find means to overcome the resistance of the Lords to it.

To this end Mr. Asquith sought from the King a promise that he would exercise his prerogative and create a sufficient number of new peers to pass the Parliament Bill through the House of Lords. Before he could give his decision the King died. Conferences between the Liberals and the Conservatives followed to see if any compromise solution could be found. The Labour Party was not invited to participate in these conferences—thus further emphasizing the small importance attached to its views by the two major parties—and apparently made no effort to be included. These conferences, after dragging on for some time, failed, and the new King, George V, then gave Asquith an undertaking to create, if necessary, sufficient Liberal Peers to carry the Parliament Bill through the Lords, but only if the mandate for such a change in the Lords' powers were renewed at a fresh general election. A new election, the second in twelve months, was then held in December, 1910.

Financially crippled by the Osborne judgment, and under heavy attack from many of the most vocal in the ranks of its own movement, the Labour Party entered this election under grave handicaps. Yet it held and indeed slightly improved its position, returning with a strength of forty-two as against forty before the election— one of the new members being George Lansbury.

It did so, however, in circumstances which tended to increase rather than decrease its dependence upon the Liberals. Of the forty-two members returned, twenty-seven owed their success in large part to the fact that no Liberal candidate had been put up against them, so that they had been able to command Liberal as well as Labour votes in their constituencies. Of the remaining fifteen, eleven, including such leaders as Keir Hardie, MacDonald and Snowden, had been elected in two-member constituencies, with a Liberal as the other member. They, too, had enjoyed the support of Liberal voters.

While, no doubt, it was equally the case that many Liberals had been returned with the help of Labour votes, it was manifest that the Parliamentary Labour Party depended upon Liberal support to a much greater degree than was healthy for a party whose primary reason for existence had been the need to break free of the old Lib-Lab tradition as the first step to the achievement of the true aims of Labour.

Ten years after the historic meeting in the Memorial Hall, when the decision had been taken to form a Socialist and trade-union alliance, that alliance had only succeeded in creating a parliamentary party half the size of the Irish Nationalist group, and one which, in practice, was hardly more free of Liberal influence than the old trade-union Lib-Lab group had been. Moreover, its power of independent action was even more restricted after the December election than before. The Liberal Government had now only 270 members as against the Conservatives' 293 and was, therefore, absolutely dependent upon Labour and Irish Nationalist votes to keep it in office. But kept in office it must be to carry through the constitutional change so badly required. Nor, even apart from this, dare Labour take any independent action to imperil the Government's position, for to do so would be to force another general election which it was in no position to fight, and bring with it the risk of the return of the Conservatives to power.

No wonder that, to many of those, including Keir Hardie himself, who had worked with such vigour and such hope for the establishment of an independent party, the reality now seemed much less inspiring than the dream had been.

The Labour Party was faced ten years after its birth with its greatest enemy; the one that alone could destroy it—the frustration and disillusionment of its own supporters.

CHAPTER IX

YEARS OF UNREST

THE disillusionment with political action that ran throughout so much of the Labour and trade-union movement in 1910 did not lift with the arrival of a new year and a new Parliament. It lasted right up to August, 1914, when the coming of the First World War threw new and more tremendous problems on to the scales.

The factors which combined to produce this disillusionment are clear. Yet, looking back, it seems in many ways altogether ironic and unjustified that it should have existed. For this was a period of great success for many of the radical policies for which the Labour movement had so long fought, if not for the Labour Party itself.

The Parliament Act, in which Labour's interests were, on any true assessment of the balance of political power in the country and the forces standing in the way of reform, no less involved than those of the Liberals, became law in 1911. Almost simultaneously a demand that had been part of Labour's case from the earliest days and had been one of the six points of the Charter—the payment of members—was accepted. A salary of £400 a year for M.P.s was agreed and became law. Henceforward the principle which had previously made parliamentary membership a preserve of the rich or the middle-class was abandoned. One of the long-standing barriers to working-class representation was removed.

Hard on the heels of this came two great measures of social reform, the National Health and the Unemployment Insurance Acts. In the same session there was a Shops Act which, although it did not go so far as Labour wished, did for the first time guarantee the shop assistant regular mealtimes and a weekly half-holiday.

And, finally, after many negotiations and much preliminary disappointment, the Trade Union Act of 1913 was passed. This

Act, although it did not completely restore the position that existed before the Osborne judgment, provided a framework within which political action by the trade unions could be carried out effectively and has in fact been carried out since. Under it any trade union was empowered to embark upon political activities if on a ballot vote being taken a majority of its members agreed and if it thereupon drew up a set of political rules which were approved by the Chief Registrar of Friendly Societies. Political activities had, however, to be financed out of a special political fund, and those members of a union who wished to do so had the right to contract out of payment to this fund—that is, they had the right to claim exemption from the political levy while remaining full members of the union in every other respect. This clause was opposed by the trade unions, but, as experience soon showed, it gave trade unions' political activity a legal foundation that was both workable and no longer subject to dispute. The alliance which had created the Labour Party was safeguarded.

Looking back, we can see this period as a time of reforming legislation of a character which basically altered the balance of political power in Britain. It opened the door for the subsequent advance of Labour and established the foundation of much of the social security legislation of today. Moreover, it was carried through by a parliament in which the progressive majority was very small. If we exclude the Irish Nationalists who, although they supported the Liberals in most issues, were primarily interested only in Home Rule for Ireland and were neither much concerned with nor represented British opinion on domestic issues, the combined Liberal and Labour majority over the Conservatives was only thirty-nine. The balance of progressive political opinion within Parliament and the country was thus quite tiny. It had been reduced at each of the elections since 1906.

The record of advance in such circumstances was a remarkable one. It might well have justified both some Labour satisfaction for the part it had been able to play in making so much progress possible and also have provided a not unsatisfactory confirmation of its belief in the feasibility of reform through parliamentary action.

The Fabian thesis, that the awakened social conscience of the middle-classes when combined with the greater political awareness of the working-class could create a situation in which the permeation of all parties with social reform and even Socialist ideas would produce immediate practical results, appeared to be justified. Moreover, even although the Labour Party had been forced into the position of a junior partner to the Liberals, its leaders could nevertheless claim with some justice that the very existence of a Labour Party had served to stimulate Liberal interest in social reform and strengthen the radical group in that Party and that Labour in Parliament had been able to exercise an effective voice in much legislation, notably that concerned with the payment of members and the Trade Union Act.

If the whole field of social legislation in the eight years from the emergence of Labour as an organized Parliamentary Party in 1906 to the outbreak of war in 1914 is reviewed the advance appears even more striking. To those measures already mentioned there must be added the Trade Boards Act, which had immeasurable effects in improving wages and conditions in the sweated industries, a Miners' Minimum Wage Act, the Acts establishing Labour Exchanges, the Old Age Pensions Act, the Act under which local authorities were given power to provide school meals, and the Lloyd George Budget, which for the first time taxed land values.

And all this had been accomplished in the face of delaying and wrecking tactics by the House of Lords which might well have made genuine progress impossible. To no small extent the social face of Britain had been changed in these years. Steps had been taken, moreover, which were to make possible even more substantial advances in the future.

Yet instead of triumph there was disillusionment; instead of elation a feeling that the Labour Party had altogether failed to live up to the high hopes which had been centred upon it. It is important to ask why, for, although some of the causes of this disillusionment were peculiar to the time and were due to special circumstances, others resulted from attitudes and conflicts within the Labour movement which were again and again to have a part in its history.

There was, of course, the fact, inevitable in the parliamentary circumstances, that Labour was overshadowed by the Liberals and was thus frequently in the position of appearing simply to endorse their proposals. From the purely party point of view it would have been much better for Labour if it had first reached parliamentary status in a period when it could have made itself the spearhead of an attack upon a reactionary government rather than the camp follower of a progressive one. That astute politician Lloyd George, who had recognized more than most the potential significance of Labour's success in 1906, and who, although he was later to be the chief instrument of liberalism's disruption, was at that time the chief hope of its radical wing, was well aware of this fact. In his promotion of social reform measures he always had, in addition to a genuine desire for social improvement, one eye upon dishing the Socialists.

Moreover, most of these social reform measures, while they went sufficiently far to make Labour's parliamentary support for them obligatory against Tory attacks, went insufficiently far to meet all the demands of the Labour rank and file. As a result the Labour Party got little credit for what was achieved and much criticism for failing to achieve more. On some of the most important social reform proposals there was, in addition, a strongly divided opinion within the Parliamentary Party itself. This was particularly the case with the National Health Insurance Bill.

This bill, which aroused the massed opposition of the Insurance Companies, the Friendly Societies, the doctors and the ladies of Mayfair who swore that never would they lick stamps for Lloyd George, was welcomed by Labour as a recognition that the State had an obligation to concern itself with the problems of sickness and disablement. But the fact that the scheme was based on a contributory system split the Labour Party. MacDonald and most of the trade-union members supported it, partly because of the belief that the contributory principle was valuable in itself, partly because of the trade-union interest in the administration of the scheme— for they as well as the Friendly Societies and Insurance Societies were invited to participate in running it and could look both to financial benefit and some access of new members as a result. Keir Hardie, Philip Snowden, George Lansbury, F. W. Jowett and Will Thorne opposed it. To them the contributory principle meant that contributions were to be exacted from workers to finance social reform schemes the cost of which ought to be borne by the community as a whole. The Fabian Society also opposed the bill, and campaigned against it in the country because the principles it embodied were contrary to those of the famous Minority Report of the Poor Law Commission which Mrs. Webb and George Lansbury had signed and which Sidney Webb had drafted.

Thus on one of the crucial social reform issues of the day the Labour Party was at sixes and sevens.

It was scarcely more united on the issue of women's suffrage. Here again there was agreement on principle but strong disagreement on methods—a disagreement whose consequences were all the more damaging because of the close alliance between Labour and the women's suffrage movement in its beginning. The women's suffrage movement owed much of its vigour to the activities of the women textile workers of Lancashire and Yorkshire. When called upon to contribute to the political funds of their unions in order to make possible an independent Labour Party they said to themselves with natural logic that what was sauce for the gander was also sauce for the goose. If political representation was necessary for men trade unionists, so was it for women trade unionists. Under their influence the I.L.P. put women's suffrage in the forefront of its programme. Mrs. Pankhurst, later the leader of the militant suffragettes, was for many years a member of the National Council of the I.L.P. Her husband had been a Socialist candidate in 1895.

But a conflict of view as to the steps by which women's suffrage should be secured began to show itself within the Labour Party at an early stage. It manifested itself first at the annual conference in 1905. A resolution endorsing a Women's Enfranchisement Bill, which aimed at giving women identical voting rights with men, was defeated on the grounds that a bill which sought merely to abolish sex disqualification would simply give votes to upper- and middle-class women so long as the political register remained as it was. Although, in fact, many working-class women would have been enfranchised by such a bill, it was argued that a reform of this character would simply increase the political power of the propertied and anti-Labour class and should be opposed. Complete adult suffrage both for men and women was the only reform which merited Labour support.

This remained the majority view of the Labour Party for many years. It was strengthened by the fact that as the suffragette campaign developed Mrs. Pankhurst and her band of militants drew very largely for their strength upon middle- and upper-class women.

Keir Hardie, who felt deeply on the injustice to women as he did on all injustice, was opposed to the majority view. So was Philip Snowden. George Lansbury went even farther.

Keir Hardie and Snowden were bitterly opposed to the excesses sponsored by the suffragettes, but Lansbury was ready to go with them all the way and was himself sentenced to three months' imprisonment for a speech at a suffragette meeting in the Albert Hall after being charged with incitement to violence under an Act of Edward III for "the apprehension of pillors, barrators and wandering robbers."

In 1912, Mrs. Pankhurst and her followers put forward a demand that Labour M.P.s should vote against the Government on every question whatever the issue involved until they were either driven from office or compelled to give women the vote. This was so extravagant a claim and would so completely have frustrated any influence that Labour could bring to bear on political events that it was at once rejected by all save Lansbury. He, however, circulated all the affiliated branches of the Labour movement asking them to endorse Mrs. Pankhurst's policy. When his action was repudiated both by the executive of the Labour Party and the council of the I.L.P., of which he was a member, he resigned his parliamentary seat for Bow and Bromley and fought a bye-election. Public opinion had by that time been bitterly antagonized by some of the militant suffragettes' actions and he was badly beaten.

Although Lansbury carried his support of the militant suffragettes farther than most, he was not alone in his sympathies. Hardie shared them. So much so, indeed, that when the annual conference voted by a large majority against support for any limited measure of female enfranchisement and authorized its parliamentary representatives to give support only to a comprehensive measure of adult suffrage, he at once announced that if this was intended to limit the action of the Party in the House of Commons he would have seriously to consider whether he should remain a member of the Parliamentary Party which he had done more than any other man to create. At a time when the majority both of the Labour Party executive and the I.L.P. council, together with the most prominent women in the Labour movement, such as Mrs. MacDonald, Margaret Bondfield, Mary Macarthur and Marion Phillips, were fighting militancy with all their power—seeing with complete clarity the threat to the whole democratic process contained in it—he sent a telegram of sympathy to militant suffragettes in prison. And this he did at the very moment when he had been re-elected leader of the Parliamentary Party which had taken its stand against the tactics of Mrs. Pankhurst and her followers.

Thus on two of the great issues of the day—National Health Insurance and Women's Suffrage—the Labour Party appeared before the public with a divided mind. Both were issues in which every division of opinion was magnified under the piercing light of acute public controversy, both were questions on which it was felt by many thousands of people that a Labour Party of all parties should have a definite policy to which all its members—or, at the very least, all its parliamentary leaders—could subscribe. Not to have one seemed to suggest a lamentable inability to offer firm leadership on great issues to the country.

Such divisions and their effect on the prestige of a party, which was in any event so small that any division within it seemed significant, were sufficiently serious.

But the *malaise* from which the Party suffered and which accounted for its failure to maintain the upward surge which had electrified the country in 1906, or indeed to win a single bye-election between the general election of December, 1910, and the outbreak of war, had much deeper roots.

In 1906 Labour and miners' M.P.s together accounted for a House of Commons total of forty-two and the sudden emergence of the Labour Party had everywhere been regarded as a portent of vast significance. By 1914 the total number of Labour M.P.s, including the miners', had fallen to thirty-eight. Not only did the Party fail to win any bye-elections between December, 1910, and the outbreak of war, it actually lost four of the seats it had held. Instead of being regarded as the portent of a vast new political movement the Party had come to be regarded by the older parties as an unimportant pressure-group with no possibility of seriously challenging them in their long-enjoyed dominance of the political scene.

Yet in this same period the total affiliated membership of the National Party had more than doubled. In 1906 it was 921,280. By

1912 it had risen to 1,895,498. The increase was temporarily halted in the following two years by the necessity for trade unions to take ballots of their members under the Trade Unions Act. But when these ballots were completed the Labour Party membership rose to 2,093,365. In 1906 there had been only seventy-five trade councils and local Labour Parties affiliated. By 1914 there were 179. In the same period the membership of the two Socialist societies rose from 16,784 to 33,230.

Yet whereas in 1906 the executive report of the Party could proudly claim: "Politicians of all parties realize that a new factor in politics has appeared . . . organized labour has at last realized its power and has learned how to use it," in the last executive report before the outbreak of war Ramsay MacDonald, the Chairman of the Parliamentary Party, and Charles Duncan, the Secretary, had to conclude their political report with the highly uninspiring observation: "The Parliamentary Party makes but one claim upon the Party outside. It asks that criticism of its work should come from knowledge. Its greatest fault is its weakness in number, but for that the constituencies and not itself are responsible."

Eight years had wrought a formidable change in the impression created by the Labour Party, both upon its own supporters and upon its opponents.

This decline in the power and the prestige of the Labour Party was not due to any decline in the attraction of the Socialist idea. On the contrary, the dynamic appeal of socialism was stronger than ever before. Many hundreds of thousands of workers were moved by it. The industrial workers were in a ferment. There was an electric quality in the air.

The disillusionment was not with socialism but with the Labour Party as an instrument of socialism.

In part that disillusionment was due to defects of leadership. Yet much of it was due to an unwillingness on the part of many Socialists and industrial workers to accept the limitations placed upon the Labour Party by its nature and constitution and by their even more serious unwillingness to accept the limitations imposed by parliamentary democracy. This dual unwillingness had a significance much more than temporary. It was to recur again and again in the history of the Labour Party.

It was on this occasion contributed to by the extravagant expectations that Labour's success in 1906 had aroused.

As MacDonald, writing in 1913, declared in *The Social Unrest:*

"The appearance of a Parliamentary Labour Party had been extravagantly hailed as the dawn of the millennium. Many trade unionists assumed that with a Labour Party in Parliament workshop agitation was no longer necessary. Legislation was to protect them in future. The party was not only to do the ordinary work of Parliament, but was to settle every workshop grievance and every industrial dispute. The Party was deluged with expressions of these expectations—sometimes from aggrieved individuals, sometimes from troubled societies—and, of course, it could not satisfy its correspondents. Much of what they asked could not be dealt with by Parliament at all; much of what was within the function of Parliament could not be done by a House of Commons in which the Labour Party was a small minority."

All this was true. Yet the disillusionment might not have been so great had the Party had a more inspiring leadership and one able to impress public opinion, and particularly working-class opinion, with the strength of its principles and the staunchness of its purpose even when circumstances robbed it of the power of parliamentary decisions. But the leaders were captive—or felt themselves to be captive—to the compromise which had been necessary to bring the Party into existence in the first place—the compromise between the Socialists and the moderate trade unionists. Because of that compromise any attempt to reach a clear statement of the political principles for which the Party was to stand had been avoided.

In its beginnings the strength of the Party had lain in its lack of a clearly defined policy; in its deliberately empirical approach to the problems of the day. It had been created to advance the cause of the working-classes. It had carefully refrained from attempting to define the long-term political, social and economic policy necessary to accomplish that purpose—because definition might force into the open differences not merely of opinion but of fundamental attitude which it was at that stage safer to leave unresolved.

In 1900 the decision to postpone any attempt to define policy had been not merely a practically wise one but the only possible one if a Labour Party on the model contemplated was to be created.

But a decade had passed and the decision not to make a decision remained unaltered. What had been sound tactics when the Party was being formed had now become a heavy strategical handicap. From time to time, it is true, resolutions in favour of socialism had been passed at national conferences of the Party. But they had been declarations of goodwill, not political directives, and had only been accepted as such. The basic issue of whether the Party was a Socialist Party or simply a reformist Party had not yet been resolved. It showed little sign of being. No one within the leadership of the Party was yet willing to face the risks involved in raising such an issue. Yet it daily became clearer that as a purely reformist Party Labour suffered from the grave disability that the Liberals had already stolen most of its clothes, even although they had cut some of them down before putting them on.

The anxiety to postpone the moment of decision was understandable. For although it offered the only possibility of arriving at a coherent policy capable of standing up to public criticism and of re-inspiring the Labour movement with something of the fire and passion that had brought it into being, it threatened considerable dangers to the Party organization itself.

Both MacDonald and Henderson, the two strongest leaders, were heavily involved personally in the Labour Party machine. MacDonald, as the first Secretary of the Labour Representation Committee, had worked hard and successfully in the early years to avoid anything that would frighten the more timid trade unionists away. He had devoted himself to building what he was far-seeing enough to know was the type of organization most likely to give a Labour Party numerical and financial strength and a firm foundation of mass support.

Moreover, although he was himself a Socialist, he was a Socialist of a peculiarly philosophical and inactive—indeed one might almost say of a non-political—kind. His socialism was not based on an understanding of the economic forces at work in society. He had little knowledge of economics, as was to be shown with tragic clarity much later in his career. What had made him a Socialist was a romanticized conception of natural history acquired during his early biological studies and transformed almost without amendment to the political struggle. He had convinced himself that there was, so to speak, a biological progression in social as in animal life from rudimentary to more perfected organisms. The "community consciousness," which was what he meant by socialism, could, he had persuaded himself, only be achieved after society had passed through all the necessary preliminary stages. The function of the intelligent man of goodwill, the man who appreciated that the true goal to which society was moving was a stage of organization fully in accord with the interests of the whole community, the function, in other words, of the Socialists, was to assist society to move forward smoothly along this road without violence or upheaval, certainly without class consciousness. As he wrote in *Socialism and Society*: "The watchword of socialism is not class consciousness but community consciousness," and again: "It is the whole of society and not merely a class in society that is moving towards class consciousness."

MacDonald, indeed, so much conceived of himself as part of a force of nature moving slowly forward to an ultimate but not very immediate perfectibility that he could write as late as 1909: "The object of Socialists who are active in politics ought not to be to form a Socialist Party, but a party that will journey towards socialism . . . socialism is a view of what society is to be when it has completed a further stage of its existence; a political party embodies working ideas for immediate activities."

There is no doubt a certain grain of philosophic truth in all this, but it was not an attitude of mind likely to produce a clear-cut and aggressive leadership for a small new party which was required to impress upon the public mind a picture of itself as something quite new and decisive in politics. MacDonald's socialism was much more that of a writer of Socialist philosophy of a kind likely to appeal to those among the high-minded and good-intentioned who are prepared to forgo lucidity if only they can be persuaded that they are on the side of the angels than that of an active leader with an explicit and coherent political philosophy capable of being applied to the issues of the day. It was to remain so throughout his career.

He was interested in politics and in the tactics of political life, but he was interested in them much more as a parliamentarian concerned with the manoeuvres of the parliamentary life than as a Socialist. He tended to reserve his socialism for his public speeches and writings. He rarely thought of it as a practical political instrument to be used in his career as an active parliamentarian.

As a writer and orator he dwelt much on the Socialist vision. But in the world of politics he was entirely content to think and work in terms of social reform—until indeed in the latter part of his life he thought of himself as the personal instrument of this force of nature which was carrying men slowly, but no doubt inevitably, to a higher state of society in which community consciousness would solve all problems: an instrument which, because it was the instrument of so great if cloudy a purpose, must be right in whatever it did.

Yet, if MacDonald's socialism was not of a kind to provide an aggressive leadership in a period of great political difficulty—and opportunity—for the Labour Party during mounting social unrest and economic disturbance, it was nevertheless of a kind to commend itself to many of the trade-union leaders of the day. They, too, were reformists who meant well by mankind—they, too, were concerned to advance slowly step by step, rather than to lend themselves to demands for a revolutionary amendment in the social and economic structure of society. They were prepared to agree, and sometimes publicly to state, that such a change would have to come and that Labour must work to that end. But without following MacDonald in his philosophical flights they felt like him that one should not try to hasten a biological process too much.

Indeed, it is probably true that there could have been no better secretary for the Labour Party in its early years than MacDonald. A less "philosophical" and more active and practical Socialist could not have played anything like so successful a part in weaning the trade unions of the day from liberalism to Labour. This was particularly so because his inactivity as a Socialist was balanced by very considerable activity as a politician and organizer and a no less considerable skill in the preparation of agenda and the management of a conference. He had, too, a natural talent—often irritating, but often tactically valuable—for evading difficult practical issues.

Because he was much the most accomplished all-round parliamentarian in the Labour Party—although never the equal of Snowden in the lucid exposition of complex economic subjects—he was also the natural leader of the Parliamentary Labour Party, if leadership was to be thought of simply in the parliamentary context. If the Labour Party had been thought of at that time as a revolutionary democratic movement concerned consistently to challenge the basic assumptions upon which the existing social and economic order were founded, and to conduct a wide campaign on all fronts in order to secure the changes inherent in that challenge, then MacDonald's qualifications for the leadership would have been less obvious. But few of those exercising the greatest influence upon the Labour Party at that time thought of it in any such terms. They thought of it primarily as the political wing of a trade-union movement still essentially reformist and even Liberal in character and having as its main function the expression of the trade-union and working-class point of view on particular issues as they arose.

The qualifications required of the parliamentary leader in such circumstances were radically different from those which would have been required if the Party had thought of itself as an aggressive Socialist Party concerned to mobilize the political power of the workers and of the scientific and idealist Socialists behind a programme of fundamental change. For the Party as it thought of itself, MacDonald had many of the appropriate qualifications for leadership, although he was suspect by some trade unionists because he was not a trade unionist and by some Socialists because his peculiarly individual conception of socialism when allied to his parliamentary ambitions predisposed him even at that stage of his career to look upon co-operation or even actual coalition with other parties in a light much more favourable than could those who had more appreciation of the actual conflicts within society.

Thus when in 1910, at the time of the constitutional crisis, Lloyd George, with Asquith's authority, approached the leaders of the other parties with tentative proposals for the formation of an All-Party Coalition Government, MacDonald provisionally accepted a place in the Coalition Cabinet and the further proposal that there should in addition be two Labour Under-Secretaries. He was only deterred from carrying the project farther—although the Conservative refusal would in any event have led to the abandonment of the scheme—by the firm refusal of Arthur Henderson and G. H. Roberts —to whom he offered the two Under-Secretary posts—to have anything to do with it.

Neither Arthur Henderson nor G. H. Roberts were at this stage of their careers convinced Socialists. They refused the Lloyd George offer brought to them by MacDonald because they had a much firmer understanding than he of the consequences such a participation in an all-party coalition would have upon the organization of the Labour Party and upon the minds of its rank and file. They were committed to an extent he never was to those trade-union and working-class loyalties which have, even in its most difficult days, always given the Labour Party a cohesion that has saved it from disaster. But they had no fundamental difference with him on general political policy. They wished no more than he to make the Party into an aggressive Socialist movement.

Henderson, who, next to MacDonald, was the leader with the most influence upon the course of the Labour Party at this stage, was concerned primarily with organization. When in 1911 he succeeded MacDonald in the secretaryship he immersed himself almost completely in it. In the long run it was immensely to the advantage of the Labour Party that he did so, for he was a superb organizer with an unshakable faith in, and loyalty to, the Labour Party as he saw it—without him it would have been in no position to take advantage of the immense movement in public opinion that followed the war. But at the time it meant that his weight, too, was thrown in the scale against any attempt to resolve the basic conflict within the Labour movement, because to do so might weaken the organization he was building up.

Thus the dilemma remained unresolved. The failure to resolve it led at the time to much disillusionment among the most active and enthusiastic in the Party's ranks and to a serious split between the Party and the more militant industrial workers. If the war had not come and brought with it its greater problems it might have permanently affected the course of Socialist development in Britain. Yet perhaps it was a wise decision not to seek to resolve it. For the Party was still made up of elements too diverse to make a genuine unity possible, and the attempt to secure unity in favour of a definite and forthright policy might at that time have shaken the organization to its foundations and thus destroyed the basis on which an effective Socialist movement was later to be built.

Moreover, the Party was suffering from the fact that the most convinced Socialists among its leaders, such as Keir Hardie and George Lansbury, were not good parliamentarians, and its most able parliamentarians, such as MacDonald, Henderson and Shackleton, were not active Socialists. Snowden perhaps was. But even his socialism was much more a form of ethical radicalism than a well-founded philosophy, and he was so much an opponent of industrial action, so doctrinaire in his approach to many problems, and so intolerant of those who disagreed with him that although his formidable intellectual powers were recognized and his honesty respected he had little personal following.

It was a party in process of development. A party in which, although the main numerical and financial support came from the trade unions, the main propaganda work in the country and the organizational work in the constituencies were in the hands of the I.L.P. Over most of the country indeed the I.L.P. was the Labour Party.

Without the enthusiasm and idealism of I.L.P. members it would scarcely have made any impact upon the consciousness of the ordinary man or woman or have been in a position to fight even as many seats as it did. Except in Barnard Castle and Woolwich, where Arthur Henderson and Will Crooks had built up local organizations with individual members, it was only through the I.L.P. that the ordinary man or woman could join the Labour Party and work for it. The I.L.P. provided most of the speakers in the country, it did most of the campaigning and practically all the propaganda. Yet if an important issue arose at a trade council or a local Labour Party, at the annual conference or in the Parliamentary Party, the final word was with the trade unions because they commanded the mass votes.

This situation might have created even more difficulties than it did if the trade unions had not, on the whole, been extremely generous in their willingness to accept the full implications of the alliance made with the Socialist societies in 1900 and very ready to agree that, although they were the senior partners in the Labour Party, it was, and must be, much more than a purely trade-union party in its outlook on affairs. Nevertheless, the weight of their influence was inevitably on the side of caution and their approach to most questions was basically empirical.

The divorce between the organization of the Labour Party and its propaganda and campaigning branch could not, moreover, avoid having consequences which were bound to add to the disillusionment of many of those who were attracted to the Labour movement by the crusading zeal of the I.L.P. There was on many occasions a discrepancy between what was said and what was actually done that was bound to blunt the edge of fine enthusiasm. The breach between faith and works, particularly in the parliamentary circumstances of the time, was often of a character to turn to frustration the zeal of those who believed themselves to be fighting for the achievement of a Socialist commonwealth.

The other member of the alliance, the Fabian Society, whose intellectual contribution had been of such value in the early days, had now ceased to take much practical interest in the Labour Party as such, although that interest was to be decisively resumed later. In the eyes of the Fabian leaders, the Labour Party at this time had become merely one instrument and that a not very important one in their policy of permeation. They had no great faith in its prospects as a potential government. As practical social scientists they preferred to concentrate their main energies on influencing those who were, and looked like remaining, the rulers of the country, although they still produced pamphlets of great propaganda value to Socialists.

The Labour Party was in a state of transition, not yet capable of assimilating and giving coherence to all the divergent groups which had gone to form it, not even certain of its ultimate course.

What was even more important was that the nation was in a state of transition also. It was moving from the security and stability of the Victorian and Edwardian ages into the perils and upheavals of the Georgian. A great many new social forces had simultaneously been set loose which buffeted opinion first this way and then that and assailed in one way and another all the organizations of society, the Labour Party amongst them, so that it was impossible for anyone to set a clear and constant course amidst the raging elements.

The speed of industrial advance, the material progress of the businessmen and manufacturers and the failure of the workers to share to anything like a just degree in their advance, the awakened social conscience of the middle-classes, the emergent political demands of those who had for so long been regarded as inferior beings—women and working-classes alike—the urge for social reform and the opposition of vested interests to it—all these combined to mark the conflicts within society more clearly than almost ever before and to do so in an atmosphere less sympathetic to compromise than at almost any time.

It was not only within the Labour movement that the disillusionment with parliamentary action existed. It is one of the ironies of history that in a period when parliamentary action secured within a matter of eight years a more rapid advance in social reform than there had been at any previous time the whole process of peaceful and constitutional change was under constant attack. It was as though there were something electric in the air—a presage of the vast international storm that lay ahead—which predisposed men and women to violent means.

With an almost mystic elation, young and middle-aged women turned to the violences of the women's suffragette movement until in the end their militancy seemed to have little relationship with the cause it had been created to serve. Whether it helped or hindered the parliamentary battle for equal suffrage no longer mattered— violence and sacrifice had become ends in themselves.

In Northern Ireland, officers of the Crown, incited and encouraged by Conservative members of Parliament, prepared to forget their oath of loyalty and take up arms to prevent Home Rule for Ireland if Parliament should by the constitutional processes of democratic decision decide that it was a desirable policy.

And all over Britain workers turned their backs on the established methods of negotiation, conciliation and arbitration, ignored very often the advice of their elected trade-union leaders, expressed their scorn of parliamentary processes and came out on strike in a series of industrial disputes that threatened to engulf the country in a vast social upheaval. Nor were the workers alone in their intransigence, it was matched by that of employers who again and again inflamed industrial passions by the employment of the lock-out.

In 1908 only 399 industrial disputes were reported to the Labour

Department of the Board of Trade. By 1911 the number had risen to 903. By 1913 to 150 a month—1,800 a year. In 1909 the number of people directly involved in industrial disputes was only 170,000, by 1911 it had risen to 831,000, and by 1912 to 1,233,000. In the same period the total number of working days affected by strikes and lock-outs rose from 2,560,000 to 38,142,000. There were economic reasons for these strikes, of course: rising prices and fantastically rising profits, while wages remained almost stationary; much publicized wealth alongside appalling poverty. But what was symptomatic of the period was the unwillingness on both sides to negotiate, the anxiety to bring things to a head.

The first rumble of the approaching storm came from the north-east early in 1910, when 30,000 Northumberland miners struck work in defiance of their own union in protest against the three-shift system laid down in the Coal Mines Regulation Act. They stayed out for three months. This was followed by a strike on the North Eastern Railway and by stoppages among the Nottingham miners, the Glasgow thread workers and the Bradford textile workers. Then the employers in the boiler-making industry entered the lists and locked out all the members of the Boilermakers' Society. This in turn brought out the iron founders. In the Rhondda Valley, 10,000 mine workers came out at the Cambrian collieries and stayed out for more than a year, the situation being much worsened by the decision of the Government to send troops to the mines. In Lancashire, after a month of fruitless negotiations, 100,000 cotton operatives were locked out by the mill-owners.

This was only the beginning. Two days before the Coronation of George V the seamen and firemen came out in Southampton and Hull. Rapidly the strike spread to Manchester, Bristol and Liverpool and then to London, where the whole of the docks were brought to a standstill under the leadership of Tom Mann, who had recently reorganized the seamen, carters and dock workers in the National Transport Workers' Federation, and who had to assist him his old companion of that earlier dock strike of twenty years previously, Ben Tillett. Police and military were drafted into the provincial ports and the Home Office and War Office were preparing to take similar action in London when the strike ended. Six days before it did so the movement spread to the railways. On 5 April,

1911, railwaymen in Liverpool struck unofficially. Ten days later the executives of the three principal railway unions—whom the companies had refused to recognize or negotiate with—jointly delivered a twenty-four-hour ultimatum to the railway companies threatening a national stoppage unless the companies met them to negotiate a settlement. At once the Prime Minister, Mr. Asquith, intervened with an offer to refer the issues to a Royal Commission and a threat to use troops if a national stoppage took place.

The unions replied to this threat of troops by calling their members out and 200,000 railwaymen struck. On this occasion the leaders of parliamentary Labour were able to play a decisive role. Asquith, with Lloyd George's aid, was persuaded not to heighten the tension by carrying out his threat to use troops. MacDonald and Henderson between them then persuaded Lloyd George, who had more perception of the danger than Asquith, and who was deeply anxious about the critical international situation which had arisen following the dispatch of a German gunboat to Agadir, to induce the companies to accept the unions' demands for direct negotiations. A settlement on lines drafted by the Labour Department of the Board of Trade was reached, a Royal Commission to examine conditions appointed and a conciliation scheme which included trade-union recognition set up. The result was the National Union of Railwaymen, formed by the fusion of the three railway unions.

Now the movement spread again to the miners. The Miners' Federation balloted all its members on a minimum wage demand. The demand was put up to the mine-owners, who rejected it. A national strike ballot was taken and in February, 1912, over 1,000,000 miners all over the country came out. Once again the Government was forced to intervene—this time with the offer of a Minimum Wages Bill and the strike ended after a month.

Almost immediately afterwards the London dockers came out again and stayed out for sixteen weeks until the strike was broken by the employment of 25,000 soldiers and sailors. In all parts of the country and in almost all trades there were smaller stoppages.

This immense upsurge of industrial action, although it seemed for the time being to turn almost the whole force of working-class power from political and parliamentary channels, did not, of course, do so entirely. Two of the greatest stoppages—and the two that had the most successful results—those of the railwaymen and the miners, were official strikes backed by the full force of the established trade unions and supported by the Labour Party in Parliament. During both of them the Parliamentary Labour Party was able to give great help in negotiations with the Government, leading to a Royal Commission in the case of the railwaymen and to a Minimum Wages Act in the case of the miners.

But many of the disputes in that stormy period which, now that it is shrouded in the mists of memory, is sometimes quoted as an age of peace, prosperity and good living for all, were of a different and unofficial character. Nor did the aid given by the Labour Party to the railwaymen and the miners alter the political attitude of those who led many of the strikes and who in many cases thought of them as campaigns in a political revolutionary movement.

"We most certainly favour strikes," declared Tom Mann in the *Industrial Syndicalist* of March, 1911. "We shall always do our best to help strikers to be successful and we shall prepare the way as rapidly as possible for the General Strike of national proportions. The workers will refuse any longer to manipulate the machinery of production in the interests of the capitalist class and there will be no power on earth to compel them to work when they thus refuse."

The insurrectionist phase of the British Labour movement which appeared to have ended with the great strikes and Trafalgar Square demonstrations of the late 1880s and early 90s now seemed to have returned. The mood of militancy and of faith in direct action as opposed to parliamentary action spread.

It was fed by a spate of syndicalist pamphlets and by the explosive journalism of the recently founded *Daily Herald*. The *Herald*, after starting life in 1911 as a halfpenny bulletin issued by London printers on strike, managed to scrape together £300. With this tiny sum "the miracle of Fleet Street" launched itself on the world as a rebel Socialist daily backed by, among others, George Lansbury, who became its editor two years later, and supported by a team of brilliant middle-class writers with a dazzling lack of reverence for anything under the sun and a cartoonist of a mordant power not seen in British journalism for many a long day—Will Dyson.

It is symptomatic of the temper of the times that, chronically short of money as it always was, without resources or official support, the *Daily Herald* flourished and got itself talked about all over Britain, while the *Daily Citizen*, which was launched as an official daily paper with the financial backing of the trade unions in October, 1912, collapsed within less than three years after a meritorious but unexciting career during which it faithfully supported official Labour and trade-union policy.

The *Daily Herald* with its lampoons, its disregard for libel, its ferocity, its ridicule, its joyous delight in battle and its readiness to support any strike anywhere, was more in tune with the mood of many thousands of workers than was the sober *Citizen*.

That mood reached its crescendo, perhaps, in the ferment that came in 1913 as a result of the lock-out of Dublin workers led by James Connolly—who was to fall three years later in the Easter Rising—and Jim Larkin and their appeal for sympathetic strike action by British trade unionists.

The Dublin lock-out posed the conflict between capital and labour in its most naked form. It was the result of an organized effort to destroy trade unionism in Dublin by the Mayor, William Martin Murphy. He persuaded Dublin employers to serve notice on all their workers that they would be locked out unless they signed a declaration that they would not belong to the Irish Transport Workers' Union which Connolly and Larkin had organized as a new type of general workers' union spreading into many trades.

This was to return to the methods of the 1830s, when Owen's Grand National Consolidated Union was smashed by the method of the employers' boycott. Not only did the unskilled workers in the Dublin slums rise to the challenge with a courage and loyalty that excited admiration all over the world, they found passionate allies among some of the greatest spirits in Ireland.

George Russell (A.E.), the great Irish poet, accused the Dublin employers of "an insolence and ignorance of the rights conceded to workers universally in the modern world as incredible and as great as your inhumanity," and told them to "Cry aloud to heaven for new souls." Countess Markievicz and others, who were later to be leaders of the Irish revolutionary movement, organized soup kitchens to help feed the workers locked out. Mayor Murphy called out the police to aid the employers and, reading aloud the reports of their baton charges to a great meeting in London, Bernard Shaw protested that it was as safe to let loose a pack of mad dogs in the streets as a party of police in Dublin city.

The *Daily Herald* organized a massed meeting of support for the Dublin workers in the Albert Hall and followed it with others all over the country. The Co-operative movement sent food ships across the Irish Sea to succour the grimly fighting and starving people in the Dublin tenements. But demonstrations and food ships were not enough for Connolly and Larkin. They wanted sympathetic strike action and they came to England to try to get it.

Larkin had long campaigned for a militant trade-union policy with, as its strategical master plan, the establishment of general unions with workers from a wide number of trades among their members. These workers were then to be required to pledge themselves not to touch "tainted goods"—to undertake, that is, to stop supplies going to any firm with whom workers of the union were in dispute.

He now wanted this principle applied by the English unions to the Dublin lock-out. He demanded that they should call upon their members not to handle anything for any firm involved in the lock-out. The British unions refused to accept any such principle. If they did, as the Railwaymen's Union pointed out, it would scarcely be possible to think of any dispute anywhere in which the railwaymen would not at once find themselves involved.

Thereupon Larkin, a man of vast physique with the shoulders of a prize-fighter and an oratorical style that matched his appearance, toured Britain denouncing the English trade-union leaders as reformists and traitors, arousing the fires of militancy with all his power. In Dublin the battle dragged on for nine months and then ended with victory for neither side; the men refused to give up their union, the employers refused to recognize it, although they found it impossible to boycott its members.

Although the English trade unions refused to accept Larkin's case for sympathetic strike action along syndicalist lines, three of the most powerful of them took, early in 1914, a significant step towards the application of the principles of joint action he had advocated. In the spring of 1914, a conference of the Miners' Federation, the National Union of Railwaymen and the National

Transport Workers' Federation decided to form a triple alliance.

The National Transport Workers' Federation had been organized by Tom Mann. The miners, and particularly their younger leaders like Arthur Cook, had been greatly influenced by syndicalist ideas.

The triple alliance embraced a combined force of more than a million and a quarter workers. Its declared aim was to concert action between the three unions in order to secure acceptance of individual programmes presented simultaneously by all three with simultaneous strike action if all or any one section of the programmes were rejected.

It began as a triple alliance, but those who sponsored it had, as Robert Smillie, the President of the Miners' Federation, acknowledged, an even wider conception in mind. "It may well be found advisable to extend the scope of the alliance in the general interests of labour as a whole."

How far the movement would have gone if the war had not come, and to what extent the whole conception of democratic parliamentary action which the Labour Party embodied would have been affected by the mounting faith of large masses of workers in the potency of direct action for both industrial and political ends, it is impossible to say. On the very eve of the war, industrial unrest appeared to be rising to a new climax. Fresh disputes in the Scottish mines and on the railways were boiling up. The building workers of London were on strike. And then on 4 August, war, the danger of which had been much discussed but whose imminence the great mass of ordinary people had scarcely believed possible, was declared.

The violence of the industrial clash, the fanaticism and sacrifice of the women suffragettes, the intransigence of the Tories in Ulster, the bitter battle against reform of the Tories in the House of Lords, were all submerged in a greater violence and a vaster sacrifice. The early twentieth century, which, as we look back nostalgically telling each other of the pleasures and gaieties of Edwardian times, seems so peaceful and so serene, but which was in truth torn and rent almost continuously by social and political strife, by the clash of irreconcilable interests at home and the rivalries of imperial powers abroad, had flowered to its climax.

For the next four years war was to govern the nation's life and out of it a new and stronger Labour Party was to be born.

PART THREE

CRISIS AND CONFLICT

CHAPTER X

THE OPPOSITION TO THE WAR

LOOKING back, it seems incredible that one of the greatest wars in history should have come upon the peoples of the world as unexpectedly as the war of 1914–18. Yet so it was.

There was dangerous tension. All over Europe the powder-trains were laid, waiting for a match to set the explosion going. There was rivalry between Russia and Germany and in both countries war-parties were anxious for external diversions to stifle mounting internal unrest. There was suspicion between France and Germany and a secret understanding between Britain and France which bound Britain not only to France, but, through her, to Russia.

There were plenty of causes from which war could come—German fear of encirclement; Austrian-Hungarian hatred of Serbia, who had gained more than her share of power in the Balkans out of the weakness of Turkey and whose independent existence provided a rallying ground for the dissident Serbian and Croatian minorities in the Austrian-Hungarian empire; increasing German influence in Turkey which seemed finally to threaten the Russian dream of advance to the Dardanelles. No great war begins without cause, and there were more than enough causes of war in the rivalries and ambitions which rent the greater and lesser Powers of the Continent.

Nevertheless, far into July, until only a week or two before war began, although there were those in Berlin, in St. Petersburg and in

Vienna who planned for war and even those who hoped for war, there was no immediate expectancy of war in any of the capitals of Europe. Still less was there any in the towns and villages, the fields and factories and workshops where the ordinary men and women lived and worked.

In Germany the Kaiser went off light-heartedly enough for his usual summer cruise in the Norwegian fiords, his chief Minister departed for a shooting party, and General von Moltke, the head of the army, went off to take a cure in a foreign spa.

In France the President and Prime Minister departed for a ceremonial visit to Russia from which they did not return until 29 July.

In Vienna the Russian Ambassador, persuaded that all was quiet, went on leave.

In Britain the Cabinet was preoccupied with industrial disputes, with the danger of civil war in Ulster and with the latest manifestations of the militant suffragette movement. Ten days before the declaration of war, Sir Edward Grey, the Foreign Secretary, so little expected war to arrive that he went off for a short fishing holiday in Hampshire. The other members of the Cabinet all left London for the week-end.

The Labour Party was no less unprepared. How could it be otherwise? The fear of war, the possibility that it might be hatched some time in the seething rivalries of the great imperialist Powers and the secret diplomacy of their Foreign Offices, was present in the minds of Socialists. That and suspicion of Britain's foreign policy.

This suspicion had been formally expressed two and a half years earlier in January, 1912, at the annual conference at Birmingham when a resolution was passed declaring that.

"This conference, believing the anti-German policy pursued in the name of the British Government by Sir Edward Grey to be a cause of increasing armaments, international ill-will and the betrayal of oppressed nationalities, protests in the strongest terms against it. The Conference is of opinion that this diplomacy has led the present Government to risk a war with Germany in the interests of French financiers over Morocco, to condone the Italian outrages in Tripoli, the Russian theft in Mongolia and in joining

213

hands with Russia in making an assault on the independence of Persia."

The suspicions remained. But there was no immediate expectancy of war—at any rate, of war on an international scale.

The assassination of the Austrian Archduke Franz Ferdinand in Sarajevo on 28 June, although it had shocked world opinion, had not made men anticipate that war was nearly upon them. Even when, three and a half weeks later, Austria, on the pretext of Serbian complicity in the assassination, delivered to the Serbian Government a forty-eight-hour ultimatum, the acceptance of which must violate Serbian independence, Sir Edward Grey told the British Cabinet that, although the situation was serious, he was hopeful that the conversations which were taking place between Russia and Austria would lead to a settlement. Having said which he went off on a fishing week-end. This was the first occasion on which the matter was even discussed at the Cabinet and then it was raised by Grey only as an afterthought at the end of a long Cabinet meeting.

As for the ordinary man in the street, he had been told nothing. He had no reason to suspect that an assassination of an archduke of whom he knew little, in Sarajevo the capital of Bosnia, a territory of which he knew less, would, in the state of international rivalry then existing, be used by Austria as an excuse to make impossible demands upon Serbia, the refusal of which—or for that matter their virtual acceptance—would provide her with a pretext for invasion. He did not know she would be encouraged and incited in her demands by Germany, that an Austrian threat of invasion of Serbia must be regarded by Russia as a German-Austrian threat to herself and bring her in, that France was committed to assist Russia in the event of war and finally that the British Foreign Secretary had committed Britain to aid France.

Indeed, this last link in the chain which was now waiting to pull the nations headlong into war had not even been made known by Asquith and Grey to the Cabinet until six years after the discussions and arrangements which forged it. When it was disclosed to them the Cabinet was appalled, but felt that British honour was too far committed to go back.

Moreover, the existence of any secret agreement binding Britain militarily to France and thus, because of the Franco-Russian Alliance, to a Russian Government which was hated and suspected by the vast majority of the British people, because of its autocratic and tyrannical character and the infamies of which it had been guilty, had been repeatedly denied.

To a question in the House as to whether there was any commitment, unknown to Parliament, which bound Britain to go to the assistance of France in the event of war with Germany, Grey replied that no such obligation existed. In March, 1913, when Lord Hugh Cecil stated, during the course of a debate, that "There is a very general belief that this country is under an obligation, not a treaty obligation but an obligation arising out of an undertaking given in the course of diplomatic negotiations, to send a very large armed force out of this country to operate in Europe," the Prime Minister intervened and stated, "I ought to say that is not true."

At an early stage in the negotiations with France, Asquith, Grey and the very small circle of members of the Cabinet fully cognizant of what was proceeding had agreed, in the words of a memorandum approved by Grey, not to make Parliament aware of the obligations that were being incurred. They had further agreed that it would not even be "wise to bring the question before the Cabinet."

It is not surprising, therefore, that the general public was totally ignorant of the significance to them of the events on the Continent up to the very eve of the declaration of war and that the leaders of the Labour Party, deeply suspicious of Asquith and Grey though they were, had no reason to believe that war was already on the move.

On 29 July, five days after the Austrian ultimatum, the Socialist International Bureau met in Brussels with Keir Hardie and Bruce Glasier as the British representatives. By then Austria had declared war on Serbia. All over Europe the troops were massing. But, although the fear of war dominated the discussions, no one, "not even," as Bruce Glasier reported, "the German representatives, seemed apprehensive of an actual rupture between the Great Powers taking place until at least the full resources of diplomacy had been exhausted."

The Socialist International—the Second International—had been founded in 1889 as the successor to the first International

Working Men's Association which, with a constitution drafted by Karl Marx, had been born at a London conference convened by George Odger, Secretary of the London Trades Council, but had soon fallen to pieces under the strain of internal dissensions. The Second International was entirely Marxist in its basis. The non-Marxist British Labour Party was, therefore, a somewhat strange adherent. Indeed its affiliation had for this reason been opposed by H. M. Hyndman and the Social Democratic Federation, who regarded themselves as the true representatives of British socialism in the International. But, in 1907, the Labour Party was accepted as a member under an ingenious formula devised by Karl Kautsky which declared that the British Labour Party, although it did not recognize the class struggle, carried it on and had an organization which, being independent of the bourgeois parties, was based upon the class struggle.

Now the Bureau of the International had met to arrange an international Socialist conference. Despite the gathering momentum of the preparations for war there was no suggestion that the arrangements for such a conference should be abandoned, although, in view of the state of war in Austria, it was decided to alter the meeting-place from Vienna to Paris and to advance the date from 23 August to 5 August.

In the evening, when the members of the Bureau had completed their arrangements for the conference, a great meeting to demonstrate against international policies which might lead to war was held. Seven thousand people attended. They heard Vandervelde of Belgium, Haase of Germany, Jaurès of France, Keir Hardie of Britain, all declare that the workers—the common people of the world—would not allow war, whatever their rulers willed. Jaurès, turning emotionally towards Haase, thanked him, in the name of the working people of France, for the demonstrations of the Social Democrats of Germany in favour of peace.

Next morning the members of the Bureau dispersed to their several countries to make arrangements for the forthcoming international Socialist conference. Forty-eight hours later they received with stunned horror the news that Jaurès, to whom they had looked as one of the great forces for international peace, had been assassinated while sitting with a friend outside a Paris café.

As the news of fighting in Serbia and general mobilization in Austria and Russia came streaming in, the hope that war would be averted shifted in Britain to the conviction that Britain must remain out of the conflict, able to exercise her great influence as a peace-maker and thus bring hostilities to an end at the earliest possible moment.

In Downing Street this view was pressed hard by Lloyd George, Lord Morley, Sir John Simon, John Burns and others. On the Sunday morning, 2 August, two days before the British declaration of war, Morley, who was the leader of those within the Cabinet who believed that Britain should remain neutral and work for a restoration of peace, estimated that there was a majority of eight or nine behind him.

The conviction that Britain could and must stay out was at that moment held by the majority of the British people. They saw no moral or other reason for intervention in what appeared to them to be a struggle for power between the autocracies of Germany and Austria-Hungary on the one side and those of Russia and her allies on the other. The Governor of the Bank of England called on Lloyd George at the Treasury to inform him on behalf of the City that the financial and trading interests of the City were totally opposed to intervention.

Under the headline, "Why We Must Not Fight. England and the Crisis," the *Daily News*, the most influential Liberal newspaper in London, published on the morning of Saturday, 1 August, an article by its editor, A. G. Gardiner, which declared, "If we crush Germany in the dust and make Russia the dictator of Europe and Asia, it will be the greatest disaster that has ever befallen Western culture and civilization." In its columns it published a mass of letters from leaders of opinion of all kinds protesting against the idea of British participation in war. "For England to join in this hideous war," wrote the Bishop of Lincoln, "would be treason to civilization and disaster to our people. God save us from the war fever."

All over the country on the afternoon of 2 August great demonstrations called by the Labour Party, but joined by many who were not among its members, were held to demand that Britain should not go to war. In Trafalgar Square a vast crowd, the vastest according

217

to the *Manchester Guardian* seen in that square for many years, heard Keir Hardie, Arthur Henderson, George Lansbury, Will Thorne, Mary Macarthur, Marion Phillips, Margaret Bondfield, Mrs. Despard, R. B. Cunninghame Graham, Robert Williams, denounce war as a needless horror and cheered the denunciation of an alliance with the Russia of the Tsars. "Do not," said Cunninghame Graham in the greatest speech of his career, "do not let us do this crime or be parties to the misery of millions who have never done us harm."

At another Labour demonstration Robert Smillie declared that if a cessation of work all over Europe would halt the war the miners would pledge themselves to join in such a course.

It was still believed that the Socialist International would hold together and that by combined international action the Socialist parties of the world could play a decisive part in making war impossible. The Trafalgar Square demonstration and the great Socialist demonstrations held simultaneously throughout the country on that Sunday afternoon had been called as a result of a manifesto drafted by Keir Hardie and Arthur Henderson as president and secretary of the British section of the International Socialist Bureau.

"The long-threatened European war is now upon us," this manifesto declared. "For more than a hundred years no such danger has confronted civilization. It is for you to take full account of the desperate situation and to act promptly and vigorously in the interests of peace.

"You have never been consulted about the war. Whatever may be the rights and wrongs of the sudden crushing attack made by the militarist Empire of Austria upon Serbia, it is certain that the workers of all countries likely to be drawn into the conflict must strain every nerve to prevent their Governments from committing them to war.

"Everywhere Socialists and the organized forces of Labour are taking this course. Everywhere vehement protests are made against the greed and intrigues of militarists and armament-mongers. We call upon you to do the same here in Great Britain upon an even more impressive scale. Hold vast demonstrations in London and in every industrial centre. Compel those of the governing class and their Press, who are so eager to commit you to co-operate with Russian despotism, to keep silence and respect the decision of the overwhelming majority of the people, who will have neither part nor lot in such infamy. The success of Russia at the present day would be a curse to the world.

"There is no time to lose. Already, by secret agreements and understandings of which the democracies of the civilized world know only by rumour, steps are being taken which may fling us all into the fray. Workers, stand together therefore for peace, combine and conquer the militarist enemy and the self-seeking imperialists today once and for all.

"Men and women of Britain, you have now an unexampled opportunity of showing your power, rendering a magnificent service to humanity and to the world. Proclaim that for you the days of plunder and butchery have gone by. Send messages of peace and fraternity to your fellows who have less liberty than you.

"Down with class rule! Down with the rule of brute force! Down with war! Up with the peaceful rule of the people!"

The great concourse of people which gathered in Trafalgar Square and in the provincial cities to answer this call and listen to the speeches of the Socialist leaders still believed that the war which now seemed certain could be prevented from spreading over all the face of the world. They passed with acclamation a resolution put from the platform at each meeting which said:

"We protest against any step being taken by the Government of this country to support Russia either directly or in consequence of an undertaking with France, as being not only offensive to the political traditions of the country but disastrous to Europe, and declare that we have no interest, direct or indirect, in the threatened quarrels which may result from the action of Serbia. The Government of Britain should rigidly decline to engage in war but should confine itself to efforts to bring about peace as speedily as possible."

The crowds dispersed. Those in London joined the others who now thronged Whitehall and Downing Street, most of them silent and anxious but some singing the Marseillaise.

The speakers at Trafalgar Square went to Ramsay MacDonald's flat in Lincoln's Inn, there to wait for his return from a lunch with

Lloyd George, Sir John Simon, George Lambert and Charles Masterman—all of them, at that stage, members of the anti-war group in the Cabinet and strong critics of Grey's foreign policy. MacDonald had also been in touch with Lord Morley—a great personal friend. When he arrived, it was to report that opinion within the Cabinet was hardening in favour of war and that, whereas in the morning Morley had believed there was a majority against British intervention, he now doubted whether more than two or three would stand with him against it. This movement of opinion within the Cabinet was due to the accumulating evidence, not yet known to the general public, that Germany intended to violate Belgian neutrality, was already massing her forces along the Belgian frontier, and had delivered an ultimatum to the Belgian Government demanding free passage for her troops through Belgian territory to attack France, against whom and against Russia she had that same day declared war.

To the majority of the Cabinet this was the decisive issue—as it was to be the decisive issue for the majority of the country and the majority of the Labour Party when it became known. In fact, the secret understandings entered into with France by Asquith and Grey would in any event—and certainly in their view—have made it difficult for Britain to stand aside. So much so that Grey, with Asquith's support, made it clear to the Cabinet that if Britain did not honour the obligations he had undertaken to France he must resign. But this the ordinary people did not know. For them it was Belgium, and the tearing up by Germany of "the scrap of paper" that pledged the Great Powers to protect her neutrality, that irrevocably tipped the scales.

On Monday morning the Parliamentary Labour Party met—and, still without knowledge of the impending German attack upon Belgium, decided that when Parliament met in the afternoon they would continue to oppose British intervention.

On those instructions, but also from his own deep personal conviction, MacDonald replied to the moving and historic speech in which Grey made it clear that Britain was so committed that to draw back was in the Government's view impossible—a speech which drew immediate assurances of support from Bonar Law for the Conservatives and John Redmond for the Irish Nationalists.

"The Rt. Hon. gentleman has," said MacDonald, "delivered a speech the echoes of which will go down to history. The speech has been impressive; however much we may resist the conclusion to which he has come, we have not been able to resist the moving character of his appeal. I think he is wrong. I think the Government which he represents and for which he speaks is wrong. I think the verdict of history will be that they are wrong. We shall see. . . . If the Rt. Hon. gentleman had come here today and told us that our country is in danger I do not care what party he appealed to, and to what class he appealed, we would be with him and behind him. . . . But he has not persuaded me that it is. He has not persuaded my hon. friends who co-operate with me that it is and I am perfectly certain that when his speech gets into cold print tomorrow he will not persuade a large section of the country. If the nation's honour were in danger, we would be with him.

"But there has been no crime committed by statesmen of this character without those statesmen appealing to their nation's honour. We fought the Crimean War because of our honour. We rushed to South Africa because of our honour. The Rt. Hon. gentleman is appealing to us today because of our honour. If the Rt. Hon. gentleman could come to us and tell us that a small European nation like Belgium is in danger and could assure us that he is going to confine the conflict to that question, then we would support him. What is the use of talking of coming to the aid of Belgium, when as a matter of fact you are engaging in a whole European war which is not going to leave the map of Europe in the position it is now? The Rt. Hon. gentleman said nothing about Russia. We want to know about that. We want to find out what is going to happen, when it is all over, to the power of Russia in Europe. . . . Finally, so far as France is concerned we say solemnly and definitely that no such friendship as the Rt. Hon. gentleman describes between one nation and another could ever justify one of those nations entering into war on behalf of another. . . . So far as we are concerned, whatever may happen, whatever may be said about us, we will take the action of saying that this country ought to have remained neutral, because in the deepest parts of our hearts we believe that was right and that that alone was consistent with the honour of our country and the traditions of the Party that are now in office."

When MacDonald sat down there was no applause. He was followed later in the debate by Keir Hardie and Arthur Ponsonby, both of whom opposed British intervention. But they were now members of a tiny minority. MacDonald had been right in his consistent criticism of Grey's foreign policy over many years. He was right when he said that Grey had made no attempt to isolate the issue of Belgian neutrality and make Britain's position on that clear from the start—indeed if he had, if he had early made it plain to Germany that any dishonouring of the treaty pledges to Belgium must compel British intervention, instead of waiting until the German troops were already massed on the frontier and the military machine could no longer be put in reverse, he might, in the judgment of Lloyd George and other members of the Cabinet, have averted war altogether. That is by no means certain. British intervention would probably, as the German General Staff calculated when they weighed the military advantages of an attack through Belgium against the political disadvantages, have been, in any event, unavoidable at this stage. But in his criticisms of Grey's handling of affairs and of the consequences of a policy of Continental agreements that had been made without public knowledge, MacDonald was right.

He was wrong, however, in his judgment of the effect upon public opinion of Grey's speech and of the German threat to Belgian independence which, even before the act of invasion on the morning of 4 August, swung British opinion almost solidly behind a British declaration of war.

On Sunday morning a majority of the Cabinet had been against intervention. Now only two cabinet ministers, Morley and John Burns, and one junior minister, Charles Trevelyan, still held to that view. On Monday morning the Parliamentary Labour Party had been wholly against war. By Monday night MacDonald and Hardie had become simply the intransigent leaders of a minority drawn mainly from the ranks of the I.L.P. It was, however, a minority which inside and outside Parliament included some of the best-known national leaders and propagandists of socialism. In addition to MacDonald and Hardie themselves, there were F. W.

Jowett, Jimmy Maxton (then chairman of the Scottish I.L.P. Council), W. C. Anderson and Philip Snowden, who was at that moment on a visit to New Zealand but who, when he returned, made plain an opposition to the war even more consistent than that of MacDonald. MacDonald, as his speech in reply to Grey had shown and as his later response to recruiting appeals was also to show, was somewhat divided in mind. He was bitterly opposed to Grey and his policy, but ready to support the war, if it could be shown, as in his view it had not been shown, that it had a just cause.

Grey's speech and the positive threat to Belgium had, however, already converted the majority of the Labour Party. They, too, had opposed the foreign policy which had preceded and led up to this dreadful climax. They agreed with MacDonald's criticisms of Grey—but they felt that all this was no longer relevant. Whatever its antecedents the issue was now clear. There could in their view be only one response.

The majority of the public agreed with them. On Sunday the crowds had gathered in Trafalgar Square to demonstrate against war. On Monday evening the crowds that massed the streets from Trafalgar Square along Whitehall to the House of Commons had come to demonstrate in favour of war. On the following day, as the news of the German reply to the British ultimatum was awaited, they gathered again along Whitehall and outside Buckingham Palace in an enthusiasm which reached its climax outside the Palace that night when it became known that war had been declared. There was little doubt now about the general mood. The German attack on Belgium had wiped out all doubts for most people; they wanted, as H. G. Wells with his genius for expressing the public mood in a phrase declared, "to be done for ever with this drilling, trampling foolery in the heart of Europe."

But the Labour movement, although the majority of its members, like the majority of the country, were convinced that the war was just and inevitable, was far from unqualified in its support of the Government. On 5 August, the day after the declaration of war, the National Executive of the Party met in London and passed a resolution which was subsequently endorsed at a joint meeting with the Parliamentary Party. This made the Labour attitude plain.

It declared: "That the conflict between the nations in Europe in which this country is involved is owing to Foreign Ministers pursuing diplomatic policies for the purpose of maintaining a balance of power; that our own national policy of understanding with France and Russia only was bound to increase the power of Russia both in Europe and Asia and to endanger good relations with Germany.

"That Sir Edward Grey, as proved by the facts which he gave to the House of Commons, committed, without the knowledge of our people, the honour of the country to supporting France in the event of any war in which she was seriously involved and gave definite assurances of support before the House of Commons had any chance of considering the matter.

"That the Labour movement reiterates the fact that it has opposed the policy which has produced the war and that its duty now is to secure peace at the earliest possible moment on such conditions as will provide the best opportunities for the re-establishment of amicable feelings between the workers of Europe."

The following day, at the instance of Arthur Henderson, a conference of all sections of the Labour and Socialist movement was called at the House of Commons, to consider measures to safeguard workers' interests and defend social conditions during the war.

At this conference representatives attended not only from the Labour Party itself, but from the Trades Union Congress, the General Federation of Trade Unions, the I.L.P., the Fabian Society, the British Socialist Party, which had been formed in 1911 by a fusion between the Social Democratic Federation and a number of left-wing groups which had broken away from the I.L.P., the Co-operative Union, the Co-operative Congress, and many of the largest individual trade unions, such as the Miners' Federation, the National Union of Railwaymen and the Transport Workers' Federation. It thus represented a meeting of every shade of opinion within the Labour movement—pro-war and anti-war alike. Out of it was established the War Emergency Workers' National Committee, with J. S. Middleton as secretary, which remained in operation all through the war and did more than any other single organization to keep the Labour movement in existence as a movement united in ultimate aims despite the fierce conflicts of opinion brought by war.

But in those first days of war the conflicts were uppermost. On 7 August Ramsay MacDonald resigned his leadership of the Parliamentary Party and was succeeded by Arthur Henderson. Six days later the I.L.P. announced its uncompromising opposition to the war.

"Out of the darkness and the depth," declared its manifesto, "we hail our working-class comrades of every land. Across the roar of guns we send sympathy and greeting to the German Socialists. They have laboured unceasingly to promote good relations with Britain as we with Germany. They are no enemies of ours, but faithful friends.

"In forcing this appalling crime upon the nations it is the rulers, the diplomats, the militarists who have sealed their doom. In tears of blood and bitterness the greater democracy will be born. . . . Long live Freedom and Fraternity. Long live International Socialism."

The I.L.P. believed that British Socialists should co-operate, not with governments, whether their own or others, but only with other Socialists. They remembered the eve-of-war meetings of the International Socialist Bureau and hoped still for international Socialist action which would bring the war to an end. But the Second International was already breaking up. The German Socialists in the Reichstag had voted war credits for the Kaiser's Government. Vandervelde, the Belgian Socialist leader who was chairman of the International Bureau, had joined the Belgian Cabinet, Marcel Sembat in France had become a member of the French Cabinet. In Russia, it is true, the Social Democrats refused to vote for war credits for the Tsarist Government, but they, too, co-operated in other ways.

In every country there was a minority of Socialists who opposed the war. Like Keir Hardie and the other I.L.P. workers, Liebknecht, Haase and Ledebour of Germany continued to serve the vision of an international working-class solidarity as they saw it, believing that it could cut through all frontiers and, "across the roar of guns," make possible an international Socialist co-operation to end the war.

Yet even those who hated war most and continued to oppose

it recognized now that the chief responsibility lay with German militarism and that there could be no peace until that militarism was destroyed. Thus when, in February, 1915, the British section of the Socialist International brought together the Socialist parties of Britain, France, Belgium and Russia in an Inter-Allied Socialist Conference in London, over which Keir Hardie presided, the conference, first referred to the deep-lying general cause of the war which it saw as a "monstrous product of the antagonisms which tear asunder capitalist society." But having said this it also declared that:

> "The invasion of Belgium and France by the German armies threatens the very existence of independent nationalities and strikes a blow at all faith in treaties. In these circumstances victory for German imperialism would be the defeat and the destruction of democracy and liberty in Europe."

For the majority of the Labour and trade-union movement the necessity to defeat German imperialism lest it should destroy all democracy and liberty in Europe was from 4 August the paramount consideration of policy. Because of it the T.U.C. and the General Federation of Trade Unions united in agreeing, on 24 August, to an industrial truce under which all strike action should be banned and on 29 August the National Executive of the Labour Party agreed both to accept an electoral truce for the duration of the war and to take part in a national recruiting campaign.

And because of it, a few months later on 19 May, 1915, Arthur Henderson became a member of a Coalition Cabinet despite his and the Labour Party's long conviction of the necessity for independence.

CHAPTER XI

LABOUR JOINS THE GOVERNMENT

THE history of the Labour Party is not simply the history of a political and economic movement. It is the history also of men and women—of their comradeships, their loyalties and their conflicts. Because of this, one finds again and again within it the traditional qualities of great drama: the clash of personalities, the entrances and exits, tragic and moving, of men and women stirred by dreams and passions and fidelities which drive them along different pathways in pursuit of the same purpose.

Entrances and exits! As 1915 dawned, Keir Hardie, "that old-fashioned man," as Ramsay MacDonald described him, "that man like a great boulder of whinstone telling of the freshness of the hills," was nearing his end.

On the first Sunday of that New Year, ill and weary and under medical attention, he spoke for the last time at Hamilton where, thirty-five years before, he had been driven from the pits and had begun his life as a Labour agitator. He spoke to men who knew him, to many who had worked in the pits with him in those far-off days, the men to whom he had dedicated his life and who had for him the respect that his immense fidelity and integrity in their service had won. But now many of them were on the other side. They could not share his opposition to the war. They could not follow him in the course he had set. For the first time there was a breach between them.

In February he spoke for the last time in Parliament—the Parliament which had excited itself so inordinately about his first appearance and in which he had been the target of so much bitterness. He spoke against a wartime proposal to allow children under twelve to be employed on farms. There could have been no more dramatically fitting subject for his last appearance in that historic assembly—he who knew so much of child-labour from his own experience. A month later he wrote his last article for the *Labour Leader*, the paper he had founded, which had been for so long the vehicle of his thoughts. And at Easter he attended his last I.L.P. Conference—the I.L.P. which more than any man he had brought into being and which of all things had been closest to his heart.

It was held in the schoolroom of a Primitive Methodist church in Norwich. Other public halls in the city had been closed to it because of opposition to the anti-war policy of the I.L.P. His last words were to protest against the sending of members of the Russian seamen's union to Siberia and "all the infamies of the bloody cruelty of Russia." After that there was silence until in September, worn-out, broken-hearted, old before his years, he died at the age of fifty-nine.

On his last visit to Parliament he met in the Lobby the eighty-year-old Lord Morley who shared his opposition to the war and had resigned from the Cabinet because of it. There was between these two men, so different in their backgrounds but alike in the incorruptible qualities of their characters, a mutual respect. Lord Morley stopped and shook hands.

"You have been ill," he said. "What was the matter? Was it the war which so weighed upon your soul and spirit that it made your body sick?"

"I could only smile a vague assent," wrote Hardie. And, indeed, Morley's diagnosis was the true one. The war and the collapse of the ideal of international socialism that it had brought, the break, as he saw it, in the ranks of Labour and the decision of the majority of the Parliamentary Labour Party—which he had created—to support the war he opposed, robbed him of the spirit to live. Despite his prophetic vision, he was granted no view of the future to solace him in those hours. He saw, as he thought, his life work, and the cause which to him was greater than life, broken in pieces about him, and he no longer wished to live.

On the outbreak of war he went to his constituency and there he was not allowed to speak. Those who opposed his views on the war—with some who had always hated him—packed the hall where he appeared and drowned his words with songs and the ringing of bells. Friends had to walk on each side of him to the house where he was staying to protect him from the jeering and shouting crowds. When he reached the house he sat down by the fire and lit his pipe. He was silent for a time, looking into the fire. And then to William Stewart, with whom he shook hands before Stewart went off to catch a train down the valley, he said: "Now I understand what Christ suffered in Gethsemane as well as any man living."

Entrances and exits!

In May of that same year in the very month that Hardie, disillusioned and broken in health, was moved from his lodgings in Nevill's Court, off Fleet Street, to hospital, Arthur Henderson, a man governed by a loyalty to the cause of Labour no less than his and who was in the course of time to make a contribution to it hardly smaller than his own, joined a Coalition Government of Liberals and Conservatives as a Cabinet Minister the better to advance the successful prosecution of the war which Hardie opposed. Through such different doors do the compulsions and conflicts of loyalty lead men governed by the same purpose.

Hardie and Henderson. These men, alike in so little, had both an integrity that no assault of fate or fortune could shake. Both were men of the working-classes, without desire or pretence to be otherwise. Both gave to the Labour movement a fidelity single-hearted and incorruptible. Yet at the end of Hardie's life they found themselves, though respecting each other still, implacably opposed in their courses. Here are the authentic ironies and tragedies of drama.

Hardie's work was ended, though its influence was to live long after him. Henderson—although he had already given much service to the Labour movement—was, in a full sense, only just beginning his real work. And he, too, twenty years later, was to die, as Hardie had and as so many of the pioneers before them had, at a moment when all that he had lived and worked for seemed shattered and broken; when the twin causes of socialism and peace on which he had spent himself seemed alike defeated and when old comrades with whom he had worked all his political life had become separated in a conflict infinitely less bridgeable than that which divided Hardie and him in that May, 1915.

But his work, like Hardie's, was to live on.

Now at that moment in 1915 it seemed to Henderson, as it

did to the majority of those in the trade unions and the Parliamentary Labour Party, although not to those in the I.L.P., that, however critical they might be of the diplomacy that had led to the war, there was but one course open to them—a course that forced them inevitably to reject the view that Hardie held. To them it was clear that the war must be fought until victory was secured, for they knew that defeat would spell the end of the democracy whose values they cherished and on whose foundations alone the Labour movement they served could build a new society.

"Had Labour been hostile, the war could not have been carried on effectively," wrote Lloyd George in his *War Memoirs*. "Had Labour been lukewarm, victory would have been secured with increased and increasing difficulty."

The leaders of Labour were no less aware of this than Lloyd George.

Nevertheless, the decision to join a Coalition Government in which Labour could be only a very junior partner was not taken lightly.

Already the majority of the members of the Labour and trade-union movement had demonstrated their willingness to make their maximum contribution to the war effort—at the risk, as it sometimes seemed, of splitting the Socialist movement irretrievably. The trade unions had declared an industrial truce prohibiting strikes for the duration of the war. The political Labour Party had accepted a political truce. Its leaders had agreed to take part in the recruiting drive, although they did so in the teeth of the opposition of many of their own left-wing or pacifist supporters. As the demand for men and munitions grew, they agreed to "dilution"—to the employment, that is, of unskilled workers in industries and on jobs that had formerly been restricted to skilled workers, although dilution seemed at times as though it might threaten standards achieved only with difficulty after prolonged industrial struggle.

Moreover, these threatened standards were themselves in many cases pitiably low. In the engineering industry the wages for a skilled fitter ranged from 30s. to 41s. a week. Henderson and the trade-union leaders, aided by women such as Mary Macarthur, fought to safeguard these rates from destruction under the impact of dilution. But, as they did so, the voice of many of the employers was heard in the trade journal, *The Engineer*, which declared categorically:

> "The fact of the matter is not that women are paid too little but that men are paid too much for work that can be done without previous training. High wages are paid on the false assumption, now almost obscured by trade-union regulations, that it takes long to learn the craft. Everyone knows now, as all managers knew long ago, that the whole argument of high wages based on long training has been carried by the board."

In an atmosphere in which, while profits soared, wages of 30s. a week could be denounced as absurdly high and a minimum of £1 a week for women was bitterly opposed, it was not easy for the leaders of Labour to persuade their followers that patriotism demanded the setting aside of the strike weapon and co-operation with the representatives of those who sought to exploit them.

Patriotism began to assume a one-sided air. It was, it seemed, to be patriotism for the workers but profits for the employers.

"I am quite satisfied," wrote a high official of the Industrial Commissioner's Department in a memorandum which went to the Minister of Munitions, "I am quite satisfied that the labour difficulty has been largely caused by the men being of opinion that, while they were being called upon to be patriotic and refrain from using the strong economic position they occupy, employers, merchants and traders were being allowed the fullest freedom to exploit to the fullest the nation's needs."

Yet, because of their conviction of the national necessity, representatives of the Trades Union Congress, the General Federation of Trade Unions and thirty-three trade unions concerned in munitions went, under Arthur Henderson's chairmanship, to meet Lloyd George and Walter Runciman at the Treasury in March and agreed to waive trade-union practices for the duration of the war in return for undertakings—never fully carried out—that there would be some limitation of profits.

By now it was clear that all hopes of a short war ending in speedy victory were illusory. The allied offensive in France had failed. The Dardanelles expedition had failed. Officers and soldiers on leave from the front were bringing back tragic stories of shortage of shells.

Finally, in the second half of May, Lord Fisher, First Sea Lord, presented his resignation to the Prime Minister, giving as his reason his acute disagreement with Winston Churchill, the First Lord. Asquith bowed before the storm which faced him from all sides, agreed to reform his administration and offered to replace the existing Liberal Government with a Coalition.

It was against this background of crisis and anxiety as to the course of the war that the invitation came to Arthur Henderson, as leader of the Parliamentary Labour Party, to join a Coalition of twelve Liberals, eight Conservatives and one non-party minister, Lord Kitchener. Junior ministerial posts were also offered to two other Labour representatives.

At a first consideration the Parliamentary Labour Party decided to reject the invitation by nine votes to eight. This vote was not, however, based solely on the opposition of a majority to any participation in a war government—the attitude of the I.L.P. members. It was due also to the feeling of others that there ought to be no such collaboration without the sanction of a Party Conference.

When the National Executive of the Party met on the same day it took a different view and voted in favour of acceptance by nineteen votes to eleven. There was thereupon a joint meeting and finally the Parliamentary Party accepted the National Executive view. The decision to join the Government was endorsed. Henderson became President of the Board of Education with a seat in the Cabinet— although in fact his real appointment was that of Labour Adviser and his duties at the Board of Education were nominal, educational policy having been one of the earliest war casualties. William Brace, a Welsh miners' leader, became Under-Secretary for Home Affairs and G. H. Roberts, Junior Lord of the Treasury.

This decision to join the Coalition divided the Labour movement. It was opposed by the I.L.P., and not only the I.L.P. but by many, such as J. R. Clynes, who were in support of the general pro-war policy. It seemed to them to represent an abandonment of that policy of independence upon which the Labour Party had been founded. Nor was Henderson himself altogether happy about it. He disliked holding a post—even although only nominally—as President of the Board of Education, for which he felt himself unfitted, and in circumstances which made it impossible for him to do anything effective in education or even have time to acquaint himself with the work of his department. This discomfort was increased by the fact that Ramsay MacDonald, and other I.L.P. leaders who had a much closer knowledge of educational matters than he had himself, were highly critical of the Government's educational policy—or rather lack of policy—so that Henderson was put in the position of defending a department for which he was only nominally responsible, and of which he had little knowledge, against the attacks of fellow-leaders of his own party who knew much more about the matter than he did and were not averse to showing it.

After a time he succeeded in ridding himself of this particular embarrassment by persuading Asquith that a full-time President of the Board of Education, able to devote himself to planning for the future, was essential and that he himself ought to become Labour Adviser in both name and fact. But although this change solved one problem it left many others.

To be Labour Adviser to a predominantly Liberal and Conservative Government, most of whose members were by tradition and upbringing incapable of recognizing the full significance of the emergence of a working-class movement or of accepting it as a full partner in the national effort, was bound to be a difficult task.

He became the principal target of the pacifist wing of the Party. That was sufficiently serious for one whose political life was governed primarily by his belief in the necessity to build a strong united party.

What was even more serious was that he also became an object of suspicion to many industrial workers who had been persuaded that Labour collaboration with Liberals and Tories in a Cabinet—in which Henderson as the sole representative of a minority had responsibility without power—was merely a pretext to secure the acquiescence of workers in an attack upon conditions under the excuse of the necessities of war.

Trade-union protection of wage rates had been waived, but the pledge given to limit profits had not been carried out to anything like the full extent promised. Men working for private firms felt that under wartime restrictions they were losing their freedom, not as part of a common effort, but simply to advantage employers.

"I am as much a slave of Sir William Beardmore as if I had a letter B branded on my brow," said David Kirkwood when Lloyd

George and Arthur Henderson went to Beardmore's works on Clydeside on Christmas Eve, 1915, to examine the cause of delays in the delivery of heavy artillery.

Moreover, although dilution would in any event have been unavoidable if the output of munitions was to be increased with the rapidity demanded by the course of the war, the problems with which it faced the trade unions had been enormously increased by indiscriminate recruiting. This had taken into the Army thousands of skilled men who would have been infinitely more useful to the nation in the munition factories. Yet, even when the national need for skilled workers was made clear, the Army refused to release them. Furthermore, the need for a rapid industrial recruitment of unskilled workers was used by many employers as an excuse to destroy standards obtained by skilled workers after a long struggle—standards the maintenance of which was felt to be absolutely essential by men in the trenches no less than by those remaining in the factories.

"Trade unionists," as Lloyd George himself wrote, "flocked to the standard of their country when volunteers were called for to face death, but men at the front, daily confronted with death and needing shells to protect and defend themselves, wrote home to their fellow trade unionists entreating them not to surrender any of the privileges of their craft, although strict adhesion to these privileges was impeding the supply of the munitions they so badly needed."

Trade unionists had indeed flocked to the colours in response to the national call. By April, 1916, nearly 3,770,000 men were actually in service and, when the married men who had "attested" under the Derby Scheme but had not yet been called up and the "starred" single men were added, the total was over 4,660,000. The bitterness of men who felt that they and their class had responded magnificently both in the field and in the factories to the national need and that this very willingness was being used against them was deepened by the miserly treatment of soldiers' wives and families, by accusations of poor time-keeping and drunkenness thrown out against workers on unreliable evidence and lightly accepted by Cabinet Ministers, and by the rapidly rising cost of living.

Yet still the need for men increased as the huge armies on the

Continent found themselves locked in a type of warfare altogether contemptuous of human life.

To meet this need, a Military Service Bill was laid before Parliament by the Government to compel single men who had not attested under the Derby Scheme to go into the Army before married men. This bill brought to a climax the Labour revolt. A joint meeting of the National Executive and the Parliamentary Party at once instructed Labour Members of Parliament to oppose it in all its stages and Henderson and his two Labour colleagues tendered their resignation to the Prime Minister.

They felt, as did many others, that such a measure of conscription—of the military necessity of which they were by no means convinced—was a negation of the democratic principles for which the nation was fighting. Moreover, behind military conscription the trade unions saw a threat of industrial conscription which might permanently destroy the freedom and negotiating power of the workers.

Sending his resignation to Asquith, Henderson begged him to realize "the intensity of feeling which the Government's proposals had evoked."

This intensity of feeling was, he said, shared not simply by "a manageable minority who would oppose compulsion in all circumstances and would be influenced by no arguments, but also by the much larger number who have given the Government loyal support during the war, but who believe that, in the circumstances of today, compulsion, or this particular measure of compulsion, is unnecessary or dangerous, or both."

Expressing with complete precision the feelings that were so rapidly creating anger and frustration within the great mass of the Labour movement, he declared that:

"They think it unnecessary because they have not been given any clear idea of our military objective or obligations, and dangerous because they doubt our capacity to maintain continually increasing forces without risk to our finance and trade. . . . But no one who has studied the recent history of Labour will doubt that it is the fear of encroachment on civil and industrial freedom— on a man's right to choose his own trade and his own master and to make his own terms of service—that makes the opposition to military compulsion a question of principle and almost of passion with men whose devotion to their country is wholly beyond question."

Asquith, despite his general lack of understanding of the needs and moods of Labour, could not fail to realize the critical situation that would follow from such a conflict with it. He at once met the Labour Party Executive and gave a pledge—honoured, as it turned out, for less than six months and possibly beyond anyone's power to honour for long in the circumstances of the war—that conscription would not be extended to married men. He gave also explicit undertakings that there would be no industrial conscription.

On this the Labour Executive agreed to withdraw the resignation of Henderson and his two junior colleagues for the time being and to refer the matter to a full Party Conference at Bristol in the last week of January.

This was the first conference held since Labour had joined the Coalition. By 1,622,000 votes to 495,000 it endorsed the decision to join the Government, but by 1,716,000 votes to 360,000 it declared its opposition to conscription. The resolution on conscription was, however, so amended that it did not specifically instruct the Party's parliamentary representatives to demand the repeal of the Conscription Bill which had actually been passed into law a week before. A much more specific motion pledging the Party in and out of Parliament to agitate for repeal was lost, although only by 649,000 votes to 614,000 with over 800,000 abstentions.

In these circumstances and in view of the assurances given to the National Executive by Asquith, Henderson felt entitled to stay in the Government. Nevertheless, these votes demonstrated clearly the divisions within the Party and the confusion into which it had been thrown by the conscription issue.

There were now three major groups within the Labour movement. Their nature is important not only because of the immediate conflicts they produced, but because of their continuing consequences in the history of the Labour Party long after the war was done.

The majority of the Party and the majority of the trade unions, although often suspicious of the Government's methods and

decisions, were fully resolved of the necessity for complete co-operation in the war effort, even when it meant collaboration with political
opponents many of whose economic and social policies they disliked.
They accepted the defeat of German militarism as the overriding
national necessity and were ready to make great sacrifices to secure
it. But, at the same time, they were watchful and suspicious of the
development of militarism within Britain itself and were not prepared
fully to accept the doctrine of a fight to the finish which increasingly
dominated the thinking of those in command.

The I.L.P., following the lead of Hardie, MacDonald, Snowden
and others, was for the most part anti-war. This anti-war feeling,
which had important consequences upon the fortunes of the Labour
Party, derived from two sources. There were those, of whom
MacDonald was one and Snowden perhaps to an even greater
degree another, who based their opposition to the war primarily on
their criticism of the policies which had preceded it. They saw in it
a conflict between rival imperialisms in which, although Germany
might be the most guilty, none of the allied countries was innocent.
They believed that, in such circumstances, the Labour Party should
safeguard its independence in order to use its influence to secure an
early and just peace, although they accepted the fact that while the
war was on its members could not stand aside from the national
effort. But they felt that to join the Government was, in Snowden's
phrase, "to take away the freedom of independent criticism which
at a time like this may be the most valuable service a small party
can render to the nation."

There were others in the I.L.P. who went further than this and
who were opposed—as MacDonald and Snowden were not—to the
war on completely pacifist grounds. To them no war in any circumstances could be justified. They considered war itself so evil
that none but evil consequences could flow from it, however
just the cause in which a nation took up arms might seem at the
time.

Finally, there was a growing industrial wing within the Labour
movement which opposed collaboration with the Government not
so much on grounds of opposition to war policy as because they saw
in it a betrayal of the class interests of the workers. They were not
for the most part Marxists. Few of them probably were aware of

Lenin's thesis that the workers should transform the imperialist war into a civil war, nor would they have accepted it if they had been. But they were aware that war had increased the power of the working-classes if they cared to use it, and they were also aware, emotionally at any rate, that this increase in power was being fought by employers many of whom saw in the war an opportunity to break the industrial strength of the unions. To them the industrial truce represented a betrayal of working-class interests and co-operation in a capitalist government collaboration with the enemy.

Many of them were stirred by the syndicalist ideas which had been gathering strength so rapidly up to the outbreak of war. More of them were influenced by conflicts with employers within their own industries and a sharp awareness of the profiteering that was being carried on under the cloak of war. They were affected, too, by rising prices.

They turned to direct industrial action in defiance of their official trade-union leaders because they felt, or many of them did, that so long as the official trade-union policy of full co-operation in the war stood they could not depend upon their leaders to fight their battles for them.

Out of this complex of feelings came strikes on Clydeside and elsewhere—by 1916 the number of days lost through strikes had risen to 4,000,000—and the rise of the shop stewards' movement as a challenge to the established trade-union organization. Out of it, too, came increasing bitterness between the trade-union and political leaders and the new leaders thrown up by the rank and file in the factories.

This bitterness reached its climax when, without Henderson's knowledge, the Government ordered leaders of the Clyde Workers' Committee, David Kirkwood among them, to be deported from Glasgow.

Yet, rent and torn by conflict as the Labour movement sometimes appeared to be, bitter as the controversies at its annual conferences were, the Party succeeded in doing what no Socialist Party on the Continent succeeded in doing. It succeeded in remaining a single party.

It was divided in policy, but it remained an organized single party. There was no permanent break in the ranks. This was the more remarkable in that, politically, the Party was in a highly anomalous position.

The Parliamentary Party was small and divided. Its best-known leaders were, with the exception of Henderson, opposed to the majority view. In the country its position was even more difficult. Its main political organization in the constituencies had always rested with the I.L.P. To the great majority of ordinary people the speeches at I.L.P. meetings were not only the authentic but almost the only voice of Labour. Yet the I.L.P. no longer represented the view of the Labour Party, as shown at its annual conferences. It was emphatically opposed to the full co-operation in the war which the trade-union members supported.

At the same time as it found itself in this anomalous position the political recognition secured by the Labour Party was greater than ever before and was shortly to be increased when Lloyd George succeeded Asquith as head of a reorganized government.

But this recognition, although given to the political party and primarily to Henderson as its leader, derived not from political but industrial causes. It arose, not from any great support for the Labour Party as a political force in the country, but from the fact that it was the political voice of the industrial workers. Such recognition as was given was not due to belief in the importance of the political Labour movement and certainly not of the Socialist movement or to any sympathy with its political aims. It was due entirely to recognition of its practical importance in wartime as the political representative of the trade unions.

Its wartime effectiveness was thus very largely that of a trade-union pressure-group. Asquith and Lloyd George cared nothing for its Socialist following. They regarded Socialists in wartime as at best a nuisance and at worst traitors. But they were well aware—and Lloyd George especially—that without the support of the trade unions the war could not be won. The only importance of the Labour Party to them was that it could act in political matters as the spokesmen of the organized industrial workers. The trade unions were equally aware of this. Many of them in addition hated as violently as did Asquith or Lloyd George or Bonar Law the anti-war views which the I.L.P.—the Socialist wing of the Party—persisted in maintaining.

There was a constant danger that out of this fact there would develop a cleavage which would permanently alter the character of the Party and destroy the original conception of an alliance between the organized workers and the Socialist societies on which it had been founded.

The credit for preventing this from happening must go primarily to Henderson. He saw what he conceived to be his own duty clearly, but he possessed the tolerance and the magnanimity which enabled him to understand that others might, no less sincerely, be impelled to follow a different course. He opposed all attempts to drive those who took a minority view out of the Party. He accepted criticism and abuse without losing his own generosity of spirit or allowing himself to be stirred by the passions of the moment. He never lost sight of the necessity for holding the Party organization together for the future.

Nor, as he so well might have done, did he seek to use the circumstances of the time to advance his own claim to leadership either during the war or afterwards. For him, the interests of the Party always came before his own and, although he was a trade unionist whose great strength came from the confidence of the trade-union leaders in his political judgment and integrity, the idea to which he gave his continuing allegiance was not that of a trade-union party only, but of a Labour Party in the widest sense of that term.

It was this loyalty which drove him to accept and continue to hold office in a Coalition Government despite the criticism it brought him. He could see no future for the ordinary people of Britain or for the Labour Party which sought to represent their interests unless the war was won.

"I have been asked why I did not resign," he said in answer to bitter criticisms at a Labour Party Conference over the deportation of the Clydeside workers' leaders. "I should be resigning every day to please some of you. I am not sure I should not resign if I were to please myself. But I am not here either to please myself or you. I am here to see the war through."

It was that loyalty which persuaded him to accept an even larger share of responsibility when, in December, 1916, the Asquith Government fell and Lloyd George stepped into the first place.

In the manoeuvres which led to that change Henderson had

no part. Although they were in many ways so different and so unsympathetic in outlook, he liked and respected Asquith. He did not either like or trust Lloyd George, although Lloyd George had an infinitely greater awareness of the power that rested in the working-classes than Asquith possessed.

When the climax of the long campaign conducted against Asquith by Lloyd George was reached, and Henderson, along with Asquith, Lloyd George, Bonar Law and Balfour, was called to a meeting of Party leaders at Buckingham Palace, he urged that Asquith should stay on.

But, at a meeting of the ministers who supported Asquith that same evening, he alone refused to pledge himself not to serve in any administration of which Asquith was not the head. Instead, he urged Asquith to agree to serve either under Lloyd George or Bonar Law in order that "a truly national administration might be formed."

In this, as in Labour Party matters, the cause was to him more important than any person.

To Lloyd George when he was invited to form a government —Bonar Law having declined to do so because of Asquith's refusal to serve under him—it was a matter of great moment to secure Labour co-operation. He was faced, he knew, with the bitter hostility of at least half the Liberal Party and with the angry contempt of the majority of the Tory ministers—although he had the support of Bonar Law and shortly afterwards secured that of Balfour and Carson. To create a national administration that would last for longer than the six weeks the political pundits were prophesying for his premiership, he must produce a ministry broadly based on all parties.

Moreover, apart altogether from the sheer business of political tactics in which he had long been adroit, he had a deeper under-standing than any other minister of the absolute necessity of Labour co-operation and of the causes of labour unrest.

But the Labour Party was bitterly critical of the intrigues which had led up to the overthrow of the Asquith Government and of the campaign against Asquith in the Northcliffe newspapers which had preceded it—and which, it was generally suspected, had been fed if not directly inspired by Lloyd George.

When Lloyd George saw Henderson on the morning after the

King had invited him to form a Government, Henderson informed him that the Parliamentary Party and the National Executive were divided as to whether Labour should or should not support his government. They wished to see him before coming to a final decision.

A meeting was arranged at noon. It is significant of the cohesion of the Labour Party that, despite its severe internal dissensions, the deputation that called to cross-examine the new Prime Minister, before deciding whether or not the Government should be supported, included the leaders of both sides within the Party. MacDonald and Snowden were present as well as Henderson, J. H. Thomas, and J. R. Clynes, with—somewhere between the two main wings of the Party—Sidney Webb, who now represented the Fabians on the National Executive.

It was a stormy and controversial meeting. Lloyd George opened by offering a number of important pledges. He informed the Labour representatives that he proposed to set up an inner War Cabinet of five non-departmental ministers responsible for the higher direction of the war and offered Labour a seat on this War Cabinet. He told them also that he would set up a new ministry—a Ministry of Labour—to deal with all man-power questions, and that this should have a Labour man at its head, and another new ministry—a Ministry of Pensions—which should also have a Labour minister in charge. In addition, he proposed that three junior ministerial posts should be offered to Labour.

Of hardly less importance, he undertook that there should be State control of mines and shipping during the war and that a Controller should be appointed to supervise food production and distribution. And he promised that at last—after more than two years of war during which food prices had risen by nearly eighty per cent—there should be food-rationing.

He was at once cross-examined by members of the deputation —and not simply on the immediate issues which he had covered in his speech to them, but at even greater length on his general policy as regards the war and the peace.

Would Labour be consulted in the Peace negotiations? It was inconceivable, he replied, that it should not be.

Was it his intention to continue the war until a decisive victory

242

had been achieved which would enable the Allies to dictate their own terms of peace or would he be prepared at any time to give favourable consideration to reasonable proposals put forward either by neutrals or by the enemy? If the proposals were reasonable he replied they would be listened to. Negotiations with Germany were not ruled out, but, before entering into them, the Allies must have a clear idea of what she meant.

Was he contemplating industrial conscription? No. There must be full mobilization of labour, but no change from the former administration was contemplated.

So the cross-examination continued, MacDonald and Sidney Webb being the most persistent questioners.

The deputation then retired to consider its decision on what was later described in the report of the National Executive to the Annual Conference as "probably the most serious position the Party has had to face in the whole of its existence."

The recognition now offered to Labour was substantial. Parliamentarily, it was a small party of under forty members and was, moreover, seriously and, as it sometimes seemed, incurably divided. Yet it was being offered a seat in the War Cabinet, the control of two new ministries with whose sphere of activity the Labour movement was particularly concerned, three junior appointments, undertakings on mining, shipping and food-rationing which it had long been pressing for and the promise of a voice in making the peace when the time should come.

Such an offer was clearly due to the new Prime Minister's appreciation that the strength of its influence with the organized workers was far in excess of its small parliamentary strength. The offer represented a substantial advance in authority from anything previously obtained and a considerable recognition of Labour's real position in the new balance of society that war was bringing with it.

But it also involved partnership in a government whose leadership many, perhaps most, Labour people distrusted. And although Labour's status in the new government would be much greater than in the old it would still remain a junior partner, able perhaps to influence but not to determine the ultimate course of policy.

The National Executive and the Parliamentary Party remained divided. MacDonald, Snowden and the other I.L.P. leaders were still against participation. So were some of the trade-union leaders, but Clynes and J. H. Thomas, who had been against participation in the first coalition, were in favour. So was Henderson. Finally, after long discussion, it was decided by the small majority of seventeen votes to fourteen to accept. Henderson joined the War Cabinet, John Hodge became the first Minister of Labour, and G. N. Barnes the first Minister of Pensions. William Brace, G. H. Roberts and James Parker had minor posts and, when a Ministry of Food was set up with Lord Rhondda as its head, J. R. Clynes became its first Parliamentary Secretary and later, when Lord Rhondda died, its head.

Labour was now deeply involved in government. The decision to participate, although it had been reached in the first place only by a very small majority, was confirmed at the Annual Conference in Manchester on 23 January, 1917, by an overwhelming one: 1,849,000 votes to 307,000.

But if the decision had the mass support of the great majority of the "middle-of-the-road" trade unionists whose votes were decisive at an annual conference and who shared Henderson's conception alike of the national need and of the responsibility of the Labour movement in face of that need, it was by no means accepted by many of those most politically active in the movement.

It was attacked at the Annual Conference in bitter speeches by Philip Snowden, Fred Bramley and other I.L.P. leaders, by the delegate of the British Socialist Party and, on the trade-union side, by Ernest Bevin, making his first appearance at a Labour Party conference as a delegate of the Dock, Wharf, Riverside and General Workers' Union led by Ben Tillett.

The split in the ranks of Labour appeared to be widening. Not only was there a deep division on political policy, but the Conference met at a period of acute industrial unrest. A few weeks before there had been a great strike in Sheffield. In Manchester itself, as the Labour delegates gathered in the city, the engineering shops were seething with an unrest that was soon to spread over all the industrial areas until, within a few weeks, a quarter of a million engineering workers were to be on strike. The shop stewards' movement, operating often in opposition to the official trade-union leaders, was growing in strength and influence and was to become the leader of a series of strikes throughout the country.

For a moment Henderson, with the support of the majority of the organized Labour movement, was a leading member of the Lloyd George Government. Because of that, the conflict between those who supported him and those who attacked him on both the political and industrial sides of the movement seemed likely at times to threaten the whole basis upon which the Labour Party had been built.

Yet within two months the first Russian revolution was drastically to alter the political scene. And within six months Henderson himself was to resign from the War Cabinet on an issue of principle which made him the target of bitter attack by some within the Labour movement who had previously applauded him—but which was to forge a new alliance between himself, MacDonald and Sidney Webb and in the end to establish the Labour Party on a firmer foundation than it had ever been before.

CHAPTER XII

THE LEADERS WHO STAYED OUTSIDE

IF THE position of Arthur Henderson and those other leaders of the Labour and trade-union movement who supported the Government in its war policy and were in consequence subjected to severe attacks from many of their former colleagues was not an enviable one, that of MacDonald, Snowden, Lansbury and the others who opposed the war from the start was even less so.

They were subjected to the anger and vilification of the overwhelming mass of the Press and to the bitter hatred and contempt of the majority of public opinion. They were denounced as traitors and pro-Germans. Many of their meetings were broken up.

Yet because they, like Henderson, followed with courage and integrity the road along which their convictions impelled them—even although it was at first a road so different from his—in the end their stand added greatly to the moral stature of Labour and brought into its ranks many men and women capable of a great intellectual and moral contribution to its cause.

There were, as has been pointed out in an earlier chapter, some among the leaders and members of the I.L.P. and its wartime supporters who were out-and-out pacifists and who believed that nothing should be done to assist the national war effort.

That was not, however, the mood of MacDonald, Snowden and most of the other principal parliamentary leaders. They had opposed the foreign policy that led up to the war, but now that it was upon the world they by no means took the view that its outcome was a matter of small account or that it should be ended by a British cease-fire. They did not, as some of the pacifists and Socialist groups in France did for example, and as some of the pacifist groups in Britain would have preferred, vote against war credits. They accepted the fact that, so long as the war was on, everything possible must be done to provide the Services with the means to fight.

But they attacked from the beginning the idea that all the war guilt was on one side and that the war could only be ended by outright victory—by the knock-out blow, as Lloyd George later described it. They believed that an honourable and a just peace could be secured by negotiation—and that it was more likely that a democratic and peaceful Europe would come to pass in the future from such a peace than that it would from a war fought to the bitter end.

Therefore, from the very outbreak of war they set themselves to do two things—to expose the real causes of the war as they saw them and to campaign consistently and continuously for a peace by negotiation—a peace in which there would be neither victor nor vanquished.

They believed that the second was conditional upon the first. Only if the real causes of war were understood, only if it were seen that although the major guilt for the war might rest on the shoulders of the German rulers they did not bear the guilt alone, would the passions that war had aroused be reduced and a public mood established that would make possible a negotiated peace that should be just and stable. Moreover, only if the true causes of the war were understood would the terms of peace when it came be such as to make possible the avoidance of future war.

This was a clear and consistent policy, although it may have given insufficient weight to the true force and objectives of German militarism, and consequently to the impossibility of securing German acceptance of a just peace, so long as the Kaiser and his generals believed in the possibility of victory. But to many during the war it appeared neither clear nor consistent. Those who advocated it, and MacDonald in particular, were attacked on the one side for faltering in their opposition to war when they accepted some of the practical policies that flowed inevitably from it, and reviled on the other as pro-Germans and believers in peace at any price.

It must be confessed, however, that while the policy itself was consistent, MacDonald himself did not always seem so in his application of it.

Snowden, when asked to take part in a recruiting campaign, replied straightforwardly that he could not do so because it would be wrong of him to ask men to fight in a war of which he did not approve and that in his view enlistment was entirely a matter for individual conscience—but that if men believed that liberty called them to fight for liberty, then they would go and would be deserving of all honour for going under so noble an impulse.

MacDonald, however, when he received a similar request from his constituency, Leicester, declined to attend the recruiting meeting, but wrote a letter to the mayor in which he said among other things: "Well, we cannot go back now, nor can we turn to the right or the left. We must go straight through. History will in due time apportion the praise and blame, but the young men of the country must, for the moment, settle the immediate issue of victory . . . I want the serious men of the trade-union, the Brotherhood and similar movements to face their duty. To such men it is enough to say, 'England has need of you,' to say it in the right way. They will gather to her aid. They will protect her. And when the war is over they will see to it that the policies and conditions that make it will go like the mists of a plague and the shadows of a pestilence."

The announcement by the mayor that he had received a letter from Ramsay MacDonald was greeted with contradictory shouts of "Read it" and "Burn it." When it was read it created some not unnatural confusion—a confusion which spread as its contents became more widely known. In the somewhat unprecise language to which MacDonald tended to turn in moments of difficulty it seemed to put forward an appeal to fight for "King and Country" not very different from that of the recruiting posters and quite contrary to the policy of the I.L.P., one of whose principal leaders he was. MacDonald, however, denied that it did so when tackled about it at a later meeting and it is probable that he meant to express opinions pretty much the same as those of Snowden.

Certainly, although some of his speeches at this time—as later —were neither precise nor lucid, his general attitude to the war was clear and was maintained with great courage.

This attitude sprang for him, as for most of those in the Labour movement who shared his views, from the profound conviction that the British people had been brought into the war very largely on false pretences and that the mood which governed the Asquith Government, and still more the Lloyd George Government, was such as to make impossible an honourable and just peace worthy of the sacrifice the ordinary men and women of Britain were being called upon to make.

The reasons why he believed that the British people had been taken into the war on false pretences, and why he considered Britain should have remained neutral, were set out with a considerable force and intellectual skill in an article he wrote for the *Labour Leader* on 14 August, which was later reprinted by the I.L.P. as a pamphlet. This article, unlike many of MacDonald's speeches, is a model of close analysis and argument. When read in full even at this distance of time it helps to make clear the qualities of intellectual leadership which gave MacDonald in his prime so dominating a position in the Labour movement and which are now sometimes forgotten in the tragedy and futility of his later years.

In it he declared: "The European war is the result of the existence of the Entente and the Alliance, and we are in it in consequence of Sir Edward Grey's foreign policy. . . . It is a diplomatists' war, made by about half a dozen men. . . . When we ask ourselves with the fullness of knowledge 'Why has this evil happened?' the only answer we can give is, because Sir Edward Grey has guided our foreign policy during the past eight years."

As proof of this charge he analysed the "correspondence respecting the European crisis" which had just been published as a White Paper.

In his view, this correspondence showed quite clearly that although Grey strove to the last to prevent a European war he did so against a background of his own previous policy which both made war and Britain's involvement in it inevitable, and which led him to reject every undertaking by Germany which would have enabled Britain to remain neutral and use her influence to restore peace. He traced the development of the Entente between Britain, France and Russia and the Alliance between Germany, Austria and Italy and showed that the nature of the diplomacy of which the Entente and the Alliance were the principal parts made a conflict between them inevitable. He showed further that Germany's aggressive attitude had been increased, and could in part be explained, by the fact that time was tipping the balance of power against her—the Entente "was forcing her to fight within two years."

In the light of all these facts he reached the conclusion that "taking a narrow view, Germany with Russia is mainly responsible for the war; taking a longer view, we are equally responsible."

Was it the case, he asked, that if war came between Germany and Austria on the one side, and France and Russia on the other, Britain must intervene? Had the German attack on Belgium, the tearing up of the scrap of paper, made her participation inevitable?

MacDonald held that if entanglements with France had not prevented him, Grey could have prevented the attack on Belgium, the event which overnight brought a complete change in British public opinion and without which the vast majority of the British people and probably the majority of the Cabinet also would not have supported war. And he further charged Grey and Asquith with withholding the truth from Parliament in order that the moral indignation of the British people, without which it would have been impossible to implement the secret pledges to France, should be unchecked by the actual truth.

He pointed out that an examination of the correspondence given in the White Paper showed that the Germans had made repeated efforts to secure British neutrality and that Sir Edward Grey had made no attempt to examine these offers and improve them. The German Ambassador had even gone so far as to propose his own conditions of neutrality and had suggested that the integrity of France and her colonies might be guaranteed. Grey had, however, refused to discuss the matter. Moreover, the fact that such an offer had been made was suppressed by both Asquith and Grey in their speeches to the House of Commons.

Furthermore, he accused Grey of misleading Parliament also about the true nature of the threat to Belgium in that he had told the House of Commons that the German offer to secure the integrity of Belgium, if passage of her troops was allowed, was unacceptable because it did not also guarantee the "independence" of Belgium. In fact, MacDonald pointed out the documents showed that the German offer had been to guarantee both Belgium's integrity and independence. And he said that the fact that Germany's military plans in the event of war included an attack on France through Belgium had been known for years and that Grey had done nothing at all to deter Germany from such a step in time to prevent war.

It was a formidable indictment, although MacDonald in his justifiable attack on Britain's pre-war policy and Grey's culpability gave insufficient attention perhaps to the paramount influence of Germany's militarist ambitions and to the fact that her real motive in seeking British neutrality was to make her domination of the Continent easier. Nor perhaps did he make it sufficiently plain that the real culpability of Asquith and Grey lay in their refusal to face Germany in time with the fact that Britain would fight. But his analysis of the general course—and the consequence—of Britain's foreign policy was masterly—and damaging.

Much of this case was restated by an even sharper pen in Bernard Shaw's "Commonsense about the War," which appeared in the *New Statesman* in November.

Shaw, however, did not make MacDonald's mistake of underestimating German militarism. And having demolished the official Foreign Office case for the war he characteristically proceeded to present it with a better case of his own. This did not prevent him from being attacked by all who supported the war, including the Labour *Daily Citizen*, nor from being thanked by Keir Hardie who, although a pacifist, which Shaw was not, was profoundly moved by so honest an examination of British policy. "Only a Celt," he wrote to Shaw, "could have done it."

MacDonald's indictment, being presented without any Shavian paradoxes, was, however, more quickly understood by statesmen and other patriotic persons who needed time and assistance to grasp what Shaw was driving at. At once MacDonald became the target of their most bitter attack. He was accused of deliberately helping Germany to poison the wells of world opinion against Britain. He was labelled "the most hated man in Britain." There were demands that the Government should take action against him.

MacDonald was not a pacifist in the full sense that Hardie, Lansbury, Maxton, Dr. Alfred Salter and some others of the I.L.P. leaders were. He was not so much a moral opponent of all war as an intellectual opponent of the foreign policy that he believed had produced this war and whose principles would also, he believed, govern the peace if war were fought to the bitter end. That was why to some of his pacifist supporters he sometimes seemed inconsistent. His attitude was more complex than theirs and placed him under greater personal strain—the more so that he was a man who liked popularity and now felt himself misjudged.

But the factual indictment which he and Snowden—the latter with a more certain conviction of his own rightness than MacDonald's, for such conviction came natural to him—launched against Grey and Asquith, and their later exposure of the post-war implications, as they saw them, of the Lloyd George policy of the "knock-out blow," added immense intellectual reinforcement to the moral convictions of the pacifists.

But if there were differences of view and of emphasis between MacDonald and the pacifists in the I.L.P., they were agreed as to the place of Socialists during the war.

MacDonald defined that place in one of the most moving and emotional speeches of his career at a memorial meeting to Keir Hardie in the City Hall, Glasgow, on 8 October, 1916, a year after Hardie's death.

"Assume that Hardie and his friends and the Party to which he belonged, the Party he founded; assume that they honestly held the opinions they enunciated," he said to the great audience that crowded the hall, "I ask: what was our duty? Our duty was to tell the country not to trust to militarism in order to save itself, but to tell it that this war, created by an old order of diplomacy, was inevitable, not because the Devil was about in some nation more than in another, but because the whole fabric was rotten at the core and was bound to fall."

And in another passage: "When a shipwreck takes place every man does not fly up to the captain's deck or go to the boats; every man has his own work to do, different from other men's work, and the safety and security of all depends not upon every man doing the same work as his neighbour, but on a subdivision of labour, so that individual services are co-ordinated to give the maximum security and the maximum amount of safety. When the bugles of war broke out we went to our appointed places. What was the appointed place of international Socialism? We knew perfectly well. We had read our histories. We knew that a perfect typhoon would rage round all our liberties, uprooting them, breaking, crushing and scattering them—north, south, east and west. Our appointed place was to stand by those liberties and defend them. Hardie knew that if we lost our democratic sense, if we put on one side our democratic political instincts, militarism would come across the seas; militarism would come to our own land; militarism would sit on our own thresholds; and, whilst our soldiers were fighting it on the Continent, our military authorities would give it hospitality, harbourage and welcome."

And finally: "The moment the peoples of Europe question things—the moment they ask why, how and wherefore—that moment the spell of war will be broken. They will come together in their sorrow and demand peace and lay the foundations of peace. . . . It is the old order that is crumbling and breaking to fragments, filling the air with its dust and the noise and confusion of its downfall. . . . We go back into the world to do our duty, to reconstruct society, to rebuild the fabric that has fallen, to make good the walls that have been crushed; to put a new idea, a new beauty, a new holiness into the lives of the peoples of Europe."

This then was their duty as MacDonald and his fellows of the I.L.P. saw it—to defend the cause of civil liberties, to ask questions, to stimulate in the minds of men and women, not only in Britain but throughout Europe, the attitudes and the ideas which would bring them together to end the war.

It was not an easy or a popular task. To the majority of the public those who set themselves to do it, whatever their motives, were pro-German enemies of their country. They were the "stop-the-war party"—at a time when to talk of stopping the war seemed treachery.

There were police raids on the I.L.P. Some of its pamphlets were seized. *Forward*, the Scottish Socialist paper, was suppressed. And although, in general, free speech was not destroyed, the I.L.P. struggled against mounting public opposition.

This public disfavour—so great that in the heat of war it seemed likely to destroy any possibility that the Socialist views of the I.L.P. would ever again be able to secure a sympathetic hearing —was balanced by a profound sense of dedication among the members of the I.L.P. itself and by an actual increase in its membership. It was faced with the bitter enmity of the vast majority, but the minority which turned to it—a minority that was to grow as the war proceeded—came to it with a deepened loyalty and passion.

Moreover, it attracted to itself and made joint cause with a number of prominent Liberals and intellectuals who shared MacDonald's and Snowden's suspicion of both the Asquith and the Lloyd George foreign policy. This was to have important and valuable consequences to the Labour Party after the war. It was to help to give the Socialist movement a wider and more classless appeal and was to enrich its philosophy with the traditions of what was best in Liberal thought—the toleration, the belief in freedom of speech, the objective search for truth, the conviction of the importance of the individual.

For the moment, however, the moral and intellectual partnership between the I.L.P. and men like Charles Trevelyan, Arthur Ponsonby, Norman Angell, E. D. Morel and Bertrand Russell, appeared merely to represent an association of the unpopular and the defeated. Not merely of the unpopular, but of the persecuted. Both E. D. Morel and Bertrand Russell were sent to prison (as were also several I.L.P. leaders, among them Maxton and R. C. Wallhead) —Russell for an article published by the No-Conscription Fellowship, Morel, who on the eve of the war had received a presentation of honour from heads of all the Churches and members of all political parties for his exposure of slavery in the Congo rubber plantations, for the crime of sending some of his pamphlets on the war to the great French writer, Romain Rolland, who was living at the time in Switzerland—a neutral country to which it was technically an offence to transmit printed matter.

When conscription came, and many members of the I.L.P., along with members of the Society of Friends and others who were pacifist on religious grounds, refused to serve in the Army, the unpopularity of the I.L.P. as their political defender grew. So did the number of those imprisoned for their political and religious beliefs. More than 1,540 were sent to prison with sentences of two years' hard labour—the maximum period for which a sentence of hard labour is allowable and in the eyes of many legal authorities the most severe sentence that can be inflicted—more severe than penal servitude, for in penal servitude the conditions of imprisonment are much easier.

As Bernard Shaw wrote in a letter to the *Manchester Guardian* commenting on the two years' sentence on the I.L.P. leader, Clifford

Allen, founder of the No-Conscription Fellowship: "A prisoner can be killed by sentencing him to hard labour for a continuing offence and renewing his sentences as they expire." Seventy-one of the conscientious objectors so sentenced did in fact die.

To defend free speech, the right of conscientious objection, the wages and conditions both of the skilled workers and the dilutees; to fight profiteering, and militarism, these were the immediate tasks that those Socialists who stood aloof from the coalition set themselves to do. They had the assistance of the *Labour Leader*, which after one attempt at suppression was allowed to carry on its campaign unmolested; *Forward*, which was suppressed for a time, and Lansbury's weekly *Herald*, which conducted its anti-war campaigns with the same dash and wit as had characterized it in its pre-war days.

But although these were their immediate tasks, they did not lose sight of their ultimate aim which was to seek to create an atmosphere in which peace by negotiation would become possible. The instrument through which that could be accomplished was, they believed, international socialism.

Immediately after the outbreak of war, the International Socialist Bureau was removed from Brussels to neutral territory at the Hague, where Camille Huysmans, the Belgian Secretary, accompanied it. In January, 1915, what was to prove an even more important development took place. The Socialists of the four neutral countries, Sweden, Norway, Denmark and Holland, set up a committee of neutrals under the leadership of the Swedish Socialist, Hjalmar Branting, in order to be ready for any opportunity that might occur of intervening to restore peace.

It was a firm article of I.L.P. faith that war guilt rested not on the people of any country but on their leaders. Within a few weeks of the outbreak of war, therefore, it sought to arrange an international Socialist conference to which German and Austrian Socialists should be invited along with the Socialist Parties of the allied and neutral countries. But French Socialists refused to take part in any meeting at which Germans were present so long as any German soldier remained on French soil. The project had, therefore, to be dropped. In its place there was an Allied Socialist Conference. This met in London in February, 1915.

It supported the allied cause, and under the influence of the

French and Belgians went much farther than most of the I.L.P. in placing the sole guilt for the war on German shoulders. But at the same time it declared its determination "to resist any attempt to transform this defensive war into a war of conquest," stated emphatically that the Socialists of the allied countries were "not at war with the peoples of Germany and Austria, but only with the Governments of those countries by which they are oppressed," and urged that when the war was over there should be set up an "international authority to settle points of difference among the nations by compulsory conciliation and arbitration."

The allied Socialists hoped that this message would stimulate peace activities within Germany and Austria by holding out the prospect of a just and honourable peace by negotiation if militarist ambitions were abandoned. So it might have done if the Governments of the allied countries themselves had not been far from believing that the war could be ended by anything short of outright victory.

Seven months later, in September, 1915, a well-known Italian Socialist, Odelino Morgari, arrived in England on a mission from Italian and Swiss Socialists and met the I.L.P. leaders. He invited them to take part in an international Socialist conference at Zimmerwald, to organize a strong peace propaganda. They agreed and F. W. Jowett and Bruce Glasier were nominated as the British delegates. But the British Government stepped in and refused them passports.

Even if they had been allowed to go they would hardly have found themselves among men who shared their views. For the Zimmerwald Conference proved to be a conference not of democratic Socialists but of revolutionary Socialists, which the I.L.P. members certainly were not. At it there were delegates representing Germany, France, Italy, Russia, Poland, Rumania, Sweden, Norway, Holland and Switzerland. Not all of them were revolutionaries, but the most dominating personalities present were—chief among them, Lenin.

This conference declared for an immediate peace without annexations and for the revolutionary class war. It denounced the industrial truce and all Socialist groups which in any country had supported the war programmes of their government. It did so in such terms indeed that when the I.L.P. was sent a copy of the manifesto for its endorsement it had no option but to disassociate itself

THE TIGER : "Curious! I seem to hear a child weeping."

A PROPHETIC CARTOON

Will Dyson, the "Daily Herald's" cartoonist, made this drawing in 1919.

J. R. CLYNES

Trade-union leader and Labour M.P. for 35 years, held office in the governments of 1916, 1924 and 1929.

J. H. THOMAS

Railwayman and Cabinet Minister, was the general secretary of the N.U.R., 1918–1931.

from the condemnation of other Socialist groups, while supporting the declarations in favour of working-class action for peace.

As the war dragged on, the possibility that an opportunity would arrive for such working-class action seemed momentarily to come nearer.

In Germany at the end of 1915 the Social Democratic Party pressed the Imperial Chancellor to state under what conditions he would be prepared to enter into peace negotiations. To this the reply was made that the German Government would give consideration to any peace proposals put forward by Great Britain.

Immediately Philip Snowden put a similar question to Mr. Asquith. He received the reply that, "If proposals of a serious character for a general peace were put forward either directly or through a neutral power by any governments they would first be discussed by the Allied Governments, and until this contingency arises I cannot give any other pledge." The Prime Minister promised, however, that if proposals for peace were put forward the Government would take Parliament into its confidence at the earliest possible moment.

This gave the I.L.P. and those who were associated with it some hope. They received even more from the evidence that came to them of a growing peace movement in Germany.

Early in 1916, therefore, Philip Snowden again raised the issue in the House of Commons. He produced evidence from German newspapers and from the spokesmen of the German Socialist Party indicating willingness to enter upon peace talks and quoted a cautious speech by the German Chancellor which also seemed to suggest a similar willingness.

Those who thought as he did, said Snowden, recognized that the British people had given overwhelming testimony to their belief in the righteousness of the national cause. If peace now were to mean new injustices and new enmities, and by leaving militarism unsubdued were simply to establish the conditions for fresh wars in the future, then they would agree that even the prolongation of the war with all its horrors and ruin would be preferable.

But, he said, there was on the contrary abundant evidence that the longer the war continued the greater would be the difficulty of arranging a just settlement. "No victory in the field," he declared, "can establish the conditions of a permanent peace unless there is the willingness and the decision to recognize that the real interests of all nations lie in respecting and safeguarding the interests of all. The ruthless subjugation of Germany would be the worst preparation for a just and lasting peace in Europe." He urged, therefore, that the possibility of a negotiated peace should be explored.

He received a short and uncompromising answer. The will of the British people was to continue the war to "a decisive military victory," said Asquith, and he contemptuously dismissed the voices of the I.L.P. and the Liberals who joined with them as "the twittering of sparrows in a thunderstorm."

Two months later, however, a new voice which could not quite so easily or contemptuously be dismissed was heard—that of President Wilson.

Wilson announced American willingness to suggest or negotiate a movement for peace. Germany and Austria at once declared their readiness to take part in a meeting in a neutral country of delegates from all the belligerent states. To this the Allies replied that while they welcomed President Wilson's message they considered that it was impossible for such a meeting to bring about a peace that would give them the reparation and the guarantees to which they were entitled.

Members of the Cabinet, who were by now by no means single-minded in their belief that peace by negotiation should be ruled out, nor all equally confident of victory, had in fact had numerous talks with Colonel House, President Wilson's private envoy, who had been testing peace prospects for him. It was in some part as a result of these that they came to the conclusion that there was no possibility of satisfactory issue from such negotiations as Wilson suggested. The war must go on.

Lest there should be any doubt of that, Lloyd George decided to make the British attitude, as he saw it, quite clear in an interview with the United Press of America—although characteristically he did not trouble to tell his fellow-members of the Cabinet that he intended to do so before giving the interview.

Britain, he declared in this interview, was not prepared to stop the war because of the squalling done by Germans or for Germans. The war would be fought to a finish. To a knock-out blow.

Three months later, Lloyd George became head of the Government, with Henderson as Labour's representative in his War Cabinet. Any prospect that the I.L.P. might be able to induce British opinion to think favourably of peace negotiations seemed ended.

Nor, although he did not go so far as Lloyd George in demanding a knock-out blow, did Henderson differ greatly from him at the time in his conception of the necessities of British war policy.

"The war has gone on too long for some people of this country," he said. "And it is possible that in the military situation we may become war-weary. But I want to warn everyone of the danger of a premature peace."

Thus as 1917 dawned the prospects of peace seemed not nearer but more distant and the division in the ranks of the Labour movement greater than ever.

So it seemed. But within three months of the formation of the Lloyd George Government something happened that was soon to change altogether the complexion of things.

In Petrograd women textile-workers acclaiming International Woman's Day called upon their fellow-workers to join them in making it a one-day strike against the war. Their call was answered. Ninety thousand workers joined them in the streets, shouting for bread and peace. There were no riots. The day closed peaceably. But the mood of protest did not pass. On the following day at least half the industrial workers in the city came out on strike. They thronged the streets shouting for peace. The authorities grew frightened. They summoned to their aid the traditional breakers of strikes. They called out the Cossacks.

The Cossacks rode out. But this time they did not ride down the people. For the first time in Russian history they felt themselves to be not the enemies of the mass but a part of the mass. They refused to charge the crowds. Only when the police attempted to break up the surging mass of workers did the Cossacks draw their swords, and this time it was not on the crowds that they drew them, but on the police.

The Russian revolution had begun.

CHAPTER XIII

THE IMPACT OF THE RUSSIAN REVOLUTION

TWELVE days after the International Woman's Day demonstration in the streets of Petrograd, the Tsar of All the Russias abdicated.

Within those twelve days much had happened. The strike had spread to Moscow and the provincial cities. The example of the Cossacks had been followed by others. When the military were called out whole regiments went over to the side of the strikers. Reinforcements of "loyal" soldiers were recalled from the front. They developed the habit of disappearing on the way. And as the strike spread the cry of the people which had been for bread and peace took on a sharper note.

Now there was added to it the call for the abdication of the Tsar. At Army headquarters, whither he had gone to inspire his generals, the Tsar wavered between an obstinate but ineffective attempt at dictatorship and a sporadic readiness to make concessions. He was a ruler who possessed neither strong mind nor strong character: he had only a dim, half-imbecile tranquillity in the face of dark events, a tranquillity which came not from courage but from an invincible incapacity to understand what was happening around him; an emptiness of spirit so complete that it robbed him of all power of consistent decision. He was obstinate and conciliatory by turn. But now neither obstinacy nor conciliation would serve his purpose. He had outlived his day. Twelve days after the women textile-workers of Petrograd sent out their call to their fellow-workers—a call which had no considered revolutionary purpose and whose response surprised them—the Tsar signed his abdication.

The first Russian revolution had succeeded. But no one knew what to do with it.

It had not been planned. It had arisen from the mass of the workers and soldiers and their wives without conscious leadership. It caught even the professional revolutionaries—the Bolsheviks— by surprise. It bewildered the members of Russia's Parliament, the Duma, who were in debate in the Tauride Palace when the soldiers and workers arrived to demand the setting up of a progressive government. In response to this demand, a provisional government with a prince as its prime minister was set up—a cautious Liberal government, with one Socialist, Kerensky, among its members as Minister of Justice.

In another part of the same building the political leaders of the Petrograd workers, the Bolsheviks, the Mensheviks, the Social Revolutionaries and the Social Democrats, also debated this revolution with which the people had so suddenly presented them and which they did not know how to handle. They decided to form a Soviet of Workers' and Soldiers' Deputies to function parallel to the Provisional Government.

The Tsar had been overthrown because the people demanded peace. But the Provisional Government was not thinking of peace. Instead it immediately announced that Russia would continue the war and carry out the agreements with her allies. And to this the Soviet of Workers' and Soldiers' Deputies in the other wing of the Tauride Palace unanimously said "Amen."

They, no more than the Duma, knew what to do with the Revolution or understood the forces that had set it in motion. Perhaps only one man in the world knew what he wanted to do with it. Not Prince Lvov, who dreamed only of being able to restore the monarchy. Not Kerensky, the Socialist, who succeeded to power in May and who ruled uneasily by fits and starts for a few months, his instrument of leadership a passionate oratory unsupported by administrative skill. Only one man—Lenin—and he at that moment of the first revolution was not in Russia but in Switzerland. His time was to come later—in November. And when it came there was no longer to be any doubt as to what should be made of the revolution, nor that Russia had done with the war. Others might compromise, but Lenin knew exactly where he wanted to go and how he proposed to take the Russian people with him on the difficult and ruthless journey he contemplated.

But in these first days of March, 1917, no one else knew. There had been a revolution. What was to be its outcome? Who was to lead it? What would be its effect on the war? No one could tell.

Yet if in Russia itself there was doubt and confusion and temporizing and compromise, nevertheless upon the ears of the rest of the world, and particularly upon those of the peoples of Russia's wartime allies, the news of the revolution came like a thunder-clap portending vast events.

To the Labour supporters of the Government in Britain it came as something more. It came as a liberation—an evidence that they were right in believing that out of war good might yet come. It brought a lifting of the spirit. Now at last it was possible to talk of fighting a war for freedom and democracy without being conscious all the time of the bitter irony of describing as a democratic crusade a war in alliance with the most oppressive autocracy in Europe.

When, two weeks after the first Russian revolution, America came into the war on the allied side, it at last seemed possible to say with justice this was truly a war of the democracies against the tyranny of the old empires.

News from out of Russia was, however, scarce and not always reliable. The Russian people were known to be war-weary, but neither the extent of that war-weariness nor the predominant part it had played in the overthrow of the old regime was at first fully appreciated in Britain. Nor was it understood how near Russia was to complete economic collapse. The new Russian Government had announced its determination to continue the war by the side of its allies. Few perhaps in Britain realized how contrary to the mood of the Russian people that declaration was.

"Organized Labour in Great Britain," cabled Henderson, "is watching with the keenest sympathy the efforts of the Russian people to deliver themselves from the power of reactionary elements which are impeding their advance to victory."

Nor was this hope that the Russians, freed from a reactionary tyranny, would fight with a renewed vigour in the "War for Democracy" shaken when the first Provisional Government fell in May and was succeeded by a reorganized government under Kerensky. Rather was it strengthened. For this was a predominantly Socialist government and, therefore, one with which Labour felt a special kinship, and its first declaration to the world was to repudiate any intention of making a separate peace and to promise to develop the principles of democracy in the Army and strengthen Russia's military power. At the same time it declared in explicit terms that the peace at which Russia aimed was one without annexations or indemnities based on the rights of all nations to settle their own affairs.

This was a determination and an objective which the great middle group of the Labour movement which was supporting the war could whole-heartedly share.

Yet already there were clear signs that authority in Russia did not rest solely with the Government. While Kerensky spent his passionate oratory in the attempt to re-kindle the fire of battle among the weary and ill-equipped regiments of the Russian forces, the Workers' and Soldiers' Soviets called not only for a peace without annexations and indemnities, but for 'Peace Now."

To Henderson and the majority of the Labour and trade-union movement Kerensky represented the true spirit of Russia—the spirit that must be aided and fostered.

To MacDonald, Snowden and the rest of the I.L.P.—and to many far to the left of them among the shop stewards' movement and in the Marxist British Socialist Party—it was the soviets who spoke with the truer voice and whose demand for Peace Now should be supported.

A committee under Snowden's chairmanship was therefore, formed to organize a great convention at Leeds: "to follow Russia in her demand for the repudiation of all materialist war aims and the establishment of a peace without annexations or indemnities."

The Convention was held in the Leeds Coliseum on 3 June, under the chairmanship of Robert Smillie, the veteran leader of the miners and one of the best-loved men in the Labour movement. To it came more than 1,100 delegates from the I.L.P., the British Socialist Party, trade unions, trades councils and co-operative societies, the Union of Democratic Control and other peace societies and from women's associations.

It was in some ways one of the most representative Socialist gatherings ever held, and although it was later disowned by the National Executive of the Labour Party and the resolutions it passed in favour of setting up Workers' and Soldiers' Councils on the Russian model had no practical result, it symbolized in a remarkable way the exhilaration that the Russian revolution had created.

In many ways it was an unrealistic conference, swept by emotion and uplifted by the belief that the destruction of what had for so long seemed the most powerful and tyrannical autocracy in Europe meant that at long last the workers of the world were coming into their own. Not all who attended it thought of the results of that revolution in the same terms. To MacDonald and Snowden it meant a step—perhaps a giant's step—nearer to their aim of an honourable negotiated peace. To others it meant, as W. C. Anderson, M.P., declared passionately in his speech, "the conquest of power by the hitherto disinherited class," to others, as Robert Williams of the Transport Workers said in his, "the dictatorship of the proletariat." To yet others the triumph of revolutionary direct action and an incentive to industrial action of a similar kind in Britain.

Despite the contradictions in the minds and speeches of many of the delegates, despite the fact that the official Labour Party and most of the big trade unions stood aloof, despite even the fact that little of practical value flowed from it, the mood of the Conference was symptomatic. It represented the first reaction of many of the most active and sincere Socialists in the Labour movement to the Russian revolution. It was a reaction which bit deep. It influenced working-class attitudes to Russia long after the first flame of exhilaration had burnt itself out and long after the character of the Russian revolution itself had changed. For many years the recollection of that early exhilaration still remained to affect man's concepts of Russia when reason and experience had combined to show how greatly that first response had been betrayed by the subsequent course of events.

In those early days, however, it was not only possible to believe that Russia would find the way to a truly Socialist democracy—it seemed in the first flush of enthusiasm as though she were already on the way.

Those who crowded the Coliseum in Leeds felt that they had gathered to acclaim a triumph of liberty, and even those who, like Henderson, were more cautious in their assessment of events, could not but feel a new stirring of the pulse.

Moreover, the immediate significance of the Russian Revolution was deepened by the fact that it coincided with efforts by the reorganized Second International in Stockholm to call a world-wide international Socialist conference for the definition of war aims. The proposals for this conference had originally been made by Branting, the great Swedish Socialist leader, Huysmans, the Secretary of the International Bureau, and Troelstra of Holland. They were now given a new and urgent importance by the fact that the Russian Workers' and Soldiers' Councils took up the cry. They demanded the immediate holding of a conference to reach decisions on war aims which should be accepted as binding by all Socialist and Labour Parties in all the belligerent countries.

Previously the proposal for an international Socialist conference had seemed to have only an idealistic significance. It was in line with the aspirations and policy of the I.L.P. and of comparable anti-war Socialist groups in other countries, but not with that of most majority groups, and it seemed unlikely that a conference—even if it were possible to hold it—would have any practical impact upon governments. Now it took on a different complexion. If those who now largely determined policy in Russia were demanding such a conference it was difficult to reject it without running the risk that rejection would stimulate Russian suspicion of the war aims of her allies and thus increase the pressure for a separate peace. And if it were held, then its decisions might at once assume practical significance through their adoption by the Russian Government.

The proposal for a Stockholm conference thus almost overnight became one that governments and not merely minority Socialist movements must take into account.

The Labour Party met to consider the invitation. It was sharply divided. Finally, however, it decided to send Ramsay MacDonald, and F. W. Jowett, representing the I.L.P., and G. H. Roberts and William Carter of the Miners, representing the Labour Party, to Russia to discover the exact objectives the Russian Socialists had in mind.

Concurrently, Lloyd George, whose radical sympathies were at first greatly stimulated by the Russian revolution, was interesting himself in the proposal.

Typically, however, he did not discuss it with his Cabinet

colleagues. No doubt he was well aware that the Conservative members of the Cabinet were unlikely to have any sympathy for the idea of a conference of Socialists in a neutral country—a conference at which men such as MacDonald, whom they regarded as little better than a traitor, would actually meet Germans. But he did not at that stage even discuss it with Henderson.

Instead he sent a long telegram to Albert Thomas, the French Socialist leader, for whom he had conceived a warm personal admiration and whom the French Government had sent to Russia to report on the situation.

He asked Thomas for his advice as to whether French and British Socialist delegates ought to attend the Stockholm conference, and himself at this stage put forward very strong arguments for thinking that they should.

"I understand," he wired, "that German Socialists of both sections are to be there and also Russian Socialists. I am afraid that, unless allied cause is represented also, bad impression may be produced on Russian Socialists. Our case is, from a democratic point of view, very strong." He went on to say that in his view, if the allied case were properly put, "it might produce an important effect not only on Russian but even on German opinion and Germany might draw conclusion that it was in reality the crimes of their ruler that prevented peace. . . . On the other hand, if Socialists from France and England are prevented from attending, conclusion will be overwhelming that their 'Governments are afraid to allow them to speak freely to their Russian Allies. . . .'"

Albert Thomas cabled from Petrograd to say that he entirely agreed and had already advised the French Prime Minister in similar terms. "The effect," he wired, "would really be deplorable on the Russian Socialists if the French and British Socialists were absent and the German Socialists present."

Thereupon Lloyd George proposed that Henderson should go on a special mission to Petrograd. On 30 May he started out.

At that time Henderson himself was by no means convinced of the value of the proposed Stockholm conference. But his visit to Russia and his discussions with the Petrograd and Moscow soviets convinced him of its desirability, although, like Albert Thomas, with whom he talked it over in Petrograd, he was quite

266

firm in his view that such a conference could only be consultative and its decisions could not be accepted as binding.

As Mrs. Mary Agnes Hamilton, his biographer, says: "He did not much like Russia or what he saw of the revolution. He found more syndicalism than socialism. As for the Bolsheviks, they struck him as alien and rather fearsome. He did not like them any better than they liked him. They were out to capitalize war-weariness in the interests of a revolution of their own pattern: if they were to succeed, goodbye to Russia as an ally in the war, or Russia as a Socialist state."

Two things determined his decision to support the call for a conference. One was the immense ignorance of the Russian Socialists of the real views of the British and French Socialists. The other was that the only opposition to the Stockholm conference in Russia came from the Bolsheviks. "All are fighting and screaming for the 'unity' of the whole of Russian social democracy," wrote Lenin to Radek. "Of course we are against this." And later: "The Soviet wants a general Socialist International Congress. We want a Congress of the Left against Social chauvinists and the centre."

To Henderson it seemed clear that the Russian Socialists could only be helped in their struggle with the revolutionary Left and Russia kept in the war if they were given support and reinforcement by an exchange of ideas with the Socialists of other countries, for which the Stockholm conference would provide the opportunity.

He, therefore, cabled this view to London. At the same time he urged that passports should at once be given to the Labour Party deputation to enable them to come to Russia. He then started on his journey home.

Both he and Sir George Buchanan, the British Ambassador, were convinced that a visit by MacDonald in particular would do good. At home the Cabinet also eventually agreed and passports were issued. But the Sailors' and Firemen's Union, led by Havelock Wilson, who was on the extreme right of the trade unions, took a different view. When MacDonald, Jowett and the others of their party arrived at Aberdeen to set sail for Russia the crew refused to take them on board and the trip had to be abandoned.

Arrived home after a long, slow journey, Henderson found that Lloyd George had gone to Paris. He at once went to the Labour

Party offices to discuss matters with his executive, taking with him four Russians whom he had met on the train from Aberdeen and who were on their way to Paris, there to represent the Central Council of Workers' and Soldiers' Deputies in talks with the French Socialists on arrangements for Stockholm. He found his fellow members of the executive still much divided about the Stockholm conference, but with opinion hardening against it. Finally, however, in face of his persuasion, a majority agreed that a special conference should be called in London on 10 August to decide, and that meanwhile he, Henderson, as secretary of the Party, MacDonald as treasurer and G. J. Wardle as acting chairman of the Parliamentary Party should accompany the four Russians to Paris for discussions with the French.

When Henderson informed his fellow Cabinet ministers o what he proposed to do he met with their unanimous hostility. However, Henderson had by now made up his mind that the Stockholm conference provided the best chance of keeping Russia in the war, the best chance of keeping Russia Socialist, and also, not less important, the best chance of getting war aims considered which would not betray the ideals with which the ordinary people of Britain had entered the war. He told the Cabinet they could have his resignation if they wished—an offer which, in Lloyd George's absence, they could not accept—and went off to Paris.

His visit to that capital in the company of MacDonald created a British newspaper storm of the first magnitude. How dare a member of the War Cabinet join with a well-known pacifist and "pro-German" on such a visit, shrieked the popular Press, and notice was given to raise the matter in Parliament. From the point of view of the Labour mission the visit was a success—the French and the four Russians were alike persuaded to agree that the Stockholm conference should be consultative only—an absolute condition, as Henderson knew, of British Labour's acceptance.

But when he arrived back in London the storm broke. Lloyd George, himself only just back from Paris, had, as was his habit, changed his mind completely from a few weeks earlier. He had abandoned his own first enthusiasm for the Stockholm conference. He had lost faith in Russia's ability to continue as an effective ally and was toying with the idea that Germany might be allowed what she wanted in the East at Russia's expense in order that the Allies should the better be able to get what they wanted in the West.

There was, therefore, nothing he wanted less at that stage than a discussion of war aims with the Russian Socialists. He was very angry. So was Henderson. He invited Henderson to put his views before the Cabinet at four o'clock. Henderson arrived only to be kept waiting in the Secretaries' room—"on the doormat," as he said—for an hour while the rest of the Cabinet discussed his sins in his absence.

When Henderson was at last admitted there was no doubt at all about his state of mind or his temper. Before going to Paris he had told the Cabinet he was ready to resign. Now he challenged them to demand his resignation. For the moment the challenge was not taken. But it could not be long delayed. On 10 August the special Labour Conference met in the Central Hall, Westminster. It had been preceded by an immense barrage of Press criticism of Henderson and by confident assertions that, when the conference met, the level-headed majority would vote against Stockholm—that by now, perhaps, even Henderson had had the sense to see how impossible it was. From 10 Downing Street there had come hints that the Russian Government itself had changed its view and no longer wanted a conference.

To this barrage of criticism Henderson replied at the conference with simplicity and dignity.

"Let us," he said, "try to take our decisions without being influenced in the slightest degree by what I cannot characterize in any other way than as an unscrupulous agitation that has been carried on from outside. Let us be influenced by the interests of the nation of which we form a part and for which the workers have done so much during the war. Let us remember poor struggling Russia, and if we cannot give the newest Democracy, the infant of Democracies, all she asks I beseech you not to give her a blank refusal.

"Of this I am convinced and I want to say this with all the seriousness and deliberation of which I am capable, that if we today, representing as we do the great British Labour and Socialist movement, determine for the whole period of the war not to use

269

the political weapon to supplement our military activities, not only shall I regret it but I will venture to predict that you as a movement will regret it hereafter. Let us by all the means at our disposal, whether they be military or whether they be political, strive to secure such a victory as will ensure for the world a lasting, honourable and democratic peace."

The debate that followed was long and serious. Both those for and against the conference felt strongly, and it was significant that Henderson's Labour colleagues in the Government—notably G. N. Barnes, Minister of Pensions, who had taken his place in the War Cabinet during his absence in Russia—opposed him.

"The main fact is," said Barnes, "that if you go there you will be going to discuss terms of peace. . . . I believe that the only way of ending this war is the way in which our brave boys at the front are trying to end it."

G. H. Roberts, another Labour member of the Government, declared that Stockholm could only be an embarrassment to Kerensky and ironically congratulated Henderson on joining MacDonald's "new majority."

"To go to Stockholm," said James Sexton, "was to go to meet men who had not repudiated masters whose hands were red with the blood of Nurse Cavell, Captain Fryatt and the crew of the *Belgian Prince*."

To this MacDonald replied amidst a storm of cheers and counter cheers that the democracies of Europe must not only help Russia to consolidate its new democracy, but must make a clear statement of where they stood in peace terms, "then we can ask our German friends how far they agree and how far they disagree."

And J. H. Thomas said: "I hope we shall not hear any more about the enemies of our country and the friends of our country. I am not afraid of meeting Germans. I am as true a patriot as anybody and I am satisfied that no German will browbeat me or compel me to do anything contrary to the best interests of my country."

Finally the vote was taken. By a three to one majority, 1,846,000 to 550,000, the conference voted in favour of Stockholm.

That evening Henderson saw Lloyd George and the following morning he sent him his resignation. It was at once accepted.

270

That, as it turned out, was one of the decisive moments in the history of the Labour Party. It did not seem so at once. It did not lead to the withdrawal of Labour from the Government—the remaining Labour ministers stayed until the war ended. Moreover, as so often happens, climax was followed by anti-climax. There was no Stockholm conference after all. Disputes in the Labour Party as to whether the minority Socialist societies should be allowed to send delegates or whether only delegates from the Labour Party, as such, should be allowed, led to a change of mood, and when the special conference met again eleven days later the basic decision to send delegates was again challenged. This time it was confirmed only by a tiny majority—so tiny, indeed, as to be ineffectual for practical purposes.

There were similar divisions in the French Socialist movement, and when on 28 August the French and British Socialists met at an inter-allied conference to decide on a joint policy for presentation at Stockholm, no agreement was reached. And in a little while Kerensky's failure in Russia, the arrival of the Bolshevik Revolution and with it the opening of peace negotiations with Germany ended all possibility of the kind of conference that those who had supported the Stockholm proposal had wished for.

It seemed as though Henderson had resigned for a will-o'-the-wisp that had come to nothing, and that although at that first meeting in the Central Hall the majority of the delegates had temporarily supported him he had followed a course of which the largest part of the movement—and especially that solid middle part where his strength lay—did not approve.

But, in fact, his resignation from the Government at that moment and on that issue—fruitless although it at first seemed to be—and the new alignment of forces within the Labour Party that came from it, was to have the most profound effect on its future.

For directly out of it there was to come a new conception both of organization and policy, and this conception was to bring the formative years of the Labour Party to an end and set its feet firmly at last on the road that was to lead to power.

CHAPTER XIV

A SOCIALIST PARTY AT LAST

IN THE history of the First World War, Arthur Henderson's resignation from the War Cabinet is but an incident. It may well be that the issue of the Stockholm conference on which he resigned was in the practical sense an unreal issue: unreal because at that moment the tides of war and of revolution in Russia were moving too quickly and too implacably for their course to be altered by any conference even if one had been held: unreal also because the identity of view between the working-classes of the warring countries which alone could have given such a conference a voice sufficient to make governments listen did not exist.

But practical tests are not the only ones with validity in the long record of human history. Henderson's protest and resignation may have had no effect on the immediate course of events on which men's minds were centred at that moment. It had a profound effect on the history of the Labour Party—an effect whose full consequences were to be seen only in the fullness of time.

There have been many more brilliant politicians than Henderson in the Labour Party, many better orators—for he was on most occasions a diffuse and platitudinous speaker—many men with a greater capacity for original political thinking. There have been none, however, with higher integrity and few with an equal capacity for organization. But what most distinguished him—what more than everything else gave him his power to influence the development of the Labour Party—was his representative character. He was, so to speak, a personification of the ordinary man in the Labour Party and particularly the ordinary man in the trade union —although his abilities were not ordinary. But he thought as they did, he reacted to events as they did, he felt as they did. But a little ahead of them—breaking a path that they would follow not just because they were ready to follow him, although he was greatly trusted, but because it was in fact the road along which their own instincts guided them. He never went far ahead, he kept always within hailing distance. Nor did he ever move to extremes either of the Left or the Right. He moved in step with the majority—a few paces ahead, showing the way.

This was not due to any deliberate exercise in political calculation, and certainly not to any anxiety as to his own popularity. He did what seemed to him to be right. But because he felt and thought so much as the ordinary man and woman in the Labour movement did, what seemed to him to be right had a habit of turning out to be what they thought to be right also.

At the beginning of the war he had no doubts as to what was the right course any more than the great mass of Labour and trade-union members had—it was to defeat German militarism. He had little sympathy with those who, like the leaders of the I.L.P., talked of the allocation of war guilt and of the need to discuss peace terms before the war had well begun, he had equally little sympathy for those who thought of the war as a class war in which the workers should look only to their own class interests. He thought of the war as a battle for democracy, for a way of life, which must be won at whatever material cost. He thought of it, that is, as most of the ordinary men and women of Britain did.

And so he willingly joined the Government when asked to do so, truly reflecting, in so doing, the mood of the great majority of the Labour movement, although not of some of its most able political leaders. He came out of the Government because his visit to Russia and his battle with Lloyd George and the Cabinet over the Stockholm conference had convinced him that sheer insistence on victory was no longer enough. And in this, too, he reflected the feeling—the developing feeling—of the ordinary rank and file members of the Labour Party whom he so faithfully represented. He was called a defeatist, but he was no more a defeatist than they were.

It was simply that in his slow deliberate way, but with perceptions sharpened by his experience in Russia, he had come to feel that the true purposes of the war were beginning to be lost sight of. What had begun as a crusade was becoming merely a struggle for power in which the absolute defeat of the enemy was the goal—whatever the cost in lives and whatever the cost also in destroying the possibility of a democratic peace and a new start in Europe when the war was done.

He was neither a pacifist nor a revolutionary any more than were the ordinary trade unionists and Labour Party members to whom he was so nearly akin. He did not like what he saw of revolution in Russia—still less did he like what he felt would follow if the Russian people were not given some firm assurance that the aims the Allies fought for were aims of which all democratic men and women should approve. And in that, too, he reflected the minds of those of whom he was so true a representative.

He had seen how the refusal to state war aims cast in the minds of the Russian workers doubt on the whole democratic intentions of the allied governments—indeed, in the face of that refusal he could not but share some of those doubts. And in that also he felt as an increasing number of men and women in the Labour Party and some outside it were also beginning to feel. He did not doubt now, any more than he had earlier, the major responsibility of German militarism for the war. But he now began to feel that not all the German people still shared that militarism, even if they ever had, and that a statement of democratic war aims might bring to the Allied cause a moral, spiritual and political reinforcement which would end the slaughter and make possible an honourable and democratic peace. In refusing to make such a declaration the allied governments were, he felt, falling a prey to the very militarism they had rallied their people to defeat. And in this, too, he expressed thoughts and fears that were beginning to stir in the minds of many ordinary men and women.

In September, 1917, a month after his resignation from the War Cabinet, he went as the fraternal delegate from the Labour Party to the Trades Union Congress at Blackpool.

He was welcomed, in the words of the official report, "with a warmth of demonstration without precedent in the history of these gatherings."

Here he was at home. Here he could speak to people who understood him because he thought in the ways that they thought and looked at the world with eyes like theirs.

The Stockholm conference for which he had struggled was dead.

But the ideal remained. The ideal, as he said in his speech, of an international conference of workers that "could be the finest expression of a League of Nations because it would be a League of the Common Peoples throughout the civilized world."

He urged the delegates not to mistake military victory for final and complete success—there could be no final success until "autocratic government has been completely and for ever destroyed."

He urged them to be fair to those minority Socialists within Germany who had stood apart from the militarism of their nation. And, answering those who said there could be no talks with Germans until Germany had been utterly defeated, he said: "I would rather consult with a German minority before peace than I would with the representatives of a discredited government when a military victory has been secured."

The delegates to the T.U.C. listened to what he had to say and although not all agreed with him the majority did. The Government was not prepared to listen. Perhaps if it had been the future might have been different.

Henderson's resignation and the fact that he carried with him the loyalty of the trade unions when he resigned—although neither he nor they wished to force the issue further and make it an occasion for a withdrawal of Labour from the Government—had immediately important consequences.

Even when he had disagreed with MacDonald, Snowden and the others of the I.L.P. he had used all his influence to prevent a permanent breach developing in the Party. Now he, and with him much of the responsible majority of the movement, were moving in a direction which made possible a genuine closing of the ranks. There had never indeed, despite the bitterness that had sometimes occurred, been any differences as to the ultimate objective between the I.L.P. and the Labour Party—the differences had been one of timing and of means. Now the passing of three years, the development of international events and the course of the war had removed most of these differences.

The trade unions, who would not have followed MacDonald because they neither liked nor altogether understood him, were ready to follow Henderson because they liked him and trusted his judgment, and because he was putting into words what they themselves were coming to feel. If he had remained in the Government, however, he would have had neither the time nor the freedom needed to exercise the influence and authority which only he could bring into the consideration of Labour policy at that time.

His freedom to devote himself to the Labour Party at this particular stage in the evolution of his own Socialist and internationalist outlook was of decisive importance to its future. The more so because his own mental and emotional development coincided so closely with the movement of feeling within the Labour Party and among many Liberals who were deeply troubled by Lloyd George's "knock-out blow" policy.

Henderson had become convinced of the necessity of three things.

The first was a statement of war aims which would show the world that the Labour movement at least was firm in its democratic and non-militarist intentions—a statement to which the adherence of other international Socialist and Labour groups could later be obtained and which might serve to rally progressive opinion everywhere.

The second was a statement of Labour Party policy in preparation for the end of the war which would firmly set down the principles for which it stood nationally and internationally, politically and economically. The period during which Labour could be satisfied with a political objective that went no farther than the establishment of a minority pressure group in Parliament was over. The movement had grown up during the war. It must now think in terms of national leadership. And to do so it must have a national policy. The period during which it had been tactically wise not to attempt to define policy too closely, for fear of splitting an infant party, was over. If it was to go forward it must now state in clear terms what it stood for and wherein its objectives differed from those of the older parties.

The third thing which seemed to him necessary was a reorganization of the constitution of the Party which would turn it from a loose federation into a genuinely national party. The potentially dangerous division between those who in the last resort controlled policy and those who propagated it in the constituencies and recruited the non-trade-union membership must be ended. If it was to have a national programme the Party itself must have a national organization and one wide enough to bring in not only the manual workers but all those outside the trade unions who were attracted by Socialist ideals.

In the practical working out of this triple programme Henderson turned to allies whom perhaps only he could have persuaded to work together—Ramsay MacDonald and Sidney Webb.

He had a great respect for MacDonald's courage and ability— a respect that the disagreements between them in the early days of the war had by no means diminished. Moreover, as a practical political organizer he knew that although the trade-union movement provided the essential mass base of a British Labour Party, it could not make that party a national party unless the I.L.P. were ready to go along with it. He was himself a trade unionist, but he had none of the suspicion of some trade unionists of the political Socialist. He knew that they had something to give which the trade unions could not.

At the beginning of the war, when the War Emergency National Workers' Committee was set up, Henderson had for the first time come in regular contact with Sidney Webb, who represented the Fabian Society on it. This, too, was the first time that Webb had come into direct practical contact with the workings of the Labour movement. The two recognized each other's qualities. Webb saw in Henderson the practical, political administrator, the man of judgment, influence and of integrity who could, if he would, become a vehicle for Fabian ideas. Henderson recognized and applauded Webb's intellectual grasp of affairs, his mastery of facts, his constructive genius in the field of social problems, his immense talent for getting ideas into shape on paper.

Both learned from the experience of war. Henderson had seen the real difference of aim that existed between Labour and the oldet parties. He had been a member of a coalition Cabinet. He saw thar the ideals of the working-class movement of which he was a part could not be achieved by collaboration with others. He became what he had not been before, a Socialist as well as a Labour man—but a practical and, above all, a democratic Socialist with nothing but dislike for those who talked in terms of revolution: a Socialist morally and intellectually sympathetic to the Fabian approach. Webb for his part came to put a much higher value on the Labour Party than he had in immediately pre-war days. He became the Fabian Society's representative in the National Executive, he played a leading part in the War Emergency Committee, he understood the Labour movement better than he had. Also he had come to recognize the limitations of the original Fabian technique of permeation of the older parties. He realized now than an intellectual case was not enough: the influence of pure reason in political affairs could be over-estimated. However strong the case for socialism put up by the Fabians, and however much support they might be able to secure for individual items in their social reform programme from some members of the older parties, neither Liberals nor Conservatives were going to let themselves be argued into abandoning the positions of economic power and privilege which they regarded as theirs by right. If socialism was to come it must come through the securing of political power by a Socialist party. And the one party able and willing to become Socialist was the Labour Party.

When Henderson, freed from Government office, threw himself with all the single-minded determination of which he was capable into the task of preparing the Labour party for the future, he turned therefore to Webb as an ally and Webb at once responded. But, as Henderson the political organizer saw, it was necessary to bring MacDonald into that alliance also. And here he showed his real talent as a handler of men. Webb and MacDonald had no liking for each other. They were completely unsympathetic personalities, poles apart in their approach to political problems. MacDonald was intoxicated by the broad sweep and the cloudy vision. He disliked the particular and the precise. He was emotional and "philosophical," courageous but opportunist and ambitious, looking upon politics as an art in which he felt himself to be a master and was determined to be a leader. Webb was intellectual, precise, concerned with the exact phrase and impatient of any assertion which could not be backed by documentary evidence. Himself uninterested in the limelight, he was contemptuous of those who were, regarding them as weaker vessels fit only to be used by those with greater self-restraint. To him politics was a social science, he had little respect

for MacDonald's wordiness and inconsistencies. Yet Henderso
succeeded in getting them both to work with him. He harnessed
their divergent and alien abilities to the task to which he had set
himself.

The alliance of these three had more than a personal significance.
It represented the coming together after the divisions of war of the
three streams whose convergence had created the Labour Party in
the first place. For these three, so different from each other in
character, personified in their separate ways the three distinct groups which throughout its history have shaped the Labour
Party.

Out of this alliance a new party was born—a Socialist Party.

Their first achievement was a statement of war aims which,
while recognizing the extent of German responsibility for the war
and the necessity for just reparation to Belgium and France, declared
explicitly Labour's faith in an international order as the only means
of preventing future war.

"Whoever triumphs," it declared, "the people will have lost
unless an international system is established which will prevent war.
It would mean nothing to declare the rights of peoples to self-
determination if this right were left at the mercy of new violations
and was not protected by a Super-National Authority. That
authority can be no other than the League of Nations, which not only
all the present belligerents but every other independent state should
be pressed to join."

Despite a warning letter addressed to the Labour Party from
Lloyd George, with whose plans at that stage a declaration of war
aims by any section of the British people did not fit, and despite the
continuing feeling of a large section of the trade unions that to
announce war aims smacked of "defeatism," a special Labour
conference just after Christmas, 1917, adopted the declaration by
2,132,000 to 1,164,000 votes, taking its lead from Henderson, Mac-
Donald, Robert Smillie and J. H. Thomas. Moreover, in February,
1918, a special conference of allied Socialists adopted the statement
without material alterations, although it strengthened it in some
respects and notably in the references to a League of Nations.

At last the majority Socialist movements of the allied nations
were united in their war aims. Nor was this all.

Many others than Socialists were now concerned about allied war policy. A letter from Lord Lansdowne appeared in the *Daily Telegraph* on 29 November calling for a restatement of war aims by the allied governments. Although it had no immediate effect on practical policy and earned for its author the epithet of defeatist that had already been bestowed on Henderson, it made many men and women of all parties look more critically upon the Lloyd George policy. In December the publication in the *Manchester Guardian* and the Lansbury *Herald* of a series of secret treaties between the Allies, released from the archives of the Russian Foreign Office by the Bolshevik Government, added to the disquiet of all liberal-minded men and women—for these treaties, mostly signed after the outbreak of war, revealed with a startling clarity that the "imperialist designs" which propaganda attributed solely to Germany were shared also by allied governments.

To men and women disturbed by this disclosure the Labour Memorandum on War Aims brought inspiration and hope.

"This," said the *Manchester Guardian*, is "the answer of democracy to autocracy . . . and surely a notable one. . . . The allied governments would be well advised speedily to follow suit."

Perhaps more than any other single action this memorandum turned the eyes of progressive and idealistic people at that time towards the Labour Party. It brought into its ranks many who had hitherto stood aside, regarding it as a class party of the trade unions, but who now recognized it as a new moral force in British politics—a force demanding their allegiance. The impact of the memorandum was immediate, but it was also pervasive, it was to grow in force as the consequences of allied war policy were disclosed in the Peace Treaties.

That was the first consequence of the combination of Henderson, MacDonald and Webb and of the new forces that were moving in the Labour movement and of which Henderson was so truly representative. The second was a programme of Labour policy, set out in detail in *Labour and the New Social Order*, of which Webb was the principal draughtsman. The third was a new constitution the draft of which was circulated to all the affiliated bodies along with the draft of *Labour and the New Social Order*.

The adoption of the new Constitution in February, 1918, and

of *Labour and the New Social Order* in June, 1918—at the first Party Conference held under the new Constitution—transformed the Labour Party. These two developments made it for the first time a truly national party. And they also made it a Socialist Party.

There are few documents drafted amid the turmoil and uncertainties of the closing months of the First World War which stand the test of thirty years of subsequent history. *Labour and the New Social Order* is such a document. It is an historic document not only because of the political consequences that flowed from it, but in its own right as a statement of principles and political aims so valid that many of them were still operative when at last a Labour Government achieved power twenty-seven years later.

This programme was embodied in twenty-seven resolutions, of which the first laid it down that the task of Social Reconstruction required: "the gradual building up of a new social order based not on internecine conflict, inequality of riches and dominion over subject classes, subject races or a subject sex, but on deliberately planned co-operation in production and distribution, the sympathetic approach to a healthy equality, the widest possible participation in power both economic and political and the general consciousness of consent which characterizes a true democracy."

The second affirmed the need for increased aggregate production of commodities and services, but affirmed also that this could not be done by "reducing the means of subsistence of the workers whether by hand or brain, nor yet in lengthening their hours of work," but only by (a) the socialization of industry to eliminate inefficiency and waste; (b) the application both of more honest determination and more science and intelligence to every branch of the nation's work; (c) improvements in social, political and industrial organization, and (d) the marshalling of the nation's resources so that each need should be met in proportion to its real national importance.

The third laid down the necessity for the extension and development of the system of a legal basic wage: "so as to ensure to every adult worker of either sex a statutory base line of wages (to be revised with every substantial rise in prices) not less than enough to provide all the requirements of a full development of body, mind and character."

Another resolution proposed a deliberate policy of full employment aided by a programme of public works developments including housing, schools, roads, railways, canals, harbours, afforestation and reclamation, and laid it down that it should be a government obligation to ensure that "the aggregate total demand for labour shall be maintained year in and year out at an approximately even level."

Specifically the programme, in addition to dealing with immediate post-war problems of demobilization and housing, included complete adult suffrage with equal rights for both sexes; unemployment insurance by a system of state subventions to increase trade-union benefits; the abolition of the Poor Law; the development of health services; the nationalization of life assurance and the development of a national insurance scheme by the State in conjunction with the Friendly Societies; the nationalization of the railways and canals and of the coal and iron mines (steel had previously been covered in the memorandum on war aims as an armament industry); the State provision of electric power stations and the linking up of existing municipal and joint stock electrical distributive services; and the control of agricultural land to increase the production of foodstuffs under conditions allowing a good life to the rural population.

It demanded the continuance of war controls and audits over processes, profits and prices in capitalist industry, the retention of a system of centralized purchasing of raw materials, foodstuff and other essential imports, and the rationing of supplies of scarce raw materials to factories in accordance with national needs.

And it proposed a drastic overhaul of the system of taxation in order to ensure both progressive taxation of large incomes and higher inheritance taxes and the redistribution of the proceeds in a wide system of social services.

Thus the framework of a policy of national ownership of basic industries such as transport, power and fuel, the central direction of industries in private ownership by the control of raw materials and of profits, the maintenance of full employment and the provision of social security schemes financed by egalitarian tax methods, was laid down while the First World War was still continuing. It was not, however, until after the devastations of a Second World War

282

that Labour was to be given the power to do what it saw then was necessary and to put into effect a programme the basis and validity of which was confirmed over and over again by the depressions and crises of the inter-war years.

Such a programme going far beyond the social reform aspirations of the pre-1914 Labour Party could not, as Henderson knew, be made effective until Labour itself achieved power. No collaboration with the Liberals, even if the Liberal Party had not been hopelessly split during the war, could have achieved it. The first step to power was a reorganization of the Party organization and the adoption of a new constitution.

The old Labour Party had had no declared objective other than "to organize and maintain in Parliament and in the country a political Labour Party."

That was now changed. The new constitution drafted by Henderson and Webb declared that the object of the Party was "to secure for the producers by hand and by brain the full fruits of their industry and the most equitable distribution thereof that may be possible upon the basis of the common ownership of the means of production and the best obtainable system of popular administration and control of each industry and service."

Thus with the acceptance of this constitution the Party became at once a Socialist Party and one appealing not to the "working-classes" or the trade unionists alone, but to all "producers whether by hand or by brain." It became, that is, a classless party appealing directly for support, as the Socialist societies had always done on a restricted scale, to men and women of goodwill in all sections of the community.

But, in order to make such an appeal effective, it was necessary to transform the original federation of trade unions and Socialist societies into a nationally organized party with strong local branches of its own, while retaining what had been the essential foundation of the original federation, and was an absolute necessity of Labour strength—the block membership of the trade unions.

This was done by proposing to retain the federal pattern but to add to it, so that henceforward the Party should consist of the affiliated organizations—the trade unions and the Socialist societies "together with those men and women who are individual members of a local Labour Party and who subscribe to the constitution and programme of the Party."

Previously the only way into the Labour Party for the non-manual worker—the non-trade-unionist—had been through membership of one of the Socialist societies. In their several ways the societies had done immensely valuable work, but it was clear that they neither could, nor in fact were, recruiting the mass individual membership which a national party must have and which the Labour Party's new programme deserved.

The combined membership of the three affiliated societies—the I.L.P., the British Socialist Party and the Fabian Society—was only 75,000. But in addition to the hundreds of thousands of men and women of Liberal views who were now turning to Labour as the only hope of a better world, and whose energies and enthusiasm must be recruited if that hope was to be realized, there were 6,000,000 new women electors—the majority of them wives of working men —who were not eligible for membership of a trade union and were unlikely to join the Socialist societies in any large numbers. Individual membership of local Labour Parties was a necessity of success.

With the acceptance of the new constitution and the endorsement of the international policy contained in the Memorandum on War Aims and the domestic programme contained in *Labour and the New Social Order*, the Labour Party finally established itself. The formative years were ended.

Now at last it was an adult party certain of its own purpose; aware also at last of what it must do to impress that purpose upon the nation.

PART FOUR

FORWARD TO GOVERNMENT

CHAPTER XV

DEFEAT AND RECOVERY

Six months after it had for the first time declared itself a Socialist Party and had reorganized its constitution to allow of the recruitment to its ranks of men and women of all classes—workers by hand and brain—the Labour Party went down to crushing defeat in the Khaki Election thrust upon the nation by Lloyd George one month after the end of the war.

It was a defeat none the less crushing for the fact that the actual number of Labour candidates returned was fifty-seven, compared with forty-two in 1910. The electorate to which they appealed had been nearly doubled as a result of the widening of the suffrage. The Labour Party had more candidates in the field than ever before and the majority of the new electors were men and women of the working-classes. It could, therefore, reasonably hope for a considerable increase in its political representation as a party appealing for a wider public support than ever before. Instead, all the Party's best-known political leaders were rejected by these new electors and, when the new Parliament met in January, 1919, the Party, so far from reflecting the change in the constitution and policy of the movement and the widening of its political appeal, was more predominantly trade unionist than ever—forty-nine of the fifty-seven Labour M.P.s represented trade unions, twenty-five of them the Miners' Federation.

Yet by another five years' time, Labour was to take office as

285

the Government of the country—although a minority government it is true—with a Parliamentary Party behind it of 191 M.P.s representing all sections of the movement—eighty-seven of them from the Socialist societies and local Labour Parties. Ramsay MacDonald, whose parliamentary career many persuaded themselves was ended in 1918, was to be Prime Minister. This first Labour Government was, it is true, to rule uneasily as a minority government existing only on the sufferance of the Liberals. Its life was to be short and its end inglorious. But it marked a new stage in British history.

When Lloyd George appealed to the country in the election of December, 1918, Labour had neither the organization nor the money to fight successfully on a wide front, although in the effort to meet the immediate post-war challenge it put 363 candidates into the field—of whom 306 were beaten. The change in the constitution of the Party and the adoption of the policy set out in *Labour and the New Social Order* had preceded the election by too short a time for them to have any real effect upon its organization and fighting strength.

By January, 1924, the new basis of local party organization laid down in the new constitution had been put into effect under Henderson's supervision and his surpassing talents as a political organizer had had time to bring their results. With tireless enthusiasm, energy and efficiency a new national agent, Egerton Wake, was developing constituency parties throughout the country, though it was not until 1932 that it could be claimed that there was some organization in every borough and division. And under Dr. Marion Phillips a women's organization had been created such as no other party possessed. Labour was able to put 428 candidates in the field and see nearly half of them successfully returned.

But although organization had its very important part in the remarkable upsurge of Labour representation between December, 1918, and January, 1924, the Parliamentary Labour Party which was called to take office on that latter date was a reflection of something much more profound than improved national organization. A revolutionary change in Britain's social and economic life and a permanent alteration in the former political balance of power had taken place. It was a change whose full consequences were not seen at once but whose impact was to grow steadily greater.

In December, 1918, the tide of public opinion was flowing irresistibly against the Labour Party. Lloyd George had capitalized his war success. The country was flushed with victory, and bent on exacting punishment and reparation from the defeated. It was easy in the immense relief that the war was over to believe that all now would be well.

Labour was labelled with scant honesty as the party of "defeatism." What chance had it against the candidates who carried Lloyd George's coupon as evidence of their fidelity to the national interest? MacDonald, Henderson, Snowden, Jowett, Lansbury, almost all the political leaders of the Party with the exception of Clynes and Thomas, were swept away in the storm. Moreover, not only were the majority of the Labour M.P.s who gathered in the House when the election was over without much parliamentary skill and experience, but for the most part they represented those groups within the Labour Party whose attitude to the war and to the peace was most nearly akin to that of the massed supporters of Lloyd George. In this they provided, for the time being, a true reflection of the mood of the majority of the country. The principles set out in the Labour Memorandum on War Aims and in *Labour and the New Social Order*, although they had won the devotion of a minority, had awakened for the moment no response in the minds of the majority of ordinary men and women.

Before such a response could come there had to be the bitterness of the disillusion that came with the peace negotiations and the economic depression that followed the war.

The Labour Party was now a Socialist Party organized to place steadily before the electorate not merely the Labour attitude to immediate practical issues, but the moral, political and economic principles which must shape the Socialist conception of a new social order. But its growth between 1918 and 1924 was not due simply to its success in propagating those principles. It was due to the fact that the whole course of social and economic development following the war underlined the moral of the Socialist thesis.

The nearly 4,350,000 electors who voted for Labour in 1924 were brought to a belief in Labour policy not simply by successful propaganda, but by the harsh logic of events. The Labour Party was—and was to continue to be—not the creator of a social and economic revolution, but its instrument. Its growing strength was due to the manifest fact that whatever successes the old economic system had been able to claim in the past it was not adequate to deal with the economic problems that now pressed upon Britain with such implacable force.

Britain's long industrial predominance was ended although the extent of the shift of economic power from Europe to the New World was not yet fully realized, and was not indeed to be completely realized until the consequences of a second world war made the knowledge inescapable. The favoured position which her early start in the industrial revolution had given her was no longer hers to anything like the same extent. She no longer had the same ability as formerly to dominate the flow of international trade and to be the main supplier of industrial products to the world. She was faced with competition of a character such as had not previously existed, and if she was to come through the tests which confronted her without grave damage to the standards of life of her people was required to carry through a fundamental reorganization of much of her economy.

But the "hard-faced" men who now crowded the Government benches were not prepared to contemplate any such reorganization. Nor were most of their fellows in industry and commerce. Their only answer to competition was to seek to force down the wages and living standards of the workers. To them the throwing of millions out of work was an unavoidable necessity of economic depression which, although it might be deplored, could not be cured.

Britain came out of the war with her power to produce increased but with most of her main products, and especially her coal, her iron and steel and her cotton, faced with new and severe competition in the markets of the world. British capitalism was confronted with a crisis of transition and readjustment caused by the immense changes in national and world economy brought by the war—and the main penalty of the crisis was paid by the workers.

In 1919 the average percentage of trade unionists unemployed during the year was 2·4. By 1921 it had risen to 14·8 and by 1922 to 15·8. Among the unorganized the situation was even worse.

It is not surprising that, in the face of such a situation, increasing numbers not of the working-classes alone but of the middle-classes

ARTHUR GREENWOOD
Policy research.

ARTHUR HENDERSON
Secretary.

J. S. MIDDLETON
Assistant secretary

EGERTON WAKE
National agent.

Victory builders in the 1920's.

THE LABOUR CABINET, 1924

FRONT ROW: *W. Adamson, Lord Parmoor, Philip Snowden, Lord Haldane, J. Ramsay MacDonald, J. R. Clynes, J. H. Thomas, Arthur Henderson.*

CENTRE ROW: *C. P. Trevelyan, Stephen Walsh, Lord Thomson, Lord Chelmsford, Lord Olivier, Noel Buxton, J. C. Wedgwood, Vernon Hartshorn, T. Shaw.*

BACK ROW: *Sidney Webb, J. Wheatley, Fred W. Jowett.*

THE LABOUR CABINET, 1929

FRONT ROW: *J. R. Clynes, Lord Parmoor, J. H. Thomas, Philip Snowden, J. Ramsay MacDonald, Arthur Henderson, Sidney Webb, Lord Sankey, Wedgwood Benn.*

BACK ROW: *George Lansbury, A. V. Alexander, Sir C. P. Trevelyan, Miss Margaret Bondfield, Lord Thomson, Tom Shaw, A. Greenwood, Noel Buxton, W. Graham, W. Adamson.*

began more and more to question the basic economic assumptions upon which private capitalism was founded and to turn to socialism as a remedy. At the same time many of those who had fought saw both the promises made to them and the ideals they had fought for ignored.

"I am not prepared to do anything in the matter. After four years of active service I have seen every ideal I fought for betrayed in the Paris Peace Conference," wrote Clement Attlee, when as Mayor of Stepney he was asked to take part in a Territorial recruiting campaign. There were many ex-Service men who were not, as he was, Socialist, but who shared this feeling of betrayal and who because of it began to look to the men who had been attacked and denounced in the war but who had stood firm for their convictions.

In 1918 Henderson's resignation from the War Cabinet and the record of MacDonald and Snowden as "pacifists" had been heavy political liabilities. As the public mood changed and the correctness of their analysis of the consequences of the Lloyd George policy was demonstrated at Versailles and in the conditions of the workers at home, their reputations rose and their courage and integrity were recognized at their true worth.

In those first years following 1918 there developed again within the Labour Party a crusading idealism such as had governed the I.L.P. in its early days. All over the country, men and women—many of them turning now to Labour for the first time—felt themselves dedicated to a cause greater than themselves—a cause which although political in form was moral in its inspiration. Those who had long been Socialists were joined by young men and women of all classes, including very many who had known the long-drawn horror of the trenches and who now saw in socialism the only possibility of averting in the future a repetition of the tragedy which had engulfed their generation. The moral and economic stirring of the working-classes was reinforced by men and women from the middle-classes and the universities who were intellectually convinced of the economic case for socialism and morally appalled by the injustices of the post-war capitalist system.

Many of these were to play a notable part in Labour's future: among them Hugh Dalton, Arthur Greenwood (who turned his back on a great future in the Civil Service to work as Research

Officer for the Labour Party), Philip Noel Baker, Will Arnold-Forster, Mary Agnes Hamilton, Barbara Wootton, Sidney Arnold, Leonard Woolf, Charles Roden Buxton, R. H. Tawney and many others.

The Liberal Party was in ruins, wrecked by the political manoeuvres of Lloyd George who had once in the days of his campaign for social reform seemed to offer it a new hope of mobilizing the social conscience of the middle-classes. To many people now the Labour Party seemed to be the true inheritor of what was most valid in the Liberal tradition. Those Liberals who had turned to it during the war were joined by others who could find in the liberalism of the early 1920s no satisfaction of the ethical purpose which guided them.

For the moment, as the Lloyd George coalition dominated the national scene, Labour's parliamentary strength was small, but the new vigour and idealism that was stirring throughout its ranks, together with the improved organization created by Henderson and Egerton Wake, had its results in a vast increase in local activity. In the municipal elections of 1919, Labour and Co-operative candidates won 412 seats, and for the first time captured control of a great city, Bradford, the birthplace of the I.L.P. Moreover, although in the 1918 election only four Labour M.P.s had been returned in the whole of Greater London, in the London Metropolitan Borough elections Labour gained 526 seats and captured control of twelve councils. On the L.C.C. it increased its strength from one to fifteen, the first indication of the revolution in London's political affairs that Herbert Morrison, now full-time Secretary of the London Labour Party at £1 a week, was to bring to pass in a few years. Outside London, Labour won majorities on three County Councils: Durham, Glamorgan and Monmouthshire.

Nationally the upsurge of Labour strength led, as so often before when the road to political advance seemed closed, to increasing emphasis on direct action.

On Clydeside, as 1919 opened, sixty thousand workers came out on strike for a forty-hour week as a means to counter unemployment, and the Riot Act was read when a great crowd under the leadership of Kirkwood, Shinwell and Gallacher gathered outside the City Chambers. The strike failed and the three leaders were sent to prison. But they represented a mood of revolutionary protest that was common and that found its expression in spontaneous strikes in many parts of the country.

In the main, however, although economic danger threatened, the lag of civilian demand was still so great that the workers were for the most part in a strong bargaining position. One after another the railwaymen, the engineers, the cotton workers and the iron and steel workers were able to win lower working hours, although wages in many industries, and particularly on the railways, were still appallingly low, and were to lead to a national railway stoppage in September. Meanwhile the Miners' Federation put forward a demand for higher wages, shorter hours and the nationalization of the mines and threatened to strike unless their demands were conceded. Moreover, they had the support of the railwaymen and transport workers in the triple alliance of which they were a part. Faced with this threat, the Government agreed to set up a Commission under Mr. Justice Sankey to report on wages and hours and on nationalization. And, at the same time, Lloyd George summoned a National Industrial Conference of trade unions and employers to consider a new charter of industrial relations.

The post-war boom was still on. The workers appeared strong and united. Trade-union membership was rising. In 1919 it rose to 5,283,000 and by 1920 had mounted to a peak of over six and a half millions. It seemed possible that, although its political strength was still small, the industrial strength of Labour was now such that it would be able to achieve a peaceful advance to better conditions.

The first signs were propitious. In an interim report, before dealing with the question of nationalization, the Sankey Commission granted the miners' demands for higher wages and a seven-hour day and held out prospects of a six-hour day to come. And for the time being the National Industrial Conference made what appeared to be remarkable progress in achieving co-operation between both sides of industry. The triple alliance of the miners, the railwaymen and the transport workers, together with the engineers, stood outside. They had no confidence in Lloyd George's intentions and refused to participate. To them the conference appeared merely as an attempt to forestall direct action by the trade unions to get the improvements they wanted—and time was to prove them right.

For the moment, however, Henderson agreed to serve as chairman of the workers' side and persuaded G. D. H. Cole, the leading intellectual of the Guild Socialist Movement, to serve with him as secretary. Largely as a result of their ability and the conciliatory and realist temper of the chairman of the employers' side, Sir Alan Smith of the Engineering Employers' Federation, a report was issued recommending a general Eight Hours Act, the setting up of a Minimum Wage Commission and the establishment of a permanent National Industrial Council equally representative of employers and workers' organizations.

And when the Sankey Commission reported, it recommended by a majority—although a bare majority only—the nationalization of the mining industry.

Momentarily the outlook appeared bright. It seemed that the war and the recognition of the increased strength of industrial labour—together with the example of revolution abroad and the anxiety to avert it at home—had brought a new atmosphere in industry and that there was now a real possibility of organized labour getting much of what it had struggled for.

The hope was illusory. The immediate post-war boom was already ending. With its ending and the consequent deterioration in the bargaining power of the industrial workers Government and employers alike abandoned the mood of conciliation and co-operation.

Although Lloyd George had pledged himself to act on the Sankey Report, he refused to do so on the grounds that the recommendation for nationalization was not unanimous. The chairman was in favour, so were the miners' representatives, but the owners, as was to be expected, were not. The recommendations of the National Industrial Conference were similarly ignored.

The solid ranks of "hard-faced business men" and Tories who had put Lloyd George in power had no longer any time for industrial co-operation. Nor had most of their counterparts in industry. They saw instead an opportunity to cut wages and break the strength of the trade unions.

So far from nationalizing the mining industry, the Government suddenly announced on 15 February, 1921, that all wartime controls over it would end on 31 March—five months earlier even than the date laid down in the Coal Mines Act. And the mine-owners, in an attempt to destroy the national solidarity of the miners, announced that in future they would not negotiate wage claims on a national but only on a district basis. The miners refused to accept. They demanded the setting up of a National Pool formed out of surpluses from the most profitable mines to maintain wages in the less profitable and a National Wages Board to fix rates. On 31 March the mine-owners locked them out.

At once the miners appealed to their allies of the triple alliance for aid. A strike of all the unions in the alliance was called for 12 April. The Government immediately proclaimed a "state of emergency." The military were marshalled, reservists were called to the colours, the parks were filled with armed troops. The danger of a clash between the workers and the Government, on a scale whose consequences no one could foresee, seemed very near. The moment of clash was briefly postponed for three days by a Government offer to meet the miners and, pending these negotiations, the strike notices were postponed until 15 April. But the negotiations came to nothing.

On 14 April a joint meeting of the Trades Union Congress Parliamentary Committee, the Labour Party Executive and the Parliamentary Labour Party met in the House of Commons and unanimously pledged support to the miners, railwaymen and transport workers. It appealed "to all sections of the Labour movement and to every citizen who cares for the well-being of the community to stand solidly against this attack on the workers' position." It seemed as though the opposing forces had taken their position and an industrial conflict of the first magnitude was inevitable. It was not to come.

For, from this joint Labour meeting, Frank Hodges, the then secretary of the Miners' Federation, went to another meeting in the House of Commons—an inter-party meeting of M.P.s. At this he stated the miners' case. When he sat down he was subjected to a barrage of questions. Would the miners consider a compromise offer which, while leaving aside the demand for a National Pool, would ensure that wages should not fall below the cost of living?

He replied that: "Any such offer coming from an authoritative source would receive very serious consideration."

With those words he signalled the end, although he did not realize it, of the triple alliance, which had seemed both to the industrial workers and to their opponents to represent the newest and strongest manifestation of the strength of organized labour. What he had said was at once reported to Lloyd George. He invited the miners to meet him to discuss a compromise solution based on such a proposal. The miners refused. At a stormy meeting the executive of the Miners' Federation repudiated their general secretary's statement and reaffirmed their previous decision that the only condition which would make a temporary settlement possible was the concession of the two principles already laid down—a National Wages Board and a National Pool.

They did so without consulting their allies in the triple alliance. But those allies were not willing to follow them in banging the door in so final a fashion. Moreover, they held that if they were to be called upon to strike in support of the miners they had a right to be consulted by the miners as to the conditions of settlement. If there was to be a triple alliance it must act together in all things—decisions which, if the alliance operated, would affect the members of all three unions could not be left to the sole discretion of the executive of one of them.

They agreed with Hodges that even a compromise offer of this kind deserved very serious consideration. When this was refused they bluntly informed the miners that in that case the terms of the alliance no longer operated and cancelled the strike notices.

The triple alliance was ended. It was perhaps inevitable that it should break under stress. The theoretical premises on which it had been founded were never practically attainable. They were that the three groups should arrange for their collective agreements to terminate on the same day, that they should then put forward simultaneous demands and jointly strike if these demands were not acceded to. In practice such a situation never arose. The wage crisis in each industry occurred not simultaneously but separately, and what had been envisaged as a joint strike in support of demands made by all became an agreement for sympathetic strike action by two of the allies in support of the other although their members were not directly involved. Moreover—and this was the real weakness of the triple alliance—at no time had there been a clear decision as to whether, if such a strike was called, control of strike policy was to be in the hands of the joint body or in the hands only of the union directly involved in the dispute.

"Only the miners can decide on what conditions they will work," said the Miners' Federation. "If our members are to be called out on strike to support you they must have some voice in determining when the strike should end," said the railwaymen and transport workers.

Because of these unsolved and perhaps insoluble problems, the triple alliance had never been so strong as it had seemed in theory. Nevertheless, its dramatic collapse on Friday, 15 April, 1921—Black Friday as it came to be called—spread dismay throughout the ranks of labour, a dismay in proportion to the high hopes that had been raised by the plans for joint action and the enthusiasm aroused for the miners' case. The miners struck alone. But all the forces were stacked against them and two months later they were driven back to work on the owners' terms.

So were the engineers when a few months later they, too, struck and were also defeated.

The post-war economic depression which many had foreseen, but against which a government dominated by Conservative businessmen had refused to prepare, was now reaching its height. Unemployment mounted to about two millions. Trade-union membership slumped as workers were thrown out of their jobs, and by the end of 1921 trade-union funds had been depleted by unemployment benefit payments of over seven million pounds.

Organization for direct action, the basis of the syndicalist philosophy which had taken hold of many of the more militant groups in the Labour movement before the war and had been revised in the light of Labour's parliamentary weakness after the 1918 election, had suffered a crushing reverse. Yet it had had its triumphs—the greatest of all eight months before this when the "Hands off Russia" movement, backed by the threat of a general strike, had forced Lloyd George to reverse his policy of armed intervention against the Bolshevists in Russia.

In that issue, however, as Ernest Bevin said when he led a deputation of all sides of the Labour movement to see Lloyd George, "democracy's inherent sense of fair play was at stake."

It was a protest against the fact that: "Tsars have murdered thousands and we have not interfered, but if a people's revolution takes place we are called upon to stamp out a 'terrible menace'." And it was backed not only by organized labour, but by a vast body of non-labour public opinion.

It did not mean that the syndicalist theory of direct action as an instrument of revolutionary political action had been accepted by the British Labour movement. It had not. Nor did it mean that British Labour approved the Soviet system. It did not then or later.

Those who did so were a small Marxist group consisting of members of the British Socialist Party, the Socialist Labour Party and the Workers' Socialist Federation. Inspired by the foundation of a Third International at a world conference called by the Bolsheviks in March, 1919, they, after many quarrels among themselves, formed a Provisional Joint Committee and summoned a Communist Unity Conference in July, 1920. Thus was born the Communist Party of Great Britain which was to play so noisy and disruptive a part in British politics for the remaining period of the fifty-year march of British Labour.

Instructed in correct tactics by Lenin himself, it applied for affiliation to the Labour Party and was refused, the first of many such refusals confirmed by great majorities at annual conferences.

Yet although the main body of the Labour movement remained unshaken in the democratic principles upon which it had been founded twenty years earlier, rejecting alike the syndicalist philosophy and the Communist, there were many occasions when belief in democratic political progress required faith and courage, and when a movement, without those roots in the national tradition from which Labour had from the first derived its sustenance, might have been tempted to turn to revolutionary paths.

The small and at that time badly led Parliamentary Labour Party was manifestly incapable of making any impact upon the course of government policy, although at home that policy was bringing with it social injustice and economic crisis and abroad was helping to set the stage for a new world war in a Peace Treaty which made the economic recovery of Germany, or indeed of Europe, impossible. Labour could protest as it did at an emergency conference in December, 1921. It could do no more.

Yet although it was politically weak and industrially on the defensive as depression robbed the trade unions of their bargaining strength, the principles it advocated were gaining ground. All over the country men and women turned with a new sense of dedication to the Socialist cause—a dedication strengthened by the democratic nature of the new organization which Henderson had built and by their knowledge that the fount of policy for the movement was not to be found simply in a small group of leaders, but in the annual conference to which resolutions came up from the trade unions, the constituency parties and the Socialist societies and at which every issue of policy was discussed.

At last, in 1922, there came a chance to test the result of all this work and to see how far the movement of public opinion had been affected by events.

Lloyd George had served his purpose so far as the Conservatives were concerned. His credit was falling fast at home and abroad. Association with him was becoming a liability rather than an asset. At the famous Carlton Club meeting on 22 October, 1922, Stanley Baldwin, stepping out from the respectable obscurity that had previously been his lot, urged Bonar Law to form a new government without Lloyd George. Bonar Law acquiesced and a Conservative Government was formed. On 15 November it appealed to the country.

In that election Labour received the support of four and a quarter million voters, two million more than in 1918, and won 142 seats, including eighty-six new constituencies. All the principal political leaders of the Party were returned with the sole exception of Henderson, who suffered for his immersion in the general problems of organization by being defeated at Widnes.

Moreover, the Party that assembled in the new Parliament was a new party in many important respects. It was more broadly based, more truly representative of all the national interests in which Labour appealed than ever before, and for the first time included among its members a number of middle-class Socialists returned for working-class areas. This was a manifestation of the classless nature of the Socialist appeal.

Many of those who had shaped Labour policy in the past or were to shape it in the future were now in the House. Those who had led the Party in the old Parliament—J. R. Clynes, J. H. Thomas, W. Adamson, Will Thorne, Ben Tillett, J. Sexton, William Graham —were reinforced by the national leaders who had suffered defeat as pacifists in 1918; Ramsay MacDonald, Philip Snowden, F. W. Jowett and George Lansbury amongst them. Moreover, the election had brought to the House for the first time many who had already won considerable reputations and served Labour greatly outside —Sidney Webb, Clement Attlee, Arthur Greenwood, A. V. Alexander, David Kirkwood, John Wheatley, James Maxton, Thomas Johnston, Emanuel Shinwell, William Whiteley—and two former Liberals with parliamentary experience, Charles Trevelyan. and H. B. Lees-Smith.

It was inevitable that the change in the composition of the Parliamentary Party should raise at once the question of leadership. At the close of the 1922 summer session J. R. Clynes had been elected leader under a party rule laying it down that the leader should be elected at the close of each session. But the new M.P.s were not interested in rules—they wanted the opportunity to choose for themselves. If Henderson had been in Parliament he would have been a strong candidate for the leadership, although in fact he did not want it, preferring to remain secretary of the Party, as he was convinced that the natural parliamentary leader of the Party was MacDonald. As it was, the issue was between MacDonald and Clynes, and MacDonald had the solid support of most of the left-wing Clydeside group led by John Wheatley, who mistakenly judged him to be much more to the Left than he was and assumed, because of his opposition to the war, that he shared their views of the nature of the class struggle.

The I.L.P. was not, however, unanimous in support of MacDonald. Snowden did not trust him as a parliamentary leader and made it plain that he did not. And many of the trade unionists, among them J. H. Thomas—who was later, curiously enough, to become almost MacDonald's closest associate—felt at that time that loyalty, if nothing else, demanded that Clynes should be re-elected.

On 21 November the new Parliamentary Labour Party met for the first time. It was moved that the officers elected in the previous session should continue—and defeated on a show of hands. Thereupon Clynes was re-nominated as chairman. At once Emanuel Shinwell, acting for the Clydesiders, nominated MacDonald. There were no other contenders. The issue was between these two.

When the result of the vote was announced MacDonald had won by five votes. Twenty-two members were absent. Of those present sixty-one voted for him, fifty-six for Clynes. It was a narrow margin for what was to be so fateful a decision.

Exactly thirteen months later, on 21 January, 1924, MacDonald became the first Labour Prime Minister of Britain.

CHAPTER XVI

THE FIRST LABOUR GOVERNMENT
AND THE ZINOVIEV LETTER

RAMSAY MACDONALD once described the first Labour Government as an "insane miracle." It was hardly that, but it was certainly a considerable political gamble—and one which, although it achieved more than it is sometimes given credit for, did not quite come off. Yet it is difficult to see how the Labour Party could have refused to accept the invitation to form a government, even though the form in which the first chance of government came condemned Labour to a minority rule in which it could do nothing except on Liberal sufferance.

The Party was growing rapidly. It had greatly increased its national prestige in the preceding year as His Majesty's Opposition. Its parliamentary leaders, and MacDonald and Snowden especially, had established new and substantial reputations by their conduct of debates. But it neither expected nor was ready to be called upon to govern the country when in November, 1923, Stanley Baldwin, who had become Prime Minister six months earlier, following Bonar Law's resignation on grounds of health, announced his intention of appealing to the country for a mandate to introduce Tariff Protection.

Labour went into the election which came in December with a spirit and an *élan* exceeding even that of 1922, but the results almost certainly surprised everyone except Henderson, that astute campaigner with his astonishing flair for judging election prospects whether they were good or bad—and perhaps Sidney Webb.

For Webb, presiding over the Labour Party Annual Conference in June, at the Queen's Hall, London, had provided the 929 delegates with a statistical analysis of Labour's progress very typical of him and had drawn from that analysis some remarkable conclusions.

It was, he pointed out, exactly ten years since the annual conference had been held in London and in that ten years the position of the Party had been transformed.

"In 1913," he said, "after more than a decade of persistent and often heroic work, the Party counted an affiliated membership of considerably under two millions. It could contest only one-tenth of the constituencies and in them could poll less than half a million votes. After three general elections it had returned only 6 per cent of the House of Commons. Its parliamentary position was ambiguous. Whilst its principles were already definite enough, its programme was still very incompletely formulated. And up and down the country its organization was often as shadowy as its programme."

He compared this position with that reached by 1923.

"Today we see the Labour Party with about four million affiliated members, being at once the poorest and quite the largest political organization in the land, locally organized in all but half a dozen out of the six hundred constituencies in Great Britain; placing some ten thousand elected representatives on the various municipal and other local councils, proclaiming not only principles but also a definitely formulated comprehensive programme over the whole range of home and foreign affairs; placing this programme before the electors in over four hundred parliamentary seats; polling in them alone four and a quarter million votes, being only a million or so fewer than the victorious Unionist Party in the whole country; returning just upon a quarter of the House of Commons; and becoming officially recognized as His Majesty's Opposition, prepared to form an alternative Ministry whenever called upon to do so."

It was certainly an astonishing advance. Webb went on to point out what it might portend.

"Those who are curious in statistics," he said, "may be interested to compute that a continuation of the rising curve of Labour votes from the 62,968 of 1900, through the 323,195 of 1906 and the 505,690 of January, 1910, the two and a half millions of 1918 and the four and a quarter millions of 1922, would produce a clear majority of the total votes cast in Great Britain somewhere about 1926. This forecast we have now to make good."

It was not, of course, made good. The curve did not continue uninterrupted—the political future is but rarely completely capable of statistical assessment. But it might perhaps have been made nearly good if events had worked out a little differently; if Labour's first essay in government had not ended quite so maladroitly; if the subsequent election had been fought with more intelligence; if Henderson rather than MacDonald had been the Party leader, or if MacDonald had escaped a little longer the clutch of personal egotism that was to eat into and destroy the immense abilities which he had first brought to the Labour movement. If! In politics there is no room for "ifs." But although the clear majority of votes for Labour by 1926 which Webb saw written as a possibility in the statistical tables did not come to pass it nevertheless remains the case that at no election after 1924 was its principal opponent, the Conservative Party, able to secure office except by alliance with some section of another party, and that, with only one setback—in 1931—the Labour vote increased at every subsequent election.

What the results of the 1923 election indicated to the practical politician, however, was not so much that Labour's position in the country was steadily advancing—the total votes it received were, indeed, at 4,348,379 only slightly above those received a year earlier—but that it was now definitely the second largest party in the country, even when the Liberals fought, as they did on this occasion, as a single party. It won 191 seats as against the Liberals' 158, although the Conservatives remained the largest party with 258 seats. Herbert Morrison, Margaret Bondfield, F. W. Pethick-Lawrence, Susan Lawrence and George Isaacs were among the new Labour M.P.s, and a remarkable feature of the results was the big advance of Labour in the Greater London Area, where the number of Labour M.P.s rose from sixteen to thirty-seven.

Although the Liberals were now the smallest of the three parties, the decision as to which of the other two parties should govern the country lay with them. Without their support the Conservatives had not a majority and with their support Labour could form a minority government. In a speech at the National Liberal Club, immediately following the election, Mr. Asquith made the Liberal position clear. The Liberals, he said, "would not lift a finger to keep the Tories in office."

No other decision was open to them by any honest standard of political judgment. The Conservatives were, it is true, the largest party. But Baldwin had gone to the country specifically to ask for a mandate to introduce Protection, and on that issue the Tories in the House were in a minority of 258 to 349, and had secured in the country only 5,544,540 votes to 8,662,581, which was the total anti-Protectionist vote of Labour and the Liberals combined.

But could and should Labour agree to form a government in conditions which would make a truly Socialist administration impossible and prevent it from carrying out the full programme on which it had gone to the country? There were divided views in the Labour movement. But when, on the day after the election, MacDonald, Henderson, Snowden, Thomas, Clynes and Sidney Webb met at Webb's house at 41 Grosvenor Road—scene of so many political tea-parties and the base from which so many adroit and successful Fabian campaigns had been launched—these six were unanimous in agreeing that it must. To refuse national responsibility would in their view, and they were undoubtedly right, inflict almost a mortal blow on Labour claims to be a great national party, capable, when called upon to do so, of forming an administration. The risks of acceptance were great, but the risks of refusal were greater, for, if the call were refused now, how could the electorate be expected to take Labour's pretensions seriously in the future?

This having been agreed, MacDonald at once retired to Lossiemouth for Christmas and Cabinet making. His first essay in the task of forming a Cabinet provided immediate evidence of how difficult a leader of a Labour Party in office he was likely to prove and how little regard he had for either the ability or the loyalty of those colleagues whom he did not find personally sympathetic, although he owed his position as leader largely to them. In his first draft Cabinet, for example, he completely ignored Henderson, the prime architect of the new Labour Party, the only member of it with Cabinet experience, and the one man who could if he had wished have successfully challenged MacDonald for the leadership. In his second he left him out of the Cabinet, but proposed that he should be chairman of the Committee of Ways and Means—a suggestion almost more insulting than being passed over entirely. Moreover, until the *Manchester Guardian* got hold of the story and killed it with scorn, he toyed with the idea of making J. H. Thomas—now a close personal intimate—the first Labour Foreign Secretary, although Thomas had manifestly, as even his friends agreed, none of the qualifications and abilities needed for that particular post.

The final result proved, however, better than the first drafts suggested. Wisely, perhaps, for he was the Party's principal expert on foreign affairs and was much more at home with international matters than with domestic issues, MacDonald decided to combine the Foreign Office with the Premiership. Clynes was Lord Privy Seal and Deputy Leader of the House; Snowden, Chancellor of the Exchequer—a post for which his gifts made him the natural, indeed the inevitable, choice; Henderson, after refusing the War Office, was Home Secretary; J. H. Thomas, Colonial Secretary; Sidney Webb, President of the Board of Trade; C. P. Trevelyan, President of the Board of Education; John Wheatley, Minister of Health; and his fellow representative of the advanced wing of the I.L.P., F. W. Jowett, First Commissioner of Works.

It was a respectable, if not a dazzling, Cabinet. But the appointment of the ex-Liberal, Lord Haldane, as Lord Chancellor, of Lord Parmoor, the ex-Tory pacifist, as Lord President of the Council, and Lord Chelmsford, who had never given any previous indications of Labour sympathies, as First Lord of the Admiralty, indicated MacDonald's congenital lack of faith in the ability of his political colleagues—and especially, with one or two exceptions, of the trade-union members of his party. This lack of faith, which had little but his own prejudices to support it, was to increase with the growth of his own personal egotism and with his conception of himself as a national rather than a party leader, a philosopher-statesman. In a Cabinet of twenty there were only five trade unionists, and these included Henderson, Clynes and Thomas, who were outstanding parliamentary as well as industrial leaders. Moreover, throughout the lifetime of the Government, MacDonald made no attempt to maintain satisfactory liaison with the trade unions, although such liaison was clearly desirable, indeed essential, in the national as well as the party interest.

Outside the Cabinet there was one appointment which, as things turned out, was to be of particular significance, that of Sir Patrick Hastings, a newcomer to the Labour Party with great legal ability but little political experience, as Attorney-General.

Among the Under-Secretaries and Parliamentary Secretaries there were several who were to justify their selection by later becoming national leaders of the Party; among them Clement Attlee at the War Office, Arthur Greenwood at Health, Margaret Bondfield at Labour, William Graham at the Treasury, A. V. Alexander at the Board of Trade, and Emanuel Shinwell as Secretary of Mines.

Having accepted the invitation to form a government, there were two courses open to Labour. It could produce a comprehensive Socialist programme in the King's Speech and challenge the Liberals to vote against it—knowing that they would be bound to accept the challenge and overthrow the Labour Government before it had well begun. Or it could try to carry through a moderate programme of social reform at home and international co-operation abroad, accepting in so doing the necessity of compromise with the Liberals on many issues.

MacDonald, Henderson and the other parliamentary leaders were unanimous in deciding on the second course. Again they were almost certainly right—although again there were risks.

To take the first course would have been dramatically satisfying and would have appealed to many of those on the left wing of the movement. But politics is a practical business. A dramatic gesture of this kind, manifestly made with the knowledge that it must bring with it parliamentary defeat, would hardly have been likely to persuade the general body of the electorate of Labour's serious intentions. Nor had Labour any mandate from the country for putting into effect a Socialist programme—and a Socialist programme, by its very nature and by the extent of the call it makes upon the co-operation and public spirit of ordinary citizens, cannot be carried through democratically without majority agreement.

"We can't have socialism without Socialists," Robert Blatchford used to tell the eager young members of the Clarion Clubs when they asked him how the Socialist dawn could be hurried forward, and that was the true answer to those who thought that the first Labour Minority Government should make Britain Socialist over-night.

There were, however, immediate problems of housing, of unemployment and of education with which a Labour government could deal and in which it could hope to make an impact by administrative action—even if sweeping legislation proved impossible in face of the Liberal veto. And in the field of foreign affairs a new approach might succeed in changing the whole atmosphere.

It was with this conception of what was possible that the Labour leaders decided to form a government. In the result, they probably did not go as far in some directions as they might well have done—in dealing with the coal industry, for example, which was left untouched—and did not show sufficient tactical skill in putting the Liberals on the defensive. In part this was due to political inexperience, an inexperience particularly marked in handling the issue which brought the Government down after less than nine months, in part to MacDonald's own preference for a mildly reformist rather than a radical policy. He was now, more than ever, the captive of the misleading comparison between biology and politics which had pleased his imagination many years before and which provided him with a satisfactory excuse for trusting to the inevitability of gradualness to produce the new society he talked of in his speeches.

It was inevitable that the impact of a Labour government should in all these circumstances fall far short of the expectations of those of its supporters who had convinced themselves that the arrival of a Socialist Prime Minister at 10 Downing Street would immediately bring with it a revolutionary change in the order of things. Their disillusionment, inevitable though it was, was increased by the obvious delight that MacDonald himself took in the social formalities of his office and the lack of any evidence of a new wind blowing in Whitehall in those matters of social convention and ritual which many besides Socialists would have been glad to see changed.

Nevertheless, the Labour Government's accomplishments in its short life of nine months were by no means negligible. It quickly abolished the "gap" between periods of benefit under the unemployment insurance scheme which had created so much bitterness and distress, and set to work on public works schemes—including road and railway construction and electrical development—to meet in some part the mounting unemployment in private industry. Rates of unemployment benefit and children's allowances were increased and the conditions of old age pensioners improved.

In education the economy policy, previously imposed under the "Geddes Axe" by a government which thought of popular education as a fit subject for reduction, was reversed. Local authorities were encouraged to go ahead with educational developments by the provision of State grants, approval was given to the building of forty new secondary schools, the proportion of free places increased, maintenance allowances raised, State scholarships restored and the grants for adult education trebled.

An Agricultural Wages Bill to restore the minimum wage which had been taken away in 1921 was introduced, and although it was mutilated by the Liberals, who deprived the Central Wages Board of the power given by the bill to overrule the decisions of the County Agricultural Wages Committees, it brought considerable improvement in the rural areas.

In housing, the Labour Government produced legislation for amending the law on rent control and for preventing evictions where non-payment of rent was due to unemployment, but was unable to carry it through in the face of Liberal opposition. But its greatest success and the most important piece of legislation put on the Statute Book during its brief period of office was John Wheatley's Housing Act, which gave subsidies to local authorities to build houses for letting at controlled rents as the essential foundation of a far-reaching programme to produce the houses required to meet the national need.

In the field of international affairs even more spectacular achievements were made—so much so that for a time the whole atmosphere in Europe was altered. Largely under MacDonald's initiative, and with the assistance of Henderson and Lord Parmoor, both of whom took a prominent and highly constructive part in international policy, the French were persuaded to evacuate the Ruhr, the Dawes Plan for scaling down German Reparations to a more practicable level was accepted and the need for a modification of the Versailles Treaty generally agreed. And through the Geneva Protocol a big advance was made towards the conception of international arbitration in the settlement of disputes as the necessary prelude to a world-wide reduction in armaments. The prospect that the League of Nations would become a workable international authority was brought nearer than at any previous time.

All this represented a heartening advance and one for which great credit must go to MacDonald. In the field of international affairs, where he felt himself able to operate as a world statesman advancing the ideals for which he had courageously fought throughout the war, MacDonald was indeed a very different man from the fumbling domestic leader with his growing dislike of his Labour colleagues and of what he felt to be the restrictions of party politics.

Yet even in foreign affairs he had his limitations. He agreed to the diplomatic recognition of Soviet Russia and to an Anglo-Russian Conference which in August, 1924, produced two draft treaties settling the outstanding differences between the two countries and preparing the way for a British trade loan to the U.S.S.R. But he did so somewhat unwillingly, partly because of his own distrust of the Russians and partly because of the bitter opposition of the Conservatives, of Lloyd George and of the majority of the popular Press. "No Money for Murderers," shrieked the *Daily Mail*, and the cry was taken up by others.

It was indeed basically Conservative and Liberal opposition to the Russian trade loan which brought about the defeat of the Labour Government before the end of the year, although the ostensible cause of that defeat was the "Campbell case."

It is perhaps a characteristic irony of politics that the fall of the first Labour Government should have been immediately due to the initiation and later the withdrawal of a charge of incitement to mutiny of a kind which might well in earlier days have been—and, in fact, had been—launched by a reactionary government against many of the founders and leaders of the Labour Party themselves. The action was both initiated and later withdrawn in complete good faith by an Attorney-General who was both new to the Labour Party and to politics and who throughout acted with the best intentions and with the highest integrity, although he was bitterly and wrongfully attacked for giving way to political pressure.

On 25 July, six months after the Labour Government had taken office, the *Workers' Weekly*, the official organ of the Communist Party, published an open letter to the Forces. In this it called upon them—quite unnecessarily in the circumstances of the time—not to allow themselves to be used in industrial disputes. This was part of a characteristic campaign by the Communist Party to try to present the Labour Government to the workers as the tool of reaction and oppression.

Two Conservative M.P.s at once asked questions about this article in the House and the attention of the Director of Public Prosecutions was drawn to it. He advised the Attorney-General, Sir Patrick Hastings, that in his opinion an action would lie under the Incitement to Mutiny Act of 1795. Without apparently considering the matter very closely, or stopping to assess what real public damage, if any, was likely to be done by the publication or whether it was sufficiently serious to justify a prosecution, the Attorney-General instructed him to take proceedings.

A week later, in reply to an angry question by John Scurr, a Labour member, the Attorney-General announced that the offices of the *Workers' Weekly* had been raided and the editor arrested and charged.

There was an immediate outburst from the Labour backbenchers. Led by James Maxton, George Lansbury, Jack Jones and others, it was directed principally not against the Attorney-General, but against the Prime Minister, whom they suspected of not being so keen as some of his Cabinet colleagues on the Russian Treaty and of being glad of any chance to attack the Communists. They were convinced—wrongly as it turned out—that he personally had instructed the Attorney-General to take this action.

Amidst the general uproar another Labour member, Tom Dickson, jumped up and asked the Attorney-General whether, if any members of the House who were speaking in their constituencies in the following week expressed similar opinions to those expressed in the *Workers' Weekly*, they would be subject to similar prosecution. "Because if so," said Dickson with a wave of his hand towards the Treasury Bench, "they will probably lose half their party."

Dickson's ironic commentary undoubtedly expressed the sentiments of a very large number of the Labour M.P.s. They saw in the action against the *Workers' Weekly* a politically inspired attack on freedom of speech of a kind that many of the most honoured of Labour pioneers and some of those at present in the House had been subjected to in the past.

Sir Patrick Hastings was both astonished and worried by the reaction. He had given no great attention to the matter in the first place and he had certainly not appreciated the passions it would arouse or the sense of injustice it would create, for he had little knowledge of the traditions and feelings of the Labour movement. He decided to look further into the action that had been taken and review the facts. As a preliminary he asked Maxton to come and see him.

From Maxton and from his other inquiries Sir Patrick Hastings learned that J. R. Campbell, the man arrested and charged, was not the editor of the *Workers' Weekly*, but only the acting editor, that he had fought in the war, from beginning to end, had been badly wounded in both feet and had been decorated for exceptional gallantry.

Sir Patrick Hastings was one of the most popular and successful advocates at the Bar, with great experience as defending counsel. When he considered these facts and thought what a defending counsel could make of them—what he himself could have made of them in other circumstances—and the amount of public sympathy that would be aroused for a prisoner with such a record, produced as the most dangerous Communist the Law Officers of the Crown could lay their hands on, he felt that he must be very sure indeed before he proceeded with the case. He examined the article again, took further legal advice on it and finally very honestly informed the Cabinet that after going further into the matter he had grave doubts whether the prosecution could succeed and therefore proposed to withdraw the case.

Meanwhile the Communist Party welcomed the publicity. It announced not merely that it would fight the case with all its energy, but that it proposed to engage Sir John Simon or Sir Douglas Hogg as counsel and to call the Prime Minister for cross-examination on, among other things, a speech he had made in the House of Commons on 4 June, 1912, defending Tom Mann who at that time had been charged with an offence exactly similar to that now brought against Campbell.

In these circumstances and in the atmosphere of political passion aroused by the proposals for a Russian loan, the withdrawal of the case was bound to create a sensation. Both the Conservatives and the Liberals at once charged the Prime Minister with interfering with the course of justice and withdrawing the prosecution for political reasons. When the House met after the recess the Conservatives followed this up with a vote of censure to which the Liberals moved an amendment proposing that a select committee should be set up to investigate the facts.

Almost to the end of the debate the outcome was uncertain. Early in its course a completely frank speech by the Attorney-General convinced very many even of the Government opponents that, whatever errors of judgment he personally might have made, the charge that he had given way to illegitimate political pressure in withdrawing the case was untrue. Moreover, Asquith did not wish to force the issue so far as to compel the Government's resignation if he could avoid it, although Lloyd George and most of the Conservatives, who were thinking much more in terms of the Anglo Russian agreement than the Campbell case, did.

But MacDonald had by now persuaded himself that his personal honour had been impugned. He had recently been the subject of a bitter personal attack by many newspapers because of his acceptance of a motor-car and the income to run it from a Scottish biscuit manufacturer who was a personal friend of his and who was given a baronetcy in the King's Birthday Honours—although, in fact, his name had been put forward originally by a previous government because of his public benefactions in Scotland. The allegation of political corruption had stung MacDonald to passionate anger— he was never one to accept criticism easily—and he was in a highly sensitive state when he faced the House in the Campbell debate. He did not come well out of the early exchanges and suffered badly under the lash of Sir John Simon, who taunted him with vagueness and ambiguity.

When he rose to reply he announced at once that if either the Conservative vote of censure or the Liberal amendment were passed, "then we go." That settled the issue. It left Asquith with no loophole for compromise.

Faced with this challenge, the Conservatives decided to support the Liberal amendment. The vote was taken and the amendment was carried by 364 votes to 198. The first Labour Government was over—brought down on an issue that need never have arisen and on which defeat was made certain by a combination of political inexperience on the part of the Attorney-General and personal irritation and misjudgment on the part of the Prime Minister.

If the end of Labour's first term of government was due to an ironic tragi-comedy of politics and personal susceptibilities, the election that followed was decided in an atmosphere of melodramatic sensationalism worthy almost of a Phillips Oppenheim novel. It left behind it one of the unsolved mysteries of politics.

For the deciding factor in this election was not the Campbell case, nor the Government's record in domestic and foreign policy, but the Zinoviev letter. And here again MacDonald's own personality played a large part.

Yet if MacDonald's personality was, as we shall see, a factor of some importance in the result, what was really significant about this election and what makes it worthy of analysis even after this lapse of time was the evidence it gave of the forces that the opponents of Labour were ready to mobilize to try to check its onward march and the appeal they were ready to make to mass-hysteria through the instrument of a violent and unscrupulous Press campaign.

Vast and serious issues faced the country. The economic situation was threatening and very shortly was to bring the country to the edge of a crisis of the greatest gravity. The issue of whether or not the League of Nations could be made an effective instrument for international co-operation and world peace was trembling in the balance. The question of whether the new forces in control in Russia could be brought into membership of the comity of nations was exercising the minds of all who were aware, however dimly, of the vast transition period that faced the world. At home unemployment, housing, industrial productivity, the demand for greater economic security—all these faced the nation with problems fundamental to its existence. Measures of great importance, among them a far-ranging Factory bill, a bill for the ratification of the Washington International Labour Convention to provide for a maximum working week of forty-eight hours, a bill for setting up a National Minimum Wage Commission, a bill for controlling prices and checking monopolies in building were still before the

House when the Government fell. The future of the mining industry was still undecided.

All these great issues were brushed aside. On none of them was British democracy seriously asked to pass its judgment by the opponents of Labour.

Instead the whole force of Conservative propaganda, ably supported by its allies and backers among the mass circulation newspapers, was concentrated on trying to frighten the public with the "Red Bogey."

The attempt to achieve a basis of trading relationship with Russia was presented with every possible embellishment of lurid propaganda as a Labour alliance with a godless power which had "nationalized women." A policy—it was suggested—which might soon come to pass in Britain also if the Socialists had their way. It is possible that those who put out this propaganda and who, on hundreds of thousands of doorsteps, did their best to persuade voters that a vote for Labour meant a vote for anarchy, murder and legalized rape, believed what they said. If so, they were manifestly unfit to participate in a sober democratic consideration of serious affairs.

But the Conservative Central Office had decided that these were the tactics by which to win an election. The Bolshevik Bogey dominated the election campaign from start to finish. And, as all successful campaigns planned for such purposes must have, the campaign had a climax. This came with the Zinoviev letter.

This letter was a communication allegedly signed by Zinoviev, President of the Comintern—the Communist Third International —Kuusinen, the Finnish Secretary of the International, and Arthur Macmanus, a British member of its Presidium, for the instruction of the British Communist Party in the action it should take to ensure the ratification of the Anglo-Soviet treaties. The original letter was said to have been sent on 15 September. At no stage was it ever available for examination, but alleged copies of it found their way first to the *Daily Mail* and, much later on, 10 October, two days after the Government's defeat on the Campbell case, to the Foreign Office. According to these copies the British Communist Party was instructed not only to support the Anglo-Soviet treaties by all legitimate means, but also to prepare for military insurrection in the working-class areas of Great Britain, to undermine the allegiance of the Army and Navy and to "paralyse the military preparations of the bourgeoisie." A strong attack on MacDonald for his anti-Soviet attitude was also contained in the note.

The question of whether there was or was not an authentic Zinoviev letter, and, if so, whether the copies received by the *Daily Mail* and the Foreign Office were true copies, has never been satisfactorily settled.

Much of the language in the published versions was very close to that commonly used in Communist documents—but, then, Communist literary style is very easy to copy. Nor were Zinoviev and his fellow Communists incapable of the wildly inaccurate misjudgment of British conditions which it contained. On the other hand, no original was ever seen—unless by the Communist Party, which, unless the whole thing were a complete fabrication, must presumably have had something and could, if the copies were inaccurate, have put the matter right by publishing the original. Nor was any action taken by the succeeding government against Macmanus, the British signatory, although, if the document was genuine, as Sir Austen Chamberlain who succeeded to the Foreign Office later declared himself satisfied that it was, a much stronger case would have lain against him for incitement to mutiny than had ever lain against Campbell—indeed an overwhelming case. A Labour Party committee of investigation set up after the election made as full inquiry as it was able but came to no final conclusion, although it expressed the view that the letter was probably, although not certainly, a forgery.

There the matter rests with a strong presumption that there probably was some letter, but that the more lurid and damaging passages in it were most likely written in by some forger who either for political or financial reasons wanted to increase the value of a document that had fallen into his hands by making it more sensational.

Be that as it may, the *Daily Mail*, when it received its copy and consulted the Conservative Central Office, at once realized that this was a "bombshell" too valuable to waste in the early stages of the election. It must be saved for an eleventh-hour sensation—

with the whole campaign leading up to it and preparing the ground for a maximum effect.

As for the Foreign Office, it sent a copy to MacDonald, who was in the midst of his election campaign, and, as a result, did not receive it until 16 October. He at once instructed the Foreign Office that the greatest care should be taken to find out whether the letter was authentic, that if it was it would have to be published, and that meanwhile a draft note to the Soviet Ambassador should be prepared ready to be sent if the authenticity of the letter were proved. This was clearly the correct, indeed the only, response he could make at that time.

The Foreign Office then drafted a note as instructed and sent the draft to MacDonald, who received it on 23 October. No final conclusion as to the note's authenticity or otherwise had by then been reached by the Foreign Office, although it inclined to the view that it was authentic. MacDonald returned the draft note with some amendments the next day. He apparently assumed, as he had every right to by normal Foreign Office procedure, that the note would be held until proof of the authenticity of the Zinoviev letter was ready to be put before him, if it ever was, and until he had given instructions for it to be sent to the Ambassador.

That same day, however, the Foreign Office heard that the *Daily Mail* had a copy of the letter and proposed to publish it on the following morning—the hour, three days before polling date, at which it was judged the bombshell would have its maximum effect having arrived. Thereupon the officials concerned took the singular and unprecedented action of issuing both their copy of the letter and the note to the Soviet Ambassador to the Press without making any attempt to get in touch with the Prime Minister and Foreign Secretary by telegraph, telephone or special courier and without his authority.

The publication of the letter and the Foreign Office note created as big a sensation as the most optimistic official of the Conservative Central Office could have hoped. Here was a letter from the Communist International giving instructions for the promotion of revolution in Britain. That was bad enough. But it was not all. Here also was a note from the Foreign Office apparently fully accepting the authenticity of the letter (as well it might, since it had never been intended that it should be sent unless and until that authenticity were proved), charging the Soviet Government with complicity in the activities of the Comintern and declaring that it must bring to an end the activities within its territory of agencies "whose aim it is to spread discontent or to foment rebellion in any part of the British Empire."

And this was the Government with whom the Labour Party had made draft treaties and to whom it proposed to advance a large loan.

Coming as the culmination of a lurid anti-Bolshevik campaign the effect three days before the end of the election was devastating. On platforms up and down the country Conservative candidates hammered home the moral drawn in the screaming headlines of the *Daily Mail* and its fellows.

Labour candidates who had been fighting the Red Bogey scare by trying to point out the advantages to British industry of a Russian trade loan did not know what to say. They could not believe that the Zinoviev letter was authentic. They felt convinced that, if there had been any suspicion that it was, they would have received some guidance from their leader. They waited anxiously for a statement from MacDonald. None came. On the day of publication he addressed a great meeting in Wales. But he made no reference of any kind to the subject which above all others was occupying everyone's mind.

Not until two days later did he refer to it—and then only to deal in bare outline with the dates on which the letter had been brought to his notice, without giving any indication as to whether or no he accepted its authenticity or agreed that the Soviet Government was itself implicated.

"We're sunk," said J. H. Thomas when he opened the morning papers on the Saturday and saw the Zinoviev headlines. All over the country flabbergasted Labour candidates looking vainly for a lead from MacDonald repeated these sentiments in their own words.

Why MacDonald gave no such lead remains a mystery. Whether he himself believed the Zinoviev letter to be authentic or not is not known. He appears at no time, until too late, to have realized its political implications and its certain effect on the election. He did not like the Anglo-Russian treaties. He was probably much annoyed by the slighting references to himself in the alleged letter. He probably hoped when it was first sent to him that it would not be necessary to do anything about it until after the election. He did not consult any of his colleagues or even attempt to prepare anything which would put the letter, if authentic, in its true perspective.

Everything that could be done to make a difficult situation disastrous he did by his silence when the letter was published.

When the election results were announced, Labour had a net loss of forty seats with only 151 of its candidates successful, the Liberal Party had been reduced to a rump of only forty-two M.P.s, and the Conservatives had a clear majority with 413 of their candidates returned.

Yet the true significance of this result was that, with every possible tactic of misrepresentation used against it, with the full force of modern propaganda employed to confuse the real issues and frighten the electorate, and with fumbling leadership of an incredible kind at the critical climax of the election, the public support for Labour was not halted.

On the contrary, although there was a loss of seats due to some extent to local pacts between Conservatives and Liberals, and even more to the failure of the Liberals to attract votes which went instead to Conservatives, the Labour vote did not fall.

Instead, it actually rose by 1,139,241 to 5,487,620. That was not much immediate consolation to the defeated. But it was a clear sign that the steady, irresistible advance in public support was continuing, that not all the electorate could be stampeded by propaganda and that Labour's ultimate success was sure.

CHAPTER XVII

THE SWING TO INDUSTRIAL ACTION
AND THE GENERAL STRIKE

FOUR and a half years separated the defeat of Labour in the
Zinoviev letter election and its return to office—this time as
the largest party in the State—in May, 1929.

They were years of crisis, of depression, of unemployment and
of drama. Years in which, after political defeat, the Labour movement, repeating once again the pattern of previous years, swung for
a time to a belief in direct action as the only road to success and
then, after the climax and frustration of the General Strike, swung
back once more to political action, stronger and more conscious
of its purpose than before.

When Labour again took office it had the votes of 8,365,000
electors behind it and there were 288 Labour M.P.s in the House.
But it was still a minority government and MacDonald was still
its leader. This time his leadership was to bring it not merely to
electoral defeat but to a tragedy of betrayal that might well have
wrecked it. He who had done so much in the years from 1900
onward to make it a living and a creative force in politics was now
to do his best to destroy it, with Snowden as his chief helpmate in
the work of destruction—Snowden, who had won so many converts
to socialism in great meetings and street-corner gatherings in the
early years. Of such are the high tragedies of politics.

Yet the tragedy was personal. The Labour Party was not
destroyed. The movement which, in the centuries of struggle and
growth, had been beaten down again and again by the malice of its
enemies and the mobilized power of privilege and reaction, and
which had always survived and re-formed to take up the fight,
survived also the defection of its leaders and went on to new strength.

For the Labour movement, which has thrown up so many remarkable leaders in its time, is greater than any of its leaders, drawing its strength never solely from the inspiration of the few, however great their individual contributions to its progress, but always from the loyalty and sacrifice of the rank and file—from the millions of ordinary men and women whose instrument it is and whole ultimate fidelity is given not to individuals but to a great cause.

When the Zinoviev letter election was over there were many among the leaders of both the industrial and political wings of the Party who were convinced that for the sake of its political health it must find a new leader. Ernest Bevin, who had already emerged as one of the most powerful and able trade-union leaders, was among them; he, indeed, had never concealed his dislike and distrust of MacDonald. So were many of the leaders of the I.L.P., including its most able writer, H. N. Brailsford, who in the *New Leader*, which he edited and which he raised to great influence, urged the Party to find a new chief. So also was Philip Snowden, who together with others went to see Henderson and urged him to allow himself to be nominated for the leadership in place of MacDonald.

Henderson refused. It is one of the ironies of history that he who more than almost any man had given his single-minded devotion and complete fidelity to the Labour Party, and whose entire interest was in its success, should have been more responsible than any other single person for insisting that MacDonald, who was to do his best to destroy it, must stay. He owed nothing to MacDonald, who had treated him badly on almost every occasion. But he believed that, by insisting on loyalty to him, he was doing the best thing for the Labour Party. That was all that mattered to him.

Yet there was much to support his view of MacDonald's indispensability at the time. Those who had served in the Government, even many of those who had been M.P.s, might have their doubts. They had experienced directly the enigma of MacDonald's personality. They had seen the indecision which lay beneath the appearance of strength, they had suffered under the vanities and egoisms of one who increasingly felt himself superior to his background, his party and his colleagues and who had schooled himself in a withdrawn aloofness from ordinary affairs that was more akin to the character of an actor playing the part of greatness than to greatness itself. They knew, or some of them did, how little practical, political content there now was in the philosophical socialism he affected.

Yet if he overacted the part of greatness, if he was personally vain and autocratic and too much delighted by the social triumphs which had come to him later in his career and without his wife's steadying influence and wise friendliness to guide him among them, he had the elements of greatness in him. In his later years he turned increasingly away from the hard intellectual discipline of creative political thought to the misty borderland of emotional response to problems, preferring the adulation of disciples to the argument of equals and the pose of a weary Atlas to the hard grind of political administration. But he had political courage of a great if intermittent kind, a vision of a new society and especially of a new international society which was true and noble, even although he sometimes preferred to talk about it rather than work for it. He was a great parliamentarian and a magnificent orator. He moved more easily in large affairs in which he could feel himself a servant of destiny than among small ones—and a successful Prime Minister must be capable of applying himself to small matters as well as large—but in the field of international relations, where he had been able to paint on a large canvas and where he could bring to bear the principles and knowledge made his own over many years, he had done magnificently—how magnificently could be seen when the change in the European atmosphere that followed the end of the Labour Government became manifest. He had all the gifts required for political greatness: a magnificent presence and voice, a power to move great crowds and inspire intense loyalty, a capacity to think not in terms of the parish but of the world—all the gifts save two, the power of cool objective thinking and the capacity for self-criticism which alone can act as a brake upon the vanity of those subjected to the histrionic temptations which beset all who play their lives upon a public stage. He would have been a great man if only he had possessed the simplicity of greatness.

But, in 1924, when Henderson brusquely dismissed all MacDonald's critics with the blunt comment that to talk of swopping

GEORGE LANSBURY

The M.P. for Bow (1922–40) speaking against the Means Test in 1936.

ELLEN WILKINSON
Their organizer and M.P. leading Jarrow unemployed to London in 1936.

leaders in the hour of defeat was not his idea of fair play, he was still the Party's strongest man and greatest public figure. His hold upon the rank and file who came under the magic of his oratory was immense. It was increased rather than diminished by defeat. The circumstances of the election, and the misrepresentation, the hysterical propaganda and the personal vilification which had been employed as the principal weapons in it, were exactly of the kind to stir the loyalty of ordinary decent men and women and rally them to his defence.

Moreover, although the sins of omission of the first Labour Government had seemed large to many while it was in office, its positive achievements took on a truer perspective as the administration of unemployment insurance under the Baldwin Government deprived many thousands of benefit and forced them to seek poor relief, as public works schemes to provide work for men who sought only the right to labour usefully and maintain their families were stopped, as educational progress was slowed down and as a new attack on the conditions of the workers was launched while internationally relations with Russia were broken off and the Geneva Protocol torn up.

Labour might not have done all that its most ardent supporters had hoped for in its brief period of government, but by comparison with what followed it was seen to have considerable achievements to its credit.

Now reaction had returned to power and industrial labour turned to the task of organizing for self-defence against an attack on wages and conditions which it had for the time being insufficient political power to prevent. The syndicalist theories of industrial action for political purposes had been abandoned—indeed, they had never held sway among more than a minority of trade unionists—but, lacking political power, the trade-union leaders were more conscious than ever of the need to concert their industrial strength in order to meet not merely attacks on wages in individual industries but a nation-wide depression of conditions.

This feeling that the trade unions must evolve an industrial policy of their own and not one that derived solely from political socialism had been increased by trade-union experience during the MacDonald administration. MacDonald had little understanding of trade-union affairs, and, except for Thomas, whom he enjoyed as an amusing companion who was in no danger of becoming a rival, had no close friends among trade-union leaders. He despised them as men who did not appreciate his qualities as a political philosopher and were impatient of the artistic and cultural bias which, as Lord D'Abernon, the British Ambassador in Berlin, had shrewdly noted when he was Foreign Secretary, he "took pleasure in proclaiming." They for their part distrusted—or many of them did—his sincerity as a Labour man.

He had markedly passed over many able and experienced trade-union leaders in selecting his first Cabinet and had preferred to appoint ex-Liberals to posts which some trade unionists could well have filled with no less ability. Moreover, he had made no attempt to establish close relations with the trade-union movement while in office or to bring them into consultative partnership on industrial policy.

While the Labour Government was still in office, therefore, the trade unions, at their 1924 Annual Conference in Hull, acting independently of the political branch of the movement, set out an industrial programme which they considered should be the goal of Labour policy. At the same time, they vested in the hands of the General Council much more authority and powers of co-ordination than formerly in order that it should be in a position to deal with industrial disputes likely to involve large bodies of workers. Thus began a development which, under the influence and in large part because of the administrative ability of Walter Citrine, the new General Secretary of the T.U.C., was greatly to increase the authority of the organized trade-union movement in the years ahead.

This greater concentration of the trade unions on their own industrial policy was immensely stimulated by the impact of the economic situation which began to develop as the Baldwin administration took over.

The Baldwin Government's decisions, taken on the advice of the Bank of England, to return to the Gold Standard and to do so at a level which compelled a reduction in British export prices, if parity was to be maintained, made an attempt to reduce general money-wages inevitable. As often before, the first attack came on the miners.

In June, 1925, the mine-owners gave notice that they proposed to terminate the wage agreement established a year earlier. At the same time they made it clear that they intended to demand heavy wage reductions and an increase in working hours. The coal industry, dependent as it was on export markets, had been particularly affected by the return to the Gold Standard at an exchange rate which made the prices formerly charged for British coal no longer competitive. And competition was increasing as the output of the German coalfields rose, following the evacuation of the Ruhr.

It is true to say that the decision by Baldwin and his Chancellor of the Exchequer, Winston Churchill, to return to the Gold Standard in May, 1925, led directly and almost inevitably to the coal lock-out and the General Strike a year later. It imposed conditions of export trade upon the industry which, badly organized and inefficiently run as so much of it was, it was totally incapable of meeting without a reorganization which the mine-owners were incapable of carrying through and unwilling to contemplate. Their only remedy was to cut wages, and in this they were supported by the Conservative Government. Indeed, as Baldwin made clear in July, 1925, the Government considered wage reductions essential not only in mining but throughout all industry.

The General Strike when it came was not, as the Government and its supporters tried to present it, a deliberate challenge to the constitutional authority of the Government. Nor was it an attempt to secure political control by industrial action. It was in no sense inspired by any syndicalist or revolutionary philosophy. Indeed, from the tactical point of view that was its weakness. The trade unions found themselves involved in a struggle with the whole forces of central government for which they had never fully planned or prepared and which was bound to fail unless it were given a revolutionary character of which they did not and could not approve, since they were firmly democratic in their political philosophy.

They found themselves involved in it, if not quite by accident, at any rate without planned intention and without any full appreciation of the logical consequence of earlier stages in the new industrial policy decided upon. For in an important sense the General Strike represented the culmination—unforeseen but almost inevitable—of the policy of unified industrial action for economic ends which flowed from the lack of confidence in political action following Labour's defeat in 1924 and from the greater concentration of authority in the hands of the T.U.C. But at no time was the road plotted fully ahead.

The new authority acquired by the General Council of the T.U.C. at the Hull Conference required the unions to give the General Council full information on any disputes. Moreover, it gave the General Council the right to distribute this information to all other trade unions likely to be concerned, to call representatives of unions into consultation if a dispute could not be solved by the usual machinery of negotiation, and to offer advice to unions on a settlement. And where a settlement still proved impossible it was empowered to organize all moral and material support on behalf of the unions concerned.

This new policy had a striking—but misleading—success in July, 1925, when the threat of an embargo on all coal transport and of a sympathetic strike on any scale considered necessary by the General Council of the T.U.C. forced the Government to intervene to prevent a coal lock-out by offering a subsidy for nine months and by setting up a Coal Commission to investigate conditions in the industry.

It was, however, a temporary victory only. The time gained was used by the Government to set up a nationwide organization—the Organization for the Maintenance of Supplies—to meet any such challenge should it be repeated in the future. When failure to reach any agreement in the mining industry and the refusal of the mine-owners to negotiate further on a national scale led to a renewal of the strike threat in April, 1926, the Government was in a very different mood. The miners had, however, the sympathy of the whole trade-union movement in their insistence on "not a penny off the pay, not a minute on the day," and when on 30 April the lock-out notices issued by the mine-owners expired and the pits stopped, a special conference of trade-union executives at once approved of strike action to any extent that the General Council should consider necessary to give the miners full support.

Even at this stage, however, the General Council did not seriously plan for a national strike. It met the Prime Minister, expecting to be able to repeat, in part at any rate, the success of the previous year. But the Government had made up its mind. There was to be no compromise. When a compromise seemed just possible on the basis of a formula drawn up in the early hours of 2 May between the Prime Minister and a group of the Cabinet and the Industrial Committee of the General Council, the possibility was almost immediately wrecked from the Government side.

This formula stated that: "The Prime Minister has satisfied himself, as a result of the consultations he has had with representatives of the Trades Union Congress, that if negotiations are continued the representatives of the Trades Union Congress are confident that a settlement can be reached on the lines of the Coal Commission's report within a fortnight." This undertaking by the T.U.C. was dependent on a withdrawal of the lock-out notices and upon further discussion with the miners' leaders who had returned to the Districts for consultation with the men.

There were further meetings at Downing Street on the Sunday evening, 3 May, to clarify the formula further and decide how far it involved the T.U.C. in recommending the miners to accept the possibility of some reduction in wages as part of a general settlement. Late that night the miners' leaders returned to London and came to Downing Street, where they and the Industrial Committee of the T.U.C. met in a conference room upstairs.

Scarcely, however, had they begun discussions when a note arrived from the Prime Minister informing them that the printers of the *Daily Mail* had refused to print a leading article attacking the trade unions in terms which seemed to the printers quite unjustifiable. The Prime Minister's note stated that the Government could not continue negotiations unless the trade unions at once repudiated "overt acts" including "gross interference with the freedom of the Press" and furthermore immediately and unconditionally withdrew strike instructions.

When the trade-union leaders went downstairs to the Cabinet Room to discuss this new development there was no one to receive them. The Prime Minister and his colleagues had abruptly decided to break off all talks and had dispersed. The General Strike was on, not because the trade unions wanted to bring it to the issue, but because the Government did.

The strike was presented to the nation as a revolutionary attempt by the trade-union movement to "force Parliament and the community to bend to its will." It was nothing of the kind. It was a sympathetic strike on behalf of the miners. At its peak it involved 1,580,000 workers in addition to the miners themselves, but several of the unions who had undertaken to strike if called upon to do so were not called out by the T.U.C. There was no disorder.

In view of the Government's determination to treat it as an unconstitutional attempt to seize power it was from the start doomed to failure. No adequate preparations had been made by the General Council, which had always hoped to avoid a strike, and there was no clear agreement among the trade-union leaders themselves on the measures that should be taken.

It is not surprising, therefore, that the strike collapsed eight days later, on 12 May, in circumstances which threw the whole Labour and trade-union movement into confusion and left bitterness and anger among the miners who continued their own struggle unaided for a further six months until they, too, were forced back to work on the owners' terms.

The decision to call off the strike—although it could not in any event have been long delayed—came after conversations between the T.U.C. and Sir Herbert Samuel, who, although acting entirely unofficially, put forward proposals which he had previously shown to the Prime Minister. While making it clear that he had no power in any way to bind the Government, he held out the very strong hope that if the strike were called off the Government would reopen negotiations for a national settlement in the mining industry. Thereupon, despite the opposition of the miners, the T.U.C. General Council decided to end the strike. They were persuaded that by doing so they would bring nearer a real chance of reaching a settlement in the coal industry. And that was, of course, the main object for which the strike had been called.

This, however, was not the Government's view. The *British Gazette*, the Government organ which had been set up under Winston Churchill's direction when the strike began, jubilantly announced that the trade unions had surrendered unconditionally without obtaining any assurances that the lock-out notices in the coal industry would be withdrawn or that strikers would be reinstated. Nor did any fresh Government intervention in the coal industry to secure a settlement follow the end of the strike.

Workers who had at first gone back to work believing they had won a victory found that in the eyes of the employers and the public and according to the declarations of the Government they had suffered ignominious defeat. So far from the coal strike being settled, the fight went on, embittered by the miners' feeling of betrayal.

The whole episode was an unhappy and a tragic manifestation of failure on the part of the trade unions to consider in advance what strike action could secure and what it could not. The trade unions put themselves into a position where defeat was inevitable because they failed to appreciate that the weapon of a national strike cannot by its very nature be used in a modern industrial state except as a revolutionary weapon, since it must inevitably call up against it all the forces of the state. They had, however, no thought of using it as a revolutionary weapon, and even if they had they would have had no support for such a course among either the great mass of trade unionists or Labour Party members. It was, however, incapable of being used successfully for the limited purposes they had in mind. In a democratic context it was bound to be defeated.

In the history of the working-class movement the General Strike represents a decisive watershed. Before this the idea of a mobilization of the workers' power in a General Strike had coloured much industrial and some political thinking. In the minds of many it had always seemed a potential rival to political action. But few of those who played with the idea had any clear conception of what it involved or had followed its implications to their logical conclusion. It was a weapon which was only powerful as a threat and which was bound to break if the threat was put into action. Now that phase was over. And, having passed it, the trade unions moved increasingly towards a more constructive industrial policy, and the Labour movement as a whole, despite the clamour in the Communist wing, set itself to work for advance exclusively through constitutional political means.

Since 1926, as G. D. H. Cole has pointed out in his careful and detailed *History of the Labour Party from 1914,* no large-scale strike has occurred in Britain. In the seven years from the end of the First World War to the General Strike the days lost by strikers averaged nearly 28,000,000 a year. Shortly before the war, in 1912, they totalled over 38,000,000. In the seven years following the strike they averaged only 4,000,000 a year and in the next seven years well under 2,000,000.

This was not because the trade-union movement was broken by the strike. It emerged from it, it is true, with heavy financial losses and with some fall in membership. But its essential solidarity was unimpaired. The change was due to a change of attitude and to a new approach to industrial problems. From now on the trade-union movement increasingly used its power to establish a framework within which successful and co-operative negotiation with employers' organizations should be possible. Of this new attitude the Mond-Turner Conference in 1928 was one of the first concrete signs. At this conference a representative group of employers under Sir Alfred Mond (later Lord Melchett) met a group of members of the General Council of the T.U.C., of which Ben Turner was chairman and in which Ernest Bevin, Walter Citrine, J. H. Thomas and Arthur Pugh were particularly active. A Joint Committee was established and did important work in promoting consultative and advisory machinery representing both sides of industry.

In the first flush of victory, however, the Baldwin Government did not, despite Mr. Baldwin's own pronouncements in favour of peace in industry, concern itself with conciliation. The trade unions were weak. Now was the opportunity to strike at them. And through them at the Labour Party.

For many on the Conservative benches, "Back to Taff Vale" became an attractive slogan, and although it was ultimately found impracticable to put the clock back the whole twenty years and curtail trade-union powers to the level imposed by that notorious decision, the Trade Disputes and Trade Unions Act of 1927 went as far towards it as political vindictiveness, curbed only by legal caution, could make possible. It made any large-scale sympathetic strike illegal and imposed heavy penalities for all who declared, instigated, assisted or took part in them. It curtailed trade-union picketing and compelled Civil Service trade unions to withdraw from their affiliation to the Trades Union Congress.

Having gone as far as they dared, or were legally advised was possible, in the direction, of the Taff Vale decision the Conservatives then sought, in the same Act, to revive some part of the spirit of the Osborne Judgment.

328

In the 1913 Act which followed the campaign against the Osborne Judgment, any trade union had been empowered to establish political funds if a majority of its members voted in favour. Having done so, it could collect dues for political purposes—any member who did not wish to contribute to the political fund having the right to "contract out." Under the 1927 Act this position was reversed. Even although a majority of members had voted for the establishment of a political fund, no political dues could be collected under the new Act unless a member confirmed his vote by an individual written application to contribute to the fund.

Instead of the minority who did not want their union to engage in political activities and affiliate to the Labour Party having to "contract out," the majority who did had to "contract in." The hope behind this clause was that many who had voted for a political fund would not take the trouble to notify their readiness to pay contributions to it and that the affiliated membership and funds of the Labour Party would consequently decline.

The intention was to cripple the Labour Party. But in that the Act singularly failed. Nevertheless, the immediate effect was severe. In the two years following the Act the Labour Party's affiliated membership fell by 1,311,000 and its total income from affiliation fees was reduced by more than a quarter. The local Labour Parties also suffered heavy financial loss. In addition, the trade unions had to restrict their own financing of candidates.

Against this, the vindictive nature of the Act had the effect of closing the ranks of Labour. It convinced the trade unions once more, as the Taff Vale and Osborne judgments had done previously, that their only political hope lay in a strong Labour Party. And it convinced the Labour Party of the need to strengthen its organization and its finances by building up a strong individual membership in the constituencies.

This new drive for individual membership, forced upon it in the first place for financial reasons as a result of the 1927 Act, was to prove a potent factor in bringing new political strength to the Labour Party.

That Labour, despite its political and industrial reverses, was in no apathetic or defeatist mood was shown by the stir of organization throughout the country, by steady gains at local elections and by great public meetings at which not only the domestic issues were put before the public, but the great issues of international policy were made real and urgent. The vigorous life which was stirring in the Party was shown, too, in the keen debates at the annual conferences which each year became more and more established as the great democratic policy-forming parliaments of the movement and at which new men, among them Herbert Morrison and Hugh Dalton, were now beginning to come to the front.

But Henderson, considering the 1924 election, was not satisfied with organization alone—although organization was essential. He was convinced that a programme more direct and defined than *Labour and the New Social Order*, significant though that had been in setting down the principles by which the Labour movement was governed, was necessary. It was the more necessary in that the I.L.P. had determined to compensate for its loss of organizational importance by establishing for itself a new influence as the pace-maker of Labour policy. It was pressing for a policy of "Socialism in Our Time" which he, and even more MacDonald, felt to be politically impracticable and which in some of its industrial aspects ran sharply counter to the views of the majority of the trade unions and to the new trend of industrial policy manifested in the Mond-Turner developments.

But to put the objections to the I.L.P. proposals was not enough. The Labour Party must itself have a definite programme to put before the country when the General Election came in 1929. Of that he was certain. With such a programme candidates would be in a stronger position than in 1924 to withstand misrepresentation and hysteria, and the electors would not be so easily persuaded to vote Conservative by misleading propaganda. MacDonald, who disliked programmes because they might tie his own hands, was not so easily convinced. But he, too, was worried by the challenge of the I.L.P. and eventually he agreed. So did the annual conference of 1927. The outcome was *Labour and the Nation*.

Labour and the Nation was not, in the form in which it was finally approved after being drafted mainly by R. H. Tawney, a concrete parliamentary programme. It did not provide a clear statement of priorities in the way that *Let Us Face the Future*, the programme on which Labour fought and won the 1945 election, did.

But it was an important and reasonably concrete statement of general policy and it gave the nation a clear view of the kind of objectives, political and economic, Labour had in view.

This statement of aims Labour put before the electorate on 10 May, 1929, when, immediately after a vote-catching Budget, Stanley Baldwin went to the country with the slogan "Safety First." The electorate found this an uninspiring appeal. It preferred the promise and adventure of the Labour declaration.

For the first time in its history Labour was returned as the largest party in the State with 288 seats, to the Conservatives' 261 and the Liberals' 57.

CHAPTER XVIII

GOVERNMENT—AND BETRAYAL

LABOUR was still not a majority party. It was still without the parliamentary power to carry through a Socialist programme.

But its parliamentary position was much stronger than in 1924. It was more experienced and had—or so it seemed—a clearer conception of what it was after. It was shortly to have for the first time in its history a national daily newspaper with a great circulation to help in putting its case before the nation. Later that year, negotiations already proceeding between the T.U.C. and Odhams Press were to put all the resources of a great publishing house behind the *Daily Herald* which had passed out of Lansbury's control into that of the T.U.C. and the Labour Party in 1922. As a result the *Herald* was at once to achieve a circulation of over a million a day and Labour was at last to have a voice in daily journalism which could compete with that of its rivals.

Moreover, it was a more broadly based party than ever before, with a greater popular vote behind it and a much more equal balance between divisional Labour Party and trade-union representation. Indeed, for the first time, the number of M.P.s sponsored by local Labour Parties was greater than those sponsored by trade unions—128 compared with 124 trade-union M.P.s and with only 25 representatives of the divisional Labour Parties in the previous Parliament.

On all counts Labour could claim now to be a truly national party. And whereas in 1924 the opportunity of office had surprised everyone, this time it had been planned for and was accepted without any misgivings.

Yet instead of triumph it was to end in defeat of the most bitter kind. Why?

In part the answer to that lies in the personalities of two men—

MacDonald and Snowden—in part in a world situation so menacing that no government could easily have come through it unscathed, and in part in a failure, responsibility for which must rest to some extent on the shoulders of all the senior members of the Government, and upon the Labour Party Executive as a whole, to understand the economic circumstances of the time and to prepare policy in the light of them.

In *Labour and the Nation* the Party had reaffirmed its socialism in more precise terms than formerly. But it had not given anything like sufficient thought to the practical application of socialism and particularly to the kind of economic and industrial action which was necessary to make even a small amount of socialism possible.

Although it had long declared that depressions and crises were inherent in capitalism, it had reached no firm conclusions as to the correct policy for a Socialist administration to follow in a period of crisis. The Socialist principles it enunciated were general. They were not backed by a concrete programme of Socialist reconstruction geared to the actual problems of the time.

Finally, although the possibility, indeed the probability, that Labour might be returned as the largest single party, but without an actual majority, had been in the minds of most of the leaders of Labour for some time, they had not come to any definite conclusion as to how far, in such circumstances, they should try to carry through a distinctive Socialist programme.

Their ill-fortune was that they inherited problems resulting from a world-wide collapse of capitalist economy. Their mistake was that although the possibility of such a crisis had long been foreseen by Socialist economists, they had no plans to deal with it. They sought instead to meet the crisis on conventional economic lines and, as was inevitable, these proved inadequate.

Yet the new Government opened its career not too badly. There had been the same initial difficulty as before over Cabinet making, and the same attempt by MacDonald to push Henderson into a position of no particular importance—even the same desire on his part to make J. H. Thomas Foreign Secretary. But, this time, Henderson knew what he wanted and was determined to have it. He wanted the Foreign Office. And he got it.

Moreover, MacDonald, having broken with the I.L.P., as had

also Snowden and, among the younger leaders, Attlee, because of its disruptive tactics, was determined that it should have no chance of seriously influencing policy. He made up his mind, therefore, to leave out Wheatley who had been the outstanding success of the first Labour Government on the domestic side. On this point he overbore Henderson, Thomas and Snowden, whom he consulted, but he agreed to include George Lansbury as a sop to the Left—although only as First Commissioner of Works, in which post he anticipated he would be able to do nothing of importance.

The new Government, although its core in MacDonald, Henderson, Snowden, J. H. Thomas and J. R. Clynes remained the same, differed in important respects from that of 1924.

Arthur Greenwood as Minister of Health, Margaret Bondfield as Minister of Labour (and the first woman Cabinet Minister), William Graham as President of the Board of Trade, A. V. Alexander as First Lord of the Admiralty, George Lansbury as First Commissioner of Works, Lord Sankey (who had become a Socialist as a result of his experiences of a Conservative Government's attitude to the coal industry) as Lord Chancellor, and Wedgwood Benn as Secretary of State for India, were all new to the Cabinet.

Outside the Cabinet there were new men in Herbert Morrison as Minister of Transport, Sir Oswald Mosley (who, after being first a Conservative and then an Independent, had joined the Labour Party and become prominent as a spokesman of the Left) as Chancellor of the Duchy of Lancaster, H. B. Lees-Smith as Postmaster-General, Sir William Jowitt as Attorney-General, F. O. Roberts as Minister of Pensions, F. W. Pethick-Lawrence as Financial Secretary to the Treasury, Hugh Dalton as Under-Secretary for Foreign Affairs, and Tom Johnston as Under-Secretary for Scotland. Susan Lawrence was Parliamentary Secretary to the Ministry of Health.

It was in many ways a brilliant team. But again, as in the previous MacDonald administration, the trade-union side of the movement was notably under-represented, although on this occasion MacDonald had not felt it necessary to go outside the Party altogether to fill any posts.

Nor were the expectations, that this was a better team than formerly, falsified by the first results as the Government got down

334

to work. In the international field, Henderson, much to MacDonald's private chagrin, proved himself not merely an able but a great Foreign Secretary. And at the Board of Trade William Graham set to work with great energy and skill to try to secure a tariff truce that would help to free the channels of world trade.

At home, although there was little socialism in the Labour Government's programme, it proved a practical and a progressive one. The Widows and Old Age Pensions Act was amended and improved, subsidies for housing which had been threatened by the Baldwin Government were maintained, and a new and improved Unemployment Insurance Act carried. As First Commissioner of Works, George Lansbury won wide popularity for himself and the Government by demonstrating what a man of energy and a cheerful love of his fellows could do in the most unexpected ways by making parks the real possession of the people.

At the Ministry of Health, Arthur Greenwood launched a bill to deal with slum clearance and, at the Ministry of Transport, Herbert Morrison produced a far-ranging Road Traffic Bill to make possible the reorganization of the road passenger transport industry on lines long urged by the trade unions. An Education Bill to raise the school-leaving age to fifteen and make provision for mainten-ance allowances was introduced and, although as a result of a con-flict over the position of Catholic and Church schools it had to be withdrawn, the Government undertook to reintroduce it in the next session. A Coal Bill which, while it did not propose nationaliza-tion, went some way to reorganize the industry was introduced. Preparations were made to amend the hated 1927 Trade Disputes and Trade Unions Act.

If the Government was far from trying to bring in socialism in our time, and was still very conscious—perhaps excessively so —of its minority position, it seemed nevertheless likely to have not unimportant achievements to its credit.

In its report to the Annual Conference in September, 1929, the Executive Committee claimed that "The Labour Government has seized the imagination of the people. Despite our parliamentary limitations, events are being shaped with a vigour and a spirit that are refreshing after the alternative inertia and reaction of the past four years." Nor was this claim altogether unjustified. Particularly in the field of foreign affairs it was possible to report a great advance. Here the Executive could truthfully report that as a result of Labour's new approach, "the outlook for a real and constructive World Peace was never more hopeful than at the present time." And although there was serious unrest in India, the calling of a Round Table Conference for the autumn of 1930 seemed to provide at least a possibility of a solution of that dangerous and intractable problem.

But at the election the Government had declared that it would place the attack on the industrial disease of unemployment in the forefront of its activity and the attack was not going well. J. H. Thomas, George Lansbury and Oswald Mosley had been given general charge of unemployment policy and it was only too clear that they were capable neither of finding an effective remedy nor of agreeing among themselves.

So far from unemployment being reduced it was rising rapidly. In June, 1929, when the Labour Government took office, there were 1,163,000 unemployed—9·6 per cent of the insured population. A year later the figure was 1,912,000—15·4 per cent. And by December, 1930, it had risen to 2,500,000—practically 20 per cent. To meet the problem considerable schemes of public works at home and in the Colonies, involving a total expenditure altogether of £120,000,000, were prepared and set going. In normal times these schemes would have represented a notable offensive against unemployment—the greatest indeed ever made by any British Government. But, in the conditions of world depression that then existed, they were incapable of making any serious impact upon the problem.

Many recognized this, among them Oswald Mosley. After quarrelling with J. H. Thomas he put forward ambitious plans of his own for the expansion of purchasing power in the home market and the "insulation" of British economy by the control of imports, bulk purchasing and public control of banking. They were rejected and, instead of staying to fight them within the Party, Mosley, already impatient of democratic processes, went off to embark on the tragic, egotistical and dictatorial journey that was to lead him to fascism.

That a minority Labour Government subject to the constant need to compromise with its political opponents should prove incapable of insulating Britain from the effects of a world-wide crisis that shook every nation in the world, bringing bankruptcy, disaster and unemployment to the most powerful industrial nation of all, America, and an economic collapse in Germany which was directly responsible for bringing Hitler to power—this cannot by any honest judgment be accounted a failure in administration. The causes of the world crisis did not lie in socialism, but in an economic philosophy and method which Socialists had always attacked. Moreover, Britain was in a particularly vulnerable position because of the permanent alteration in her economic status resulting from the First World War, the extent to which her international bankers had borrowed at short term abroad and re-lent at long term to finance international projects, many of which were fundamentally unsound, and the neglect of her basic industries because of the greater profit that could be secured by the financing of international and domestic speculative enterprises.

But, this being said, it remains the case that the MacDonald administration failed lamentably in any true economic understanding of the problem. It stuck obstinately to a course which was bound to end in political and economic disaster and lead to a betrayal of all the principles of social and economic equity for which the Labour movement had struggled throughout its lifetime.

It did so partly because MacDonald himself had no real knowledge or understanding of economic problems and no faith in the Socialist economic principles which he professed. To an incredible degree he saw an international crisis, which was bringing ruin to a large part of the world, solely in terms of his own personal position and, governed increasingly by the vanity which had always been so dangerous a part of his character, began at an early stage to contemplate ways in which the crisis could be used to allow him to become a truly "national leader."

That was one factor. The other was the character and economic outlook of Philip Snowden.

Snowden had an integrity which even his critics must admire. He was not moved in the course he took by small vanities or personal ambitions, although an intellectual contempt for most of his colleagues—including, understandably, MacDonald himself—and the decisions reached at what he regarded as trade-union dominated and emotionally unstable national conferences, played a large part in his attitude. But his political integrity and economic rectitude were both anchored to two doctrines which were entirely unsuited to the conditions of the time. One was a fanatical belief in the sanctity of free trade—the economic philosophy to which he had given his devotion in his youth, the other was a scarcely less fanatical belief in the Gold Standard. He was a Socialist in his ethical and philosophical outlook, but in his economic thinking he was a nineteenth-century Liberal—a direct descendant of Gladstone whose portrait frowned down upon him with grim approval from a wall of the Chancellor's study in 11 Downing Street.

Within the context of that economic philosophy there was no way in which Britain could meet the economic storm without the most substantial cuts in the standards of life of her people and particularly of the unemployed. Nor, although Snowden was not to appreciate it until too late, could the twin pillars of his financial orthodoxy be kept standing even with these sacrifices. Both were to fall, but not until, in the effort to preserve them, he had done his best to destroy the Labour Party he had helped to create.

If Snowden had been willing to suspend the Gold Standard at an early stage of the crisis and thus to enable British export prices to find their true level in world markets; if he had been prepared to ban exports of capital and to accept the idea of a controlled economy in which free trade would be replaced by direct agreements with suppliers and by trade pacts with the Dominions; if he had been capable of a complete reorientation of his economic thinking, then it is possible that Britain might have been able to cushion herself against some of the worst consequences of the international crisis. But he was not. The inflexibility of character which in ethical matters was a part of his moral strength in this betrayed him.

Nor at a time when mounting unemployment made inevitable an enormous increase in the total of unemployment benefits if the unemployed were not to be driven down to intolerable levels of poverty was he prepared to abandon any of the orthodoxies of Gladstonian finance. He was incapable of conceiving that Budgets might be left unbalanced in a depression as a deliberate act of policy and the deficit wiped out by a surplus in more prosperous years. He could not conceive that a strict annual accountancy was altogether inappropriate to the conditions of the time. Nor would he accept the suggestion that, even within a balanced Budget, money could be made available for unemployment payments and the maintenance of essential social services by suspending for the time being and until the crisis was past the annual Sinking Fund payments for the redemption of the National Debt.

He regarded these payments as an essential act of financial integrity—and financial integrity in the narrow orthodox sense in which he conceived it had come to possess for him the force of a moral compulsion to which it was perfectly proper that human well-being should, if necessary, be sacrificed. He was determined to balance his Budget without increased taxation or any reduction in Sinking Fund payments. There was, therefore, no alternative but to enforce large cuts in the social services and the unemployment benefits. To this course he set himself.

The setting up of a committee under the chairmanship of Sir George May, the retiring secretary of the Prudential Assurance Company, to make proposals for "effecting practical and legitimate reductions in the national expenditure," was the first step in that campaign.

The committee's investigation was, as Snowden himself later admitted, deliberately designed to frighten the country and force the hands of his colleagues.

In the first it succeeded, although the two Labour members of the committee, Arthur Pugh and Charles Latham, refused to accept the majority view. But, by adding the deficit on the Unemployment Insurance Fund to the deficit in the Budget, by making the blackest prognostications as to the future and by accepting the Snowden thesis that the Sinking Fund payments could not be touched, the majority report presented a picture of financial disaster which shocked the country. It did more. It so seriously damaged British financial credit abroad that it started a run on British banks which made a large-scale financial crisis inevitable—and with it the abandonment of the Gold Standard Snowden was fighting to preserve.

But neither Snowden nor Montagu Norman, the Governor of the Bank of England, and his colleagues in the City who throughout this period exercised great influence on Snowden, were prepared to contemplate that yet. Instead, the Bank of England hurriedly

339

sought loans from the New York Federal Reserve Bank and the Bank of France in order to find funds to meet the drain. Credits oɟ £50,000,000 were arranged. They were quite inadequate and were quickly gone.

Thereupon the Bank of England, with Snowden's approval, set about trying to negotiate a further £80,000,000 loan. It was met by the response—which it certainly did not dislike and may well have incited—that a further advance could not be made unless Britain balanced her Budget on the lines suggested by the May Report.

The stage was set for the climax. It came when the Cabinet, after accepting one by one the demands for economies made to Snowden by the bankers and to MacDonald by the Conservative and Liberal leaders with whom he was in constant touch, was brought to the very edge of acceptance of the final demand that there should be a reduction in Unemployment Benefit by ten per cent and that a Means Test for applicants should be instituted.

The majority of the members of the Cabinet had received their interpretation of the cause of the crisis and the measures necessary to meet it only from the lips of MacDonald and Snowden. They had been accustomed to regard Snowden as the unquestionable financial authority of the Party. They made no serious attempt to withstand his proposals until the very last. Only at a joint meeting of the National Executive and the T.U.C., which MacDonald and Snowden had been persuaded, with some difficulty, to attend and at which they had said little, had there been strong criticism. This had come mainly from Bevin and others on the trade-union side, who had made it clear that they could not endorse any cut in Unemployment Benefit and considered that the possibility of a revenue tariff should be explored.

But the Cabinet itself played no very creditable part in developments. Its members allowed themselves to be pushed reluctantly along the road MacDonald and Snowden and their new allies in the City and in the Conservative Party had laid down. Although they objected, they at no time seriously challenged Snowden with constructive alternatives.

Now, however, faced with the proposal for a cut in the Unemployment Benefit, they did object. They were not—or many of them were not—prepared to accept the final abandonment of Labour policy involved. Out of a Cabinet of twenty-one, ten members refused to agree that these were necessary or should be enforced by a Labour Government.

The split was too large to bridge. The Government could not continue. MacDonald, therefore, asked for the resignations of all the Cabinet. With these in his hands, he left to seek an audience with the King. In half an hour he returned to inform his colleagues that the King had agreed to hold a conference with himself, Baldwin and Sir Herbert Samuel at ten o'clock the following morning.

At twelve o'clock, two hours after this conference, the Labour Ministers reassembled at Downing Street. They all, including even Snowden, expected to be told that Baldwin had been invited to form a government, perhaps with Liberal aid.

Instead, MacDonald informed them that he himself had agreed to remain as Prime Minister of a National Government of which Baldwin and Samuel would both be members. The meeting lasted a few minutes only. There was no expression of regret from MacDonald; no indication of how long such an eventuality had been in his mind or of how many secret conversations had gone to prepare the way for it. He was clearly glad to be done with his former comrades and delighted to be a "national leader" at last. They for their part were too shocked and surprised to make any comment. Silently they dispersed as Snowden, Thomas and Lord Sankey were asked to stay behind. These three were invited to join the new Government. All accepted. Of them all Lord Sankey was the only one who had the courage to attend a Parliamentary Labour Party meeting and explain his decision—a decision based in his case on his desire to complete if he could the work on an Indian Settlement on which he was engaged.

So ended the second Labour Government.

On 7 October the "National" Government which succeeded it, after carrying through a Budget which imposed the economy cuts the Labour Ministers had rejected—and after suspending on 21 September the Gold Standard which Snowden and the City of London had declared must be kept inviolate—dissolved Parliament and went to the country. It appealed for a "doctor's mandate."

To ensure that this appeal was successful no vilification or misrepresentation of the Labour Party was spared either by MacDonald or Snowden or their new colleagues. MacDonald waved worthless mark notes in the air, declaring that the pound would have a similar fate if Labour were allowed to rule; Snowden described the mild—too mild—Labour programme as bolshevism run mad; Runciman, the Liberal leader, accused the Labour Party of taking Post Office deposits—"the savings of the poor"—to finance extravagant payments to the unemployed. Against such canards, and the hysteria which accompanied them, Labour fought in vain.

When the results were announced the Labour Party in Parliament had been reduced from 289 to only forty-six. It was back in parliamentary strength to where it was in 1910. All its Front Bench leaders, with the exception of George Lansbury, Attlee and Stafford Cripps (who had become Solicitor-General in 1930), were defeated.

To the jubilant Tories with 471 seats, and to their captives MacDonald, Thomas and Snowden, it seemed as though the Labour Party had been irretrievably destroyed and turned overnight into a mere rump of a party without possibility of recovery.

But, once again, those who convinced themselves that at last the forward march of Labour was ended were wrong. Once again, as so often before, it was to reform and fight again. And this time under new leaders, and with a purpose not broken but tempered by disaster, it was to establish itself more firmly than ever before.

The long march was halted, but it could not be stayed. For it had behind it the devotion of men and women whose fidelity no disaster or betrayal could shake and it represented a purpose whose urgency the whole configuration of national and international affairs was increasingly to make more clear.

PART FIVE

THE ROAD TO POWER

CHAPTER XIX

FRUSTRATION AND TRAGEDY
IN THE NINETEEN-THIRTIES

IT WOULD have been natural if, after the defeat of 1931, the Labour movement, with its parliamentary forces reduced again to the mere handful of twenty years earlier, had turned as in previous defeats to industrial action. It would even have been natural if there had been a strong swing to Marxism, for all the warnings of the Communists as to the kind of sabotage a democratic Labour Party would meet from the forces in control of finance and industry seemed to have been justified. Moreover, the Marxist prophecy that capitalism would collapse from its own inner contradiction seemed during this period of crisis as though it might be justified by events.

Yet Labour neither abandoned its faith in political action nor turned Marxist. It remained a democratic political party striving to fulfil its purpose by constitutional means: the purpose to which it had held so firmly through so long a period of struggle. Naturally it swung leftward and naturally also there was in the reaction against the events of 1931 a tendency to overestimate the nature of the opposition Labour would be likely to meet in putting Socialist principles into action. Neither then nor at any other time did the Labour Party envisage any other than constitutional action to carry through its Socialist programme. But it seemed possible to many at that period that it might have to prepare itself to meet and defeat political sabotage and even counter-revolutionary action when it came to power.

For the time being, however, power seemed a long way away. Yet, in truth, the most remarkable feature of that period was the steadiness of Labour organization and the continuing hold of the Labour Party on a very large section of the electorate.

In 1918 the split between the Liberal leaders and the defection of Lloyd George had wrecked the Liberal Party and helped to bring to an end its long career as one of the historic parties of the State.

The defection of MacDonald, Snowden and Thomas, despite their national prestige, their popularity, and their place in the history of the Labour Party, had no such effect upon it. The roots of its strength went down too deep for any personal challenge to shake it.

The steadfastness of the rank and file was the more remarkable in that the bitter campaign against their former party by MacDonald and Snowden coincided with the decision of the I.L.P., as a result of the long dispute in policy, to fight the election as a separate party. Labour had not only lost its two best-known leaders. The close association of the Socialist society which had done most to create it and which had been for many years the chief instrument of its propaganda was also, for very different reasons, now ended. Moreover, it was confronted with a new bid for left-wing support by Mosley's New Party. It is true this bid did not in the event come to much. Mosley had been talking largely of putting 400 candidates into the field. All he was, in fact, able to muster was twenty-nine and all of them were defeated. The Communists also put forward twenty-six candidates and all of these, too, were beaten.

There was hardly a circumstance disadvantageous to Labour which did not exist at the 1931 election. Yet, although it suffered so heavy a parliamentary defeat, its popular vote was 6,362,561—two million less than in 1929, it is true, but a remarkable number in view of the combination of "national" parties against which it fought and the scale and character of the propaganda launched against it. Here indeed, coolly regarded, was a remarkable sign of the inherent strength of the movement. In the face of catastrophe the ranks had not broken. They held firm in their fidelity to the great purpose which sustained them and to the comradeship of which they felt themselves to be a part.

This staunchness was a circumstance to sustain courage and give foundation for future hope. But it did not alter the fact that Labour was condemned to political frustration at a time when the attack on the standard of living of the workers, and particularly the unemployed, was severe, and when, as the cynical speech at the League of Nations of the new Foreign Secretary, Sir John Simon, on the Japanese attack on Manchuria soon showed, those in control of international policy were to play a major part in wrecking the bright hopes of international peace that Arthur Henderson had kindled.

Henderson and all the other nationally known leaders, with the single exception of Lansbury, who, great idealistic leader that he was, was not at his best in the day-to-day politics of parliamentary life, were out of the House. And, however hard it worked and however ably it fought, the little band of Labour M.P.s could not hope to influence the course of policy determined by the predominantly Conservative administration over which MacDonald nominally presided, but of which he was, in fact, the helpless captive.

Yet it closed its ranks and fought as best it could. Henderson had been elected leader when MacDonald went—too late by seven years—but Henderson was not in the House and, in any event, was President of the Disarmament Conference at Geneva, where world opinion gave his great qualities the due the British electorate withheld. Although he was re-elected to the parliamentary leadership as a mark of honour and respect, the task of actual leadership, therefore, fell upon George Lansbury, with Clement Attlee as deputy leader. The choice of Attlee seemed at the time fortuitous and without real significance. To many people it still continued to seem so when he later succeeded Lansbury as leader. But it was to prove of immense importance. He, more than any man, had the qualities of integrity, calm judgment and parliamentary skill which, in this crisis in its history, Labour needed to guide it and which could convert defeat into ultimate and magnificent victory. Once again, almost without knowing it, Labour had thrown up the kind of leaders its purpose required.

345

But for the time being the struggle was hard and unrewarding. It was to become even more formidable as time passed, and the small Labour forces lacked the strength to alter, however much they might challenge, a national policy which they knew was leading inevitably to international catastrophe.

Although the new National Government, with its massive and acquiescent majority, could push any measure it wished through Parliament, the reductions in unemployment benefits, the imposition of the Means Test, the cuts in pay in the public services and the economy programme brought a rising temper in the country which flared up in the naval mutiny at Invergordon in September, 1931, and in mass demonstrations and a national hunger march the following year. The crisis of private capitalism was being solved according to the traditional pattern at the cost of bitter sacrifices by the workers.

In such circumstances the Communist Party, primary organizer of the National Unemployed Workers' Movement, naturally sought to present itself to workers as the only truly left-wing movement capable of fighting a battle which it claimed reformist Labour was allowing to go by default. And it has to be admitted that Labour, although it had shed MacDonaldism and moved to a more positive socialism than ever before, was for the moment too rent by internal argument and too little decided on its strategy to provide an effective and dramatic leadership for the forces of discontent in the country. It had to adapt itself to new problems and adaptation was not always easy. In any event, there was for the time being little that could be done in face of the solidly entrenched forces of a conservatism which could perceive no cure for a crisis of under-consumption but a further reduction in the standard of living of the poorest members of the community.

One thing, however, was clear. This was that the enunciation of principles, even of principles as well thought out and as genuine as those expressed in *Labour and the Nation*, was insufficient. Labour, if it was to be effective, must consider much more carefully, not simply the Socialist objectives it wished to attain, but the means by which it could attain them. It must have not only a general policy, but a detailed programme—only thus could it avoid the danger of a repetition of the experiences of 1929, when the Labour Government had been dangerously unprepared to deal with the economic situation which confronted the nation.

In December, 1931, therefore, the Executive appointed a Policy Committee to develop, in the words of the Annual Report, "its general programme of national economic and social planning in order that the various parts may be seen in proper perspective and so that the essential unity of the programme may be emphasized."

It was the first decisive and essential step forward from a Socialist philosophy to a Socialist programme which could make that philosophy truly effective. The lesson of defeat had been quickly learnt.

The first policy reports were on "Currency, Banking, and Finance," "The Land and the National Planning of Agriculture," "The National Planning of Transport," and "The Reorganization of the Electricity Supply Industry." They were followed between 1932 and 1939 by others dealing in detail with every aspect of national policy to a degree never before attempted by a political party.

In the detailed research which preceded these reports, and in their actual drafting, leaders of every branch of the movement participated. Lansbury, Attlee, Morrison, Greenwood, Dalton, Clynes, Pethick-Lawrence, Addison, Citrine, Laski, R. H. Tawney, Barbara Ayrton-Gould, Susan Lawrence, James Walker, George Lathan, these and others set themselves to a task whose purpose was to give Labour a clearer conception than it had ever had before of the difficulties it must face and the means it must take to overcome them and, at the same time, to present to the nation a programme which would provide the electorate with all the material needed to judge the constructive purposes which Labour was setting out to achieve.

In the existing social order there was much to denounce, much to arouse passion and indignation; but denunciation and indignation were not sufficient. Labour must prepare itself for the hard constructive tasks by which alone a democratic social revolution could be made possible. And it must set the facts before the people.

This then was the task to which Labour now turned. It was one that was clearly essential. But it by no means resolved all the divisions which had inevitably followed the disillusionment of

MacDonaldism. It was not always easy for a movement which had been built on idealism and agitation and which now faced inevitable political frustration to satisfy itself with the transition, imperative though it was, to the business of hard, practical, undramatic planning.

Moreover, because of its very concentration on what was likely to be practically possible the programme seemed to many in the I.L.P. and elsewhere to be far too mild. As on other occasions in the past, the cry went up that socialism was being sacrificed to "reform." It was not so, as in the end was abundantly to be proved, but the I.L.P. and its allies, with their eyes turned backward to the days of agitation instead of forward to the days of power, could not be convinced. And in July, 1932, the increasingly uncomfortable alliance between the I.L.P. and the Labour Party was brought to an end by an I.L.P. conference decision to disaffiliate. The long association which had accomplished so much and produced so great a change in the political atmosphere of the nation was ended. It was a sorry conclusion to so magnificent and fruitful a partnership, but perhaps it was inevitable. The Labour Party was adapting itself to the practical requirements imposed upon a party which is thinking in terms of constructive government. The I.L.P. was not ready to do so.

Indeed, there was now taking place within the Party a struggle no less profound and significant for the future than that which there had been in the early beginnings of the movement between those who saw the necessity of a practical and non-doctrinaire approach capable of attracting mass support and those who would suffer no compromise with Socialist ideals as they saw them.

To the majority of the national executive and to the majority of the delegates at repeated conferences it was clear that Labour must prepare itself for government by developing a programme capable of practical attainment and of appealing to a majority of the electorate—not all of whom were likely to be convinced and ardent Socialists—as being reasonable, workable and equitable. It must be a programme, moreover, which, while Socialist in content and true to the continuing ideals which had for so long inspired and sustained the Labour movement, would take into account all the circumstances of British economy and recognize the contribution that could be made to national betterment by men and women of many different aptitudes and social backgrounds. And it must recognize also that a democratic Socialist programme must be based on popular consent and must keep the economy of the country working efficiently even while it changed it.

Such an approach, essentially practical and undoctrinaire in character, was bound to be attacked as insufficiently Socialistic by those who were unprepared to accept the limitations always imposed upon the ideal by the possible or who were impatient of the apparent slowness of the democratic method.

The break away of the I.L.P. was one manifestation of that conflict. Another was the career of the Socialist League, which, after beginning its life under the name of the Society for Socialist Inquiry and Propaganda, as a ginger group within the Labour Party, developed later into a would-be rival group putting forward its own programme. More constructive and more ready to accept both the limitations of the democratic system and the obligations of Labour Party membership was the New Fabian Research Bureau, which was founded about the same time in 1932 with Mr. and Mrs. G. D. H. Cole as its leading spirits—the Webbs of the new enterprise. Because it was ready to work within the framework of the Labour Party's constitution this group did work of immense value in clarifying Labour political and economic thinking and was able eventually to join with, and revivify, the Fabian Society and restore it from the lethargy into which it had fallen to something of its old liveliness and influence.

Even while the struggle—to some extent the unreal struggle, because there was no real conflict on ultimate aims—continued between Left and Right in the debates on national policy, the value of a practical programme presented as an administrative possibility was being shown in the field of local government and particularly in London.

Here, under the brilliant leadership of Herbert Morrison and the team of able people he had gathered round him, Labour in 1934 won a clear majority on the L.C.C. and took over the administration of the greatest city in the Empire. Moreover, having achieved power, it demonstrated so brilliantly Labour's ability to govern and to bring a new humanity into public affairs that it was returned again and again.

349

If victory in the L.C.C. election was the most spectacular evidence of Labour advance, it was far from being the only one. In the London Metropolitan Borough Elections Labour had a net gain of 472 and won a clear majority on fifteen of the Metropolitan Councils—a recognition of the administrative ability and warm human sympathy Labour Councils had already brought to local government in London and the affection and admiration with which men like George Lansbury had won in their fight to bring new hope to the East End of London. And in the country generally Labour gained control of twenty-one County Boroughs and eighteen non-County Boroughs and won 117 seats in the provincial County Council Elections.

In Parliament Labour's power might be small, but its hold in the country was manifestly increasing and it was demonstrating what was at this stage most essential for progress, that within its ranks idealism and administrative capacity went in partnership.

Yet the road to power was not easy. If the readjustments in political thinking required by the necessity to develop a practical domestic programme were considerable, those required in the field of international affairs were even greater as the forces of aggression in Japan, in Italy and in Germany gained strength.

The Labour Party had from the first pledged itself to the support of the League of Nations—indeed, the concept of a League of Nations had been part of Socialist international thinking long before the League came into existence. Whatever their other failures, both Labour Governments had brought to bear the whole influence of Britain to increase the authority of the League. Arthur Henderson, as President of the Disarmament Conference, which position he continued to hold after he ceased to be Foreign Secretary, had won the admiration of all who wanted peace throughout the world by his indomitable struggle to give practical reality to ideals which inspired the League.

But now Hitler ruled in Germany. And in Italy Mussolini dreamed of imperial conquest. Aggression was stirring in Europe and was soon to be on the march. The practical issue of how far those who believed in a League of Nations were prepared to go in giving it the power to prevent aggression could not any longer be avoided. It was an issue on which the Labour Party had not defined its attitude—indeed, had almost deliberately refrained from defining its attitude because of the internal conflicts that an attempt at definition might produce.

The pacifist tradition was still strong in the Party. So was the conviction, product of the disillusionment of 1914–18, that all wars even when they were ostensibly fought to serve democratic purposes were merely a part of the struggle between rival imperialisms. Moreover, there was no confidence among Socialists that if it gave support for armaments to make possible a strong League of Nations policy those armaments would, in fact, be used for that purpose by a government which Labour distrusted completely, and whose whole international policy was based increasingly on the appeasement of aggressors.

Yet the decision as to Labour's attitude towards the League as a defensive power against aggression could not be avoided. It was made inevitable when on 3 October, 1935, Italian troops entered Abyssinia.

That year the Labour Party Conference was meeting in Brighton. It met only a few days after the attack on Abyssinia had begun.

Arthur Henderson, who more than any man had in these latter years voiced on an international platform the practical international ideals of Labour, was ill. He came to Brighton hoping to be well enough to take part in the debates, but before the conference opened he had a relapse and had to be taken from his Brighton hotel to a London nursing home.

There he lay dying as the conference opened and as the news of the first moves in that European aggression he had fought so hard to avert grew hourly more menacing. He had devoted his life to two things—the Labour Party and the cause of peace. Like Hardie, to whom in his integrity, his lack of self-interest and in the great contribution he had made to the Labour Party he was akin, he was to die when the twin causes he had served with so great a fidelity were in eclipse. But, like Hardie's, his work and his name were to live on, honoured for ever by those who reap the reward of their labours.

At the conference George Lansbury, who also had been ill but had now returned to the leadership, rose to oppose the resolution drafted by the Executive and moved by Hugh Dalton. This resolution called upon the Government "in co-operation with other nations represented at the Council and Assembly of the League to use all the necessary measures provided by the Covenant to prevent Italy's unjust and rapacious attack upon the territory of a fellow-member of the League."

Stafford Cripps had already opposed the resolution, but from a different standpoint from that of Lansbury. To Cripps the League of Nations had become "nothing but the tool of the satiated imperialist powers" from which, therefore, power should be withheld. For Lansbury the issue was one of Christian pacifism. He could not support any policy which looked to the employment of force to attain its ends. He spoke with a sincerity that stirred the delegates —the more so that he had made it clear that if the Executive's resolution were carried he recognized that he must resign from the the leadership of the parliamentary party.

But although they were moved emotionally, neither Lansbury's pacifism nor Cripps's "anti-imperialism" altered the view of the vast majority of the delegates. By 2,168,000 votes to 102,000 they carried the resolution calling for League action against Italy.

But the long debate and Lansbury's resignation created in the minds of the public an impression of confusion and lack of decision which the actual vote did little to counter. And when on 25 October Parliament was dissolved and Mr. Baldwin went to the country to seek, as he said, a mandate for British support for collective security, it suffered from that fact. In the popular judgment Labour was not willing to face up to the realities of the international situation and Mr. Baldwin was. As a result of that tragic misjudgment the "National" Government was returned with 420 members, a massive majority which gave it an unshakable dominance over British policy until that policy—one completely opposite to that on which the election was won—brought a new world war. Labour had 154 M.P.s, an increase of ninety-six. But the total was still not much more than half that of 1929—and was too little to give it any effective power to influence national policy.

Now, however, many of the old leaders were back, among them Morrison, Dalton, Alexander and Shinwell, to add to the debating strength of Attlee, Greenwood and Aneurin Bevan.

There had been at one time a pretty general expectation that

ERNEST BEVIN
General Secretary of the Amal-
gamated Transport and General
Workers' Union 1922–40, Minis-
ter of Labour 1940, Foreign
Minister 1945.

HERBERT MORRISON
Secretary of the London Labour
Party 1915–40, Leader of the
L.C.C. 1934–40, Home Secre-
tary 1940-5, Lord President of
the Council 1945.

THE LABOUR GOVERNMENT, 1945

FRONT ROW: *Viscount Addison, Lord Jowitt, Sir Stafford Cripps, Arthur Greenwood, Ernest Bevin, C. R. Attlee, Herbert Morrison, Hugh Dalton, A. V. Alexander, Chuter Ede, Ellen Wilkinson.*

CENTRE ROW: *Sir Ben Smith, J. Wilmot, Aneurin Bevan, George Isaacs, Viscount Stansgate, George Hall, Lord Pethick-Lawrence, J. J. Lawson, J. Westwood, E. Shinwell, Tom Williams, G. Tomlinson, A. Barnes.*

BACK ROW: *W. Whiteley, Sir Edward Bridges (Permanent Secretary to the Treasury), Sir Frank Soskice, J. B. Hynd, Earl of Listowel, E. J. Williams, Lewis Silkin, J. Griffiths, Lord Winster, P. J. Noel-Baker, Wilfred Paling, Sir Hartley W. Shawcross, Norman Brook (a Secretary to the Cabinet)*

C. R. ATTLEE

Joined the Fabian Society 1908, M.P. for Limehouse since 1922, Leader of the Labour Party 1935–40, Prime Minister 1945.

immediately after the election Attlee, who had succeeded Lansbury as leader—and who had been acting leader during all the period of Lansbury's illness before that—would be replaced either by Morrison or Greenwood. But when a vote was taken he received in the first ballot fifty-eight votes to Morrison's forty-four and Greenwood's thirty-two, and in the second ballot, when Greenwood dropped out, he received eighty-eight to Morrison's forty-four votes, which remained unchanged.

Those Labour M.P.s who had been in Parliament in the difficult days from 1931 had come to appreciate Attlee's qualities as leader. They knew his integrity, his quiet strength, his ability to hold together the varying groups within the Party, and they voted almost solidly for him. Thereafter he who had seemed earlier so unlikely a contender was to prove himself a leader of the kind Labour most needed and was to hold the leadership for longer than anyone before in the history of the Party.

It was, however, a party doomed to frustration which he led in the four years that remained until the outbreak of war—a frustration deepened by the certainty that war was coming and that the Conservative policy of appeasement of the dictators was making it inevitable.

Labour could protest. It could challenge the Government again and again, but it could make no impact on the massive and quiescent Conservative majority which lined up so faithfully, first behind Baldwin and then behind Chamberlain, as they gave way before the dictators.

It was a situation bound by the nature of things to bring frustration—and with frustration disunity.

This sense of frustration was inevitably increased by the policy of non-intervention in Spain, support for which was forced upon British Labour in part by the fact that the Popular Front Government in France had sponsored it. It found its expression first in the demand for a United Front with Communists and then for a Popular Front with those of all parties who could be persuaded to fight appeasement. But the vast majority of Labour members were not ready to accept either. The United Front was not ready because it was impossible to co-operate successfully with a Party which was, despite its occasional protestations to the contrary, unalterably opposed to the democratic philosophy which is the foundation of the Labour Party's socialism; the Popular Front because there was, in fact, nothing to be gained by an association which would have reduced the strength and homogeneity of Labour itself without making possible an overthrow of the Government. The Government could not be overthrown unless a considerable number of Conservatives themselves could be awakened to the peril and the dishonour of the course they were supporting. And they, despite the warnings of their own greatest leader, Churchill, and, despite the resignations of Anthony Eden and Duff Cooper, refused to be awakened.

In those four years Labour in Parliament made some tactical errors, among them the decision, until an advanced stage, to vote against rearmament—not because need to rearm to meet the Nazi menace was not accepted, it was—but as a demonstration of lack of faith in the foreign policy and integrity of the Government. It often seemed divided in counsel and disunited in action as it searched for a way to stop the drift to international tragedy and war.

But at no stage did it ever make the mistake of condoning or appeasing fascism. From the beginning, in Parliament, in the declarations of the National Council of Labour—representing the Labour Party, the T.U.C. and the Co-operative movement—and at its annual conferences it proclaimed the evil nature of nazism and the shame and peril of appeasement. But its forces were too small to divert the Conservatives in power from the course they had chosen.

That was the tragedy of Labour in those years—and the tragedy of the nation also.

CHAPTER XX

POWER AT LAST

THE part of the political Labour Party, of the trade unions and of the whole Labour movement in the struggle of the free world against nazism which began when Germany invaded Poland on 1 September, 1939, is a part of history. There is no need to retell it here.

Nor is there need to restate the reasons why, so long as Neville Chamberlain remained head of the Government, Labour, while putting the whole force of its massive strength behind the war effort, rejected the invitation to participate in the Government. It would have been impossible for any Labour man to have worked with confidence under a Prime Minister Labour so much distrusted and whose blindness and folly had contributed so greatly to world disaster. So long as he was in charge, Labour felt that it could work best for victory outside the Government.

When in May, 1940, the failure of Chamberlain as a war leader became so clear and the anxiety of country and Parliament so great that even he was forced to recognize that he must reconstruct his Government, it was the Labour Party which forced him to realize also that reconstruction must involve his own departure from the principal office. Labour refused to enter a government under him, although Clement Attlee informed him that it would be willing to serve under another leader who could and would mobilize the whole forces of the nation for victory. This decision sealed the fate of the Chamberlain administration. It made possible the national administration under Churchill which was essential to victory.

The story of the great coalition that followed is part of the imperishable history of all time. In that government of wartime unity, Attlee, Bevin, Morrison, Dalton, Alexander, Cripps and other Labour men played an immense part. They were able to do so because they truly represented the movement they led.

"If we come in without the movement we are nothing to you. We come in only provided that we have the support of our movement." With these words Attlee replied to the invitation of the new Prime Minister when, immediately after seeing the King, Winston Churchill asked that he and other leaders of Labour should join the new Government.

The support of the movement was certain. Labour was determined to fight without ceasing, and with every ounce of its power the war, against nazism and fascism—to a realization of whose menace and horror it had sought to rouse the nation from the very first. After their meeting with Churchill, Attlee and Arthur Greenwood, the Deputy Leader, at once went to Bournemouth, where the annual conference of the Labour Party was being held. At a specially summoned joint meeting of the National Executive and the General Council of the Trades Union Congress they informed their comrades on the political and industrial side of the movement of their interview with the new Prime Minister. They received unanimous support.

On the Monday morning, 13 May, 1940, Attlee spoke to the great assembly of delegates asking them to endorse the decision of the Executive that Labour should take its share of responsibility as a full partner in the new Government.

"We are here," he said, "to take a decision not only on behalf of our own movement but on behalf of labour all over the world. We have to stand today for the souls in prison in Czechoslovakia, in Poland, yes, and in Germany. We have to stand for those whose freedom is threatened all over the world. We have to fight for the freedom of the human spirit."

How that fight was fought and won and the part that Labour played in it needs no retelling.

The Great Coalition was a war coalition. When the war in Europe ended it came, as it was right that it should, to an end. For although on the organization of the nation for victory in this war upon which the whole future of civilization depended there was no dispute, it was otherwise on the issue of how the nation should be organized to meet the perils and opportunities of peace. On that there could be no permanent agreement between Labour and Conservatives.

The principles for which the Labour movement had fought from its first beginnings were as valid as ever and those principles could only be made effective by a Socialist government. Indeed, they had now a new validity and a more urgent importance if this time the ideals for which ordinary men and women had fought and the hopes that had sustained them through all the horror and tragedy of war were not to be dispersed and broken in peace as they had so quickly been after the First World War.

It was in this conviction that Labour entered the election of July, 1945, precipitated by Mr. Churchill immediately the European war ended, although Labour had proposed that the coalition should continue until the autumn in order that it could be fought on a new and improved register of voters and that Service voters could be given adequate time to consider all the issues. It was in this conviction that it won.

Here was a situation in which the electorate was called upon to face great issues. Let them be faced reasonably, calmly, with the seriousness that they required. That was Labour's desire. It, therefore, put before the voters in *Let Us Face the Future* a more detailed and specific statement of its programme than had ever been presented to the electorate by any political party in British history.

But it was not the Conservative Party's desire. Nor was it Mr. Churchill's desire. The great national leader of the war years became overnight a party propagandist who, in his opening broadcast to the electors, could find it possible to accuse those who had been his comrades in every phase of the great battle for freedom of wishing to destroy freedom—of finding "odious" the free Parliament which he and they had fought together to sustain against every menace the power of totalitarianism could bring to bear against it and of wishing to bring to Britain "some form of Gestapo." In that first broadcast he could even find it possible to produce, once more, one of the oldest and most outworn of all the devices of Conservative propaganda and to declare "there is no man or woman in this country who has, by thrift or toil, accumulated a nest-egg, however small, who will not run the risk of seeing it shrivel before their eyes."

357

Such tactics had succeeded before. They were the well-worn ammunition of Tory propaganda. But this time they were not to succeed.

When, on the following evening, it was Attlee's turn to broadcast to the nation, he showed at once how different was Labour's conception of the intelligence of the British people. Capably, reasonably, logically he set out the issues on which he believed the electorate must decide and the constructive proposals Labour had to make.

On that note—or, rather, on these two alien and jarring notes —the election was fought. And because Labour refused to allow itself to be diverted from its purpose by any of the misrepresentations launched by the Conservative Party and its supporters in the Press, but held firmly to its belief that British democracy was an adult democracy whose members wished to consider serious issues seriously, it won.

The first decisive stage in the journey which had begun forty-five years before in the Memorial Hall, Farringdon Street, in February, 1900, but whose roots went back through all the centuries of struggle, had at last been reached. Labour was in power with an absolute majority at last.

The 393 Labour members who crowded the Government benches when the new Parliament met represented, not the victory of a class party, but of one that had appealed successfully to men and women of goodwill among all classes. It was the manifestation not simply of a transitory mood at one general election, but of a genuine and cumulative increase over many years of popular support for Socialist policies that had been advanced with increasing precision in every phase of the Labour Party's history.

This support did not derive simply from successful political advocacy, although that had played its part. It came from the logic of events and the maturing development of circumstance. These had shaped the minds of men and women increasingly and inevitably to an understanding of the validity and inevitability of Socialist principles which had originally been advanced against so great a weight of public opposition.

Never in the history of any parliament had the Government benches provided a more completely representative cross-section of

British society than was produced by this election. Here were men and women from the elementary schools, the State secondary schools and the public schools, from Oxford and Cambridge, from the newer universities and from none. Side by side on those benches sat miners, textile workers, agricultural labourers, factory operatives, railwaymen, lorry drivers, housewives, clerks, barristers, doctors, company directors, industrialists, teachers, university lecturers, engineers, farmers, business men, officers of the Services; men and women of varied ages and all income groups brought together, not by the materialist compulsions of Marxist philosophy nor the defence of any vested interest, but by a common democratic inspiration and a common faith in the great ethical principles of socialism.

In the Government itself, the classless nature of this party which had come into being as a federation of Socialists and trade unionists, but which had from the first shown itself more than the political instrument of an economic interest, was also clear. Here, working together as colleagues in a great enterprise, were men and women possessing a greater diversity of experience and drawn from a greater number of social groups than in any previous peacetime government in the history of Britain. The Labour Party had truly become what Keir Hardie and his comrades in the early pioneering days had sought to make it: a classless Socialist Party.

But it had achieved power in circumstances very different from any he had ever foreseen and in conditions of the most critical kind. Britain had emerged from the war victorious but dangerously weakened economically. She faced in the field of both international and imperial affairs, problems of an altogether new order of magnitude.

A vast and revolutionary change in her economic and industrial life had become necessary if she was to survive, and this change had to be carried out in conditions of peculiar difficulty.

Before the war her economy had been that of a great exporting country, an international banker, a world-wide transporter of goods, and the possessor of large foreign investments.

Her export trade had been secured by a high degree of specialization in the output of machinery, textiles and industrial products manufactured from imported raw materials.

She had been able to maintain the standard of life of her people only with the assistance of a large income from export trade, from shipping services, from the overseas operations of bankers and merchants, and from the investments made abroad by industrialists out of their profits in the nineteenth century.

Not since the beginning of the nineteenth century, when her total population was only 12,000,000 people, had she been self-sufficient.

Nearly three-quarters of all the food she ate had come from abroad, fifty-five per cent of her meat, seventy-five per cent of her wheat, eighty-five per cent of her butter, all her tea, cocoa, and coffee, three-quarters of her sugar. Every year before the war more than 20,000,000 tons of imported food had been brought across the seas and unloaded at her docks.

Moreover, with the single exception of coal, the raw materials upon which her major industries depended were largely or wholly imported; all the cotton, all the rubber, five-sixths of the wool, practically all the petroleum, two-thirds of the iron ore, most of the timber. Altogether nearly 25 per cent of her entire national income, or, in other words, a quarter of the combined value of all the goods and services produced by her people, went in paying for imports of one kind or another.

This economy had been destroyed by the war. In order that the fullest advantage could be taken of the geographical position which made her territory the most suitable base from which to launch allied air and land attacks against Germany, export industries had been cut to an irreducible minimum.

To pay for essential imports of war materials and food, the wartime Government had taken possession of £3,700,000,000 of overseas investments belonging to public corporations and private investors and sold one-third. Of those that were not sold the majority were in countries which had been overrun by the enemy. They could not be realized, they produced no income, much of the physical wealth they represented was destroyed. Yet the income from these investments had been essential to Britain's pre-war economic balance.

In addition, £152,000,000 of the gold and dollar reserves of the nation had been liquidated and overseas debts totalling £2,879,000,000 incurred to cover war purchases and the cost of maintaining military forces. As a consequence, despite the immense assistance given under Lend-Lease, Britain faced the future, when the war ended, a debtor country for the first time in her history.

Less than one-half of her pre-war export trade still remained. Because of the rise in world food prices, the income from this was sufficient to finance only one-quarter of the pre-war volume of imports. Half of her pre-war merchant shipping fleet of 18,000,000 tons had been sunk. Most of her overseas banking income had gone. A large part of her industrial equipment was desperately in need of replacement, for instead of spending, as would normally have been the case over five years, £1,000,000,000 to maintain and renew plants and factories in the civilian industries, this money had been spent on munitions of war. Her coal industry, which had before the war been the source of her greatest exports, had deliberately been reduced in size. Collieries had been closed down, essential equipment allowed to go unrepaired and unrenewed, workers drafted to industries of more immediate military importance. The same had happened in the textile industry, where 260 mills were closed in 1941.

In addition she had suffered physical damage of a total value of £1,500,000,000 to factories, railways and docks by air attack; more than 4,000,000 houses, one out of every three in the whole country, had been destroyed or damaged.

She had new commitments for Government expenditure on relief for war-stricken countries and on occupation forces, amounting to more than £200,000,000 a year. So fundamentally had the balance of pre-war economy been altered that there was no hope of restoring even the pre-war position except by a vast re-deployment of manpower and industrial resources and by discovering new ways of increasing industrial productivity.

To secure the overseas income to pay for essential food and raw materials it was necessary to raise physical exports to three and a half times the level to which they had been allowed to fall during the war, and to secure and hold an export trade at least one and three-quarter times the volume of that achieved in the peak days of her industrial activity when Britain was the greatest exporting country in the world—with all such an increase involved in the movement of workers to new industries and the development of new plants and processes. For the first time in her industrial history Britain was actually short of men and women.

The situation which faced the new Labour Government was thus of an unprecedented difficulty and complexity. If it was to be met successfully, it required a revolution not only in national economy but in men's and women's attitudes. It was not a problem of recovery to normal, difficult enough as even that would have been, but of response to a situation altogether new in the history of the nation.

All the conditions existed to produce an economic collapse and mass unemployment greater even than had followed the First World War—unless Labour could show itself capable of applying its Socialist principles in dealing with those basic problems of economic security which the Conservatives and their allies had proved so incapable of solving in 1918 and onwards. The task was of a magnitude to dismay any government. Moreover, although it had been enormously increased in complexity and urgency by the economic consequences of the war, its roots went much farther back and were to be found in the economic and political policies of a generation or more.

Even before the Second World War Britain had found it increasingly difficult to balance her overseas payments. She had walked a razor edge between stability and instability, and by 1938 was spending abroad £40,000,000 a year more than her overseas income.

The undermining of her position as a great creditor nation, which had brought with it such major problems as the Second World War ended, had begun a quarter of a century earlier during the First, although neither Britain nor the rest of the world had then been ready to accept the fact.

Even the illusion of choice was now gone. What was involved was not merely some halt in progress, a temporary living on capital while the economy was adjusted to meet new conditions. What was now in question was Britain's survival as a great economic Power and her very ability to feed her closely packed population and keep her industries running.

Nor did the economic problem stand alone. Problems no less formidable also faced the country in international and imperial affairs.

Britain's international influence had rested in the past upon her position as a balancing Power in Europe and upon the authority she exercised as the centre of a vast commonwealth and empire covering nearly one-quarter of the land surface of the globe, embracing more than one-quarter of its population, and jointly possessed of a sufficiency or actual surplus of more basic raw materials than any other group. The war had vitally affected her position in both these respects.

For centuries the primary purpose of British policy in Europe had been to prevent the domination and dictatorship of the Continent by a single Great Power. Now the end of the latest of the wars, fought to prevent the dominance of the Continent by one Power, saw also the destruction—for the time being certainly, and possibly for ever—of the whole pattern of strong independent states in Europe. Only one great land Power remained in Europe: Soviet Russia. And Soviet Russia soon made it clear that she was determined to exploit to the full the opportunity thus provided and extend her influence, if she could, not merely from the Baltic to the Black Sea, but westward to the frontiers of Germany and beyond.

Britain's position as the moral leader of Western Europe was strong. But the essential basis of a stable democratic political life for Europe was economic recovery, and this required a degree of assistance that was for the time being beyond Britain's single capacity. Yet, until economic recovery was possible, the foundations of political democracy in Europe were built on moving sand.

That was the situation in Europe.

Britain's position as the centre of a world-wide commonwealth and empire was subject to even greater stresses. The vast problem of Indian independence—that independence which Labour had always supported—had now a new urgency. To India's neighbour, Burma, the war had brought invasion and destruction and had left behind it an equally insistent desire for independence. Ceylon, small in size but strategically of enormous importance as a naval base, was similarly stirred. All over the East a movement of nationalism was spreading, fanned by a deepening resentment of what was regarded as an alien white domination. And this great movement in the East was a portent also of what might soon be expected in Africa and the West Indies.

There was yet a further problem. The life and safety of the British Commonwealth depend on freedom of communications. To link the territories which compose it, not less than 80,000 miles of sea routes must be kept open and free from the threat of any impediment. The effective strength of the naval and air forces, without which this freedom of passage might at any time be placed in jeopardy, rests on the command of bases at strategic points all around the globe.

In no area of the world is this more true than in the Eastern Mediterranean and the Middle East. Twenty per cent of Britain's imports and ninety per cent of the oil produced by British-controlled oilfields pass through the Mediterranean.

Nor does the importance of the Mediterranean lie only in its position as a commercial route. It derives directly from the fact that its domination by an enemy power in the event of war would disastrously weaken Britain's position throughout the Middle East, which is an area of primary significance to her and will remain so as long as the British Commonwealth lasts. It is a corridor through which run essential imperial communications by land and sea, and is at the centre of essential air routes. Unless this area is peaceful there can be no assurance of security for the Commonwealth and no assurance of world peace. It is, therefore, a primary British interest—as it is a world interest—that the nations which compose the Middle East should not lose their independence and fall under the domination of one Great Power which would thus be in a position to menace the African continent, and irrupt into the Indian Ocean, along the vast arc of whose shores is grouped some two-fifths of the total area of the British Commonwealth and its associates: the Union of South Africa, Southern and Northern Rhodesia, Tanganyika, Kenya, British Somaliland, Aden, India, Ceylon, Burma, Malaya and Australia.

Throughout this area Britain found herself faced at the end of the war with grave new problems. Egypt, whose importance as a strategic base and supply centre had once more been demonstrated during the war, was in a state of nationalist fervour which sought satisfaction in the demand for an early withdrawal of British troops and the speedy revision of the Anglo-Egyptian Treaty of 1936.

Throughout the countries of the Middle East there was a

stirring of two great forces: the force of nationalism, and the force of social revolt engendered by the war. The Middle East could no longer stand aside from the world movement towards greater equality; it was against the interests of all who wanted world peace, and most certainly counter to both the practical interests and the moral imperatives of a Socialist Britain that it should.

But to carry through such changes peacefully required a degree of economic assistance from outside that Britain alone was for the time being in no position to give. If they were not carried through peacefully, or were suppressed and thwarted by rulers unwilling to recognize the need for change, the Middle East could become a breeding ground for violence and revolt, and the whole series of relationships upon which British security in this area had been founded might be thrown into confusion.

Britain's greatest interest in 1945 was to develop the power and authority of the United Nations. That was both an idealistic and a realistic policy. But it soon became clear that, although the United Nations represented a hope, the actual hard fact of the world situation was that the war had established a strategic revolution and that there were now three effective world Powers and three only—America, Russia and Britain. Everywhere the frontiers of the spheres of influence regarded by each of the three Great Powers as essential to its own security ran together. If they could co-operate, none of them need have any anxiety. If not, none of them could feel safe.

Russia was not ready to co-operate.

Instead of wishing to continue the comradeship of war, and instead of welcoming the coming of a Socialist Government to Britain, Russia set herself to destroy it if she could. To her the election of a Socialist Government in Britain presented an ideological obstacle to the westward expansion of Communist influence in Europe. It had established a powerful counter-attraction to communism, a new magnet in whose direction the European Left might be drawn. It offered the possibility of a new hope for the masses of Europe that robbed communism of its exclusive appeal. Therefore, to the Communists, it was an enemy to be attacked by every means.

These were the formidable difficulties which faced Britain in every aspect of her national life in 1945 when for the first time in political history a Labour Government was elected to power. The economic life of the nation, its very ability to support and feed its people, was threatened; the disintegration of the Commonwealth and Empire was a possibility which no observer, whether friendly or otherwise, could ignore; the position of Britain as a Great Power capable of exercising influence over the course of world events and helping to establish the foundations of world peace was gravely menaced.

It is against this background that the achievements of Labour, now at last in a position to test the validity of its Socialist principles and demonstrate the capacity of its leaders, must be judged. They are remarkable achievements.

The first essential, not merely of any possibility of improving the social condition of the great mass of ordinary men and women, but of survival, was economic recovery. This is what has been accomplished as a result of Labour policy.

Despite shortages of material which have slowed down or interrupted work in many industries; the physical destruction or damage of more than 25,000 factories by air attack; the wearing out and non-replacement during the war of machinery and equipment in factories, mines, docks, and power stations and of locomotives and railway wagons; a winter, in 1947, of snow, frost, and floods worse than anything recorded for more than a century, which cost the country £200,000,000 in lost production and killed large numbers of sheep and cattle; a summer of drought that ruined many crops; despite these and many other factors that, by any reasonable calculation, should have made a huge reduction in national productivity unavoidable, British industry has been brought to the highest level of aggregate output and the greatest volume of export trade in its history. Previous all-time records have been broken in major industry after major industry.

No other country in Europe has achieved its pre-war level of steel production. But the British steel industry, operating under Government direction and control, has far surpassed every previous record of output.

The tonnage of merchant ships under construction has been brought to more than double the immediate pre-war figure: more than half of all the merchant shipbuilding in the world is being carried out in British yards.

Output of railway wagons is above pre-war, output of motor trucks more than double the pre-war level. Internal-combustion engines, boilers, steam-raising accessory plant, steam-turbo-alternators, textile machinery, coal cutters, coal conveyers, all are being produced at a greater rate than ever before. The production of agricultural tractors is five times as great as it was in 1938, that of tractor-drawn ploughs more than six times. Three times as many mowers and threshing machines are being produced.

Agricultural production has been brought to a higher level than pre-war in all the main crops; grain by sixty-three per cent, potatoes and vegetables by over a hundred per cent, sugar beet by sixty-five per cent, liquid milk by forty-six per cent.

Indeed, the levels of production in industry and agriculture under Socialist direction would—if the international economic conditions of pre-war days had still prevailed—have made possible a higher level of national prosperity than at any previous time in the national history.

Much remains to be done. The trade unbalance between Europe and America and the world-wide exchange problems resulting from the war confront Britain especially with problems of immense magnitude.

But the rate of British recovery has far surpassed that of any other European nation and has far and away exceeded what was done in 1918. Full employment has been maintained and the fear of unemployment removed from the lives of the workers.

How has this been achieved? By the application to the national economy of the Socialist principles consistently put before the electorate by the Party and worked out in detail in a great series of reports presented to electors before the election. Everything the Labour Party undertook to do in its election programme the Attlee administration has done. It is the first administration in British political history that has carried through every one of its promises.

There were many non-Socialists who argued that the economic situation which Labour found itself called upon to solve was so serious that Socialist measures ought to be left aside for the time being. That was to mistake altogether their inspiration and purpose. They were in the eyes of the Labour Party the essential foundations of a new order of society: the more serious the crisis the greater was the need to lay those foundations rapidly. It is on these foundations that the economic recovery has been built. Without them it would not have been possible.

The national control of banking and investment, the public ownership of coal, electricity, gas, transport and steel, these are the essential foundations of a sound and equitable national economy in the Socialist view. Every one of them (with the exception of steel which is due to pass into public ownership in 1950) has been accomplished in the five years of Labour administration.

But British socialism has never been doctrinaire. Public ownership of all the basic common service industries has been integrated in a new democratic pattern which includes the general planning—but not actual control or ownership—of much private industry.

Britain has led the way in European recovery because, for the first time, the economic problem has been related to every part of the industrial system and a partnership of a quite new kind set up between Government, trade unions and employers on Central Advisory Councils, Regional Boards for industry and other bodies.

Because of Socialist planning, Britain has now a good chance of recovering from the economic battering of the war, of climbing back to a satisfactory trade balance and of making herself thereafter independent of any need for further American aid—although for Britain, as for every other Western European nation, American aid was a first essential of recovery after the war.

But although economic planning has always been a part of Socialist policy, it represents only one aspect of the advance towards a new social pattern that shall be more just and equitable.

Economic planning is essential because, without the socialization of major industries and the central planning of the rest of the national economy, it would not be possible to achieve an increase in national productivity sufficiently large to carry a great programme of social reform without budgetary difficulty.

But alongside increased industrial production there has been achieved a substantial advance towards greater financial equality.

Over the whole range of industry average weekly earnings for men and women have been raised to over £5 a week, which is nearly double the pre-war average.

Some of this increase has been absorbed by higher prices, but basic food costs have been kept stable by subsidies. But when all adjustments are made the average wage-earner is now receiving real wages at least ten per cent, and in some cases as much as thirty-five per cent, higher than before the war. The lowest-paid workers have benefited even more.

An egalitarian tax policy has substantially reduced direct taxation on lower incomes while drastically increasing it on higher. Nearly 3,000,000 people in the lower income group who paid income tax when the Labour Government came into power no longer do so. The taxes paid by many millions more, including a considerable number in the middle-class income groups, have been reduced.

A new pattern of society is being created in which there are few people with high incomes and none with very low ones.

The number of those who after paying tax have a net income of between £3 and £10 a week has risen from 6,320,000 before the war to 13,175,000 now. The number of those in the upper sector of this group, that is, with net incomes after tax of between £5 and £10 a week, has been increased by nearly three times—from only 1,820,000 before the war to 5,225,000 now. The number of those with net incomes between £500 and £1,000 a year has also risen by nearly forty-five per cent. But above this figure there has been a sharp decline as a direct consequence of a budgetary policy specifically designed to produce a more egalitarian society.

At one end of the scale, the low wages of the past have been ended; the number of those with net incomes above £150 a year has been more than doubled, and the number of those in the middle group between £5 and £10 a week net nearly trebled. But there are twenty-five per cent fewer people with net incomes above £1,000 a year than there were before the war, and very high incomes have practically disappeared. Only some 35,500 people now have a net income above £2,000 a year, less than 900 have a net income of more than £4,000 a year, and there are only forty-five people in the whole country with a net income of above £6,000 a year. A new income pattern is emerging in Britain.

At the same time a more just and equal society has been brought nearer by a great advance in social services.

The school-leaving age has been raised to fifteen, free part-time education at County Colleges until the age of eighteen for all leaving school before that age, and the payment of fees abolished in all primary and secondary schools coming under the local education authorities. Well over 440,000 more children are at school than before the war.

Facilities for university education have been increased, government financial grants to the universities raised to five times the pre-war level, and the number of State scholarships more than doubled. Poverty is no longer a bar to the highest education. Each year between five and six thousand more new students are entering the universities than before the war, large numbers of them, including many in the two older universities of Oxford and Cambridge, with financial grants from the Ministry of Education or from local education authorities sufficient to cover their living costs during their university careers. Britain is moving rapidly towards a unified educational system within which privilege will have been abolished.

This educational change, combined with the narrowing of the gap between the highest and lowest incomes, is bringing a change in the British social pattern as significant as that which followed the rise of the middle-classes in the Industrial Revolution. But this time social barriers are being broken down over a much wider area. The whole programme of social reform has that purpose in view.

At the same time, the National Health Service has not only made the best medical service available to all for the first time, but has made a contribution to equality in the field of medicine comparable to that made in education. The full service, with its hospitals, health centres, maternity and child-welfare clinics, its teams of doctors and its specialist services, will take time to perfect. But the principle has been established, and every member of the community, rich or poor, can turn to the service as of right. Need, not money, has been made the test.

This principle, that essential need shall be the test, has also governed food policy.

The rationing system has been, as during the war, designed to secure absolute equality in the distribution of basic foods so long as there exists a shortage which might otherwise lead to unequal distribution. The control of food prices, which costs in subsidies £485,000,000 a year, the equivalent of a contribution of 14s. a week towards the cost of the household budget of a family of four, has kept basic foods at price levels that make them equally available to everyone. Claims upon essential food supplies have thus been determined not by income but by need, in the same way that claims upon educational and health services are being determined.

As a result of this policy the retail price of about eighty-five per cent of all the food normally consumed by families with earnings up to £6 or £7 a week, including all basic foodstuffs, has been kept down to a level much below that which would otherwise have ruled. At the same time, the provision of free milk and the extension of midday meals to school-children, the giving of special facilities for running canteens in factories, workshops, and mines, and the development of civic restaurants run by municipal authorities on a self-supporting non-profit-making basis, have further increased the real incomes of those in the lower income groups and contributed to the redistribution of national income which is the purpose of the general egalitarian policy.

So, too, with housing. Here also the test has been need. More houses have been built than in any other country affected by the war, and they have been built for rental to those whose need is greatest in a programme planned from the start to deal with the urgent problem in the fairest way.

Many public services are, however, organized locally by municipal authorities, who obtain the funds to finance them by levying a rate of so much per pound on the value of property in their districts; with the result that a rich district where property values are high can receive from, say, a shilling rate an income ten or fifteen times as great as that received by a poor area where property values are low. Under such conditions a rich and varied civic life was formerly made impossible in just those areas where it was most needed. Now as a result of Labour policy all counties and county boroughs whose rateable values are below the average are receiving equalization grants from a central fund. This will spread benefits

371

over the whole community and help to reduce the gap between the amenities in rich and poor areas which was formerly such a feature of British life. Greater equality, that was an essential Labour aim. But greater security is no less vital.

Under the National Insurance Act every person in the country is now a contributing member in a comprehensive scheme to which the national Treasury, and, in the case of employees, employers also contribute. Standard benefits have been provided in sickness, unemployment, or on retirement, of 26s. a week for a single person and 42s. a week for a couple living together, with a further allowance of 7s. 6d. a week for the first child and 16s. a week for an adult dependent. In addition, there are maternity grants, widows' pensions, and grants to cover funeral expenses.

The Industrial Insurance Act has made available benefits of 45s. a week for six months to all those injured while at work, and a disability pension, in case of permanent incapacity, of 65s. a week, plus 16s. for a wife and 7s. 6d. for the first child—or £4 8s. 6d. a week in all.

Combined with the scheme of family allowances, under which an allowance of 5s. a week is paid for every child, after the first, up to the age of fifteen or a year longer if the child is still at school, whether the parents are in or out of work, healthy or sick, old or young, and irrespective of income, these measures have provided a more complete system of social security than that in any other country in the world.

This is the measure of the extent to which Labour in power has transformed the lives of ordinary men and women.

These social insurance and national assistance projects, like those aimed specifically at creating greater equality, show the general design of the new social pattern, which the Labour Government has established, and are helping to shape that pattern.

The difficulties that face Britain, intensified though they are by immediate post-war complications, have roots going far back into her previous economic, social and industrial system. It is only by changing this system and by adapting herself to new circumstances, as formerly she adapted herself successfully to the changes demanded by the Industrial Revolution, that Britain can regain her position as a great democratic world power.

She is doing so because the Socialist principle which has inspired the Labour Party from its birth has been put into action by men and women who have brought to the service of the State not only great administrative capacity and wide experience of affairs, but a philosophy of life.

A social revolution has been carried through. It has been carried through according to a pattern in which public ownership of the basic sources of financial and economic power is linked with the planning of private enterprise within the framework of a national economic policy; in which financial and social reform measures are reducing the gross disparities between rich and poor, in which claims upon essentials of all kinds are increasingly determined by need rather than income.

Despite world shortages there is a higher average standard of living in Britain than ever before. There is greater equality. There is greater security.

That is the accomplishment of the Labour Government at home. What of matters abroad? In the Commonwealth a new era of partnership has been opened.

Instead of conflict and disintegration, the roll of members of the Commonwealth enjoying Dominion status has, as a result of a great gesture of imaginative statesmanship, been extended by three Asiatic names, India, Pakistan and Ceylon. Burma, although she has chosen independence outside, instead of inside, the Commonwealth, has done so under conditions and according to such mutually agreed terms as regards trade and defence that her association with Britain is almost as close as if she had chosen to remain within the Commonwealth.

In the Colonial Empire, also, history is on the march. Great advances in political self-government, in economic expansion, in the development of trade unions, in education, and in the union of territories whose political and economic advance can be made more rapid by membership in a larger unit, are taking place.

Through the £125,000,000 Colonial Development and Welfare Fund, the £100,000,000 Colonial Development Corporation, and the £50,000,000 Overseas Food Corporation, large sums are being made available for programmes that will both raise the standard of living of native peoples and increase the economic resources of the Empire as a whole. All colonial governments have been asked to take over the ownership of mineral resources and arrange for their national development. New constitutions have been established with elected legislative councils in many territories; in the legislative councils of Nigeria and the Gold Coast there are now African majorities, and in East Africa the Africans sit alongside Europeans and Indians in the main governmental bodies. In West Africa a new state is being slowly born.

British trade-union officials have gone out to the Colonies to help develop local trade-union movements, the British Co-operative movement is assisting in the development of producers' and distributors' co-operatives, university colleges are being established and delegates from a council representing the British universities have visited East Africa, West Africa and the West Indies to advise on the extension of higher education.

Throughout the Colonial Empire, from the West Indies and the Bahamas to West Africa, East Africa, and Malaya, great new schemes of social, political and economic reconstruction are taking form.

The East African groundnuts scheme financed by the Overseas Food Corporation, which involves the clearing of thousands of acres of bush, is but the first of many such developments. Similar possibilities are being explored in Gambia, the Gold Coast and Nigeria. In Uganda a great new hydro-electric scheme to harness the waters of Lake Victoria, where they flow, with immense smooth power, over the Ripon and Owen Falls, is under way and may play as large a part in the industrialization of Central Africa as coal did in the industrialization of Britain.

The natural resources of many parts of the Colonial Empire are immense. In the past they were largely undeveloped. That era has ended. Development will take time. But the next few years are likely to see material and political advances which will alter the Colonial Empire almost out of recognition and immensely strengthen the whole fabric of the British Commonwealth.

In international affairs, although Russian policy has prevented the advance to peaceful co-operation that was hoped for, the Soviet thesis of an early collapse of British power has been proved wrong.

So far from collapsing or weakening under Russian pressure, and thus destroying any possibility of ultimate international co-operation for world peace, Britain has stood firm and has given new leadership to all the democratic forces in Europe.

It was the response of a Socialist Foreign Secretary, Ernest Bevin, that made the great conception of Marshall Aid a practical possibility. It is British leadership in Europe that has brought Western Union into being and that has, in partnership with America, shaped the Atlantic Pact. The forces making for world peace have been steadily strengthened.

In a situation of immense difficulty and danger the forces of democracy have been sustained and defended.

At home, in the Commonwealth and Empire, in foreign affairs, Labour has overcome menacing problems and made great achievements—although much remains to be done and some major problems, particularly in the international economic field, remain to be solved.

The men and women who struggled and fought against all the forces of privilege, and were so often defeated in that long struggle out of which at last the Labour Party was born, dreamed of a society in which insecurity and gross inequality should cease. The pioneers who met in the Memorial Hall in Farringdon Street in February, 1900, set themselves to achieve such a society knowing that the road to it would be difficult and dangerous. Now, despite the immense difficulties of the post-war years, the foundations of that society have been laid.

In five years of Labour rule, and in the face of an economic and international situation which threatened the very foundations of British existence, more has been done to make Britain a true social democracy than ever before in the nation's history. Because of what has been accomplished millions of ordinary men and women now know a security they never knew before and the gates of opportunity stand wider open than they have ever been.

CHAPTER XXI

THE CONTINUING PURPOSE

IN 1900 when the delegates of the trade unions and the Socialist societies gathered in the Memorial Hall to consider whether they should form a Labour Party, no working man had ever been allowed a decisive voice in the government of Britain. Even the suggestion that a working man should seek to represent his fellows in Parliament was shocking to many of those in power—the idea that those who by their labour produce the wealth of Britain should have a genuine voice in the government of Britain was unthinkable.

Although the conscience of the middle-classes was stirring, and although Gladstone and Disraeli had each in their several ways brought new impulses and a new vision to the political life of Britain, it was still accepted almost as a law of nature that millions of men and women should live in poverty while a few had wealth and power almost beyond computation.

That the children of the working-classes should leave school and go to labour for a pittance in mines and factories at an age when those of the middle- and upper-classes were scarcely out of the nursery, that they should live in hardship and die in poverty, that they should be automatically excluded from higher education and should in all things be treated as members of a lower and almost an alien race—this to all but a handful of fanatics and visionaries seemed an immutable requirement of the universe.

We have marched forward a long way since then, and the measure of the change in the fifty years between is the measure of the revolution that a Labour Party has helped to bring about in the political and social life of Britain.

The Labour Party has been at once the manifestation and the expression of the economic emergence of the working-classes in the swiftly altering industrial pattern of the half-century. But to give political expression to the hopes and needs of the industrial workers, to voice their demand for a true share in the government of their country, this has been only a part of the service of Labour.

It has fought for the material advance of ordinary men and women and it has been successful. It has fought for greater economic security, for greater equality, for a fair deal for all—and in its years of power it has shaped British society to a new pattern which for the first time includes these things among the natural rights of ordinary men and women so that the lives of the common people of Britain have been given a new shape and a new significance. In five years many of the economic and social ills, not merely of fifty years ago, but of twenty-five or even ten years ago, have been banished from memory.

But the impulses which created British socialism and have made the British Labour Party the greatest party in the State within so brief a period of political history, have never been solely material impulses. The ideals which governed its coming to life, which supported it through so many difficulties and sustained it in all reverses, were never solely economic.

Economic security, greater economic equality, the public control of the primary sources of economic power for the good of all, a fair return for their labour to all who work whether by hand or brain, these are the necessary foundations of a Socialist society, not its ultimate and final justification.

For the true end of socialism is not materialist. The vision that sustained the pioneers, and that still inspires those who are their heirs in a magnificent adventure, is the vision of the dignity and importance of ordinary men and women and of a true commonwealth in which all shall be neighbours, working together each according to their ability for the enrichment and happiness of all.

It is in truth a new society that socialism seeks to build—a society bound together not simply by the bonds of economic interest, but by a common moral and spiritual purpose and a common reaching after the values which alone can make a civilization truly great. The commonwealth it seeks to establish is a commonwealth of free men and women liberated not only from ancient tyrannies but from those no less powerful and destructive compulsions of competing self-interest which modern industrial capitalism has imposed. A commonwealth in which men and women may live their lives freely and graciously and in which there shall be room for

377

all the infinite expressions of human personality. A commonwealth in which men and women may work for purposes worthy of them and in which they may also have, let it be said, a great deal of fun.

The foundations have been laid. Some of the essential economic and social changes have been carried through. The worst inequalities and injustices of the past have been overthrown. In the face of the most formidable national and international difficulties socialism in power has held to the course it set itself and achieved successes which have won the admiration of the world. Against odds so tremendous that it seemed impossible to avoid economic and social disasters as great or greater even than those which followed the First World War, it has carried through a peaceful revolution which has not only changed the face of Britain but set an example to all nations. It has added a new and exciting chapter to the British story —a chapter which in the perspective of history will be seen to be one of the greatest in that long and proud history.

But it is only a beginning that has been made. The feet of Labour stand firmly on the soil of Britain from which it draws so much of its strength, but its face is turned steadily forward. It is a part of the wave of the future; that wave that shall carry men and nations to new splendours and a new harmony and make possible a flowering of the human spirit such as we have never known.

The march is not over. It is only just beginning. These fifty years and the years that went before them are but the prelude to the greater story. Now, as it makes ready for a new advance, Labour calls to its ranks as throughout its history a great company, the company of those of all ages and all classes who are not afraid to fight for the progress of mankind and to give their fidelity to the cause of the brotherhood of man.

Here is no summons to easy victory. The forward march will be no easier than that which has gone before. The challenges to be met and overcome are no smaller; the demands upon those who would serve no lighter than they have ever been. Who would have it otherwise? This is a companionship summoned for no mean or paltry purpose but for one of the great causes of history.

No service is too great for such a cause, for it is the cause of all mankind. No enemy can in the end defeat it, for it has allies in the hearts of men and women everywhere.

AUTHOR'S NOTE

I have drawn on many sources for the material used in this history of the rise of the Labour Party, so many that it is not possible to mention all. But I should like to pay special acknowledgment to the debt I, along with all other students of Labour history, owe to Professor G. D. H. Cole for his British Working Class Politics 1832–1914 *and* A History of the Labour Party from 1914 *and for much other writing, and to Mrs. Cole for her* Makers of the Labour Movement, *also to Max Beer for his* History of British Socialism *and to Herbert Tracey for his* Book of the Labour Party. *I have drawn inevitably upon many political autobiographies and biographies and must mention particularly Mrs. Mary Agnes Hamilton's biography of Arthur Henderson and William Stewart's* Life of Keir Hardie. *The original documents quoted in* From Cobbett to the Chartists, *edited by Max Morris, and* Labour's Formative Years, *edited by James B. Jeffreys, have also been invaluable. The annual reports of the Labour Party have naturally been an indispensable source of information, together with much contemporary journalism. To the writings of Professor Tawney and Professor Laski I owe a great deal, but my greatest debt is to all those in the Labour movement whom I have had the honour to number among my friends and who have taught me the spirit and meaning of socialism.*

INDEX

INDEX

The publishers acknowledge permission from Picture Post Library to reproduce the picture of Mr. Bernard Shaw.